LAWRENCE AND THE ARABS

LAWRENCE

from a bust by Eric Kennington

LAWRENCE AND THE ARABS

ROBERT GRAVES

WITH A NEW INTRODUCTION
BY DALE MAHARIDGE

Illustrations edited by Eric Kennington
Maps by Herry Perry

SEVEN STORIES PRESS
New York • Oakland • London

Names: Graves, Robert, 1895-1985, author. | Maharidge, Dale, writer of introduction.
Title: Lawrence and the Arabs : an intimate biography / by Robert Graves ; introduction by Dale Maharidge.
Description: [2nd edition] | New York : Seven Stories Press, 2018. | Includes bibliographical references.
Identifiers: LCCN 2018008489 | ISBN 9781609808204 (pbk.)
Subjects: LCSH: Lawrence, T. E. (Thomas Edward), 1888-1935. | Great Britain. Army--Biography. | Soldiers--Great Britain--Biography. | World War, 1914-1918--Campaigns--Middle East. | Middle East--History.
Classification: LCC D568.4.L45 G7 2018 | DDC 940.4/15092 [B] --dc23
LC record available at https://lccn.loc.gov/2018008489 ISBN e-Book edition: 9780795336904

Printed in the USA

College professors and high school and middle school teachers may order free examination copies of Seven Stories Press titles. To order, visit www.sevenstories.com, or fax on school letterhead to 212-226-1411.

9 8 7 6 5 4 3 2 1

CONTENTS

INTRODUCTION TO THE NEW EDITION
by Dale Maharidge.......................... vii

AUTHOR'S INTRODUCTION TO
THE FIRST EDITION xi

LAWRENCE AND THE ARABS 3

APPENDICES 457

INDEX 471

LIST OF ILLUSTRATIONS

LAWRENCE *from a bust by Eric Kennington* . . . . .frontis

'AIRCRAFTMAN SHAW' 38

MAP: THE ARAB AREA 52

THE EMIR FEISAL 63

THE EMIR ABDULLA *from a drawing by Eric Kennington* 83

THE VILLAGE OF DATE PALMS 113

FEISAL'S ARMY ENTERING WEJH 132

AUDA *from a drawing by Eric Kennington* 154

MAP: THE RIDE TO AKABA 161

AUDA AND HIS KINSMEN
    copyright American Colony Stores, Jerusalem 170

THE PILGRIM-RAILWAY 191

AKABA 213

MAP: LAWRENCE'S RIDES 225

DEMOLITIONS ON THE RAILWAY 250

ALI IBN EL HUSSEIN *from a drawing by Eric Kennington* 261

AZRAK 275

FAHAD OF THE BENI SAKHR
    from a drawing by Eric Kennington 280

ABDULLA EL ZAAGI *from a drawing by Eric Kennington* 302

MAHMAS 309

MULE TRANSPORT NEAR ABA EL LISSAN
    copyright French Army Photo Dept. 327

MAP: THE CAMPAIGN IN THE NORTH 342

BUXTON'S MEN BLOWING UP MUDOWWARA STATION 347

AT GUWEIRA *copyright French Army Photo Dept.* 358

AN ARMOURED FORD IN THE DESERT
    copyright Imperial War Museum. 365

LAWRENCE AND HIS BODYGUARD AT AKABA 377

FEISEL JUST AFTER HIS MEETING WITH ALLENBY
    copyright Imperial War Museum. 397

LAWRENCE AT VERSAILLES 414

'T.E.' ON 'BOANERGES,' THE MOTOR-BICYCLE 442

INTRODUCTION TO
THE NEW EDITION

T. E. Lawrence was totally badass. There were the many military feats: blowing up seventy-nine railroad bridges in the Arab war against the Turks; riding camels some thousand miles per month over a year-and-a-half period; dodging daggers, bullets, bombs. The man who was a modern before his time: vegetarian, who spoke to women as he would to a man. The cosmopolitan: so fluent in Arabic that he could speak numerous regional subdialects. The mad bad boy: he wore Arabian clothes—a robe and silk-and-gold headdress—to a Buckingham Palace reception, causing a "rebuke." In Damascus, a superior officer admonished him for his "scandalous" and "disgraceful" outfit, saying he should be shot, which elicited hysterical laughter from Lawrence; the officer slapped him. No matter. Lawrence didn't care what anyone thought of him. And he hadn't yet reached the age of thirty.

If you're like me, someone who follows news on the Middle East but is far from expert on the region, you first approach *Lawrence and the Arabs* with a bit of trepidation, fearing the need for substantial understanding of history and politics of those lands to fully appreciate this volume. Nothing could be further from reality. This is the book one should read to gain some of that knowledge. Today's reader, connecting the dots between events from a century ago and contemporary headlines, keeps muttering "aha!" A new understanding emerges.

Robert Graves does more than document the extraordinary story of one British officer and the Arabian leaders in the eastern desert campaign during World War I. The genius of the publisher was to ask a poet to take on the role of biographer. In Graves's account, the desert also becomes a character. The lyrical poet includes descriptions of ridges of "sun-browned flints" and flowering saffron plants creating a golden view over a great expanse. The dark poet, the one that dominates, constantly shows the unrelenting and merciless desert; foul waters that must be drunk; the stunning extremes of summer sun that kills a man short on water within hours and winter cold so bitter as to cause otherwise fierce warriors (with the exception of Lawrence) to beg off; snakes so venomous that the only recourse after a man was bitten was the Howeitat treatment, which was to "bind up the bite with snake-skin plaster and read chapters of the Koran to the patient until he died." Graves concludes that outside some cities in the north, the "desert would always remain barbarous and primitive." A reader thinks of Paul Bowles, who later wrote of another desert, the African Sahara, "How fragile we are under the sheltering sky. Behind the sheltering sky is a vast dark universe, and we're just so small."

Landscapes shape people. One comes away from *Lawrence and the Arabs* with the feeling, *how can this region be anything other than tribal?* That word of course has become a pejorative. Western judgment makes "tribal" synonymous with "backward." Tribal takes on a different meaning when viewed through the prism of Lawrence—it very much seems like the natural order of things in this harsh environment, while foreign powers, which formed artificial nation-state boundaries in the Middle East, seem most naive and arrogant. Outside meddling in the region continues today, the spawn of this history.

A Syrian friend expressed feelings of admiration-frustration about Lawrence to me some months short of the one-hundredth anniversary of his riding into Damascus as the Turkish fled. Lawrence's spirit lives on in the Middle East, for good and ill. Lawrence wrote that "my object with the Arabs was always to make them stand on their own feet." But he wasn't able to influence the postwar order. During the conflict, he wasn't an early-day Rambo with a condescending white superior Western attitude. He wouldn't have survived a fortnight there if that were true. "Aurens" was loved by many Arabs at the same time his nation's leaders were selling them out in the secret Sykes-Picot treaty involving the United Kingdom, France, and Russia, which divided up the region in advance of the war's end, codified later at Versailles—Lawrence tried and failed to defeat Sykes-Picot there. Lawrence discovered the covert treaty as the war was being prosecuted but kept this information from his Arab comrades in arms, not for sinister reasons, but apparently to forestall them losing spirit. This of course also helped the British cause. Was this bad? Should he have told them as soon as he learned and allowed the chips to fall where they may? The reader can judge.

During the rebuke over his Arabian dress at Buckingham Palace, Lawrence told the person of importance who admonished him: "When a man serves two masters and has to offend one of these, it is better for him to offend the more powerful."

Lawrence was both a British officer and a "white Arab." Yet Lawrence remained very much loyal to the British master. Graves notes that he was a man who "hovered somewhere midway between the one thing and the other." He was the consummate outsider, which makes reading about him today so satisfying.

—Dale Maharidge
March 2018

AUTHOR'S INTRODUCTION
TO THE FIRST EDITION

Early this June I was invited by the publishers to write a book about Lawrence. I replied that I would do so with Lawrence's consent. Shaw, as I must call him, for he has now taken that name and definitely discarded 'Lawrence,' cabled his permission from India, and followed it up with a letter giving me a list of sources for my writing and saying that since a book was intended about him anyway he would prefer it done by me. He thought that I could write a book accurate enough in its facts to discourage further unauthorized accounts and that he could trust me not to spare his own feelings wherever I wished to draw any critical conclusion. And he hoped that the book would have exhausted all public interest by the time that he had finished with the Royal Air Force and returned to civil life.

I have his most generous permission, with that of his trustees, to use copyright material at my discretion—but certain limits were given—both from *Revolt in the Desert* and from *Seven Pillars of Wisdom* (of which that is an abridgment), a book that will not be issued for public sale in Shaw's lifetime. Unfortunately owing to pressure of time my completed typescript could not be submitted to Shaw before publication and I apologize to him for any passages where my discretion has been at fault. I did, however, write and ask him specific questions and sent him rough drafts of nearly all my material. I must, however, draw a clear line between Shaw's approval of my writing the book if it had to be written, and my own responsibility for the facts and opinions given here.

These chapters contain much that is of interest, I hope, even to readers of the *Seven Pillars of Wisdom*; and readers of *Revolt in the Desert* may be glad of a narrative that is continuous. Critics must remember that Shaw, when preparing the *Seven Pillars* for private circulation, had in mind an audience of not more than a couple of hundred people and that he consequently had greater freedom in his vocabulary than I have had; and could also assume a specialized knowledge of Eastern history, geography and politics in his audience that I am not permitted to assume.

I have tried to give a picture of an exasperatingly complex personality in the easiest possible terms. I have tried also to make a difficult story as clear as may be by a cutting-down of the characters that occur in it; mentioning by name only the outstanding ones and explaining the rest in such terms as 'a member of the body-guard,' 'a British Staff-officer with Feisal,' 'a major-general,' 'a French colonel,' 'the chief of the Beni Sakhr,' etc. (Geography has been similarly simplified; the maps have been designed so that few places occur on them that are not mentioned in that part of the story to which they refer, and few or no places are mentioned in the story that are not to be found on the maps.)

This is not the method of history, but history, which is the less readable the more historical it is, will not eventually be hindered by anything I have written. I have attempted a critical study of 'Lawrence'—the popular verdict that he is the most remarkable living Englishman, though I dislike such verdicts, I am inclined to accept—rather than a general review of the Arab freedom movement and the part played by England and France in regard to it. And there has been a space-limit.

For information about Lawrence I am greatly indebted to Mrs. Fontana, Mrs. Thomas Hardy, Mrs. Lawrence (his mother), Mrs. Kennington, Mrs. Bernard Shaw, Field-Marshal Viscount Allenby, Colonel John Buchan, Colonel R. V. Buxton, Colonel Alan Dawnay, Mr. E. Forster, Mr. Philip Graves, Sir Robert Graves, Dr. D. G. Hogarth, Mr. Cecil Jane, Mr. Eric Kennington, Mr. Arnold Lawrence (a younger brother), Sir Henry McMahon, Private Palmer of the Royal Tank Corps, Serjeant Pugh of the Royal Air Force, Mr. Vyvyan Richards, Lord Riddell, Mr. Siegfried Sassoon, Lord Stamfordham, the Dean of Winchester, Mr. C. Leonard Woolley, and others.

For permission to use copyright photographs, to *The Times*, the Imperial War Museum, the French Army Photographic Department, Major Goslett, Colonel R. V. Buxton, Dr. D. G. Hogarth, Serjeant Pugh, Mr. Eric Kennington, and Aircraftman Shaw himself.

R.G.
August, 1927

*Onager solitarius in desiderio animi sui
attraxit ventum amoris.*
JEREMIAH

LAWRENCE AND THE ARABS

I

I write of him as Lawrence since I first knew him by that
name, though, with the rest of his friends, I now usually
address him as 'T. E.': his initials at least seem fixed and
certain. In 1923 when he enlisted as a private soldier in the
Royal Tank Corps he took the name of 'T. E. Shaw': and has
continued in that name in the Royal Air Force, confirming
the alteration by Deed Poll. His enlistment in 1922 was in
the name of 'Ross' and these two are not, he admits, his only
efforts to 'label himself suitably.' He chose 'Shaw' and 'Ross'
more or less at random from an Army List, though their
shortness recommended them and probably also their late
positions in the alphabet; troops sometimes get lined up in
alphabetical order of names and Lawrence avoids the right of
the line by instinct. He was tired of the name Lawrence,—
and found it too long—particularly of the name 'Lawrence of
Arabia' which had become a romantic catchword and a great
nuisance to him. Hero worship seems not only to annoy Lawrence but, because of a genuine belief in his own fraudulence
as its object, to make him feel physically unclean; and few
who have heard or read of *Lawrence of Arabia* now mention
the name without a superstitious wonder or fail to lose their

heads if they happen to meet the man. A good enough excuse for discarding the name Lawrence was that it never had any proud family traditions for him. Mr. Lowell Thomas, who has written an inaccurate and sentimental account of Lawrence, links him up with the Northern Irish family of that name and with the famous Indian Mutiny hero 'who tried to do his duty': this is an invention and not a good one. 'Lawrence' began as a name of convenience like 'Ross' or 'Shaw,' and Lawrence was never of the tribe which does things because public duty is public duty. He acts in all things for his own best reasons, which though perhaps—I might say 'certainly'—honourable are never either public or obvious. The Arabs addressed him as 'Aurans' or 'Lurens,' but his nickname among them was *Emir Dinamit*, or Prince Dynamite, for his explosive energy. Old Auda, the fighting chief of the Howeitat, used to called him 'The World's Imp,' which is better still.

He was born at Tremadoc in North Wales in August 1888. This proved useful because later at Oxford University he could enter Jesus College, which financially favours Welsh students, as a Welshman. Actually he is of very mixed blood, none of it Welsh; if I remember rightly it is Irish, Hebridean, Spanish, and Norse. This again has always been useful; mixed blood has meant for Lawrence a natural gift for learning foreign languages, a respect for the manners and customs of strange people and, more than this, the power of entering a foreign community and being accepted after a time as a member of it. He has, also, no sense of the superiority of the English over foreigners. This he puts down merely to his general disrespect for humanity; but a strong natural bias towards the English may be suspected if only as towards the speakers of English, a language for which he cannot conceal his affection.

His father, now dead, came from County Meath in Ireland, of Leicestershire stock settled in the time of Sir Walter Raleigh. He was a great sportsman. The mixed blood is chiefly from this side. His mother who two years ago went off unconcernedly to end her days with a mission in Central China—but has recently been sent back home much against her will because of political troubles there—is a woman of decision and quiet power: with features like Lawrence's. She told me once: 'We could never be bothered with girls in our house': and, conveniently, she had five sons and no daughters. This home-atmosphere possibly accounts for Lawrence's world being so empty of women: he was brought up to do without female society and the habit has remained with him. That he has a fear or hatred of all women is untrue. He tries to talk to a woman as he would talk to another man, or to himself. If she does not return the compliment by talking to him as she would to another woman, he leaves her. He has no false sense of chivalry. He is not a courtier but neither is he a boor.

His childhood was spent in Scotland, the Isle of Man, Jersey, France and Hampshire. In France he attended a Jesuit school, though neither he nor his family were Catholics. From Hampshire the family came to Oxford where Lawrence went to the City of Oxford School. Of his boyhood at Oxford there are stories that show that he began being the person Lawrence early. He took an interest in archæology which elder people thought unwholesome in a boy, and when old buildings were pulled down or excavations made was always on the spot. He had a secret arrangement with the city workmen to give him any pieces of pottery or other finds that they made and was soon an actual expert on the pottery of the Middle Ages. He had a theory which he intended to prove in a book that the dating of ancient pottery in England is all wrong, much of what is called Roman pottery being really Saxon: but that book he has never found time to write. At the age of thirteen he began a series of bicycle tours round England by himself and in pursuit of a study of mediæval armour made a large collection of brass-rubbings from old monuments in country churches. He made a point at his home of never saying when or where he was going or when he would be back. He liked to return at night by an upper window and be found in bed the next morning. To avoid surveillance later he refused to sleep in the house at all, but used a summer-house in the garden (he built it himself) as his bedroom. He explored the many streams about Oxford in a canoe: (and in after years brought a canoe with him at great expense to Mesopotamia, where it was the first canoe ever seen on the River Euphrates). Not content with the streams above ground he began exploring the underground streams of Oxford City. Probably he made a map; maps were his speciality. He made eight tours of France in his school vacations, studying the cathedrals and castles, and living on practically nothing. When he was sixteen he broke a leg while he was wrestling with another boy at the Oxford City School. He said nothing until school ended for the day and then returned home, not able to walk, on a borrowed bicycle. (He has never grown since that date.)

He took no interest in school games because they were organized, because they had rules, because they had results. He will never compete in anything. He was interested in machinery—(he is still an expert on racing cars and such-like, and after the War occupied part of his leisure with the help of the makers of the Brough Superior motor-cycle in testing and reporting on their next year's models). He read widely, carefully and rapidly in several languages, his chief study being mediæval art, particularly sculpture. What is more remarkable is that while he was still at the High School he began thinking about that very revolt of the Arabs against the Turks which is the main story of this book.

At Jesus College in the University, where he won a scholarship, he read for the History School; or was supposed to do so. As a matter of fact the three years were spent chiefly in reading French Provençal poetry and mediæval Chansons de Geste. Mr. Vyvyan Richards, a fellow-undergraduate, has told me: 'There was a mystery in the College about a strange undergraduate who never appeared in the daytime but spent hours of the night walking round the quadrangle by himself; I was one of those appointed to investigate; that was how I first discovered Lawrence. I patronized him at first as a second-year man does a first-year man, but I soon stopped that. I remember once I was teasing him for his theories about pottery; we were walking on the New College mound which is supposed to have been thrown up in the Civil Wars. I kicked up a bit of pottery and said to him, "You'll tell me next that this proves something." "Thank you," he said, "as it happens it does. It goes to prove that this mound is considerably older than Cromwell's time." That silenced me. He never took any part in College life and never dined in Hall. Once in winter he arrived at my lodgings after midnight and asked me to come bathing. He wanted me to try the sport of diving through the ice: I thought it too dangerous, so he went off alone. He had a wonderful library, and was much interested in printing. It has been said that he printed books with me; but this is not true; there was much planning about it, but it never came off.'

Lawrence only lived one term in the College itself: the

remainder of the time he was allowed to live at home. He read all night and slept in the mornings. He was not only a non-smoker and total abstainer but a vegetarian. In all his University life, as at school, he never took part in or watched a single organized game, though I believe he did a certain amount of roof-climbing, an unorganized night-sport which is entirely against University regulations. He is said to have invented the now classic climb from Balliol College to Keble College, a distance of perhaps a third of a mile, with only a single drop in between. This Lawrence neither confirms nor denies. He had a lively admiration for his tutor R. L. Poole and only once 'cut' a tutorial, then wrote to apologize. Poole replied: 'Don't worry yourself at having failed to come to me last Tuesday. Your absence gave me the opportunity to do an hour's useful work.' He apparently only attended three courses of lectures in the whole of his three years and found these unprofitable.

Mr. Cecil Jane writes of this period:

> 'I coached him in his last year at the Oxford City School and saw a great deal of him all through his time at Oxford. He would never read the obvious books. I found out in the first week or two that the thing was to suggest rather out-of-the-way books. He could be relied upon to get more out of a suggestive sentence in a book than any ordinary man would get from a volume. His work was always on his own lines, even to the hours when he came to me. Shortly after midnight to 4 a.m. was a favourite time (living at home he had not to bother about College regulations: it was enough for his mother to report that he was "home by twelve"). He had the most diverse interests

historically, though they were mainly mediæval. For a long time I could not get him to take any interest in late European History—was very startled to find that he was absorbed by R. M. Johnston's *French Revolution*. While he was at school still I used to be surprised by his fondness for analysing character: it was a little habit of his to put questions to me in order to watch my expression: he would make no comment on my answer but I could see that he thought the more. In many ways he resembled his father, quite one of the most charming men I have known—very shy, very kind. Lawrence was not a bookworm though he read very fast and a great deal. I should not call him a scholar by temperament and the main characteristic of his work was always that it was unusual without the effort to be unusual. He liked anything in the nature of satire; that is why he appreciated Gibbon's notes so much. He was very diffident about his own work; he never published his really admirable (but small) degree thesis. He was very robust, a little difficult to know, and always unexpected.'

When the time came for his final examinations for his degree Lawrence was unprepared. He was advised to submit a special thesis to supplement his other papers. He chose as his subject 'The influence of the Crusades on the mediæval military architecture of Europe.' Even before he went to the University, he had specialized in mediæval fortifications and had visited every single twelfth-century castle in England and France; it now remained for him to go to Palestine and Syria and study the Crusaders' castles there. He decided to go out in the summer months of 1909, his last long vacation. He had learned a smattering of Arabic from a half-Irish Arab, then lecturing at Oxford, who advised him, if he went, to save expenses by living on the hospitality of the Syrian tribes. It was to be his first visit to the part of the world where he later became famous.

Before he left he visited Dr. D. G. Hogarth, the present Keeper of the Ashmolean Museum at Oxford, whom he met on this occasion for the first time but who has been his close friend ever since—'the man to whom I am indebted for every good job I have ever had except my enlistment in the Royal Air Force.' He told Hogarth that he was going to visit Syria to study Crusaders' castles but wished to know where he would be likely to find remains of the ancient Hittite civilization. Hogarth told him what he wanted but said, 'This is the wrong season to visit Syria: it is too hot there now.' 'I'm going,' said Lawrence. 'Well, have you the money? You'll want a guide and servants to carry your tent and baggage.' 'I'm going to walk,' Lawrence said. 'Europeans don't walk in Syria,' said Hogarth, 'it isn't safe or pleasant.' 'Well, I do,' said Lawrence. He went and was away for four months, returning to Oxford late for the next term. He had been on foot, in European dress and brown boots, carrying only a camera, from Haifa on the north coast of Palestine to the Taurus mountains and across to Urfa by the Euphrates in Northern Mesopotamia. He brought back sketch-plans and photographs of every mediæval fortress in Syria and also a collection of Hittite seals from the Aintab region for Hogarth. He had had two bouts of fever, Dr. Hogarth tells me, and had once been nearly murdered. The fever is perhaps hardly worth mentioning: Lawrence has had fever so often that he is quite used to it. He got malaria in France when he was sixteen and has had countless returns of it since. When he was eighteen he got Malta fever and since then has had dysentery, typhoid, blackwater fever, smallpox and other varieties.

The murder story has often been told, but incorrectly. What happened was that Lawrence on his way to Syria had bought a copper watch at Paris for ten francs. By constant use the case had been polished till it shone. In a Turkman village near the banks of the Euphrates where he was collecting Hittite antiquities he took out this watch one morning; the villagers murmured 'Gold.' A villager stalked Lawrence all day as he went on his journey and towards evening ran ahead and met him, as if accidentally. Lawrence asked the way to a certain village. The Turkman showed him a short cut across country; where he sprang upon Lawrence, knocked him down, snatched his Colt revolver, put it to his head and pulled the trigger. Though loaded it did not go off: the villager did not understand the mechanism of the safety catch, which was raised. He tried the trigger again and then in anger threw it away and battered Lawrence about the head with stones. The appearance of a shepherd fortunately frightened him off before he had succeeded in cracking Lawrence's skull. Lawrence got up, crossed the Euphrates to the nearest town (Birejik) where he could find Turkish policemen. There he presented the order that he had from the Turkish Ministry of the Interior requiring all local governors to afford him every help, and collected a hundred and ten men. With this force, whose ferry-fare he had to pay across the river, he re-entered the villa.

Contrary to the usual story of a desperate fight and the burning of the village, there was no violence. Lawrence, with fever heavy on him, went to sleep while the usual day-long argument went on between the police and the villagers. At night the village elders gave up the stolen property and the thief. The true version of the story is better if only because it has this more satisfactory ending that the thief afterwards worked in the diggings at Carchemish under Lawrence; not too well, but Lawrence was easy with him.

During this walk he lodged every night, when off the beaten track, in the nearest native village, taking advantage of the hospitality which poor Syrians always show towards other poor; and began his familiarity with Arab dialects. Lawrence is not an Arabic scholar. He has never sat down to study it, nor even learned its letters—in any case twenty years' study are needed before anyone can call himself an Arabic scholar and Lawrence has had a better use for his time. But he is fluent in conversational Arabic, and can tell pretty accurately by a man's accent and the expressions he uses from what tribe or district of Arabia, Syria, Mesopotamia or Palestine he comes. On his return to Oxford he was awarded a First Class Honours Degree in History on the strength of his thesis, and the examiners were so impressed that they celebrated the event by a special dinner at which Lawrence's tutor, Poole, was the host.

It is circumstantially related that the piece of archæological news which most delighted Oxford concerned the burial of Crusaders in the Holy Land; that it was known already that a knight who had been on one Crusade and died at home had his legs and the legs of his effigy crossed at the ankle, that a knight who had been on two Crusades had his legs crossed at the knee, but that Lawrence found that Crusaders who had died in the Holy Land itself were buried with their toes turned inwards. The incrustations of the Lawrence legend are typified in this completely false and widely current story. In the first place, Lawrence made no such discovery. In the second, he does not believe that the crossing of the legs of the effigies has anything to do with the Crusades. Let me take the opportunity of contradicting a further absurd story of Lawrence's adventures about this time among the head-hunters of Borneo. Somebody has confused him, I suppose, with Rajah Charles Brooke of Sarawak; Mr. Lowell Thomas gives the story, alleging a British Museum mission.

The desert took a strong hold on Lawrence. He went riding out on one occasion (a year or two later) over a rolling plain in Northern Syria to examine a ruin of the Roman period which the Arabs believed to have been made by a prince of the border as a desert-palace for his queen. The clay with which it was built was said to have been kneaded not with water but with the precious essential oils of flowers. His guides, sniffing the air, led him from one crumbling room to the next, saying, 'This is jessamine, this is violet, this is rose.' But at last an Arab said, 'Come and smell the sweetest scent of all,' and they went to the main hall, where they drank in the calm, empty, eddyless desert wind. 'This,' said the Arab, 'is the best, it has no taste.' The Bedouin, Lawrence recognized, turns his back on perfumes and luxuries and the petty business of towns because in the desert he is without doubt free: he has lost material ties, houses, gardens, superfluous possessions and all other such complications, and has won instead a personal liberty in the shadow of starvation and death. This was an attitude that moved Lawrence greatly, so that, I believe, his nature has ever since been divided into two conflicting selves, the Bedouin self always longing for the bareness, simplicity, harshness of the desert—that state of mind of which the desert is a symbol—and the over-civilized European self. The European self despises the Bedouin as one who loves to torture himself needlessly and who sees the world as a hard pattern of black and white (of luxury or poverty, saintliness or sin, honour or disgrace), not as a moving changing landscape of countless subtle colours and shades and varieties. Again, the conflict is between the fanatic who is always either on the crest or in the trough of his emotions, who loves and hates violently, and the over-civilized man whose chief aim in life is to keep an equal mind even if he undoes himself by the very wideness of his sympathies. These two selves are mutually destructive, so Lawrence has finally fallen between them into a nihilism which cannot find, in being, even a false god in which to believe.

Magdalen College, on Hogarth's prompting, gave him a travelling scholarship for four years, and this enabled him to continue with his archæology. In 1910 he first went with Dr. Hogarth and Mr. Campbell-Thompson on the British Museum expedition to excavate Carchemish, the ruined Hittite capital on the Syrian bank of the Euphrates. Hogarth had engaged him on the strength of his Syrian walking tour and his knowledge of pottery. He was not a trained archæologist as yet, but an odd-job man at fifteen shillings a day and made it his main business to look after the gangs and keep them happy. For the rest, he had the photography, the pottery, the piecing together of broken sculptures and, later, engineering work in laying or lifting the light railway that carried earth from the diggings to the dumps. But the gangs came first. While they were happy the work was sure to go well. Lawrence knew them all by name and even the names of their children for whom they would beg quinine when there was fever about. Only he never knew any one of the men by sight; a peculiarity of Lawrence's which will be discussed later.

In the winter of 1910, in the off-season for digging, Hogarth arranged for Lawrence to visit Sir Flinders Petrie's camp in Egypt, to study the most advanced technical methods in digging. The camp was in a village near the Fayoum and the work was the uncovering of pre-dynastic remains of about the year 4000 B.C. Sir Flinders Petrie was at first not impressed with Lawrence's appearance, and it is said reprimanded him for appearing at the camp in football shorts and a blazer. 'Young man, we do not play cricket here.' The absurdity of Lawrence as a cricket enthusiast is not the least comic point in the tale. However, Sir Flinders Petrie soon realized that he was a useful man to have with him, and tried to get him to join the camp again another year. But Lawrence thought that Egyptian excavations were dull compared with Hittite excavations. The Hittite was still an unknown civilization; with the Egyptians the main problems were solved and all that remained was to fill in unimportant gaps. The only personal recollection I heard from Lawrence about this digging in Egypt was that often in the evening when the sun suddenly sank and it got very cold he and his fellow-workers used to wrap themselves round and round for warmth in the white linen cloth which had been buried with these pre-dynastic Egyptians for their next-world wear (it was a period before mummy-wrappings) and walk home that way smelling of spices.

As an archæologist Lawrence soon won reputation. His memory for details is extraordinary, almost morbid. A friend once joked about him 'there is something of the thin-lipped Oxford don about Lawrence'; but that was no more than saying that Lawrence has a vast well-ordered store of accurate technical knowledge on every conceivable subject and does not like to hear amateurs talk inaccurately when he is about.

Half a dozen decisive words from Lawrence and superfluous talk ends. I was present once when an American writer who only knew Lawrence as a soldier began to teach him about Arabic art. Very soon finding himself in deep water the writer shifted to ground where he thought he was safe: he began to talk about Aztec stone carvings in Central America. Lawrence listened politely and corrected him on a technicality. After that the American stopped talking and listened. Field-Marshal Allenby, who is interested in archæology (and during the War took away the command of at least one officer because he pulled down an ancient building), told me: 'When Lawrence and I talked archæology it was always Father Lawrence talking to a little schoolboy. I listened and learned.'

Probably Lawrence's knowledge is not so vast as it appears and the impression of omniscience that he conveys is due rather to a faculty of forgetting what he calls utterly useless knowledge such as higher mathematics, class-room metaphysics and theories of æsthetics, and of fitting together harmoniously what he does know. A small knowledge which is in harmony with itself will seem uncanny to those with a much greater store of facts that do not hold together. Still, Lawrence's knowledge must be pretty extensive. In six years he read every book in the library of the Oxford Union—the best part of 50,000 volumes, probably. His father used to get him the books while he was at school and afterwards he always borrowed six volumes a day in his father's name and his own. For three years he read day and night on a hearthrug, which was a mattress so that he could fall asleep as he read. Often he spent eighteen hours a day reading, and at last got so good at it that he could tear the heart out of the most formidable book in half an hour. In reviewing Lawrence's life, one has to accept casually such immoderate feats; they are part of his nature and the large number of them that can be verified excuses one's credulity for others of the same remarkable character that are pure fiction.

Lawrence has been known to give information, when provoked, even where it could hardly be expected to be appreciated. 'What are you grinning at, you there?' shouted a sergeant- instructor to him one day about two years ago, when he was in the Tank Corps. 'Do you really want to know, Sergeant?' said Lawrence. He did. So Lawrence explained a joke in a late-Greek dialogue of Lucian's that he had been turning over in his mind during arms-drill. He quoted for a quarter of an hour and the sergeant and squad listened without interruption in the greatest interest. Again, in a hut in the Air Force a comrade once asked him, 'Excuse me, Shaw, but what does "iconoclast" mean?'—he acted as a handy cross-word dictionary—and then Lawrence outlined a brief history of the religious politics in fifth-century Constantinople which first gave rise to the word. But this is merely a good-humoured joke on himself: he despises mere knowledge, though he accumulates it and stores it carefully from old habit. He despises it because it is imperfect, because he sees *knowledge* as the opposite of *wisdom*. He never bluffs; and he dislikes bluffers. They say that in his first days in the Royal Air Force three years ago he helped some of the fellows who were taking German as an extra part of the education course. This came to the notice of one of the officers, who heard that Aircraftman Shaw had been seen reading a book called *Faust*. The next day, finding Shaw with his book, the officer began to show off: 'What a wonderful writer Goethe was! *Faust* is a masterpiece, don't you agree? Now, *this* is a passage that has always appealed to me very much' (pointing over Shaw's shoulder). 'Yes,' said Shaw, 'but this is not Goethe's *Faust* but Jacobsen's *Nills Lyhne* in Danish.' His knowledge does not help him much in the Royal Air Force. The Education Officer at Uxbridge asked him: 'And you, what is the subject in which you feel particularly weak?' The other fellows had said 'French' and 'Geography' and 'Mathematics.' Lawrence replied simply and truthfully, 'Polishing greasy boots.'

This is getting too far ahead of the story, which is still about Lawrence as an archæologist before the War. In 1911 he was again at Carchemish with Hogarth. The report of the Carchemish excavations which lasted from 1910 to 1914 is published by the Oxford University Press. After 1911 Dr. Hogarth left the operations in charge of Mr. G. Leonard Woolley, who re-engaged Lawrence. A visitor, Mr. Fowle, has given a description of the life at the camp when he visited it in 1913. The Turks had given permission to the excavators to build only a single room; Lawrence and Woolley kept the letter and broke the spirit of the order by building a large **U**-shaped building and then partitioning it off into compartments each with a separate door into the courtyard that this single room enclosed. The compartments to the right were used for storing antiquities and for photographic work (Lawrence's particular care); the sleeping-rooms of the excavators and their guests were on the left. The middle of the **U** was a living room with an open fireplace, well-filled book-cases and a long table covered with current British journals and the archæological journals of all the world. According to Mrs. Fontana, wife of the former Italian Consul at Aleppo, the house, which was of mud-brick, was paved with a Roman mosaic found in the upper layers of the excavations. She relates how Lawrence would cross the

Euphrates in his canoe to get flowers from an island on the far side to liven up the place; a dangerous voyage, it seemed to her, for the Euphrates has a very powerful current. In its marvellously soft water he used to bathe every day. He had also got the workmen to make him a long clay water-chute and taught them the sport of tobogganing down it into the river.

Woolley and Lawrence had soon come to be on the best possible terms with their workmen, who were of mixed races: Kurds, Arabs, Turks, and so on. Local brigands were working for them at the diggings, including the leaders of the two most notorious brigand bands, the Kurdish and the Arab, and the two Englishmen were so well known and respected that they were made judges of various local disputes between villages or persons. Mr. Fowle relates that Lawrence had recently been away to settle a case where a man had kidnapped a girl from her father's house but had not been able to get the father's consent to a marriage.

In Woolley's bedroom was an ancient wooden chest containing thousands of silver pieces for the payment of the workmen. It was unlocked and unguarded; because if any man had come to steal from it the other workmen would soon have found him out and taken matters into their own hands and probably killed the thief. Lawrence and Woolley found that the way to get the best results was to pay the workmen an extra sum of money for any antiquity that they found, according to its actual value. The workers accepted the sum offered without question, whether they were given gold or small silver, and the more willingly because the Englishmen accepted nothing that was not paid for. If the object offered was valueless it was returned to them. They came to take a real interest in the work and Mr. Fowle records the excitement with which the uncovering of a Hittite stone carving was watched, and the burst of applause and firing of two hundred revolvers when the four-thousand-year-old figure of a superb stag was revealed.

Lawrence himself, as Dr. Hogarth tells me, preferred sleeping outside the hut on a knoll, the ancient citadel of the city, close to the river. Here would gather the diggers and amuse him with stories, many of them scandalous, about the old Sheik of Jerablus (the modern village on the site of Carchemish) and his young wife, and about the Germans in their camp a quarter of a mile away. A railway was being made from Constantinople to Bagdad and at the site of Carchemish the railway had to cross the Euphrates. German engineers were building a bridge. The Germans could not be bothered to get to know their workmen by name, but used numbers painted on their coats as the quickest way of recognizing them. They even allowed members of tribes who were blood enemies to work side by side and many deaths happened this way. The Germans envied Lawrence and Woolley because they could always get as many workmen as they wanted. On one occasion when the Englishmen had to turn away fifty men for lack of money to pay them with, the men refused to go but stayed on without pay until money might come again.

With the Germans there was good feeling. Woolley and Lawrence gave them permission among other things to cart off for their new buildings such stones from the diggings as were of no archæological interest. But the chief engineer, Contzen, was a difficult man to remain friendly with. He was a rough drinking fellow, the son of a Cologne chemist. The back of his neck was too thick for Lawrence's taste: it lapped over his collar. He came once to ask permission to dig away some mounds of earth which, though inside the excavation area, were close to the bridge where he wanted earth for an embankment. This was refused because the mounds of earth were the old mud-brick city walls of Carchemish and of great archæological importance. He grew angry at that and breaking off all friendly relations decided to wait until the digging season ended and the Englishmen went away. So when Woolley had gone to England and Lawrence to the Lebanon mountains, Contzen recruited local labour for digging away the walls. There was an Aleppo Arab called Wahid the Pilgrim left in charge of the diggings in the absence of the Englishmen, who, hearing what Contzen was about to do, went over to the German camp and told him that without orders from Woolley or Lawrence he could not allow the work to begin. Contzen answered that he would start the next day and ordered Wahid to leave the camp. Wahid sent a wire to Lawrence in the Lebanon, saying that he would hold up the work until further orders. He went the next morning with a rifle and two revolvers and sat on top of the threatened wall. A hundred workmen began laying a light- railway from the embankment to the foot of the wall, and Wahid addressed them, promising that he would shoot the first man who drove a pick into the wall, and then would shoot any German within range. The workmen, many of whom were of the English camp but doing temporary work in the off-season, stopped work and sat down at a safe distance. Contzen came up and threatened, but Wahid levelled his rifle and told him to keep his distance: Contzen did not dare to do more. All that day the two parties sat and watched each other, and all the next day. That night the Germans began a little revolver practice in their courtyard, shooting at a lighted candle: Wahid climbed up on the wall and fired half a dozen shots over their heads, shouting to them to stop their noise and go to bed: and they obeyed.

Lawrence wired to Wahid to hold on; he was now in Aleppo seeing to things. Wahid wired back that the Germans were becoming dangerous, and that the next morning he was going to the camp to kill Contzen. Then he made his will, got drunk and prepared for the morning. Lawrence in Aleppo found he could do nothing with the local Turkish Officials in whose care the diggings were supposed to be, so he wired to Constantinople, and got an unexpectedly quick reply: the Turkish Education Minister was ordered to go up to Carchemish in person and stop the work. Lawrence wired an order to Wahid to offer no further resistance to the Germans. He sent the wire by the railway telegraph, and the railway people, who naturally were on Contzen's side in his embankment-making, knew nothing of the orders from Constantinople to stop the work and thought that the opposition was at an end. Lawrence and the Minister were given a motor trolley, on which they travelled at once. Wahid, getting the wire, was deeply disappointed and went off to drown his sorrows in drink. Contzen set his gang to work on the wall. They had hardly moved two or three feet of earth and mud-brick when up came the Minister in a fury, with Lawrence behind him, and made Contzen tear up the rails and dismiss his extra workmen, abusing him for his dishonesty. Wahid was publicly congratulated.

After this there was further trouble with Contzen. (Though not with the German camp as a whole as has been said: Woolley and Lawrence kept open house and the better Germans used to visit them regularly and dine with them.) One day, Ahmed, one of the house-servants of Woolley and Lawrence, on his way home from shopping at the village, met the foreman of a gang of railway workers. The foreman owed him money and a dispute started. A German engineer came up and flogged Ahmed without inquiring into the cause of the dispute: it was enough that the railway work had been delayed. Lawrence went to Contzen, and told him that one of the engineers had assaulted his house-servant and must apologize. Contzen consented to make inquiries, called up the engineer, and asked him for his account of the affair. He then told Lawrence angrily, 'It is all a lie. This gentleman never assaulted your servant; he merely had him flogged.'

'Well, isn't that an assault?'

'Certainly not. You can't use these natives without flogging them. We flog every day.'

'We have been here longer than you and have not flogged a man yet, and don't intend to let you start on them. Your engineer must come to the village and apologize to Ahmed in public.'

'Nonsense. The incident is closed,' and Contzen turned his back.

'On the contrary,' said Lawrence (one can hear his small deadly voice), 'if you don't do as I ask I shall take the matter into my own hands.'

Contzen turned round again. 'Which means—?'

'That I shall take your engineer to the village and compel him to apologize.'

'You will do nothing of the sort,' said Contzen, scandalized; but then he looked at Lawrence again. In the end the engineer came to make his public apology, to the vast satisfaction of the village.

Later the Germans found themselves in great trouble. They had established a local bakery to prevent their men sending parties for bread to their home-villages every ten days. This bread- getting meant that thirty or forty men missed a day's work. The Germans let the bakery to a town-bred Syrian (one of a most dishonest race), who decided to make his fortune. He used bad corn and so the bread was too sour to eat. The Germans had arranged that the money for the bread supplied should be deducted from the men's pay. When the workmen refused to eat the bread and again sent home to the villages for their own, the price of the week's bread that they had refused was deducted from their pay. Not only the bread contract but the contract for getting men to work on the railway had been given to adventurers; as Contzen's successor Hoffmann discovered to his disgust. Complaints of the men not getting the money due to them were so numerous that he decided to pay them himself. Unfortunately he accepted the figures given him by the contractors, and there was trouble at once.

The first man who came to the pay-table had been offered fifteen piastres a day, which was a good wage, and had been working six weeks: he was down in the books as entitled to only six piastres a day. After deductions for bread which he had not had, water which he had got from the river himself, and so on, he was found to be owed only twenty-seven and a half piastres for six weeks' work. The man protested. Hoffmann's Circassian guard slashed him across the face with a whip. The man stooped to pick up a stone; his friends, who were Kurds, did the same, and the guard fired. A brisk battle started, stones and a few guns on one side, revolvers on the other. Lawrence and Woolley hearing the noise came up to persuade the men, about seven hundred of them, to cease fire. Lawrence has a gesture which he uses in emergencies of this kind. He lazily raises both hands, clasps them behind his head and remains silent and apparently wrapped in thought. It attracts attention more readily than any noise or violent motion, and when he has his audience quiet all about him he says what is to be said with the gentle, humorous wisdom of an old nurse subduing a noisy schoolroom. The Kurds ceased fire: but the seven Germans did not. They continued to use their revolvers from the hut where they had taken refuge, and the Circassian raised his gun towards Woolley and Lawrence as they came up begging the Germans to stop. The Germans had quite lost their heads and went on firing, though the Kurds were not firing back: it was only with the help of Wahid and a former brigand chief called Hamoudi, that Lawrence and Woolley prevented the whole mass of workmen from rushing down to do massacre. It was more than two hours before the Kurds could be drawn off: then it was found that the Germans only had cuts and bruises to show while the Kurds had eighteen men wounded and one killed.*

The Germans had wired for help to Aleppo at the first alarm, saying that their camp was being fired on: the telegram was mistranslated and a special train arrived with the Aleppo Volunteer Fire Brigade, brass helmets and all. After they had been sent back, a detachment of two hundred Turkish soldiers came and was stationed in the German camp. But all railway work ceased for a week because the dead man belonged to a Kurdish clan across the river, and his friends refused to allow the bridge-building to be carried on in their territory. The German Consul at Aleppo finally had to ask the Englishmen to settle the matter between the railway people and the Kurds. Woolley agreed and blood-money was fixed at

---

* This account appears in Woolley's *Dead Towns and Living Men*: the slight differences in the story are due to emendations by Lawrence.

£120. The German Consul refused, saying that the Germans had acted in self-defence, but he was soon made to see that a tribal matter must be settled by tribal custom. The Kurdish chief agreed to accept the money but only out of favour to the English, and things were patched up: in future the money for the workmen was to be paid to the Kurdish head-men direct from the Company for the payment of the workers, and the chief was to be himself responsible that the work was properly carried on. For these services Lawrence and Woolley were offered Turkish decorations, but refused them.

This ex-brigand chief Hamoudi and a younger man called Dahoum, who was trained by Lawrence as a photographer, came on a visit with him to England. They enjoyed Oxford, particularly the sport of bicycle riding, which was new to them. They had women's bicycles because of their long robes, and got into trouble for the delight that they took in bicycling round and round the policeman who stands in the centre of 'Carfax,' the principal cross-roads of the city. They slept out in the garden. Their one regret was that they could not take the hot-water-taps back with them: Lawrence could not make them understand that these would not work in a Syrian mud-brick village as they did at No. 2 Polstead Road, Oxford. And they would stand in the public lavatories and stroke the white glazed 'beautiful beautiful bricks.'

Among the women for whom Lawrence has had the greatest respect was the late Miss Gertrude Bell, one of the great English travellers in Arabia before Lawrence's day. (Among these, by the way, who include Palgrave, Doughty and the Blunts, he does not reckon Sir Richard Burton who, he says, did not travel single-mindedly as the others did, wrote so difficult an English style as to be unreadable, and was both pretentious and vulgar. Among non-English travellers, he speaks highly of Burckhardt and Niebuhr.) Gertrude Bell visited the Carchemish camp one morning in 1911 and since news of her coming had arrived before her, the village was in a great state of excitement. At the time there were only three Englishmen in the camp: Dr. Hogarth who was married, Mr. Campbell-Thompson who was widely known to be engaged, and Lawrence who wore the red tasselled belt to his white flannel shorts which marked the bachelor in those parts. It was decided by the diggers that Gertrude Bell was coming to marry Lawrence and all preparations were made for a festival When, therefore, she said good-bye the same evening and prepared to go off there was a great clamour. It was thought that she had refused Lawrence and so insulted the village. Lawrence managed to quiet them down by an ungallant but successful lie before stones were thrown and Gertrude Bell, who had been puzzled by the demonstration, never learned the truth until Hogarth told her some years later: it amused her greatly.

There were two digging seasons at Carchemish: between June and September the local harvest claimed the workmen, and between November and March the rains rained and the snow snowed and the Euphrates flooded the lowlands into a marsh. In the off-seasons Lawrence did not usually return to England but wandered instead all over Syria and the Near East studying antiquities, learning Arabic and getting in touch with the members of the various Arab Freedom Societies of which an account will be given in the next chapter. He had already begun to take steps for the fulfilment of his schoolboy ambition to help in the Arab Revolt. But his immediate object was to collect information for writing a history of the Cru-

sades. This is another book that he has never found time to
write. He did, however, complete a travel-book called 'Seven
Pillars of Wisdom,' later destroyed in manuscript, about seven
typical Near-Eastern cities: Cairo, Smyrna, Constantinople,
Beyrout, Aleppo, Damascus, Medina.

He was, among other things, a student of world-politics and
saw that the alliance between the Turks and the Germans would
have dangerous results. The Constantinople-Bagdad railway
was part of a German scheme for establishing an Eastern
Empire with the Turks as allies. He had already paid a visit to
Lord Kitchener pointing out the danger of letting the Germans
get control of the port of Alexandretta which is in the crook
between Asia Minor and Syria, but Kitchener told him that he
knew all about it, He had repeatedly warned the British Foreign
Office of the complications that would follow—the French
had ambitions for the control of Syria too—but Sir Edward
Grey's pacific policy allowed no alternative. Kitchener's final
words to Lawrence were that within three years there would
be a world-war which would settle this lesser question with a
greater. 'So run along, young man, and dig before it rains.' It
has been said that Lawrence's way of calling public attention in
Europe to the concealed threat to world-peace in the building
of the railway that linked Berlin with Bagdad was this: that he
loaded sections of drainage pipes on mules and transported
them by night to the hills which commanded the bridge; that
he mounted them on piles of sand to resemble guns; that, as he
expected, the Germans observed them through field-glasses, got
excited and wired to Berlin and Constantinople that the British
were fortifying the hills; that the European press was excited for
days. There is no word of truth in all this comic-paper stuff. To
begin with, Lawrence had no drainage pipes at his disposal.

The following are extracts from letters of Lawrence from Carchemish. The first is dated September 1912:

'To-day is the end of Ramadan, and they are surging in and out of the courtyard firing revolvers, and bringing me portions from the feast going on in the village. I have twelve sheets of bread, wrapping up twelve packets of parched corn, with grapes and cucumbersin abundance. But I can't yet talk Arabic!

'There is a splendid dress called "of the seven kings":—long parallel stripes of the most fiery colours from neck to ankle: it looks glorious: and over that they wear a short blue coat, turned up at the cuffs to show a dull red lining, and they gird themselves with a belt of thirteen varicoloured tassels, and put a black silk and silver weave of Hamath work over their heads under a black goat-hair head-rope. You have then only to add a vest of gold-embroidered silk, and white under-tunics to get the idea of one man's dress (I have forgotten Kurd knitted socks in nine primary colours, and red shoes), and there are ninety and nine, all different, eating a sheep before the door!

'All is well here (after bad waves of cholera and smallpox) and I expect to get back at Christmas.'

The second letter is dated December 1913:

'I have gradually slipped down, until a few months ago when I found myself an ordinary archæologist. I fought very hard, at Oxford and after going down, to avoid being labelled: but the insurance people have nailed me down, now ... I have got to like this place very much: and the people here—five or six of them—and the whole manner of living pleases me. We have 200 men to play with, anyhow we like so long as the excavations go on, and they are very splendid fellows many of them—I had two of them, head-men, in England with me this summer—and it is great fun with them. Then there are the digs, with dozens of wonderful things to find; and hosts of beautiful things in the villages and towns to fill one's house with. Not to mention Hittite seal-hunting in the country round about, and the Euphrates to rest in when one is over-hot. It is a place where one eats lotus nearly every day.'

In the winter of 1913 Dr. Hogarth was asked to suggest an archæologist who might join the surveying party in the peninsula of Sinai—the desert between Palestine and Egypt in which Moses kept the Jews wandering until he had made a fighting people of them. He recommended Woolley, but Woolley could not spare the three months that he was wanted for, so he and Lawrence went together for six weeks and divided the work between them. They got on well with the surveyor, Captain Newcombe, an Engineer officer who afterwards was in Arabia with Lawrence, and made important discoveries of ancient remains. They mapped out, not too seriously perhaps, the probable route of the Israelites' marches and found the place which may have been Kadesh Barnea where Moses struck the rock and water gushed out. They went as far as Petra and Maan in Arabia, places that figured importantly in Lawrence's campaign four years later. Their report appears in a book called *The Wilderness of Sin*, published in 1914 by the Palestine Exploration Fund. The survey could not be complete without certain bearings taken at the Red Sea port of Akaba, but the Turks had refused permission, for military reasons. Lawrence told Newcombe that he would go and look at Akaba. He got there without opposition and took what notes he wanted. Then he had a sudden desire to explore the ancient ruins on a little island called Faroun Island which lies a quarter of a mile from the coast. He asked permission to use the one boat that was on the beach. The Turks refused and a large party drew the boat up on the beach so that he could not possibly move it. That did not stop Lawrence. In the middle of the day when all Turkish soldiers go to sleep he made a raft out of three of his large camel water-tanks. These copper tanks hold eighteen gallons apiece and measure about three feet six inches by one foot three inches, and are nine inches deep; they make excellent rafts. The wind took him safely across and he inspected the ruins, but he had difficulty on the return journey. The water was full of sharks, too.

The survey, it should be explained, was ordered by Kitchener for military purposes. But it was disguised as archæology. The Palestine Exploration Fund got permission from the Turks for it and the task of Lawrence and Woolley was, they found on arrival, to provide the archæological excuse for Newcombe's map-making activities.

II

A brief description of Lawrence:—He is short (five feet, five and a half inches), with his body long, I should judge, in proportion to his legs, for he is more impressive seated than standing. He has a big head of a Norse type, rising steeply at the back. His hair is fair (not blond) and rather fine: his complexion is fair and he could go unshaved longer than most men without showing it. The upper part of his face is kindly, almost maternal; the lower part is severe, almost cruel. His eyes are blue grey and constantly in motion. His hands and feet are small. He is, or was, of great physical strength: he has been seen to raise up a rifle at arm's length, holding it by the barrel-end, until it was parallel with the ground—yet no one would suspect him of being more than tough. In Arabia he won the respect of the desert fighters by his feats of strength and agility as much as by his other qualities. The pass-test of the highest order of fighters was the feat of springing off a trotting camel and leaping on again with one hand on the saddle and a rifle in the other. It is said that Lawrence passed the test. Of his powers of physical endurance the story will tell.

Here are a few first impressions of Lawrence; difficult to

reconcile:—'*That* commonplace looking little man!' (a poet). 'Face and figure of a Circassian dancing-girl' (an American journalist-lecturer). 'A little man with a red face like a butcher' (Royal Tank Corps). 'Face like a cheap writing-pad; a proper swede-looking (i.e. bumpkin) chap' (Royal Air Force). 'A comical little x—' (Royal Tank Corps). 'A young man of considerable physical beauty: it is the sober truth that I have not seen such burnished gold hair before or since, nor such intensely blue eyes' (a visitor at Carchemish). 'A very quiet, sedate manner, a fine head but insignificant body' (a major of the Camel Corps).

He has a trick of holding his hands loosely folded below his breast, the elbows to his sides, and carries his head a little tilted, the eyes on the ground. He can sit or stand for hours at a stretch without moving a muscle. He talks in short sentences, deliberately and quietly without accenting his words strongly. He grins a lot and laughs seldom. He is a dead shot with a pistol and a good rifle-shot. His greatest natural gift is being able to switch off the current of his personality whenever he wishes to be unnoticed in company. He can look heavy and stupid, even vulgar; and uses this power constantly in self-protection. When he first joined the Royal Air Force he was sent one day to nail down carpets under the direction of an Air-Marshal's wife. She had known him well, but Lawrence to avoid general embarrassment did not wish to be recognized, and so she did not know him. As a matter of fact he is hardly ever recognized in uniform by people who used to know him. The tight collar and peaked cap are a disguise and there is nothing immediately remarkable about his appearance, no irregularity of feature or gesture or carriage. When the current is not switched off there is a curious feeling of force whenever he is in the room, a steady force, not an aimless disturbing one, and the more powerful because it is so well controlled; so that those who do not accept him as a friendly being are apt to fear him. I have even heard it said 'Lawrence must have direct dealings with the Supernatural.' This is, however, nonsense. The power is from within and not from without. I have noticed that he dislikes being touched; a hand laid on his shoulder or knee is an offence; he can understand the Oriental notion that 'virtue' (he would, I think, call it 'integrity') goes out of a man when so touched. He will never shake hands if he can avoid doing so nor will he ever fight hand to hand. He does not drink or smoke. This is not due to deliberate teetotal conviction or because he regards these things as poison, but principally because he has no occasion to drink or smoke. Most people begin drinking and smoking out of mere sociability: Lawrence always avoids sociability of any sort. He is uncomfortable with strangers: this is what is called his shyness. He regards drinking, gluttony, gambling, sport and the passions of love—the whole universe for the average man—as unnecessary; as, at the best, stimulants for the years when life goes flat.

He avoids eating with other people. Regular mealtimes are not to his liking. He hates waiting more than two minutes for a meal or spending more than five minutes on a meal. That is why he lives mainly on bread and butter. And he likes water better than any other drink. It is his opinion that feeding is a very intimate performance and should be done in a small room behind locked doors. He eats, when he does eat, which is seldom, in a casual abstracted way. He came to visit me one breakfast-time on his racing motor-bicycle: he had come about two hundred miles in five hours. He would eat no breakfast. I asked him later what the food was like in the camp. 'I seldom eat it: it's good enough. I am now a storeman in the Quartermaster's stores, so I don't need much.' 'When did you last have a meal?' I asked. 'On Wednesday.' Since when apparently he had some chocolate, an orange and a cup of tea. This was Saturday. Then I think I put some apples near him, and after a while he reached for one. Fruit is his only self-indulgence. (Shelley, by the way, had this casual habit of eating, though he did not thrive on it like Lawrence: and he had Lawrence's gift of entering and leaving a room unnoticed if he wished.) It is his occasional habit to knock off proper feeding for three days—rarely five—just to make sure that he can do it without feeling worried or strained. One's sense of things gets very keen by this fasting, he finds, and it is good practice for hard times. His life has been full of hard times.

Lawrence also, when his own master, avoids regular hours of sleep. He has found that his brain works better if he sleeps as irregularly as he eats. In the Royal Air Force he is always in bed at 'Lights Out' and sleeps until after midnight. Then he dozes, thinking more or less until reveille. At night, he finds, the minds of others are switched off and that gives his mind longer range, free of their vibrations. He avoids as far as possible all social relationships, all public events. He joins no clubs, societies, groups. He answers few letters but the immediately pressing ones and not always those. On visiting Oxford in 1922 after two months prolonged to six in the East, he found his table stacked with correspondence; perhaps two or three hundred letters. He had given orders to have nothing forwarded. He read them all carefully and sent off a single answer—a telegram: the rest went into the waste-paper basket. Usually he will answer a pre-paid telegram. Or, it would be more true to say, he will use the reply-form, though not necessarily to the sender. He *never* answers a letter addressed to him as 'Lawrence': this warning may save some of my readers money in stamps. When he does write a letter it is not of the sort that finds its way into the waste-paper basket. A Lawrence letter is always practical, considered, full, helpful, informative. This sort of thing . . . 'When you go to Rheims, go alone. Sit down at the base of the sixth pilaster from the west on the south side of the nave aisle and look up between the fourth and fifth pillars at the third window of the clerestory on the north side of the nave . . .' (1910).

He is one of the rare people who have a sensible attitude towards money. He neither loves it nor fears it, for he has found it useless to help on the two or three occasions when he has greatly desired things worth while. He can be a financier if and when it pleases him: for the most part he is not bothered about his bank-balance. At the moment he has no bank-balance at all, and has taken great care not to make a penny out of any of his writings on the Arab Revolt. Apart from this he has done his best to earn money with his pen, and has made £35 in four years' anonymous effort. He calls these earnings the jam on his Royal Air Force bread and butter. He writes with great difficulty and corrects much; and takes no pride or pleasure in anything that he has written. Most of these earnings are from translation-work and none of them from creative or original writing. He never intends to write another real book. He usually writes, by the way, in indian ink because it makes a good mark on the page. His handwriting is unpretentious and at first sight almost school-boyish; but always legible. It varies very much with his mood, from large and square to small and narrow, from upright to a slight backward slant. I believe that the one thing that he likes is to find some one who knows more than himself or can do something better than himself. To such a person he will attach himself and learn all that is to be learned. And if he meets someone who can actually think faster or more accurately than himself and can even anticipate him in his apparently erratic but most carefully considered behaviour, so much the better. At the same time he has a savage conviction of his own general insufficiency which he will not allow to be contradicted by particular occasions on which he has been proved to excel others. It is not modesty but a sincere faith in his own unworthiness suggesting the cries in the Church Litany and will not stand contradiction.

Perhaps his most unexpected personal characteristic is that he never looks at a man's face and never recognizes a face. This is inherited; his father one day stepped on his toe in the street and passed on with an apology, not knowing him. He would not recognize his mother or his brothers, even, if he met them without warning. Long practice has made Lawrence able to talk for twenty minutes at a time to whoever accosts him without betraying that he hasn't a notion who the person is. Yet he can remember names and details of taste and character, and words and opinions and places vividly and at great length. He does his best to see people; but is constantly getting into trouble for not recognizing and saluting officers when they are out of uniform; for nobody is willing to believe his excuses.

He has never been dogmatic about any creed or political conviction: he has no belief in a philosophic Absolute. He has no use for crowds or any person whose only strength is that he is a member of some society or creed. He clearly also expects people to find themselves and be true to themselves, and to leave their neighbours to do the same: he would wish every

AIRCRAFTMAN SHAW

in 'Scruff order'

man to be an everlasting question-mark. He can be relentless to the point of cruelty: the shock of his anger, which is a cold quiet laughing anger, is violent. To hear him, say, dismissing an impostor who claims to have served during the War in the East in such and such a unit, or reminding a bully of men deliberately sent to their death by him in such and such a province, is a terrifying experience. But when the offender is gone, the anger goes too and leaves no trace.

Lawrence does not like children (or dogs or camels) in mass, in the usual sentimental way. He likes a few children (as also a few dogs, a few camels). From the rest he shrinks. He is afraid of them, and he is sorry for them, as for creatures forced, without having their wishes consulted, into an existence in which, if they are good creatures, they will necessarily find disappointment. This will not prevent him at times from talking really to a child, treating it as an independent person and not merely as a clever echo of its parents.

He has, it seems, no use for the human race as such or interest in its continuance. He has no sentimentality about universal brotherhood, like Swift; he has no use for the works of men.

And he has come to this view, I think, by the same road as Swift, by an overwhelming sense of personal liberty, a largeness of heart, and an intense desire for perfection so obviously unattainable as hardly to be worth starting for.

We may conclude that when, in 1922, his dislike of the crowd became too strong and he saw that it was becoming a definite limitation for him, when he found in fact after the apparent triumph of the Arabian adventure that in avoiding the mask of a popular hero he was withdrawing more and more and becoming unwholesomely interested in just being himself, he took a violent course—he enlisted and bound himself to a life in which he was forced perpetually to be a member of the crowd. The Army and Air Force are the modern equivalent of the monastery, and after five years he does not regret his choice of a life as nearly phys-ical as an animal's, in which food is provided, and drink, and a round of work in harness and a stable afterwards until the new day brings a repetition of the work of yesterday.

What is called Lawrence's 'love of publicity' can best be explained as a burning desire to know himself, for no one can be himself except by first knowing himself. To publicity in the sense of what is published about him he is indifferent; he is never more than amused at what he has read about himself. But it ceases to be amusing to him when he meets people who believe all they read about him and act as if legend was truth. He denies the legend, and they say 'how modest these heroes are': and he is nearly sick. He does not believe that heroes exist or ever have existed; he suspects them all of being frauds. If he is interested at times in what people may think of him this is only because their opinion may show him what sort of a man he is more clearly than any amount of self-examination can. He has been often accused of vanity because he has sat for his portrait to so many artists and sculptors—he has only four times refused to sit—but it is the opposite of vanity. A vain man has a very clear view of himself which he tries to force on his neighbours. Lawrence sits for his portrait because he wants to discover what he is, by the effect which he produces on the artist: so far from being vain he clearly has no picture of himself at all except a contemptuous one. He accepts the view that he is a complete humbug and play actor; chiefly, perhaps, because people who are themselves humbugs and actors see him so in their own likeness.

He has another reason for 'sitting' and that is because artists (in the wider sense) are the only class of human beings to which he would like to belong. He can salve the regret that, rightly or wrongly, he feels at not being a true artist, by watching artists work and providing them with a model. He has done a good deal of experimental sculpture; he told me once that somewhere, I think in Syria, there are twelve life-size statues left by him on the roof of a house. Certainly some of the decorations outside a nonconformist chapel in the Iffley Road at Oxford are his work, but unsigned and indistinguishable from the rest. I have seen silversmith work by him. He has written poems, but they fall short of his intentions more seriously even than his handicrafts, because poetry has more freedom possible to it than these. Lawrence's chief curse is that he cannot stop thinking, and by thinking I mean a working of the mind that is not mere calculation from any given set of facts, but a much more intense and difficult process which makes its own facts and tests them as it goes and destroys them when it is over. In all my acquaintance I know no more than three people who really *think*, and these three include Lawrence. He seems to be perpetually stretching his mind in every direction and finding little or nothing; 'lunging about,' as an Arab poet said, 'like a blind camel in the dark.' At least the effort seems to make the mind harder and fitter.

But this account is getting too philosophical, and the simplest conclusion about Lawrence is the best. It is not that 'He is a great man.' The greatness of his achievement is in any case historical. He, a foreigner and an unbeliever, inspired and led the broadest national movement of the Arabs that had taken place since the great times of Mohammed and his early successors, and brought it to a triumphant conclusion. It is not that he is a genius. This has come to be a vulgar almost meaningless word, attached to any competent scientist or fiddler or verse-maker or military leader. It is not even that he is an 'erratic genius,' unless 'erratic' means that Lawrence does not do the usual things that men of successful talents do; the ordinary vulgar things that are expected by the crowd. If Napoleon, for instance, who was a vulgar rather than an 'erratic' genius, had been in Lawrence's position at the close of the 1918 campaign he would have proclaimed himself a Mohammedan and consolidated the new Arabian Empire. Lawrence did nothing of the sort, though he had popularity and power enough perhaps to make himself Emperor even without an official change of faith. But it would have been foolish to expect a man who has qualities that shine in difficult weather to subdue them in calm weather. He came away and left the Arabs to employ the freedom that he had given them, a freedom unencumbered by his rule which, however just and wise, would always have been an alien rule. He would have contradicted himself had he suffered all those pains to free the Arabs and then enslaved them under himself. The trouble with him often is that he is too sane. He is impish at times but never erratic; he does nothing without good reason, though his decisions may disappoint the crowd. There was nothing erratic about Lawrence when he enlisted as an airman in 1922. When I heard of it first it did not surprise me: one learns not to be surprised at anything Lawrence does. My only comment was 'He knows his own needs,' and now I can see clearly that it was the most honourable thing to himself that he could have done. It was, moreover, a course that he had decided on in 1919 and had suggested to Air-Marshal Sir Geoffrey Salmond before the Armistice. But not till Mr. Winston Churchill had given the Arabs what Lawrence considered a fair deal was he free to please himself. Politics accounted for the three years' delay.

The least and most that can be said about Lawrence is that he is a good man. This 'good' is something that can be understood by a child or a savage or any simple-minded person. It is just a feeling that you get from him, the feeling 'here is a man with great powers, a man who could make most men do for him exactly whatever he desired, but yet one who would never use his powers, from respect for the other man's personal freedom.'

Popular suggestions made lately for employing Lawrence's talents or genius have been as numerous and varied as they have been ridiculous. The public has taken an interest in him that almost amounts to a claim for ownership: but nobody owns Lawrence or will ever own him. He is not a public Niagara that can be harnessed for any political or commercial purpose. A Colonial Governor-Generalship? What sort of appointment is that for a man who might have been an Emperor? And imagine Lawrence, who has long come to the point of disbelieving in his existence and every one else's, laying foundation stones and attending ceremonial parades and banquets! Lawrence, shortly after the War ended, was invited to attend the reception after a society wedding. He went (a man he liked was being married) in company with a young diplomatic attaché who was much impressed by the occasion. 'What name, gentlemen?' asked the flunkey at the door. Lawrence saw his companion pulling himself together for an impressive entrance and the spirit of mischief overcame him. 'Messrs. Lenin and Trotsky,' he said quickly. And 'Mr. Lenin, Mr. Trotsky!' the flunkey bawled out mechanically to the scandalized assembly: which, indeed, included Royalty.

Another suggestion has been that Lawrence should be entrusted with a mission to settle affairs in China. If Lawrence had any desire to settle affairs in China, even supposing that he felt himself capable of doing so, which is doubtful (it is quite possible that he is ignorant of Chinese), he would certainly demand an absolutely free hand. And it is then possible, indeed probable, that the solution he would provide would be one not at all favourable to European control of Chinese affairs. In any case, he had done this sort of thing once already: one does not repeat unpleasant experiences, for hire, without conviction, unless one has that sense of patriotic duty of which Lawrence is completely free. Other silly suggestions have been that he should edit a modern literary review, that he should be given an appointment in connexion with the Mesopotamian oil-fields, that he should be made director-general of British Army training or given a high post at the British Museum. All these suggestions remind one of the various methods detailed in mediæval books under the heading 'how to catch and tame a Unicorn.' People do not seem to realize that he knows himself pretty well and that he has chosen to serve in the Royal Air Force, which is not a life that comes easily or naturally to him, for a full engagement. He finds its difficulty worth coping with and is content. If he wants to do anythingelse he will do so without prompting.

It is remarkable that the most popular suggestion has been that Lawrence should head a great religious revival. In view of my conclusion about Lawrence that he can best be described simply as a 'good man' there may seem to be something in that suggestion. But it is as foolish as the rest. In the first place Lawrence has read too much theology to be a simple, successful revivalist and does not believe that religions can be 'revived', but only invented. In the second, he would not think of using his personality for any new popular campaign, military or religious, ever again. His nihilism is a chilly creed, the first article of which is 'thou shalt not convert!' In the third place

But enough. Mr. George Bernard Shaw perhaps made the most practical suggestion, that Lawrence should be given a government pension and chambers in some public building (he mentioned Blenheim Palace) and be allowed to spend his time exactly as it suited him. But I think that Lawrence would be unwilling to accept even a gift like this; such an arrangement would put him under a shadowy obligation to the public and, anyhow, he does not believe that he is worth anyone's paying. Also he might have aesthetic objections to Blenheim Palace. Also someone else already lives there. The only suggestion that I can make for the future treatment of Lawrence is simply this: that he should be left alone to maintain that rare personal liberty which so very few people are capable of maintaining.

Most of what I have written is more or less in Lawrence's favour. What is the worst that can be said against him? A great many things, perhaps, but they have mostly been said by Lawrence himself at one time or another. In the first place, he is an incurable romantic and that means that he is on doubtful terms with all institutions which claim to preserve public stability. He has loved adventure for its own sake, and the weaker side because it is the weaker side, and the lost cause, and unhappiness. Now, the incurable romantic is approved by society only if he is incompetent and fails, gloriously perhaps, but conspicuously, and so proves that the stupid ordinary people who control public security are always right after all. Lawrence's romanticism is not incompetent, it is not unsuccessful. When a European monarch one day in 1919 greeted him with the remark, 'It is a bad time for us kings. Five new republics were proclaimed yesterday,' Lawrence was able to answer, 'Courage, sir! We have just made three kingdoms in the East.'

For the real success of his romanticism—a romanticism which, as in the 'Winston' settlement of the Middle East, the big achievement of his life for which the War was a mere preparation, comes uncomfortably near realism—he is naturally very much hated by most government officials, regular soldiers, old-fashioned political experts and such-like; he is a disturbing element in their ordered scheme of things, a mystery and a nuisance. Even now, as a mechanic in the Air Force, he is a worry. They suspect some diabolic trick for raising mutiny or revolt. They refuse to believe that he is simply there because he is there. That he wants to be quit of affairs and become politically and intellectually unemployable.

Again, he is not even a single-minded romantic: he clearly despises his romanticism and fights it in himself so sternly that he only makes it more incurable. People like Lawrence are in fact an obvious menace to civilization; they are too strong and important to be dismissed as nothing at all, too capricious to be burdened with a position of responsibility, too sure of themselves to be browbeaten, but then too doubtful of themselves to be made heroes of.

The only original thing—if it is original—that I can say against Lawrence—if it is against him—is this: he keeps his enormously wide circle of friends, who range from tramps to reigning sovereigns and Air-Marshals, as much as possible in watertight compartments, each away from the other. Towards each friend he turns a certain character which he keeps for that relationship and which is consistent with it. To each friend he reveals in fact some part of himself, but only a part: these characters he never confuses. So there are many thousands of Lawrences, each one a facet of the Lawrence crystal: and whether or not the crystal is colourless and the facets merely reflect the characters of the friends whom they face, Lawrence himself has no notion. He has no intimates to whom the whole might be shown. The result of this dispersion—his friends are not casually made but chosen out, representing various departments of art, life, science, study (and he has an especial tenderness for ruffians)—is that such of his friends as are of a possessive nature try to corner him, each believing that he alone knows the real Lawrence, so that there is a comical jealousy when they meet. This may be also partly due to Lawrence being a person about whom it is easier to feel than to speak. One cannot put him into words—I cheerfully own to failure—because he is so various, because he has no single characteristic or humour that one could swear to. So his friends resent every description of him that they hear and cannot give one of their own to justify their resentment. Hence, probably, their possessive secrecy.

In getting together material for this book I have had more than one rebuff from friends who have carefully treasured some personal relation with which they thought themselves uniquely favoured. In spite of rebuffs I have tried to get bearings on Lawrence from as many angles, friendly and hostile, as possible: and if the only Lawrence that I still can see is the facet that he has consistently presented to me in the seven years that I have known him—well, let it be so: if it is only *a*

Lawrence and not *the* Lawrence, it is nevertheless more plausible than most supposedly complete individuals that I know.

I would not offer Lawrence, nor most certainly would he offer himself, or consider himself, as a model of conduct, or as a philosophic system. Circumstances and his own lifelong efforts have made him more free of human ties than other men. He can therefore dispose of himself in any market at any given time. Others cannot; they have careers, ambitions, families, wants, hopes, fears, traditions, duties—all binding them to that organized human society in which Lawrence seems to play only an accidental and perfunctory part. It is this extraordinary detachment, this final insulation of himself, which makes him the object of so much curiosity, suspicion, exasperation, admiration, love, hatred, jealousy, legends, lies. He has resolutely and painfully adopted the attitude towards organized society, 'you go your way and I'll go mine,' 'leave me alone, and I'll leave you alone,' but organized society cannot control itself in its hue-and-cry after a lost lamb that is perversely in need of no crook or fold. It is perhaps the triumph of his detachment that one can write of him in this way, as if he were a character in ancient history, confident that whatever one writes will not affect the man himself in the least, that his check will be only on infringements of copyrights that are no longer entirely his own.

For all that, he has not been able to keep himself to himself in one rather serious respect. Wherever he goes and makes his presence felt he seems to leave behind, probably unconsciously and certainly unwillingly, a number of fictitious Lawrences, people who seek to get something of the man's power by a mere imitation of what happen to be at the time his outward peculiarities. An affected lack of ease in society, an affected self-withdrawal, an inclined carriage of the head, a deliberate economy of gesture and vocabulary, a peculiar dragging of the words *yes* and *no*, a lack of emphasis at the moments of arrival and departure—whenever I meet these, I know that the Lawrence legend is stalking about, a ghost as persuasive, as destructive, as false as the Byron legends of a hundred years ago. Lawrence has a right to be Lawrence; he is his own peculiar invention. But at second and third hand he is occasionally comic, as when some ambitious, conventional, sporting, self-indulgent lion tries on his unicorn skin. But more often it goes beyond the comic stage: strong silent little men are even more insufferable than strong silent big ones. And by a cosmic joke in the worst taste the legend of 'The Uncrowned King of Arabia' has become popularly entangled with a novelist's myth of 'The Sheik of Araby.' Booksellers have wasted a good deal of time in explaining that 'Revolt in the Desert' is not a sequel to 'The Son of the Sheik.'

Now, the difficulty of writing a definite summary of what Lawrence is or was at any given time is that he makes a point of keeping his opinions and desires as far as possible in a state of solution; he prevents them, that is, from crystallizing into a motive that will affect the opinions, desires and actions of other men. When, in spite of all precautions, a motive does appear, a force is generated that is nearly irresistible, and while this lasts he stands out with glaring distinctness as a figure in history. But his greatness or power or whatever one may call it, though popularly *revealed* on such occasions, results apparently from his negative policy of being sure of nothing, believing nothing, caring for nothing, all the rest of the time. And with this paradox my study must end.

III

Lawrence once attended on the Emir Feisal, the chief Arab leader of the Revolt, when he was privately received at Buckingham Palace. Lawrence was wearing Arabian dress; the white robe, the belt, the dagger, the silk and gold head-dress, and was rebuked by a person of importance: 'Is it right, Colonel Lawrence, that a subject of the Crown and an officer too, should appear here clothed in foreign uniform?' He answered respectfully but firmly, 'When a man serves two masters and has to offend one of these, it is better for him to offend the more powerful. I am here as official interpreter of the Emir Feisal, whose uniform this is.' Lawrence's problem, whether his loyalty lay towards the Arabs or towards England when England and the Arabs were in conflict, was the most difficult problem of his life. England could claim earlier rights of allegiance—he was for two years a British army officer before he began the Arabian adventure—while his natural instinct to side with the weaker cause inclined him to press the Arab claim even against the interests of British Imperial expansion. When further it seemed that the right lay on the side of the Arabs rather than on that of his own country he was even more divided in mind.

How he came to be in this position cannot be shown without a short chapter of history and geography. The first thing to be explained is what is meant by 'The Arabs.' The Arabs are not merely the inhabitants of the country called Arabia: the word includes all those Eastern races which speak the language called Arabic. The Arabic language is spoken over an area as big as India, lying between a line formed by the extreme eastern coast of the Mediterranean, the Suez Canal, the Red Sea, and a second line farther east parallel with it formed by the River Tigris and the Persian Gulf as far as Muscat on the Indian Ocean. This rough parallelogram of land, which is much longer than it is wide, includes Syria, Palestine, Transjordania, Mesopotamia and the whole of the Arabian Peninsula. The people who live in it are called Semites, the children of Shem. The Semites were cousins by blood even before they were given a common religious language, Arabic, by Mohammed's conquests and his *Koran*. Arabic, Assyrian, Babylonian, Phœnician, Hebrew, Aramaic and Syriac, the principal Semitic languages, are all related to each other rather than to the languages of African Ham or Indo-European Japhet. Into this Semite country many foreign peoples have from time to time forced a way, but none have kept a footing for long. Egyptians, Persians, Greeks, Romans and Franks (the Crusaders) have in turn tried, but their colonies have gradually been destroyed or swallowed up by the Semites. The Semites have themselves sometimes ventured out of their area and in turn been drowned in the outer world. France, Spain and Morocco to the west, India to the east, were reached in the great days of the Mohammedan conquests. But with few scattered exceptions the Semites have never been able to live outside their old area without changing their natures and customs.

This Semite country has many different climates and soils. On the west is a long range of mountains running all the way

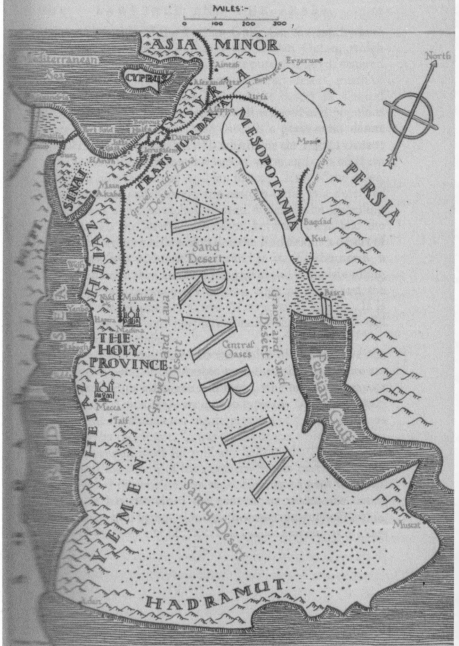

from Alexandretta in Northern Syria, through Palestine and the land of Midian till it reaches Aden in Southern Arabia. It has an average height of two or three thousand feet, is well watered and well populated. On the east is Mesopotamia, a plain lying between the rivers Euphrates and Tigris, its soil one of the most fertile in the world, and below Mesopotamia another but infertile plain stretching from Kuweit along the Arabian side of the Persian Gulf. On the south there is a long range of hills facing the Indian Ocean, which supports a fair population. But these outer fringes of watered country frame an enormous waste of thirsty desert, much of it still unexplored. In the heart of the desert in Central Arabia there is a large group of well-watered and populous oases. To the south of these oases is a great sand desert stretching to the inhabited hills which line the Indian Ocean: it is impassable to caravans for lack of water and cuts off these Southern hills from true Arabian history. East of the oases, between them and Kuweit, the eastern limit, is a desert of gravel with some stretches of sand which make travelling difficult. To the west of the oases, between them and the populated western hills which line the Red Sea, is a desert of gravel and lava with not much sand in it. To the north, a belt of sand and then an immense gravel and lava plain filling up everything between the eastern edge of Syria and the banks of the Euphrates where Mesopotamia begins. It is over the western and northern deserts that Lawrence did most of his fighting.

The hills of the west and the plains of the east are the most active parts of the Arabic area, though being more exposed to foreign influence and trade, whether European or Asiatic, the Arabs there are not so typically Semitic in character as the inhabitants of the deserts and of the central oases protected by the desert. It was on the desert tribes that Lawrence depended most for military help in the Arab Revolt, and it was the Arabs of the northern Syrian desert to whom for personal reasons he was most anxious to give freedom. Lawrence has described the process by which the desert tribes come into being. The south-western corner of Arabia, south of the holy city of Mecca, is called Yemen. It is a fertile agricultural district famed for coffee but much overpopulated: and for the surplus population there is no easy outlet. To the north is Mecca, where a strong foreign population drawn from all the Mohammedan world jealously bars the way. To the west is the sea and across the sea lies only the Sudanese desert. South is the Indian Ocean. The only way out is east. So the weaker tribes on the Yemen border are constantly pushed out into the bad lands, where farming becomes less and less easy, and farther out still until they become pastoral and finally are forced into the actual desert. There they work about from oasis to oasis perhaps for several generations until they may be strong enough to establish themselves again as agricultural Arabs in Syria or Mesopotamia. This, writes Lawrence, is the natural circulation that keeps Arabia healthy.

The great deserts are not, as might be supposed, the common property of all the Arab tribes to wander about in according to their pleasure. The territories are strictly divided up between the various tribes and clans, who may graze their camels and flocks only in their own pastures. Thus any clan new to the desert must either fight or pay tribute to maintain itself in any fixed territory. It may pass through and be given free hospitality, but after three days the journey must be renewed. As if the natural hardships of desert life were not enough, the old-established desert tribes are at constant feud with each other, and until the Arab Revolt began had no common thought or motive. (There are moreover outlaws, men with no tribe, who rob and kill any man they meet.) The Bedouin's curse has always been the curse of Ishmael, to have his hand against every man and every man's hand against him. Yet on the whole he keeps to a very strict code of honour in his tribal warfare.

The two most important cities in Arabia are the holy cities of Mecca and Medina. Mecca is about fifty miles inland, about half-way down the Red Sea: Jiddah is its port. Medina, two hundred and fifty miles to the north of Mecca, is about one hundred and fifty miles inland behind the range of hills. Every year for more than a thousand years there has been a great pilgrimage to these cities from all over the Mohammedan world. The most famous route is from Damascus in Syria, twelve hundred miles south across the Arabian deserts. Until recently this was a painful journey on foot or camel back, from which thousands of pilgrims, mostly old men who made this pilgrimage as the final religious act of their life, used never to return. One of the chief sources of wealth for the desert tribes was then this yearly pilgrimage. They sold food and animals to the pilgrims and were paid for the caravan's safe passage through each tribe's territory. If the money, however, was not paid they would raid the caravan and cut off and rob the stragglers. The Bedouin Arab had a great contempt for the pilgrims, mostly townsmen from Syria and Turkey, and regarded them as his natural prey. A railway was at last built from Damascus to Medina, and the pilgrims were able, just before the outbreak of the War, to set out in reasonable hope of a safe return. There only remained the stretch between Medina and Mecca not yet linked by a railway. The Damascus-Medina railway was built for the Turks by German engineers. The pretext for building it was a pious one; the real reason was to give Abdul Hamid, the Sultan, access for his troops to the Holy Cities, other than by the Suez Canal.

The Turks, like the Arabs, need some explanation. They are not of the race of Shem but visitors from Central Asia; they were late converts to Mohammedanism as the Prussians to Christianity, and made their home in Anatolia, in Asia Minor. They are, like the Prussians, before anything else a fighting people. They are dull, brutal and enduring: their chief virtue is the soldierly one of united action against their neighbours, whom they divide and conquer like the Romans. After the first exciting days of Mohammedan conquest, when the Arabs overran half the known world, the huge new empire had to be knit together. The Arabs had no ruling power themselves and had to rely on the non-Semitic peoples whom they had conquered to provide a system of government. This was the opportunity of the Turks. They were first the servants, then the helpers, then the rulers of the Arab races. Finally they became tyrants and burned and destroyed everything that annoyed their soldier-minds by its beauty or superiority. They robbed the Arabs of their richest possessions and gave them nothing in return. They were not even great road-makers and bridge-builders and marsh-drainers like the Romans. They neglected public works and were the enemies of art, literature and ideas.

The Arabs by their early conquests in Spain and Sicily had been really helpful to European civilization in the Dark Ages: the Arabic origin of many early scientific terms is a reminder of the refreshment that Arab thought provided. True, they were imitative rather than creative, and the ideas that they brought were merely the remnants of Classical learning caught from the Greek city of Alexandria in Egypt before it died. But compared with the Turks they have always seemed cultured, prosperous, even progressive. Turkish rule was a parasite growth, strangling the Empire as ivy strangles a tree. It was cunning at setting subject communities at each other's throats, and teaching them that the local politics of a province were more important than nationality. The Turks gradually banished the Arabic language from courts, offices, the Government service and superior schools. Arabs might only serve the State, now a mere Turkish Empire, by becoming imitation Turks.

There was of course great resistance to this tyranny. Many revolts took place in Syria, Mesopotamia and Arabia; but the Turks were too strong. The Arabs lost their racial pride and all their proud traditions. But of one thing they could not be robbed, the Koran, the sacred book of all Mohammedans, to study which was every man's first religious duty, whether Arab or Turk. Not only was the Koran the foundation of the legal system used throughout the Arabic-speaking world, except where the Turks had lately imposed their more Western code, but it was the finest example of Arabic literature. In reading the Koran every Arab had a standard by which to judge the dull minds of his Turkish masters. And the Arabs did succeed in keeping their rich and flexible language, and actually in filling the crude Turkish with Arabic words.

The last Sultan of Turkey, Abdul Hamid, who reigned during the first few years of this century, went even further than those before him. He was jealous of the power of the Arab Grand Sherif of Mecca, who was the head of the priestly family of sherifs (or men descended from the prophet

Mohammed) and ruled with great honour in the Holy City.* Previous Turkish Sultans finding the Sherif of Mecca too strong to be destroyed had saved their own dignity by solemnly confirming in power whatever Sherif was elected by his family, which numbered about two thousand persons. But Abdul Hamid, who, for autocratic reasons, laid new stress on his inherited title of Caliph or Ruler of the Faithful (the orthodox Mohammedans), wanted the Holy Cities to be under his direct rule; until now he had been safely able to garrison them with soldiers only by means of the Suez Canal. He decided to build the pilgrims' railway and to increase Turkish influence among the tribes of Arabia by money, intrigue, and armed expeditions. Finally, not content with interfering with the Sherif's rule even in Mecca itself, he even took away important members of the Prophet's family to Constantinople, as hostages for the good behaviour of the rest.

Among these captives were Hussein, the future Sherif, and his four sons, Ali, Abdulla, Feisal and Zeid, who are important in this story. Hussein gave his sons a modern education at Constantinople and the experience which afterwards helped them as leaders of the Arab revolt against the Turks. But he also kept them good Mohammedans and when he returned to Mecca took good care to cure them of any Western softness. He sent them out into the desert in command of the Sherifian troops that guarded the pilgrim road between Medina and Mecca, and kept them there for months at a time.

---

* Mr. Lowell Thomas has described Lawrence as a Sherif of Mecca. This is plainly ridiculous. Whatever mixed blood Lawrence has in him he certainly is not a pedigreed descendant of the Prophet. He has never been to Mecca and would not offend the Arabs by so doing.

IV

Four years before the War, Abdul Hamid was deposed by a political party known as the Young Turks. The Young Turks believed in Western political ideas learned from the American schools founded in Turkey, and in military methods learned from their advisers, the Germans; but French culture and government gave them their clearest model to imitate. They objected to Abdul Hamid's idea of a religious empire ruled by a Sultan who was both head of the State and spiritual ruler. They favoured the Western idea of a military state—Turkey—ruling its subject races merely by the sword, with religion a matter of less importance. As part of this policy they sent Hussein and his family back to Mecca. This nationalist movement in Turkey was really one of self-protection. Already Western ideas about the rights of subject races to govern themselves had begun to crumble up the Turkish Empire. The Greeks, Serbs, Bulgars, Persians and others had broken away and set up their own governments. It was time for the Turks to protect what was left by adopting the same nationalist policy.

After their first success against the Sultan the Young Turks began to behave foolishly. They preached 'Turkish brotherhood'; meaning no more than to rally together all men of Turkish blood. Turkey should be the absolute mistress of a subject empire in the modern French style; not merely the chief state of a religious Empire only bound together by the Arabic language and the Koran. They also hoped to get back into their state the Turkish population which was at the time under Russian rule in Central Asia. But the subject races, who far outnumbered the Turks, did not understand this. Seeing that the Turks even in their own country were dependent on Greeks, Albanians, Bulgarians, Persians and others for the running of all their government offices and doing all their business except the simple military-part, they thought that the Young Turks meant to have an Empire something like the white part of the British Empire, one in which Turkey was to be the head of a number of free states, self-governed but contributing to the general expenses of the Empire. The Young Turks saw their mistake and immediately made their intentions quite plain. Led by Enver, the son of the late Sultan's chief furniture-maker, and a soldier-politician who had worked his way up, it was said, by murdering in turn every superior officer who stood in his way, they stopped at nothing. The Armenians began to take up arms for freedom. The Turks crushed them—the Armenian leaders failed their followers— and massacred men, women and children in hundreds of thousands. They massacred them not because they were Christians but because they were Armenians and wanted to be independent. Such wholesale barbarity was made possible for Enver and his friends by the nature of the Turkish private soldier, who has been described as the best natural soldier in the world. This means that he is brave, enduring and so obedient that he allows himself to have no feelings except those that he is ordered to have. He will butcher and burn even in his own country if so ordered, and will be merciful and affectionate if so ordered. He merely tries to do his duty.

The Arabs, who had also begun to talk of freedom, were more difficult to deal with because more numerous and because being (unlike the Armenians) Semites they were more powerfully affected by the idea. For Semites can be swung on an idea as on a cord (the phrase is Lawrence's). The Syrian Arabs, since they were nearest to Europe, first caught fire, and the Young Turks took what measures they dared to take short of massacre. The Arab members of the Turkish Congress were scattered, Arab political societies were suppressed. The public use of the Arabic language except for strictly religious purposes was forbidden all over the Empire. Any talk of Arab self-government was a punishable offence. As a result of this oppression, secret societies sprang up of a more violently revolutionary kind. One of these, the Syrian society, was numerous, well organized, and kept its secret so well that the Turks, though they had suspicions, could not find any clear evidence of its leaders or membership, and without evidence dared not begin another reign of terror of the Armenian kind for fear of European opinion. Another society was composed almost entirely of Arab officers serving in the Turkish army, who were sworn to turn against their masters as soon as a chance offered. This society was founded in Mesopotamia and was so fanatically pro-Arab that its leaders would not even have dealings with the English, French and Russians, who might otherwise have been their allies, because they did not believe that if they accepted European help they would be allowed to keep any freedom that they might win. They preferred a single bad tyranny which they knew well to a possible new tyranny of several nations whom they did not know so well; and at the end of the War members of the society were still commanding Turkish divisions against the English. The Syrian society, however, looked for help to England, to Egypt, to the Sherif of Mecca, to anyone in fact who would do the Arabs' work for them.

These freedom societies grew until in 1914 the War broke out: then European opinion did not matter much and the Turks, with the power given them by the general mobilization of the Army, could act. Nearly one-third of the original Turkish Army was Arabic-speaking, and after the first few months of the War when they had recognized the danger the Turks took good care to send Arab regiments as far away as possible from their homes, to the northern battle fronts, and there put them into the firing line as quickly as possible. But before this, a few Syrian revolutionaries were found to have been appealing to France for help in their campaign for freedom, and here was an excuse for a reign of terror. Arab Mohammedans and Arab Christians were crowded into the same prisons, and by the end of 1915 the whole of Syria was united by a cause that suppression only made stronger.

Early in the same year the Young Turks were convinced by arguments and pressure from the part of their German Allies that in order to win their war, which was pressing them very hard, they must work up some religious enthusiasm, proclaim a Holy War. In spite of their former decision to give religion an unimportant position in the empire, Holy War was necessary for more than one reason; they wanted the support of the religious party in Turkey, they wanted their soldiers, now badly fed and badly equipped, to fight bravely in the confidence of going straight to Paradise if they were killed; and they also

THE EMIR FEISAL
and his Negro Freedmen

wanted to encourage Mohammedan soldiers in the French and British armies to throw down their arms. In India particularly, such a proclamation was expected to have an immense effect. The Holy War was therefore proclaimed at Constantinople and the Sherif of Mecca was invited, or rather ordered, to confirm the proclamation.

If Hussein had done so the course of the War might have been very different. But he did not wish to take the step. He hated the Turks, whom he knew for bad Mohammedans without honour or good feelings, and he believed that a true Holy War could only be a defensive one, and this was clearly aggressive. Besides, Germany, a Christian ally, made a Holy War look absurd. He refused.

Hussein was shrewd, honourable and deeply pious. His position, however, was difficult. The yearly pilgrimage ended with the outbreak of war and with it went a great part of his revenues. As he was for the Allies an enemy subject, there was danger of their stopping the usual food-ships from India. And if he angered the Turks they might stop food from coming to him by the desert railway; and his own province could not grow food enough for its population. So having refused to proclaim the Holy War he begged the Allies not to starve his people out for what was not their fault. The Turks, in reply to his refusal, began a partial blockade of Hussein's province by controlling the traffic on the railway. The British, on the other hand, allowed the food vessels to come as usual. This decided Hussein. He decided to revolt (as his neighbour Ibn Saud of the central oases had successfully done four or five years previously) and had a secret meeting with a party of British officers on a deserted reef on the Red Sea coast near Mecca. He was given assurance that England would give him what help he needed in guns and stores for his war. He had also just been secretly asked for his support by leaders of both secret societies, the Syrian and the Mesopotamian. A military mutiny was proposed in Syria. Hussein undertook to do his best for them. He therefore sent Feisal, his third son, to report to him from Syria what were the chances of a successful revolt.

Feisal, who had been a member of the Turkish Government and was therefore able to travel about freely, went and reported that prospects were good in Syria, but that the war in general was going against the Allies; the time was not yet. If, however, the Australian divisions then in Egypt were landed, as was expected, at Alexandretta in Syria, a military mutiny of the Arab divisions then stationed in Syria would certainly be successful. The Arabs could make a quick peace with the Turks, securing their freedom, and after this even if Germany won the world-war they might hold what they had won.

But he was not in touch with Allied politics. The French were afraid that if British forces were once landed in Syria, they would never leave it; and Syria was a country in which they were themselves interested. A joint French and British expedition would not have been so bad, but the French had no troops to spare. So, as it has been responsibly stated, the French Government put pressure on the British to cancel their arrangements for the Alexandretta landing. After much delay the Australians were landed with numerous other British and Indian troops and a small French detachment to give an Allied colouring, not in Syria, but the other side of Asia Minor, at the Dardanelles. It was an attempt, nearly successful, to capture Constantinople and so end the eastern war at a blow. After the landing the English asked Hussein to begin his revolt; on Feisal's advice he replied that the Allies must first put a screen of troops between him and Constantinople; the English, however, were no longer able to find troops for a landing in Syria even with French consent.

Feisal went up to the Dardanelles to watch how things went. After several months the Turkish army, though successful in holding its position, had been crippled by enormous losses. Feisal, seeing this, returned to Syria, thinking that the time was at last come for the mutiny, even without Allied help. But there he found that the Turks had broken up all the Arab divisions, sending them to the various distant war-fronts; and his Syrian revolutionary friends were all either under arrest or in hiding, and numbers had already been hanged on various political charges. He had lost his opportunity.

He wrote to his father to wait until England grew stronger and Turkey still weaker. Unfortunately England, quite apart from the difficulties of the *Entente*, was in a very bad position in the Near East, forced to withdraw from the Dardanelles after losses as heavy as the Turks had suffered. The English politicians were content to take the blame for not having landed troops at Alexandretta, the one really sensible place, rather than give away their French colleagues; and the rumour went round England 'The Greeks let us down.' Bulgaria, too, had lately joined with the Turks and Germans, so that the French insisted on the Dardanelles troops being landed not at Alexandretta, even this time, as had been intended, but at Salonica. To make matters worse, a British Army was surrounded and starving in the town of Kut, on the Mesopotamian front. Feisal's own position grew very dangerous. He had to live at Damascus as the guest of Jemal Pasha, the Turkish general in command of the forces in Syria, and being himself an officer in the Turkish army had to swallow whatever insults the bullying Jemal threw at the Arabs in his drunken fits. Feisal had, moreover, been president of the secret freedom society in Syria before the War and was at the mercy of its members; if he was denounced by any of these—perhaps a condemned man might try to buy his life with the information—he was lost. So Feisal had to stay anxiously with Jemal at Damascus, and spent his time rubbing up his military knowledge. His elder brother Ali was now raising troops down in Arabia, giving as the excuse that he and Feisal intended to lead them in an attack against the English in Egypt. But the troops were really intended for use against the Turks as soon as Feisal gave the word. Jemal with his brutal Turkish humour would send for Feisal and take him to see the hanging of his Syrian revolutionary friends. The doomed men dared not show that they knew what Feisal's real intentions were, for fear that he and his family would share their fate—Feisal was the one leader in whom Syria had confidence. Nor could Feisal show them what his feelings were by word or look; he was under the watchful eye of Jemal. Only once did his agony make him lose self-possession; he burst out that these executions would cost Jemal all that he was trying to avoid. Then it took the strongest efforts of his friends at Constantinople, the leading men of Turkey, to save him from paying the price of these rash words.

Feisal's correspondence with his father in Mecca was an extremely dangerous one: old family retainers were used to take messages up and down the pilgrims' railway, messages hidden in sword hilts, in cakes, sewn between the soles of sandals, or written in invisible ink on the wrappers of harmless packages. In all his letters Feisal begged his father to wait, to delay the revolt until a wiser time. But Hussein trusted in God rather than in military common sense and decided that the soldiers of his province were able to beat the Turks in fair fight. He sent a message to Feisal with the news that all was now ready. Ali had raised the troops and they were waiting for Feisal's inspection before starting for the front.

Feisal told Jemal of his father's message (without, of course, explaining its hostile significance) and asked permission to go down to Medina. To his dismay Jemal replied that Enver Pasha, the Turkish Commander-in-Chief, was now on his way to the province and that Enver, Feisal and himself would attend the inspection together. Feisal had planned to raise his father's crimson banner of revolt as soon as he arrived in Medina and so take the Turks unawares: but now he was saddled with two uninvited guests, the two chief generals of his enemy, to whom, by the Arab laws of hospitality, he could do no harm. They would probably delay his action so long that the secret of the revolt would be given away.

In the end, however, everything passed off well, though the irony of the review was almost unbearable. Enver, Jemal and Feisal watched the troops manœuvring in the dusty plain outside the city gate, rushing up and down in sham camel-fights or playing the ancient Arab game of javelin-throwing on horseback. At last Enver turned to Feisal and asked, 'Are these all volunteers for the Holy War?' 'Yes,' said Feisal, with another Holy War in mind. 'Willing to fight to the death against the enemies of the faithful?' 'Yes,' said Feisal again, and then the Arab chiefs came up to be presented, and one of the prophet's family drew Feisal aside privately, whispering, 'My lord, shall we kill them now?' Feisal answered, 'No, they are our guests.'

The chiefs protested that it must be done, for so the war could be ended in two blows. They tried to force Feisal's hand,

and he had actually to go among them, just out of hearing of Enver and Jemal, to plead for the lives of these two uninvited guests of his, monsters who had murdered his best friends. In the end he had to make excuses and take the party quickly back into the town under his personal protection and from there escort them all the way to Damascus with a guard of his own slaves to save them from death on the way. He explained this action as being merely great courtesy shown to distinguished guests. But Enver and Jemal were most suspicious of what they had seen and at once sent large Turkish forces by the railway to garrison the holy cities. They wanted to keep Feisal captive at Damascus; but telegrams came from the Turks at Medina asking for him to return at once to prevent disorder, and Jemal reluctantly let him go. Feisal was forced, however, to leave his suite behind as hostages.

Feisal found Medina full of Turks, an entire Army Corps of them, and his hope of a surprise rush, winning success with hardly a shot fired, had become impossible. His chivalry had ruined him. However, he had been prudent too long now. On the same day that Feisal's suite escaped from Damascus, riding out into the desert to take refuge with a desert chief, Feisal showed his hand: he raised the banner of revolt outside Medina.

His first rush on Medina was a desperate business. The Arabs were badly armed and short of ammunition, the Turks were in great force. In the middle of the battle one of the principal Arab tribes broke and ran, and the whole force was driven outside the walls into the open plain. The Turks then opened fire on them with artillery and machine guns. The Arabs, who only used muzzle-loading guns in their tribal battles, were terrified: and thought that the noise of the bursting shells was equalled by their killing powers. Feisal as a trained soldier knew better, and with his kinsman, young Ali ibn el Hussein, rode about on his mare among the shell-bursts to show that the danger was not so great as the tribesmen feared. But not even Feisal could draw the Arabs to the charge. Part of the tribe that had first broken approached the Turkish commander and offered to surrender if its villages were spared. There was a lull in the fighting and the Turkish general invited the chiefs to talk over the matter; secretly at the same time he sent troops to surround one of the suburbs of the city which he singled out for his object lesson in Turkish terror. While the conference was in progress these Turks were ordered to carry the suburb by assault and massacre every living creature in it. It was done, horribly. Those who were not butchered were burned alive—men, women and children together. The Turkish general and these troops had served together in Armenia and such methods were not new to them.

The massacre sent a shock of incredulous horror across Arabia. The first rule of Arab war was that women and children too young to fight must be spared and that property which could not be carried off in fair raiding should be left undamaged. Feisal's men realized what Feisal knew already, that the Turks would stick at nothing, and they fell back to consider what must now be done. They were in honour bound, because of the massacre, to fight to the last man; and yet their arms were plainly worth nothing against modern Turkish (and German) rifles and machine-guns and artillery. The Turks in Medina realizing that they were henceforward in a state of real or threatened siege, made their situation better by driving out into the desert many hundreds of the poorer

Arab townsmen whom they would otherwise have had to feed.

Feisal's attack on Medina had been timed to the day of his father's attempt on the Turks at Mecca. Hussein was more successful; he succeeded in capturing the city itself at the first rush, but it was some days before he could silence the Turkish forts that commanded the city from the hills outside. The Turks were foolish enough to shell the holy Mosque which was the goal of the yearly pilgrimage. It contained the Kaaba, a cubical shrine into whose walls was built the sacred black stone worshipped there as a rain-bringing charm long before Mohammed's time and the one exception that Mohammed was forced to make in his orders against the worshipping of idols. The black stone was said to have fallen from Heaven and what is more, probably had; it is apparently a meteorite. In the bombardment a Turkish shell killed several worshippers praying before the Kaaba itself and a second shudder of horror ran through the Mohammedan world. Jiddah, the port of Mecca, was also captured with the assistance of the British Navy; and the whole province with the exception of Medina, was after a time cleared of Turks.

From their camp to the west of Medina, Feisal and Ali sent messenger after messenger to the Red Sea port, Rabegh, which was on the roundabout road between Medina and Mecca. They knew that the British, at their father's request, were landing military stores there. Yet they got nothing from Rabegh but a little food and a consignment of Japanese rifles, rusty relics of the fighting at Port Arthur ten years before, which burst as soon as fired. Their father remained in Mecca.

Ali went at last to see what was happening: he found that

the local chief at Rabegh had decided that the Turks were bound to win and so had decided to join them. Ali made a demonstration and got help from another brother, Zeid, and the chief fled as an outlaw to the hills. Ali and Zeid took possession of his villages and found in them great stores of arms and food landed from the British ships. The temptation to settle down for a spell of ease and comfort was too much for them. They stopped where they were.

Feisal was left to carry on the war alone a hundred and fifty miles away inland. In August 1915 he visited another port on the Red Sea farther north than Rabegh, called Yenbo, where the British Navy had landed a force of marines and captured the Turkish garrison. Here he met a British colonel who was acting under orders of the High Commissioner in Egypt, and asked him for military help. After some time he was sent a battery of mountain guns and some maxims which were to be handled by Egyptian Army gunners. The Arabs with Feisal rejoiced when the Egyptians arrived outside Medina, and thought that they were now the equal of the Turks. They went forward in a mob and drove in first the Turkish outposts and then the supports, so that the commander in the city was alarmed. He reinforced the threatened flank, bringing up heavy guns which opened long-range fire on the Arabs. One shell burst close to Feisal's tent where he was sitting with his Staff. The Egyptian gunners were asked to return the fire and knock out the Turkish guns: but they had to admit that they were helpless. The Turkish guns were nine thousand yards away and their own—twenty-year-old Krupp guns—only had a range of three thousand. The Arabs laughed scornfully and retreated again to their defiles in the hills.

Feisal was greatly discouraged. His men were tired; he had

had heavy losses. Money was running short and his army was gradually melting away. He did not like having to carry on entirely by himself while his brother Abdulla remained in Mecca and Ali and Zeid at Rabegh. He fell back with his main body to a position nearer the coast, leaving local tribes to carry on his policy of sudden raids on Turkish supply columns and night attacks on the outposts. It was at this point in the history of the Revolt that Lawrence appeared and turned the tide.

V

At the outbreak of the War Lawrence had of course to give up the idea of continuing at Carchemish, which was in Turkish territory. He was, at the time, in Oxford—it was the off-season for digging—and he much resented this interruption of what had been to him a nearly perfect life. He tried to join an Officers' Training Corps at Oxford, but without success. He tried again in London; but it was no good. It has been incorrectly said that he was marked as 'physically below fighting standard': this would, however, be quite believable. Perhaps the only other man in England who was Lawrence's equal in physical strength and endurance was Jimmy Wilde, the fly-weight boxer, a World's champion who not only beat every other man of his own weight but for years was unbeaten by boxers weighing a whole stone heavier than himself. Wilde was rejected as being of 'emaciated physique' and not fit for active service. But in Lawrence's case it was only a temporary glut of recruits that was responsible for his being turned away. Dr. Hogarth heard that Lawrence was at a loose end and got him given a week's trial, as a favour, by Colonel Hedley, the head of the Geographic Section of the General Staff at Whitehall. Three weeks later Hogarth met

Hedley and asked him, 'Did you find young Lawrence any use?' 'He's running my entire department for me now,' said Hedley shortly. Lawrence's task here was making maps of Sinai, Belgium and France.

Four months later, on Turkey's entering the War, Lord Kitchener ordered all members of the Sinai Survey expedition of 1913–14 to be sent immediately to Egypt, where their knowledge would be useful in view of a possible Turkish invasion of Egypt. General Maxwell wired that they were not wanted. Kitchener wired back that they were already on their way. In Cairo Lawrence naturally went to the Military Map Department of the Intelligence Service, where again he made his presence felt. About certain parts of Syria and Mesopotamia he knew even more than the Turks themselves. At the same time he was engaged in general intelligence as staff-captain at General Headquarters, Egypt. He was charged with making out a periodic report to the General Staff as to the position of the various divisions and smaller units of the Turkish Army: this information came from spies or from prisoners captured on the various fronts. Although a most valuable officer he was not popular with the senior military officers about him, particularly with those fresh from England who did not believe that a civilian like Lawrence was competent to talk about military subjects. There was annoyance, for instance, when he interrupted two generals discussing a reported movement of Turkish troops from So-and-So to Such-and-Such by saying: 'Nonsense; they can't make the distance in twice the time you give them. The roads are bad and there's no local transport. Besides, their commanding officer is a very lazy fellow.' Also he was looked on with disfavour for going about without a military belt, in patent-leather shoes, and not wearing the right-coloured socks or tie. His reports, too, were not written in the style favoured. The War Office handbook of information about the Turkish Army, of which he was joint editor for fourteen editions, contained such comments as 'General Abd el Mahmoud commanding the —th Division is half-Albanian by birth and a consumptive; an able officer and a gunnery expert; but a vicious scoundrel, and will accept bribes.' These personal comments were thought unnecessary: the theory held by the British was that their officer opponents were gallant fellows entitled to every courtesy. An objection was also raised to such scholarly footnotes as a comparison between the new Boy Scout movement in Turkey and the Corps of Pages kept in Egypt in the time of the Janissaries. The General Staff disliked history and suspected a joke. Among Lawrence's other tasks was questioning suspected persons; he had the gift of being able to tell at once from small points in a man's dress and from the dialect he spoke more or less what he was and where he came from. Two recorded examples will serve. An ugly-looking ruffian was caught on the Suez Canal, suspected of being a spy. He said he was a Syrian. Lawrence, overcoming his usual aversion to looking a man in the face, said 'He's lying; look at his little pig eyes! The man's an Egyptian of the pedlar class.' He spoke sharply in the pedlar's dialect, and the man admitted who he was. On another occasion, but later in the War, when Lawrence had greatly improved his accuracy, a fine-looking Arab came in with information. Lawrence's colleague said: 'Here's one of the real Bedouin come to see you.' Lawrence said, 'No! He's not got the Bedouin walk or style. He's a Syrian Arab farmer living under the protection of the Beni Sakhr tribe,' and so it proved.

In 1915 Cairo got so full of generals and colonels with

nothing to do but send unnecessary messages about and get in the way of the few people who were doing any work, that it was mere comic opera. No less than three General Staffs fully officered were collected in Egypt, and it was impossible for any one of them to define exactly where its duties began and ended. There was current a wicked parody of an old Egyptian-Christian creed, in which occurred the phrase, 'And yet there are not three Incompetents but one Incompetent.' One of the most intimate glimpses we get of Lawrence in 1915 is of a small grinning second-lieutenant, with hair of unmilitary length and no belt, hiding behind a screen in the Savoy Hotel with another equally unmilitary colleague, softly counting 'One, two, three, four!' . . . through a hole in the screen. They were counting generals. An important conference was going on in the room, for generals only. His colleague swears to me that Lawrence counted up to sixty-five. He himself only made it sixty-four, but one of the Brigadier-Generals may have moved.

Lawrence went on several journeys to the Suez Canal, where a weak Turkish attack had been made and a strong one was always expected, and one to the Senussi Desert in the West of Egypt (I believe to discover the whereabouts of British prisoners captured by the hostile Arabs there). He was also sent to Athens to get contact with the Levant group of the British Secret Service, whose agent in Egypt he was for a time until the work grew too important for an officer of his low rank to perform. He also was engaged in getting information about the anti-British revolutionary societies in Egypt and, because the Egyptians are not as loyal in their secret societies as the Syrians and Mesopotamians, was always having visitors; one party after another came offering to betray the names of its fellow-members until he had seen nearly the whole society. Lawrence's chief difficulty was to prevent the various parties meeting each other on the office-stairs. Social life in Egypt bored him. 'It's a bad life this,' he wrote at the end of March 1915, 'living at close quarters with a khaki crowd very intent on "Banker" and parades and lunch. I am a total abstainer from all of these and so a snob.' In April 1916 he was sent to Mesopotamia. He had an official task in which he was not much interested and a private intention known only to a few colleagues whom he could trust.

In Mesopotamia an army composed of mixed Indian and British troops had been marching up the Tigris from the Persian Gulf and had at first met with success, but sickness, transport difficulties, bad strategy and strong Turkish forces had held up the advance, which became a retreat: and soon General Townshend with a large force was cut off and besieged in the town of Kut. Provisions were failing and the fall was believed to be a certainty because reinforcements could not arrive from India in time. Lawrence's official task given him direct from the War Office at London was to go as member of a secret mission to the Turkish commander who was besieging Kut: to persuade him not to press the siege. It was thought possible that a large bribe might work because it was known that the Turks were themselves in difficulties. They had few troops—the Arabic-speaking regiments were openly mutinous—and a Russian army to the North had just captured the town of Erzeroum, the capital of Kurdistan, in the famous snow battle. The Russians were pressing on towards Anatolia, the Turks' home province; so that at any moment the siege might collapse. As a matter of fact the capture of Erzeroum had been 'arranged'—Colonel Buchan's novel *Greenmantle* has more than a flavour of truth—and the War Office hoped that the same success could be repeated at Kut. Nevertheless bribes would be useless, Lawrence had told those who sent him, and would only encourage the Turks. The Turkish commander, being a nephew of Enver, the chief Young Turk, never needed to worry about money.

The British Generals in Mesopotamia were not pleased with the idea of this conference. Two of them told Lawrence that his intentions (which they did not know) were dishonourable and unworthy of a soldier (which he never acknowledged himself to be). Now, this Mesopotamian Army was under the orders of the Government of India and though Lord Kitchener, who was in general command of the Imperial British Forces, had early in the War approached two leaders of the secret freedom society of Mesopotamia to offer to help in a mutiny which might have cleared Mesopotamia of the Turks at a single blow, his hand had been held. The Indian Government was afraid that if the Arabs mutinied it would be not able to grant Mesopotamia those benefits of British protection which had been granted to Burma some years before; the Arabs would want to remain free. So the help that Kitchener would have given was withheld and the mutiny did not come about. Instead, an army was sent from India to act without the Arabs: with disastrous results. The British and Indians were looked upon as invaders as unwelcome as the Turks and were not only given no help but were constantly being raided and robbed by the local Arab tribes.

Lawrence's private intention, which was the real reason of his coming, had been to see whether the situation in Mesopotamia would allow of local co-operation on Nationalist lines between the British and the Euphrates tribes, whom he knew well from his Carchemish days. Some of these were already in revolt—he hoped further to get in touch with the great Ruwalla tribe of the Northern Syrian desert—and with his assistance might soon have cut all Turkish communications by holding up river traffic and raiding supply columns until the army before Kut would be in a state of siege itself. Kut could hold out until he had made his preparations; if only eight more aeroplanes could be found for dropping provisions into the town. But he found that it was hopeless. The policy of wresting Mesopotamia without Arab help and making it part of the Empire was to be stubbornly maintained; sooner, almost, than recognize the Arabs as a political force the English would leave the country to the Turks. The result was that Lawrence did not do what he intended.

The conference with the Turkish General to which he and two others went across the Turkish lines with a white flag and with handkerchiefs bound over their eyes, was merely an attempt to ransom, on grounds of humanity or interest, those of the garrison of Kut whose health had suffered by the siege and whom captivity would kill, and to persuade the general not to punish the Arab civilians in Kut who had helped the British. After these things had been not very satisfactorily settled—they got nearly a thousand of the sick exchanged against healthy Turks; they should have got three thousand—the conference developed into a mere exchange of courtesies. In these, however, Lawrence and Colonel Aubrey Herbert, who was with him, would not join. When the Turk said, 'After all, gentlemen, our interests as Empire builders are much the same as yours. There is nothing that need stand between us,' Herbert replied shortly: 'Only a million dead Armenians,' and that ended the conference.

Lawrence had one more task; to explain to the British Staff in Mesopotamia, on behalf of the High Commissioner of Egypt, that the help promised to Sherif Hussein did not include a support of his claim to the Caliphate, the spiritual headship of the Mohammedan world, as was believed in India, with alarm. The official Caliph was still the ex-sultan Abdul Hamid. Having done this, he came away. Kut surrendered (half its garrison died in captivity and the Turks hanged a number of the Arab civilians) and the remainder of the British Army, whose advance the local Arabs continued to resent, lost enormous numbers of men and spent another two years in reaching Bagdad.

Things were going from bad to worse. The British High Commissioner, who had made the promises to Sherif Hussein on behalf of the British Foreign Office, found himself in difficulties. The general commanding the British forces in Egypt, who took his orders only from the War Office, did not believe in the Revolt and was not going to waste men, arms or money over it. His rule was 'No side shows.' It is possible also that he did not like the High Commissioner, a civilian, to be interfering in military matters. So, outside Medina, Feisal, waiting every day anxiously for the artillery and other stores which had been promised him, and with his own private treasure nearly spent in paying his armies, was left in disappointment and inaction. After the landing of a few native Egyptian troops and stores at Rabegh nothing much more was done; and it seemed that the Revolt was already over. Many of the staff officers at Cairo looked on all this as a great joke at the expense of the High Commissioner. They laughed that Hussein would soon find himself on a Turkish scaffold. As plain soldiers they had a fellow- feeling for the Turk, and could not see the tragedy and dishonour that they were intending. To make matters worse a French military mission was arranging an intrigue against Hussein in his towns of Jiddah and Mecca, and was also proposing to the harassed old man military schemes that would have ruined his cause in the eyes of all Mohammedans.

In Cairo Lawrence had come to be more plagued than ever by generals and colonels, and he discovered that since his great interest in the Arab Revolt was known he was about to be put in a position where he could not do much more to help it. He decided to get away in time. He asked for permission to go, but it was not given, so he began making himself so obnoxious that the General Staff would be only too glad to be rid of him. He was already known as a conceited young puppy and began a campaign of pin-pricks, correcting the grammar of the most senior officers and commenting on their ignorance of the geography and customs of the East. The break came in this way. The chief of staff one day rang him up on the telephone. 'Is that Captain Lawrence? Where exactly is the Turkish Forty-first Division now stationed?' Lawrence said, 'At So-and-So near Aleppo. The 131st, 132nd, 133rd regiments compose it. They are quartered in the villages So-and-So, So-and-So, and So-and-So.'

'Have you those villages marked on the map?' 'Yes.'

'Have you noted them yet on the Dislocation files?'

'No.'

'Why not?'

'Because they are better in my head until I can check the information.'

'Yes, but you can't send your head along to Ismailia every time.' (Ismailia was a long way from Cairo.)

THE EMIR ABDULLA

from a drawing by Eric Kennington

'I wish to goodness I could,' said Lawrence, and rang off.

This had the desired effect; it was decided to get rid of Lawrence somehow. He took the opportunity to ask for ten days' leave to go for a holiday on the Red Sea in company with a Foreign Office official, Storrs (afterwards the first Christian Governor of Jerusalem since the Crusades), who was visiting the Sherif on important business. He got his leave, and at the same time made arrangements to be transferred from the Military Intelligence Service to the 'Arab Bureau,' which was under the direct orders of the British Foreign Office. The Arab Bureau was a department that had just been formed for helping the Arab Revolt and was run by a small group of men, some of them, like Lloyd and Hogarth, old friends of Lawrence's, who really knew something about the Arabs— and about the Turks. Lawrence's transfer was arranged directly between the War Office and the Foreign Office in London, so that gave him time. He intended to do much in his ten days' leave.

VI

Lawrence and Storrs arrived at Jiddah, the port of Mecca on the Red Sea, in October 1916. (At this point Lawrence begins his public account of his adventures, the book *Revolt in the Desert*).

The Sherif's second son Abdulla came to meet the two Englishmen, riding on a white mare with a guard of richly armed slaves, on foot, about him. Abdulla had just come home victorious from a battle at the town of Taif, inland from Mecca, which he had won from the Turks in a sudden rush; he was in great good humour. Abdulla was reported to be the real leader of revolt, the brain behind Hussein, but Lawrence, summing him up, decided that he might be a good statesman and useful later to the Arabs if ever they succeeded in winning freedom (and his judgment of the present King of Transjordania was correct), but he did not seem somehow to be the prophet who was needed to make the revolt a success. He was too affable, too shrewd, too cheerful: prophets are men of a different stuff. Lawrence's chief object in coming to Jiddah was to find the real prophet, if there was one, whose enthusiasm would set the desert on fire; so he decided at once to look elsewhere.

Meanwhile Abdulla talked to Lawrence about the campaign, and gave him a report to be repeated to headquarters in Egypt. He said that the English were largely responsible for the Arab lack of success. They had neglected to cut the pilgrims' railway, and the Turks had therefore been able to collect transport and supplies to reinforce Medina. Feisal had been driven from Medina and the enemy there was now preparing a large force to advance on Rabegh, the Red Sea port. The Arabs with Feisal who were barring their road through the hills were too weak in supplies and arms to hold out long. Lawrence replied that Hussein had asked the British not to cut the railway because he would soon need it for his victorious advance into Syria, and that the dynamite which had been sent to him had been returned as too dangerous to be used by Arabs. Moreover, Feisal had not asked for more supplies or arms since the time when Egyptian gunners had been sent.

Abdulla answered that, if the Turks advanced, the Arab tribe called The Harb between them and Rabegh would join them and all would be lost. His father would then put himself at the head of his few troops and die fighting in defence of the city. At this point the telephone bell rang and the Sherif himself from Mecca spoke to Abdulla. Abdulla told him what was being said, and the Sherif answered, 'Yes, that is so! The Turks will only enter over my dead body,' and rang off. Abdulla smiled a little and asked whether in order to prevent such a disaster a British brigade, if possible composed of Mohammedan troops, might be sent to Suez, with ships waiting there to rush it to Rabegh as soon as the Turks began their march from Medina. To reach Mecca the Turks had to go through Rabegh because of the water supply, and if Rabegh could be held for a little while, he would himself soon lead up his victorious troops to Medina by the eastern road. When he was in position his brothers Feisal from the west and Ali from the south would close in and a grand attack would be made on Medina from three sides.

Lawrence did not like the idea of sending troops to Rabegh, and replied that there were difficulties about providing shipping for a whole brigade. There were no wholly Mohammedan regiments in the British Army, and a brigade was not large enough anyhow. Ships' guns would defend the beach, which was all that the brigade could defend, just as well as men on the shore. Moreover, if Christian troops were sent to the assistance of the Holy-City against the Turks, it would cause bad feeling in India, where the action would be misunderstood; already there had been great excitement in India when a small British Fleet had bombarded the Turks at Jiddah, the port of Mecca. Still, he would do his best and tell the British in Egypt what Abdulla's views were. Meanwhile might he go to Rabegh, see what the country was like and also talk with Feisal? He could find out from Feisal whether the hills could be held against the Turks if more help in arms and stores were sent from Egypt.

Abdulla consented but had to get permission from his father; which after some difficulty (for Hussein was very suspicious) was given. Abdulla wrote to his brother Ali telling him to mount Lawrence well and convey him safely and speedily to Feisal's camp. This was all that Lawrence wanted. That night a sad-looking brass band, in tattered Turkish uniforms, whom Abdulla had captured at Taif played them Turkish and German tunes, and Abdulla told Lawrence of the plans he had made some time before for winning freedom from the Turks by the simple method of detaining important pilgrims to Mecca and holding them as hostages: but Feisal had disagreed. Then Abdulla asked Lawrence how many generations back King

George could trace his ancestry: Lawrence replied, 'Twenty-six generations; to Cedric the Saxon.' (Or however many it was: I have forgotten, but of course Lawrence knew.) Abdulla proudly remarked that this was not bad, but that he could go seventeen better. Clearly Abdulla was not the prophet. Next day Lawrence took boat to Rabegh and there gave the letter to Ali.

Lawrence took a fancy to Ali, who was the eldest of the four brothers, a man of thirty- seven: he was pleasant-mannered, well read in Arabic literature, pious, conscientious; but he was a consumptive and his weakness made him nervous and moody. If Feisal was not what Lawrence hoped him to be, Ali would perhaps lead the revolt very fairly well. With Ali was another brother, Zeid, a boy of nineteen. He was calm and flippant and not zealous for the Revolt. He had been brought up in the harem and had not yet found himself as a man of action; but Lawrence liked him and he was more pleasant than Ali who did not like the idea of a Christian, even with the permission of the Sherif, travelling in the Holy Province. Ali did not allow Lawrence to start until after sunset lest any of his followers, whom he could not trust, should see him leave the camp. He kept the journey a secret even from his slaves, gave Lawrence an Arab cloak and headcloth to wrap round his uniform and told the old guide who was to go with him to keep his charge from all questioning and curiosity by the way, and to avoid all camps. The Arabs in Rabegh and the district were of the Harb tribe whose chief was pro-Turkish and had fled to the hills when Ali came to Rabegh with his army. They owed this chief obedience, and if he heard of Lawrence's journey to Feisal, a band of them might be sent to stop him.

Lawrence could count on his guide: a guide had to answer with his life for that of his charge. Some years before a Harb tribesman had promised to take the traveller Huber to Medina by this very road (which was the pilgrims' road between Medina and Mecca), but finding that he was a Christian had killed him. The murderer relied on public opinion to excuse him, but it went against him in spite of Huber having been a Christian. He had ever since lived alone in the hills without any friends to visit him and had been refused permission to marry any woman of the tribe. It was a warning to Lawrence's guide and the guide's son who went with them.

Lawrence, out of training after two years of office work in Cairo, found the journey trying, though the experience of riding a first-class camel of the sort trained in its paces for Arab princes was new and delightful. There were no good camels in Egypt, or in the Sinai desert where the animals though hardy and strong had not been properly trained. The party rode all night except for a short rest and sleep between midnight and the grey dawn. The road was at first over soft flat sand, along the coast between the beach and the hills. After some hours they struck the bed of what in the short rainy season of Arabia is a broad flood-river, but now was merely a wide field of stones, with here and there clumps of thorn bushes and scrub. Here the going was better for the camels and in the early sunlight they made a steady trot towards Masturah, where was the next watering-place out from Rabegh on the pilgrims' road. Here the guide's son watered the camels, climbing twenty feet down the side of the stone well and drawing up water in a goatskin, which he poured into a shallow trough. The camels drank about five gallons each, while Lawrence rested in the shade of a ruined stone wall, and the son smoked a cigarette.

Presently some Harb tribesmen came up and watered their she-camels. The guide did not speak to them, for they

belonged to a clan with whom his own people, their neighbours, had until recently been at war and even now had little
friendship. As Lawrence watched the watering two more Arabs
arrived from the direction in which he was bound. Both were
young and well mounted; but one was dressed in rich silk
robes and embroidered headcloth, the other more plainly in
white cotton with a red cotton head-dress, evidently his servant. They halted beside the well and the more splendid one
slipped gracefully to the ground without making his camel
kneel and said to his companion: 'Water the camels while I go
over there and rest.' He strolled over to the wall where Lawrence was sitting and pretended to be at his ease, offering a
cigarette just rolled and licked. 'Your presence is from Syria?'
he asked. Lawrence politely parried the question, not wishing
to reveal himself, and asked in turn: 'Your presence is from
Mecca?' The Arab also was unwilling to reveal himself.

Then there a comedy was played which Lawrence did not
understand until the guide explained it later. The servant stood
holding the camels' halters waiting for the Harb herdsmen
to finish their watering. 'What is it, Mustafa?' said his rich-
ly-dressed master, 'Water them at once!' 'They will not let me,'
said the servant dismally. The master grew furious and struck
his servant about the head and shoulders with his riding stick.
The servant looked hurt, astonished and angry, and was about
to hit back when he thought better of it and ran to the well.
The herdsmen were shocked and out of pity made way for
him. As his camels drank from their trough they whispered,
'Who is he?' The servant answered, 'The Sherif's cousin, from
Mecca.' The herdsmen at once untied bundles of green leaves
and buds from the thorn trees and fed the camels of this
honourable visitor. He watched them contentedly and called

God's blessing on them: soon he and his servant rode away south along the road to Mecca, while Lawrence and his guides went off in the opposite direction.

The old guide began to chuckle and explain the joke. The two men were both of noble birth. The one who played the part of master was Ali ibn el Hussein, a sherif, the other was his cousin. They were nobles of the Harith tribe and blood enemies of the Harb clan to which these herdsmen belonged. Fearing that they would be delayed or driven off the water if they were recognized, they pretended to be master and servant from Mecca. Ali ibn el Hussein afterwards became Lawrence's best friend among the Arab fighting men and at one time saved his life: he had already made a name for himself in the fighting at Medina and had been the leader of the Ateiba tribesmen in much camel-fighting with the Turks. Ali had run away from home at the age of eleven to his uncle, a famous robber chieftain, and lived by his hands for months until his father caught him. The old guide grew enthusiastic in his account of Ali, ending with the local proverb, 'The children of Harith are children of battle.'

The day's ride which began over shingle continued over pure white sand. The glare dazzled the eyes, so that Lawrence had to frown hard and pull his headcloth forward as a peak over his eyes and beneath them too. The heat beat up in waves from the ground. After awhile the pilgrims' road was left and a short cut was taken inland over a gradually rising ground of rock ridges covered with drift sand. Here grew patches of hard wiry grass and shrubs, on which a *few* sheep and goats were pasturing. The guide then showed Lawrence a boundary stone and said with some relief that he was now at home in his own tribal ground and might come off his guard.

By sunset they reached a hamlet of twenty huts where the guide bought flour and kneaded a dough cake with water, two inches thick and eight across. He cooked it in a brushwood fire that a woman provided for him and, shaking off the ashes, shared it with Lawrence. They had come sixty miles from Rabegh since the evening before and still had as far again to go before they reached Feisal's camp. Lawrence was stiff and aching, his skin blistered and his eyes weary. They stopped at the hamlet for two hours and rode on in pitch darkness up valleys and down valleys. Underfoot it seemed to be sand, for there was no noise, and the only change came from the heat of the air in the hollows and the comparative coolness of the open places. Lawrence kept on falling asleep in the saddle and being woken up again suddenly and sickeningly as he made a clutch by instinct at the saddle-post to recover his balance. Long after midnight they halted, slept for three hours and went on again under a moon. The road was among trees along another water-course with sharp pointed hills on either side, black and white in the moonlight: the air was stifling. Day came as they entered a broader part of the valley with dust spinning round here and there in the dawn wind. On the right lay another hamlet of brown and white houses looking like a dolls' village in the shadow of a huge precipice thousands of feet high.

From the houses after a while came out a talkative old man on a camel and joined the party. The guide gave him short answers and showed that he was unwelcome, and the old man to make things easier burrowed in his saddle pouch and offered the party food. It was yesterday's dough cake moistened with liquid butter and dusted with sugar. One made pellets of it with the fingers and ate it that way. Lawrence accepted little, but the guide and his son ate greedily, so that the old man went short: and this was as it should be, for it was considered effeminate for an Arab to carry so much food on a journey of a mere hundred miles. The old man gave news of Feisal; the day before he had been repulsed in an attack and had had a few men wounded: he gave the names of the men and details of their wounds.

They were riding over a firm pebbly ground among acacia and tamarisk trees and their long morning shadows. The valley was like a park; a quarter of a mile broad. It was walled in by precipices, a thousand feet high, of brown and dark-red with pink stains, at the base were long streaks of dark green stone. After seven miles they came to a tumbledown barrier which ran across the valley and right up the hill-sides wherever the slope was not too steep to take the wall: in the middle were two walled-in enclosures. Lawrence asked the old man what the wall meant. He answered instead that he had been in Damascus, Constantinople and Cairo and had friends among the great men of Egypt, and asked whether Lawrence knew any of the English there? He was very inquisitive about Lawrence's intentions and tried to trip him in Egyptian phrases. Lawrence answered in the Syrian dialect of Aleppo, whereupon the old man told him of prominent Syrians whom he knew. Lawrence knew them too. The man then began to talk local politics, of the Sherif and his sons, and asked Lawrence what Feisal would do next. Lawrence as usual avoided answering, and indeed he knew nothing of Feisal's plans. The guide came to the rescue and changed the subject. Later Lawrence found that the old man was a spy in Turkish pay who used to send frequent reports to Medina of what came past his village for Feisal's army.

After a long morning's travel, through two more valleys and across a saddle of hills, the party found itself in a third valley, where the old spy had told them that they would soon find Feisal. In this valley they stopped at a large village where there was a strip of clear water two hundred yards long and twelve wide, bordered with grass and flowers. Here they were given bread and dates by negro slaves—the best dates Lawrence had ever tasted—at the house of a principal man. The owner was, however, away with Feisal, and his wife and children were in tents in the hills, looking after the camels. The climate was feverish in these valleys and the Arabs only spent five months in the year in their houses: in their absence the negroes did the work for them. The black men did not mind the climate and prospered with their gardening, growing melons, marrows, cucumber, grapes, tobacco, which gave them pocket-money. They married among themselves, built their own houses and were well treated by the Arabs. Indeed so many of them had been given their freedom that there were thirteen purely negro villages in this valley alone.

After their bread and dates, the party went on farther up the valley, which was about four hundred yards broad and enclosed by bare red and black rocks with sharp edges and ridges, and soon came upon parties of Feisal's soldiers and grazing herds of camels. The guide exchanged greetings with them and hurried his pace; they pressed towards the hamlet where Feisal was encamped. Here there were about a hundred mud houses with luxurious gardens. They were all built upon mounds of earth twenty feet high, which had been carefully piled up, basket-full by basket-full, in the course of generations. These mounds became islands in the rainy season, with the flood-water rushing between them. At the village where they had just been there were scores of similar islands, but hundreds more had been washed away and their occupants drowned in a cloudburst some years before; an eight-foot wall of water had raced down the valley and carried everything before it. The guide led on to the top of one of these mounds where they made their camels kneel by the yard-gate of a long low house. A slave with a silver-hilted sword in his hand took Lawrence to an inner court. The account of Lawrence's meeting there with Feisal can best be given in Lawrence's own words:

'On the farther side of the inner court, framed between the uprights of a black doorway, stood a white figure waiting tensely for me. I felt at first glance that this was the man I had come to Arabia to seek—the leader who would bring the Arab Revolt to full glory. Feisal looked very tall and pillar-like, very slender, in his long white silk robes and his brown headcloth bound with a brilliant scarlet and gold cord. His eyelids were dropped; and his black beard and colourless face were like a mask against the strange still watchfulness of his body. His hands were crossed in front of him on his dagger.

'I greeted him. He made way for me into the room and sat down on his carpet near the door. As my eyes grew accustomed to the shade, they saw that the little room held many silent figures, looking at me or at Feisal steadily. He remained staring down at his hands, which were twisting slowly about his dagger. At last he enquired softly how I had found the journey. I spoke of the heat and he asked how long from Rabegh, commenting that I had ridden fast for the season.

'"And do you like our place here in Wadi Safra?"

'"Well; but it is far from Damascus."

'The word had fallen like a sword into their midst. There was a quiver. Then everybody present stiffened where he sat, and held his breath for a silent minute. Some, perhaps, were dreaming of far-off success: others may have thought it a reflection on their late defeat. Feisal at length lifted his eyes, smiling at me, and said, "Praise be to God, there are Turks nearer us than that." We all smiled with him, and I rose and excused myself for the moment.'

Any reader, by the way, who prefers Mr. Lowell Thomas's version of these incidents is welcome to his choice:

'On arrival at Jiddah, Lawrence succeeded in getting permission from Grand Shereef Hussein to make a short camel journey inland to the camp of Emir Feisal, third son of the Grand Shereef who was attempting to keep the fires of revolution alive. The Arab cause looked hopeless. There were not enough bullets left to keep the army in gazelle meat and the troops were reduced to John the Baptist's melancholy desert fare of locusts and wild honey.

'After exchanging the usual Oriental compliments over many sweetened cups of Arabian coffee, the first question Lawrence asked Feisal was, "When will your army reach Damascus?" The question evidently nonplussed the Emir, who gazed gloomily through the tent-flap at the bedraggled remnants of his father's army. "In sh' Allah," replied Feisal, stroking his beard. "There is neither power nor might save in Allah, the high, the tremendous! May He look with favour upon our cause. But I fear the gates of Damascus are farther beyond our reach at present than the gates of Paradise. Allah willing, our next step will be an attack on the Turkish garrison at Medina where we hope to deliver the tomb of the Prophet from our enemies.'"

VII

Lawrence visited the Egyptian gunners, who seemed unhappy. Egyptians are a home-loving race and they were fighting against the Turks, for whom they had a sentimental feeling, among the Bedouins, whom they thought savages. Under British officers they had learned to be soldierly, to keep themselves smart, to pitch their tents in a regular line, to salute their officers smartly. The Arabs were always laughing at them for all this, and their feelings were hurt. Next Lawrence had a long talk with Feisal and his supporter Maulud, an Arab who had been an officer in the Turkish army and had twice been degraded for talking of Arab freedom. Maulud had been captured by the British while commanding a Turkish cavalry regiment against them in Mesopotamia. But as soon as he heard of the Sherif's Revolt he had volunteered to fight the Turks, and many other Arab officers with him. So now he began to complain bitterly that the Arab army was being utterly neglected: the Sherif sent them thirty thousand pounds a month for expenses but not enough barley, rice, flour, ammunition or rifles, and they got no machine-guns, mountain-guns, technical help or information. Lawrence stopped Maulud and said that he came for the very purpose of hearing and reporting to the British in Egypt what was needed, but that he must first know exactly how the campaign was going. Feisal gave him the history of the Revolt from the very beginning, as it has been told in a previous chapter, and mentioned mischievously among other things that in the fighting with the Turkish outposts, which took place usually at night because the Turkish artillery was then blinded, the battle would begin with curses, insults and foul language: and this wordy warfare reached its climax when the Turks in a frenzy called the Arabs 'English!' and the Arabs screamed back 'Germans!' There were no Germans in the Holy Province and Lawrence was the first Englishman: but this final foul insult was always the signal for hand-to-hand fighting. Lawrence asked Feisal his plans and Feisal said that until Medina fell they had to remain on guard, for the Turks were certainly intending to recapture Mecca. He did not think that the Arabs would want to defend the hill-country between Medina and Rabegh merely by sitting still and sniping from the hills. If the Turks moved, he proposed to move too. He favoured an attack on Medina from four sides at once with four armies of tribesmen, with himself and his three brothers each at the head of an army. Whatever the success of the attack, it would check the advance on Mecca and give his father time to arm and train regular troops.

For without regular troops a steady war against the Turks was impossible; the tribesmen could not be persuaded to stay away from their families more than a month or two at a time, and soon got bored with the war if there was no chance of exciting camel-charges and loot. Feisal talked at some length and Maulud, who had sat fidgeting, cried out, 'Don't write a history of us. The only thing to be done is to fight and fight and kill them. Give me a battery of mountain-guns and machine-guns and I will finish this war off for you. We talk and talk and do nothing.'

Feisal was dead tired: his eyes were bloodshot, his cheeks hollow. He looked years older than thirty-one. For the rest, he was tall, graceful, vigorous, with a royal dignity of head and shoulders, and beautiful movements. He knew of these gifts and therefore much of his public speech was by sign and gesture. His men loved him, and he lived for nothing but his work. He always overtaxed his strength and Lawrence was told how once after a long spell of fighting in which he had to guard himself, lead the charges, control and encourage his men, he had collapsed in a fit and been carried away from the victory unconscious with foam on his lips.

At supper that night there was a mixed company of sheikhs of many desert tribes, Arabs from Mesopotamia, men of the Prophet's family from Mecca. Lawrence, who had not revealed himself except to Feisal and Maulud, spoke as a Syrian Arab and introduced subjects for argument which would excite the company to speak their minds. He wished to sound their courage at once. Feisal, smoking continual cigarettes, kept control of the conversation even at its hottest, and without seeming to do so stamped his mind on the speakers. Lawrence spoke with sorrow of the Syrian Arabs whom the Turks had executed for preaching freedom. The sheikhs took him up sharply. The men, they said, had got what they deserved for intriguing with the French and English: they had been prepared, if the Turks were beaten, to accept the English or French in their place. Feisal smiled, almost winked at Lawrence, and said that though proud to be allies of the English, the Arabs were rather afraid of a friendship so powerful that it might smother them with over-attention. So Lawrence told a story

of how the guide's son on the ride from Rabegh had complained of the British sailors there. They came ashore every
day. Soon, the guide's son had said, they would stay overnight
and settle down and finally take the country. Lawrence then
had spoken of the millions of Englishmen fighting in France
and had said that the French were not afraid that they would
stop for ever. (As a matter of fact this was not quite true: the
French peasants did have the same fear, but Lawrence had not
been in France.) The guide's son had scornfully asked whether
Lawrence meant to compare France with the Holy Province.

Feisal pondered over the story and said that, after all, the
British had occupied the Sudan, though as they said, not
wanting it; perhaps they might also take Arabia, not wanting
it. They hungered for desolate lands, to build them up and
make them good: one day Arabia might tempt them. But the
English idea of good and the Arab idea of good might be different, and forced good would make the people cry out in
pain as much as forced evil. Feisal was a man of education, but
Lawrence was surprised at the grasp that these tribesmen, the
ragged and lousy ones even, had of the idea of Arab national
freedom. Freedom was an entirely new idea to the country,
and one that they could hardly have been taught by the educated townsmen of Mecca and Medina. But it appeared that
the Sherif had wisely made his priestly family into missionaries of this idea; their words carried much weight.

The Sherif had had the sense too, in spite of his great piety
as a Mohammedan, to keep religion out of the war. Though
one of his chief personal reasons for declaring war was that
the young Turks were irreligious, he realized that this would
be an insufficient reason for the tribes. They knew that their
own allies the British were Christians. 'Christian fights Chris-

tian, why not Mohammedan Mohammedan? We want a Government which speaks our own language and will let us live in peace. And we hate the Turks.' They were not troubled by questions of how the Arab Empire was to be ruled when the Turkish Empire was ended. They could only think of the Arab world as a confederation of independent tribes, and if they helped to free Bagdad and Damascus it would be only to give these cities the gift of independence as new members of the Arab family. If the Sherif liked to call himself Emperor of the Arabs, he might do so, but it was only a title to impress the outer world. Except for the departure of the Turks everything would go on much as before in the land.

The next morning Lawrence was up early and walking by himself among Feisal's troops. He was anxious to find out what they were worth as fighters by the same means that he had used the night before with their chiefs. There was not much time to spare for getting the information he wanted and he had to be very observant. The smallest signs might be of use for the report which he was to make to Egypt, one which perhaps might rouse the same confidence in the Revolt that he had always had. The men received him cheerfully, lolling in the shade of bush or rock. They chaffed him for his khaki uniform, taking him for a Turkish deserter. They were a tough crowd of all ages from twelve to sixty, with dark faces; some looked half negro. They were thin, but strong and active. They would ride immense distances, day after day, run barefoot in the heat through sand and over rocks without pain, and climb the jagged hills. Their clothing was for the most part a loose shirt with sometimes short cotton drawers and a head shawl usually of red cloth, which acted in turn as towel, handkerchief or sack. They were hung with cartridge-bandoliers, several apiece, and fired off their rifles for fun at every excuse. They were in great spirits and would have liked the war to last another ten years. The Sherif was feeding them and their families and paying two pounds a month for every man and four pounds extra for the use of his camel.

There were eight thousand men with Feisal, of whom eight hundred were camel-fighters: the rest were hill men. They served only under their own tribal sheikhs and only near their own territory, arranging for their own food and transport. Each sheikh had a company of about a hundred men. When larger forces were used they were commanded by a Sherif, that is, a member of the Prophet's family, whose dignity raised him above tribal jealousies. Blood feuds between clans were supposed to be healed by the fact of the national war and were at least suspended. The Billi, Juheina, Ateiba and other tribes were serving together in friendship for the first time in the history of Arabia. Nevertheless, members of one tribe were shy of those of another and even within a tribe no man quite trusted his neighbour; for there were also blood-feuds between clan and clan, family and family; and though all hated the Turk, family grudges might still be paid off in a big attack where it was impossible to keep track of every bullet fired.

Lawrence decided that in spite of what Feisal had said the tribesmen were good for irregular fighting and defence only. They loved loot and would tear up railways, plunder caravans and capture camels, but they were too independent to fight a pitched battle under a single command. A man who can fight well by himself is usually a 'bad soldier' in the army sense and it seemed absurd to try to drill these wild heroes. But if they were given Lewis guns (light machine-guns looking like overgrown rifles) to handle themselves, they might be able to hold the hills while a regular army was built up at Rabegh. This regular army was already being formed under command of another Arab deserter from the Turkish army, somewhat of a martinet, called Aziz el Masri. In the British prisoners-of-war camps in Egypt and Mesopotamia were hundreds of Syrians and Mesopotamians who would volunteer against the Turks if called upon. Being mostly townsmen and therefore not so independent, they were the right material for Aziz to train. While the desert fighters harassed the Turks by raids and sudden alarms, this regular force could be used to do the regular fighting. As for the immediate danger, the advance through the hills— Lawrence had seen what the hills were like. The only passes were valleys full of twists and turns, sometimes four hundred, sometimes only twenty yards across, between precipices; and the Arabs were fine snipers. Two hundred good men could hold up an army. Without Arab treachery the Turks could not break through; and even with treachery it would be dangerous. They could never be sure that the Arabs might not rise behind them, and if they had to guard all the passes behind them they would have few men left when they reached the coast.

The only trouble was that the Arabs were still terrified of artillery. The fear might pass in time, but at present the sound of a shell exploding sent the Arabs for miles round scuttling to shelter. They were not afraid of bullets or, indeed, of death, but the manner of death by shell-fire was too much for their imagination. It was necessary then to get guns, useful or useless, but noisy, on the Arab side. From Feisal down to the youngest boy in the army the talk was all of artillery, artillery, artillery. When Lawrence told Feisal's men that howitzers were being landed at Rabegh that could fire a shell as thick as a man's thigh, there was great rejoicing. The guns, of course, would be no military use; on the contrary. As fighters the Arabs were most useful in scattered irregular warfare. If they were sent guns they would crowd together for protection, and as a mob they could always be beaten by even a small force of Turks. Only, if they were given no guns, it was clear that they would go home, and this would end the Revolt. Artillery, then, was the only problem; the Revolt itself was a real thing, the deep enthusiasm of a whole province.

VIII

ater Lawrence saw Feisal again and promised to do
what he could. Stores and supplies for his exclusive use
would be landed at Yenbo, a hundred and twenty miles
north of Rabegh, and about seventy miles from where he now
was at Hamra. He would arrange, if he could, for more volunteers from the prisoners' camps. Gun-crews and machine-gun
crews would be formed from such volunteers, and they would
be given whatever mountain-guns or light machine-guns could
be spared in Egypt. Lastly, he would ask for British Army officers, a few good men with technical knowledge, to be sent to
him as advisers and to keep touch for him with Egypt. Feisal
thanked Lawrence warmly and asked him to return soon.
Lawrence replied that his duties in Cairo prevented him from
actual fighting, but perhaps his chiefs would let him pay a visit
later when Feisal's present needs were satisfied and things were
going better. Meanwhile he wished to go to Yenbo and so on to
Egypt as quickly as possible.

Feisal gave him an escort of fourteen noblemen of the
Juheina tribe and in the evening he rode off. The same desolate
country as before, but more broken, with shallow valleys and
lava hills and finally a great stretch of sand-dunes to the distant

sea. To the right, twenty miles away, was the great mountain Jebel Rudhwa, one of the grandest in the country, rising sheer from the plain; Lawrence had seen it from a hundred miles away from the well where Ali ibn el Hussein and his cousin had watered. At Yenbo Lawrence stayed at the house of Feisal's agent, and while waiting for the ship which was to take him off, wrote out his report. After four days the ship appeared; the commander was Captain Boyle, who had helped in the taking of Jiddah. Captain Boyle did not like Lawrence at first sight, because he was wearing a native headcloth which he thought unsoldierlike. However, he took him to Jiddah, where he met Sir Rosslyn Wemyss, the British Admiral in command of the Red Sea Fleet, who was just about to cross over to the Sudan.

The Navy under Sir Rosslyn had been of the greatest assistance to the Sherif, giving him guns, machine-guns, landing parties and every other sort of help; whereas the British Army in Egypt was doing nothing for the Revolt. Practically no military help came except from the native Egyptian Army, the only troops at the disposal of the British High Commissioner. Lawrence crossed over with the Admiral and at Port Sudan met two English officers of the Egyptian army on their way to command the Egyptian troops which were with the Sherif, and to help train the regular forces now being formed at Rabegh. Of one of these, Joyce, we shall hear again: the other, Davenport, also did much for the Arab army but, working in the southern theatre of Revolt, was not with Lawrence in his northern campaign. In the Sudan, at Khartoum, Lawrence met the commander-in-chief of the Egyptian army who a few days later was made the new High Commissioner in Egypt. He was an old believer in the Revolt and glad to

hear the hopeful news Lawrence brought: with his good
wishes Lawrence returned to Cairo. In Cairo there was great
argument about the threatened Turkish advance on Mecca:
the question was whether a brigade of Allied troops should
be sent there: aeroplanes had already gone. The French were
very anxious that this step should be taken, and their representative at Jiddah, a Colonel, had recently brought to Suez,
to tempt the British, some artillery, machine-guns, and cavalry and infantry, all Mohammedan soldiers from the French
colony of Algeria, with French officers. It was nearly decided
to send British troops with these to Rabegh, under the French
colonel's command. Lawrence decided to stop this. He wrote
a strong report to Headquarters saying that the Arab tribes
could defend the hills between Medina and Rabegh quite well
by themselves if given guns and advice, but they would certainly scatter to their tents if they heard of a landing of foreigners. Moreover, on his way up from Rabegh he had learned
that the road through Rabegh, though the most used, was
not the only approach to Mecca. The Turks could take a short
cut by using wells of which no mention had been made in
any report, and avoid Rabegh altogether; so a brigade landed
there would be useless anyhow. Lawrence accused the French
colonel of having motives of his own (not military ones) for
wishing to land troops, and of intriguing against the Sherif
and against the English: he gave evidence in support of these
charges.

The Commander-in-Chief of the British Army was only
too glad of Lawrence's report as he still had no wish to help
the 'side-show.' He sent for Lawrence. But first the Chief of
Staff took Lawrence aside, talked amicably and patronizingly
to him about general subjects and how jolly it was to have

been at Oxford as an undergrad—he apparently thought that
Lawrence was a youngster who had left for the War in his first
year at college—and begged him not to frighten or encourage
the Commander-in-Chief into sending troops to Rabegh,
because there were no men to spare on side-shows. Lawrence
agreed on condition that the Chief of Staff would see that at
least extra stores and arms and a few capable officers were sent.
The bargain was struck and kept. The brigade was never sent.
Lawrence was much amused at the change in the attitude of
the staff towards him. He was no longer a conceited young
puppy, but a very valuable officer, of great intelligence, with a
pungent style of writing. All because, for a wonder, his view of
the Revolt was agreeable to them. It is recorded that the Com-
mander- in-Chief was asked, after Lawrence's interview with
him, what he thought of Lawrence. He merely replied: 'I was
disappointed: he did not come in dancing-pumps.'

The friendly Head of the Arab Bureau, to which Lawrence
was now transferred, told him that his place was with Feisal
as his military adviser. Lawrence protested that he was not a
real soldier, that he hated responsibility, and that regular officers were shortly being sent from London to direct the war
properly. But his protest was overruled. The regular officers
might not arrive for months, and meanwhile some responsible
Englishman had to be with Feisal. So he went and left his map-
making, his *Arab Bulletin* (a secret record of the progress of the
revolutionary movements) and his reports about the whereabouts of the different Turkish divisions, to other hands, to
play a part for which he felt no inclination.

IX

In December he went by ship to Yenbo, which on his advice had been made the special base for landing supplies for Feisal's army. Here he found a British officer, Captain Garland of the Royal Engineers, teaching the Arabs the proper use of dynamite for destroying railways. Garland spoke Arabic well and knew the quick ways both of destruction and of instruction. From him Lawrence, too, learned not to be afraid of high explosive: Garland would shovel detonators, fuse and the whole bag of tricks into his pocket and jump on his camel for a week's ride to the pilgrims' railway. He had a weak heart and was constantly ill, but he was as careless of his health as of his detonators and kept on until he had derailed the first Turkish train and broken the first bridge. Shortly after this he died.

The general position was now this: The advanced tribes this side of Medina were keeping up the pressure on the Turks and every day sent in to Feisal captured camels or Turkish rifles or prisoners or deserters, for which he paid at a fixed rate. His brother Zeid was taking his place in Harb territory while he made sure of the tribes who were covering Yenbo. His other brother Abdulla had moved up from Mecca to the east of Medina, and by the end of November 1916 was cutting off the city's supplies from the central oases. But he could only blockade Medina, he could not make the joint attack with Feisal and Ali and Zeid because he had with him only three machine-guns and ten almost useless mountain-guns captured from the Turks at Taif and Mecca. At Rabegh four British aeroplanes had arrived and twenty-three guns, mostly obsolete and of fourteen different patterns, but still, guns. There were now three thousand Arab infantry with Ali, of whom two thousand belonged to the new regular army which Aziz was training: also nine hundred camel corps and three hundred troops from the Egyptian army. French gunners were promised. At Yenbo, Feisal was also having his peasants, slaves and paupers organized into regular battalions in imitation of Aziz's model. Garland held bombing classes there, fired guns, repaired machine-guns, wheels and harness, and the rifles of the whole army.

Lawrence had decided that the next thing to be done was to attack Wejh, a big port two hundred miles away from Yenbo up the Red Sea. The chief Arab tribe in those parts was the Billi; Feisal was in touch with these, and had thoughts of asking the Juheina tribe, whose territory was between Yenbo and Wejh, to make an expedition against the place. Lawrence said he would go to help raise the tribe and would give military advice. So he rode inland in company with Sherif Abd el Kerim, a half brother of the Emir of the Juheina. Lawrence was surprised at the sherif's colour; Abd el Kerim was a coal-black Abyssinian, son of a slave girl whom the old Emir had married late in life. He was twenty-six years old, restless and active, and was very merry and intimate with every one. He hated the Turks, who despised him for his colour (the Arabs had little colour-feeling against Africans: much more against the Indians). He was also a famous rider and made a point of taking his journeys at three times the usual speed. On this occasion Lawrence, since the camel he was riding was not his own and the day was cool, did not object.

They started in the early afternoon from Yenbo at a canter which they kept up for three hours without a pause. Then they stopped and ate bread and drank coffee while Abd el Kerim, who made no pretence at dignity, rolled about on his carpet in a dog-fight with one of his men: after this he sat up exhausted, and they exchanged comic stories until they were rested enough to get up and dance. At sunset they remounted and an hour's mad race in the dusk brought them to the end of the flat country and a low range of hills. Here the panting camels had to walk up a narrow winding valley, which so annoyed Abd el Kerim that when he reached the top he galloped the party downhill in the dark at break-neck speed; in half an hour they reached the plain on the other side, where were the chief date gardens of the Southern Juheina. At Yenbo it had been said that these gardens and Nakhl Mubarak, the village beside them, were deserted, but as they came up they saw the flame-lit smoke of camp-fires and heard the roaring of thousands of excited camels, the shouting of lost men, volleys of signal shots, squealing of mules. Abd el Kerim was alarmed. They quietly rode into the village and, finding a deserted courtyard, hobbled the camels inside out of view. Then Abd el Kerim loaded his rifle and went on tiptoe down the street to find out what was happening; the others waited anxiously. Soon he returned to say that Feisal had arrived with his camel corps and wished to see Lawrence.

They went through the village and came on a wild noisy confusion of men and camels: pressing through these they

THE VILLAGE OF DATE PALMS
(Nakhl Mubarak)

suddenly found themselves in a dry but still slimy river-bed where the army was encamped, filling the valley from side to side. There were hundreds of fires of crackling thorn-wood with Arabs eating or making coffee or sleeping close together muffled in their cloaks. Camels were everywhere, couched or tied by one leg to the ground, with new ones always coming in and the old ones jumping up on three legs to join them, roaring with hunger and alarm. Caravans were being unloaded, patrols going out, and dozens of Egyptian mules were bucking angrily in the middle of the scene. In a calm region in the middle of the river-bed was Feisal, sitting on his carpet with Maulud the Mesopotamian patriot and a silent cousin, Sharraf, who was the chief magistrate of Taif. Feisal was dictating to a kneeling secretary while at the same time another secretary was reading the latest reports aloud by the light of a silvered lamp held by a slave.

Feisal, quiet as ever, welcomed Lawrence with a smile until he could finish his dictation. After it was done he apologized for the confusion and waved the slaves back so that the talk could be private. The slaves and onlookers cleared a space, but at that moment a wild camel broke through the ring, plunging and trumpeting. Maulud dashed at its head to drag it away, but it dragged him instead, and its load coming untied, an avalanche of camel-fodder came pouring over the lamp, Lawrence and Feisal's cousin. Feisal said gravely, 'God be praised that it was neither butter nor bags of gold.' Then he explained what had happened in the last twenty-four hours.

A big Turkish column had slipped behind the barrier of Harb tribesmen on guard in the valley where Lawrence had first met Feisal, and cut their retreat. The tribesmen farther down the valley panicked; instead of holding up the Turks by sniping from the hills they ran away in two's and three's to save their families before it was too late. Turkish mounted men rushed down the valley to Zeid's headquarters, and nearly caught Zeid asleep in his tent: however, he got warning in time and managed to hold up the attack while most of his tents and baggage were packed on camels and driven away. Then he escaped himself; his army became a loose mob. They rode wildly towards Yenbo, which was three days' journey away, by the road south of the one that Lawrence had just taken.

Feisal hearing the news had rushed down here to protect the main road to Yenbo which now lay open: he had only arrived an hour before Lawrence. He had five thousand men with him and the Egyptian gunners, the Turks perhaps had three or four thousand. But his spy-system was breaking down— the Harb tribesmen were bringing in wild and contradictory reports—and he had no idea whether the Turks would attack Yenbo, or leave it alone and attack Rabegh, a hundred and twenty miles down the coast, and so go on to Mecca. The best that could happen would be if they heard of Feisal's presence here and wasted time trying to catch his main army (which was what the military textbooks would have advised) while Yenbo had time to put up proper defences.

Meanwhile he sat here on his carpet and did all he could. He listened to the news, and settled all the petitions, complaints and difficulties that came up before him. This went on until half-past four in the morning, when it grew very cold in the damp valley and a mist rose, soaking every one's clothes. The camp gradually settled down for the night. Feisal finished his most urgent work, and the party, after eating a few dates, curled up on the wet carpet and went to sleep. Lawrence, shivering, saw Feisal's guards creep up and spread their cloaks gently over Feisal when they were sure that he was asleep. Awake, he would have refused such luxury.

An hour later the party rose stiffly and the slaves lit a fire of the ribs of palm-leaves to warm them. Messengers were still coming in from all sides with rumours of an immediate attack and the camp was not far off panic. So Feisal decided to move, partly because if it rained in the hills they would be flooded out, partly to work off the general restlessness. His drums beat, the camels were loaded hurriedly. At the second drum, every one leapt into the saddle and drew off to right or left, leaving a broad lane down which Feisal rode on his mare; his cousin followed a pace behind him. Then came a wild-looking standard-bearer with a face like a hawk and long plaits of black hair falling on either side of his face: he was dressed in bright colours and rode a tall camel. Behind was a bodyguard of eight hundred men. Feisal chose a good camping-ground not far off, to the north of the village of the date-palms.

The next two days Lawrence spent with Feisal and got a close view of his methods of dealing with a badly shaken army. He restored their lost spirits by his never-failing calm courage and listened to every man who came with petitions. He did not cut them short even when they put their troubles into verse and sang songs of many stanzas at his tent door. This extreme patience taught Lawrence much. Feisal's self-control seemed equally great. One of Zeid's principal men came in to explain the shameful story of their flight. Feisal just laughed at him in public and sent him aside to wait while he saw the sheikhs of the Harb and of the Ageyl whose carelessness in letting the Turks *get* by in the first place had brought about the disaster. He did not reproach them, but chaffed them gently about the fine show they had put up and the fine losses that they had suffered. Then he called back Zeid's messenger and lowered the tent-flap to show that this was private business.

Lawrence remembering that Feisal's name meant 'the sword flashing down at the stroke' was afraid that an angry scene would follow, but Feisal merely made room for the messenger on the carpet and said, 'Come and give us more of your Arabian Nights' Entertainment: amuse us.' The man, falling into the spirit of the joke, began to describe young Zeid in flight, the terror of a certain famous brigand with him, and, greatest disgrace of all, how the venerable father of Ali ibn el Hussein had lost his coffee-pots; one of the 'children of Harith' too!'

At Feisal's camp the routine was simple. Just before dawn a man with a harsh powerful voice who was prayer leader for the whole army would climb to the top of the little hill above the sleeping army and utter a tremendous call to prayers, which went echoing down the valley. As soon as he ended, Feisal's own prayer-leader called gently and sweetly from just outside the tent. In a minute, Feisal's five slaves (who were actually freedmen, but preferred to go on serving) brought cups of sweetened coffee. An hour or so later, the flap of Feisal's sleeping tent would be raised, his invitation to private callers. Four or five would be present and after the morning's news came a tray of breakfast. Breakfast was mainly dates; sometimes Feisal's Circassian grandmother would send up a batch of her famous spiced cakes from Mecca, sometimes a slave would cook biscuits. After breakfast little cups of syrupy green tea and bitter coffee went round while Feisal dictated the morning's letters to his secretary. Feisal's sleeping tent was an ordinary bell-tent furnished merely with a camp-bed, cigarettes, two rugs and a prayer carpet.

At about eight o'clock Feisal would buckle on his ceremonial dagger and walk across to the big reception tent, which was open at one side. He sat at the end of this, his principal men spreading out to left and right with their backs against the sides of the tent. The slaves regulated the crowd of men who came with petitions or complaints. If possible, business was over by noon.

Feisal and his household, which included Lawrence, then went back to the other of his two private tents, the living tent, where dinner was brought. Feisal ate little but smoked much. He pretended to be busy with the beans, lentils, spinach, rice, or sweet cakes until he judged that his guests had eaten. He then waved his hand and the tray disappeared. Slaves came forward to wash the eaters' hands with water: the desert Arabs use their fingers for eating. After dinner there was talk, with more coffee and tea. Then till two o'clock Feisal retired to his living tent and pulled down the flap to show that he was not to be disturbed, after which he returned to the reception tent to the same duties as before. Lawrence never saw an Arab come away from Feisal's presence dissatisfied or hurt; and this meant not only tact on Feisal's part but a very long memory. In giving judgment he had to recall exactly who every man was, how he was related by birth or marriage, what possessions, what character he had, the history and blood feuds of his family and clan; and Feisal never seemed to stumble over facts. After this was over, if there was time, he would go out walking with his friends, talking of horses or plants, looking at camels or asking someone the names of rocks and ridges and such-like in the neighbourhood.

At sunset came the evening prayer and afterwards, in his living tent, Feisal planned what patrols and raiding parties were going out that night. Between six and seven came the evening meal: it was like dinner except that cubes of boiled mutton were mixed in the great tray of rice. Silence was kept until the meal was over. This meal ended the day except for occasional glasses of tea. Feisal did not sleep till very late and never hurried his guests away. He relaxed in the evening and avoided work as much as he could. He would send for some local sheikh to tell stories of tribal history; or the tribal poets would sing their long epics, stock pieces which, with the change of names only, did service for every tribe in Arabia. Feisal was passionately fond of Arabic poetry and would often provoke competitions, judging and rewarding the best verses of the night. Very rarely he would play chess—the game was brought to Europe first by the Arabs—swiftly and brilliantly. Sometimes he told stories of what he had seen in Syria, or scraps of Turkish secret history, or family affairs. Lawrence learned from him a great deal about people and parties among the Arabs that was useful to him later.

Feisal asked Lawrence if he would wear Arab dress like his own while in the camp: it was more comfortable, and more convenient because the tribesmen only knew khaki as Turkish uniform and every time that Lawrence went into Feisal's tent and strangers were there an explanation had to be made. Lawrence gladly agreed and Feisal's slave fitted him out in splendid white silk wedding-garments embroidered with gold which had lately been sent to his master, possibly as a hint, by a great-aunt in Mecca. Arab clothes were not a novelty to Lawrence. He had frequently worn them in Syria before the War.

X

He decided to go back to Yenbo to organize the defence because Feisal's stand could not be more than a short pause. With the hills undefended the Turks could strike where and when they pleased, and they were much better armed and better trained than Feisal's Arabs. So Feisal lent him a fine bay camel and he raced back by a more northerly route, for fear of Turkish patrols that were reported to have pushed round to the road by which he had come. He arrived at Yenbo just before dawn, in time to see Zeid's beaten army ride in, about eight hundred camel fighters, without noise but apparently without any sense of shame at their defeat. Zeid himself pretended to be less concerned about it than anyone else: as he rode in he remarked to the Governor, 'Why! your town is half in ruins. I must telegraph to my father for forty masons to repair the public buildings,' and this he actually did. Meanwhile Lawrence had telegraphed to Captain Boyle at Jiddah that Yenbo was threatened and Boyle promptly replied that he would come there at once with his fleet. Then came more bad news: Feisal had been attacked in force before his troops had recovered from their fright: after a short fight he had broken off and was falling back on Yenbo. It seemed that the war was nearly over, the Revolt crushed. With Feisal were two thousand men, but Lawrence saw at once that the Juheina tribe was absent: there must have been treachery, a thing that neither Lawrence nor Feisal had believed possible from the Juheina.

Lawrence, though dead tired after three days with hardly any sleep, went to see Feisal at once and heard the news. The Turks had broken in from the south and threatened to cut Feisal off from Yenbo: their guide was a Juheina chief, hereditary lawgiver to the tribe, who had a private quarrel with the Emir of the Juheina. They had seven useful guns with which they shelled Feisal's camp. Feisal, undismayed, held his ground and sent round the Juheina to work down the great valley to the left and fall on the Turkish right wing. He then posted the Egyptian gunners on the right and began to shell the palm groves, where the Turkish centre was concealed, with his own two guns. These guns were a present from Egypt, old rubbish, but good enough, it was thought, for the wild Arabs—like the sixty thousand rifles also sent which had been condemned as useless for the British Army after hard service at the Dardanelles.

A Syrian Arab, Rasim, who had once been in command of a Turkish battery, was working these guns but without sights, range-finder, range-tables or high explosive. He was using shrapnel, old stock left over from the Boer War, the copper fuses green with mould. Most of it burst short if it burst at all. However, Rasim had no means of getting his ammunition away if things went wrong, so he blazed away at full speed, shouting with laughter at this way of making war. The tribesmen were much impressed with the noise and smoke and Rasim's laughter. 'By God,' said one, 'those are the real guns: the importance of their noise!' Rasim swore that the Turks were dying in heaps. The Arabs charged forward happily. Feisal was hoping for a big victory when suddenly the Juheina on his left under their Emir and Abd el Kerim, his brother, halted and finally turned and rode back to the camping-ground. The battle was lost: he called to Rasim to save the guns at least, and Rasim yoked up his teams and trotted off to the right towards Yenbo. After him streamed the centre and right, Feisal and his bodyguard bringing up the rear and leaving the cowardly or treacherous Juheina to look after themselves.

As the tale was still being told, and Lawrence was joining in the general curse against the Emir of the Juheina and Abd el Kerim, there was a stir at the door and who should come running in but Abd el Kerim himself! He kissed Feisal's headrope in greeting and sat down. Feisal stared and gasped and said 'How?' Abd el Kerim answered that the Juheina had been dismayed at Feisal's sudden flight: he and his brother had been left to fight the Turks for the whole night alone, without artillery, and the gallant tribesmen had resisted until they were forced out of the date-palms by weight of numbers. Half the tribe were just coming along with his brother, the other half had gone inland, for water. 'But why did you retreat to the camping- ground behind us during the battle?' asked Feisal. 'Only to make ourselves a cup of coffee: we had fought all day and it was dusk: we were very tired and thirsty.' Feisal and Lawrence lay back and laughed; and then went to see what could be done to save Yenbo.

The first thing was to send the Juheina back to join their fellows and keep up a constant pressure on the Turkish communications with raids and sniping. The Turks would have to leave so many men behind, strung out in small garrisons, to guard their supplies, that by the time they reached Yenbo the defenders would be stronger than themselves. Yenbo was easy to defend by day at least; the town was on the top of a flat coral reef twenty feet above the sea, surrounded on two sides by water, and on the other two by a flat stretch of stand without any cover for the attackers. Guns were being landed from Boyle's ships, of which he had brought five, and the Arabs were delighted with their size and number, and were much impressed by the fleet. All day long the whole army worked hard under Garland's direction at the task of fortification, using the old town-wall as a rampart for the Arabs to defend under the protection of the naval guns. Barbed-wire entanglements were strung outside and machine-guns grouped in the bastions of the wall. There was great excitement and confidence, and nearly every one sat up all night. Lawrence himself was sound asleep on one of the ships.

There was one alarm that night at about eleven o'clock. The Arab outposts had met the Turks only three miles from the town. The garrison was roused by a crier and every man took his place quietly on the wall without a shout or a shot fired. The search-lights of the ships, which were anchored close to the town, crossed and re-crossed over the plain. But no further alarm was given and when dawn came it was found that the Turks had turned back. They had been frightened, it was discovered later, by the search-lights and the blaze of lighted ships crowding the harbour, and by the silence of the usually noisy Arabs. Yenbo was saved.

A few days later Boyle dispersed his ships, promising to bring them back at an hour's notice to Yenbo if the Turks tried again. In one of these ships Lawrence went down to

Rabegh, where he met the French Colonel. The Colonel was still trying to get a mixed British and French brigade landed to help the Arabs, and tried to convert Lawrence to his views. He said that so soon as Mecca was safe the Arabs ought not to be encouraged to go on further with the war, which the Allies could manage far better than they. His plan apparently was that if the brigade were landed at Rabegh, the Arab tribes would suspect Hussein of selling his province to the English and French and stop fighting for him. This brigade would then be his main defence against the Turks, and when the war against the Turks was won on the other battlefields, Hussein could be confirmed as King of Mecca and Medina as a reward for his loyalty. The Colonel's general attitude seemed to be 'We Allies must stick together and outwit these Arabs who are savages not worth the consideration of us Westerners.'

Lawrence thought that he saw the game. The Frenchman was afraid that if the Revolt were carried farther north to Damascus, Aleppo, Mosul, the Arabs might capture these cities from the Turks and keep them after the War; and they were cities that France wanted to add to her colonial empire. Moreover, in the Sykes-Picot Treaty, made between France, England and Russia in 1916 for dividing up the Turkish Empire after the War, the French had actually agreed that independent Arab governments, though in the French 'sphere of influence,' should be established in these cities if they were freed by the Arabs themselves—an event that none of the signatories thought possible at the time; it was a matter of form, merely, to suggest it. At the time Lawrence knew nothing of this treaty, which was a secret one, but he suspected the Frenchman, and he had no intention of letting the Arabs down for the sake of the *Entente Cordiale*. The Colonel, hearing of Lawrence's and

Feisal's intention to continue with the plan of attacking Wejh that had been interrupted by the Turkish advance, did his best to discourage it. On his honour as a staff-officer (and he had a very distinguished record) he said that it was suicide to make such a move; and gave many reasons. Lawrence brushed him aside. He believed that the Arabs had a chance now of a wide and lasting success, and Wejh was the first step.

The Turks meanwhile were being hard pressed by the Juheina who, split up in small parties, made their lives wretched by constant raids, sniping, and looting of supplies: and British seaplanes began bombing their camp in the palm-groves of Nakhl Mubarak. They decided to attack Rabegh. There Feisal's brother Ali, who had now nearly seven thousand men, was ready to advance against them, and Feisal and the younger brother Zeid planned to move round inland behind the Turks and take them in a trap. Feisal had difficulty with the Emir of the Juheina, whom he asked to move forward with him; the Emir was jealous of Feisal's growing power with the tribes. But Feisal made them move without their Emir. He then rode south to raise the Harb. All was going well until he heard from Ali that his army had gone a little way forward when, hearing false reports of treachery, it had rushed back in disorder to Rabegh. Feisal could do nothing, he could not even count for certain on the Harb, who might join the Turks if they got the chance and whose territory ran down south of Rabegh.

Then Colonel Wilson, who was British representative in the province, came up to Yenbo from Jiddah and begged Feisal to leave the Turks alone and make the attack on Wejh. The plan was now to move up with the whole Juheina fighting force and the regular battalions from Yenbo; the British Fleet would give all the help it could. Feisal saw that Wejh could be taken in this way, but Yenbo was left defenceless; he pointed out that the Turks were still able to strike and that Ali's army seemed to have little fight in it, and might not even defend Rabegh, which was the bulwark of Mecca. However, Colonel Wilson gave Feisal his word that Rabegh would be kept safe with naval help until Wejh had fallen, and Feisal accepted it. He saw that the attack on Wejh was the best diversion that the Arabs could make to draw the Turks off Mecca, and started at once; at the same time sending his brother Abdulla machine-guns and stores and asking him to move to the impregnable hills sixty miles north of Medina, Juheina territory, where his forces could both threaten the railway and continue to hold up the eastern supply caravans.

The Turks were still making for Rabegh, but very slowly, and with an increasing sick list among the men and animals, due to overwork and poor food. They were also losing an average of forty camels a day and twenty men killed and wounded in raids by the Harb tribes in their rear. They were eighty miles from Medina and, as Lawrence had foreseen, each mile that they went forward made their lines of communication more exposed to attack. Their pace got slower and slower till it was no more than five miles a day, and on the eighteenth of January 1917 they withdrew, when still thirty miles from Rabegh. It was Feisal's and Abdulla's new moves which finally recalled the expedition to Medina, and for the next two years until the War ended and the Holy City surrendered, the Turks were kept sitting helplessly in trenches outside it, waiting for an attack which never came.

XI

On New Year's Day 1917 Feisal and Lawrence, who was still rather a foreign adviser than an actual fighter in the Arab cause, sat down at Yenbo to consider the Wejh expedition. The army now consisted of six thousand men, most of them mounted on their own camels. The first fierce eagerness had left them but they had gained in staying power, and the farther away they moved from their homes, the more regular their military habits became. They still worked independently, by tribes, only bound by goodwill to Feisal's command, but when he came by, they now at least fell into a ragged line and together made the bow and sweep of the arm to the lips which was the Arab salute. They kept their weapons in good enough order, though they did not oil them, and looked after their camels properly. In mass they were not dangerous: in fact their use in battle lessened as their numbers increased. A company of trained Turks could defeat a thousand Arabs in open fighting, yet three or four Arabs in their own hills could hold up a dozen Turks.

After the battle of the date-palms it was decided not to mix Egyptian troops with Arabs. They did not go well together. The Arabs were apt to let the Egyptians do more than their share of the fighting because they looked so military; they would even wander away in the middle of a battle and leave them to finish it. So the Egyptian gunners were sent home (and went gladly), while their guns and equipment were handed over to Rasim, Feisal's own gunner, and to Feisal's machine-gun officer; who in their place formed Arab detachments mostly of Turk-trained Syrian and Mesopotamian deserters. Maulud got together a force of fifty mule-mounted men whom he called cavalry and, since they were townsmen and not Bedouin, soon made regular soldiers of them. They were so useful that Lawrence telegraphed to Egypt for fifty mules more.

Now although the Arabs were of less use in mass than in small groups, it was necessary to make this march on Wejh a huge parade of tribes to impress all Arabia. Feisal decided to take all the Juheina tribe and add enough of the Harb, Billi, Ateiba and Ageyl to make it the biggest expedition in Arab memory. It would be clear that the Revolt was now a real national movement, and when Wejh was taken and the tribes returned home with the news, there would be no more petty jealousies and desertions of clans to hinder the campaign. Feisal and Lawrence did not expect any hard fighting at Wejh because the Turks had no spare troops to send to its defence or time to send them. It would take them weeks to withdraw their Rabegh expedition—the hindering of which with Harb help was now Zeid's occupation—and if the Arab army could reach Wejh in three weeks' time, they would surely take it unprepared.

Lawrence was anxious to take part in a small raid on the Turks, just to get the feel of it for future information, so on January the second 1917 he set out with thirty-five tribesmen. They rode some miles south-east until they came to a valley near the Turkish lines of communication. Ten men stayed guarding the camels, while Lawrence and the remaining twenty-five climbed over the sharp-edged crumbling cliffs on the farther side of the valley to another valley, where a Turkish post was known to be. There they waited shivering for hours in the mist. When dawn came they saw the tips of a group of Turkish bell-tents, three hundred yards below, just showing over a small spur that lay between. They put bullets through these tent-tops, and when the Turks rushed out to man their trenches, shot at them; but the Turks ran so fast that probably few were hit. From the trenches the Turks fired back wildly and rapidly in all directions as if signalling for help to the nearest big Turkish garrison—there were garrisons strung all along the road for eighty miles back. As the enemy was ten times their number already, the raiders might soon have been cut off. Lawrence decided to do no more: they crawled back over the hill to the first valley, where they stumbled over two stray Turks and carried them back to Yenbo as prisoners.

That morning the army started for Wejh, first making for a group of wells fifteen miles north of Yenbo. At their head rode Feisal dressed in white, his cousin beside him on the right in a red headcloth and reddish-yellow tunic and cloak, Lawrence on the left in white and scarlet. Next came three standard-bearers carrying an Arab flag of faded crimson silk with gilt spikes. Then the drummers playing a march, then the wild mass of Feisal's bodyguard, twelve hundred bouncing well-fed camels, with coloured trappings, packed closely together, their riders dressed in every possible combination of bright colours. This bodyguard was of camel-men called the Ageyl. They were not a desert tribe but a company of young peasants from the oasis country of Central Arabia. They had signed on for a term of years first of all for service with the Turkish Army but had soon gone over in a body when the Revolt started. Having no blood enemies in the desert and being the sons of desert traders they were most useful in the later campaign.

Beside the road were lined the rest of the army, tribe by tribe, each man standing beside his couched camel waiting his turn to join the procession. They saluted Feisal in silence, and Feisal cheerfully called back 'Peace be with you!' and the head sheikhs returned the phrase. The procession swelled, the broad column filled the valley in length as far as the eye could see, and, the drums beating, every one burst into a loud chant in praise of Feisal and his family.

Lawrence went back on his racing camel to Yenbo: he had to make sure that the naval help for the attack on Wejh would be properly timed. But first of all, feeling anxious about a possible Turkish attack on deserted Yenbo, he got a big British vessel, the *Hardinge*, formerly a troopship, to take on board all the principal stores of the town, including eight thousand rifles, three million cartridges, thousands of shells, two tons of high explosive, quantities of rice and flour. Boyle promised to lend the *Hardinge* as a supply ship for the force on its way up the coast, landing food and water wherever needed. This solved the chief problem, which was how to maintain ten thousand men with only a small supply column; and, for the rest, Boyle promised that half the Red Sea fleet would mass at Wejh; landing-parties were already being trained.

The Billi tribesmen who lived about Wejh were friendly and knew moreover that if they did not welcome Feisal's army it would be the worse for them, so it seemed certain now that Wejh would be taken. Boyle promised to take on board the *Hardinge* an Arab landing-party of several hundred Harb and

Juheina tribesmen. While this was being settled Lawrence heard that the three regular British officers who had been instructed to help Feisal direct the campaign were now on their way from Egypt. One of these, Vickery, arrived first. He was an artillery officer, with a good knowledge of Arabic; and what Lawrence thought that the Arabs needed, a trained staff officer.

On the sixteenth of January Vickery, Boyle, Feisal, Maulud, Lawrence, met in Feisal's camp, now half-way to Wejh, to discuss the advance. It was decided to break the army up into sections and send them forward one after the other, because of the difficulty of watering a whole army at the same time at the few wells or ponds on the line of march. These sections should then meet on the twentieth of January at a place fifty miles from Wejh where there was water, and make the last stage together. Boyle agreed to land tanks of water two days later at a small harbour only twelve miles from Wejh. On the twenty-third the attack was to be made; the Arab landing-party would go ashore from the *Hardinge* north of the town while Feisal's mounted men cut all the roads of escape south and east. It all looked very promising and there was no news from Yenbo that was not good. Abdulla was moving up to his position north of Medina, and news came that he had just captured a well-known Turkish agent, a former brigand, who was going with bribes among the desert tribes, and was on his way to Yemen far down in the south where a Turkish garrison was cut off. Abdulla took with this man twenty thousand Turkish pounds in gold, robes of honour, costly presents, some interesting papers and camel loads of rifles and pistols. It was the greatest good fortune.

In the tent with Vickery and Boyle, Lawrence had forgotten

FEISAL'S ARMY ENTERING WEJH

his usual calm and said that in a year the Arab army would be tapping on the gates of Damascus. There was no response from Vickery, who was angered at what he thought was a romantic boast that could only come from a man like Lawrence who did not know his job as a soldier. Lawrence was disappointed in Vickery, who was so much a soldier that he did not realize what the Arab Revolt was. It was not like a war in which large trained armies, with complicated modern equipment, manoeuvre from town to town, seeking each to destroy or cut off the other. It was more like a general strike over an immense area. The only big army was the Turkish and even that was not free to move about as it liked, because of the difficulties of the country. Lawrence knew that his boast had not been a vain one; five months later he was secretly in Damascus arranging for the help of its townsmen when Feisal's forces should arrive to free them. And a year later he did in fact enter the city in triumph and become temporary governor. Vickery had not seen that with a grand alliance of Semites, an idea and an armed prophet, anything might happen. Had Lawrence only had a sounder military training than the casual reading of military history for his degree at Oxford (and in his teens the occasional captaincy of a non-militaristic Church Lads' Brigade when his brother needed a substitute!) and if now he had been given a free hand, it would have been Constantinople and not Damascus that the Arabs should have reached. The conflict between Vickery and Lawrence, however, was not as between two British military advisers with different views. It was really as between a British military adviser and a white Arab; for though it was not quite clear yet to himself, this was what Lawrence was becoming.

The next morning there was trouble with the second batch of fifty mules which had arrived for Maulud and was landed by the *Hardinge* along with the other stores. The mules were sent without halters, bridles or saddles, and once ashore stampeded into the little town near by, where they took possession of the market-place and began bucking among the stalls. Fortunately among the stores taken for safety from Yenbo were spare ropes and bits, so that after an exciting tussle the mules were captured and tamed. The shops were reopened and the damage paid for.

Lawrence remained with Feisal's army for the rest of the advance. From this half-way halt they started on January the eighteenth at midday. The Ageyl rode spread out in wings for two or three hundred yards to the right and left of Feisal's party. Soon there came then a warning patter of drums from the right wing—it was the custom to set the poets and musicians on the wings—and a poet began to sing two rhyming lines which he had just invented, about Feisal and the pleasures that he would provide for the army at Wejh. The men with him listened carefully and took up the verse in chorus, repeating it three times with pride and satisfaction and challenge. Before they could sing it a fourth time, the rival poet of the left wing capped it with a rhyme in the same metre and sentiment. The left cheered with a roar of triumph, then the drums tapped again, the standard-bearers spread out their great crimson banners, and the whole bodyguard right, left and centre broke simultaneously into the Ageyl marching song. The Ageyl sang of their own towns left behind and the women whom they might never see again, and of the great perils ahead of them. The camels loved the rhythm of the song and quickened their pace, while it lasted, over the long desolate sand-dunes between mountains and sea.

Two horsemen came riding after them. Lawrence knew one of these as the Emir of the Juheina, the other he could not make out. But soon he recognized the red face, strong mouth and staring eyes of his old friend Colonel Newcombe of the Sinai surveying party, who was now come here as the chief British military adviser to the Arabs. Newcombe quickly became friendly with Feisal, and the rest of the journey was made even happier by his enthusiasm. Lawrence, comparing notes with him, was glad to find that they both had the same general views. The march was uneventful. Water was the one problem, and though water-scouts went ahead to find what they could, the advance was delayed by its scarcity, so that it was clear that Feisal would be two days late for the rendezvous with the *Hardinge* on the twenty-second. Newcombe rode ahead on a fast camel to ask the *Hardinge* to come again with its water-tanks on the twenty-fourth, and to delay the naval attack if possible until the twenty-fifth.

Many helpers joined Feisal during his advance; the Billi chiefs met him at their tribal boundary, and later Nasir rode up, the brother of the Emir of Medina. His family was respected in Arabia only second to the Sherifs of Mecca, being also descended from the Prophet but from the younger son of Mohammed's only daughter. Nasir was the forerunner of Feisal's movement; he had fired the first shot at Medina and was to fire the last shot beyond Aleppo, a thousand miles north, on the day that the Turks asked for an armistice. He was a sensitive, pleasant young man who loved gardens better than the desert and had been forced unwillingly into fighting since boyhood. He had been here blockading Wejh from the desert for the last two months. He and Feisal were close friends. His news was that the Turkish camel-corps outpost barring the advance had been withdrawn that day to a position nearer to the town.

The last three days of the advance were painful; the animals were without food for nearly three days, and the men came the last fifty miles on half a gallon of water and with nothing to eat: many of them were on foot. The *Hardinge* was at the rendezvous on the twenty-fourth and landed the water promised; but this did not go far. The mules were allowed first drink, and what little was left was given to the more thirsty of the foot-men. Crowds of suffering Arabs waited all that night at the water-tanks, in the rays of the search-lights, hoping for another drink if the sailors came again. But the sea was too rough for the ship's boat to make another trip.

From the *Hardinge* Lawrence heard that the attack on Wejh had already been made the day before; for Boyle was afraid that the Turks would run away if he waited. As a matter of fact the Turkish Governor had already addressed the garrison saying that Wejh must be held to the last drop of blood: after his speech he had got up on his camel and ridden off in the darkness with the few mounted men whom he had with him, making for the railway a hundred and fifty miles inland across the mountains. The two hundred Turkish infantry left behind decided to follow his orders rather than his example, but they were outnumbered three to one and the fleet shelled them heavily. The landing was made by the sailors and the Arab force, and Wejh was taken. But the *Hardinge* had come away before the end, so the advancing force could not be sure whether it would find the town still in Turkish hands.

At dawn on the twenty-fifth the leading tribes halted at a spot a few miles from the town and waited for the others to come up. Various small, scattered parties of Turks were met; most surrendered, only one put up a short fight. When they reached the ridge behind which Wejh lay, the Ageyl bodyguard dismounted, stripping off all their clothes except their cotton drawers, and advanced to the attack: their nakedness was protection against bullet wounds, which would strike cleaner this way. They advanced company by company, at the run, and in good order with an interval of four or five yards between each man. There was no shouting. Soon they reached the ridge-top without a shot fired. So Lawrence watching knew that the fighting was over.

The Arab landing-party was in possession of the town, and Vickery, who had directed the battle, was satisfied. But when Lawrence found that twenty Arabs and a British flying officer had been killed, he was not at all pleased. He considered the fighting unnecessary; the Turks would soon have had to surrender for want of food if the town had been surrounded, and the killing of dozens of Turks did not make up for the loss of a single Arab. The Arabs were not pressed men accustomed to be treated as cannon-fodder like most regular soldiers. The Arab army was composed rather of individuals, and its losses were not reckoned merely by arithmetic. And because kinship is so strong a force in the desert, twenty men killed meant a far wider range of mourning than a thousand names in an European casualty list. Moreover, the ships' guns had smashed up the town badly, which was a great loss to the Arabs, who needed it as a base for their future attacks inland on the railway. The town's boats and barges, too, had been sunk, so the landing of stores was a difficulty, and all the shops and houses had been looted by the Arab landing-party as a compensation for their losses. The townsmen were mostly Egyptians who could not make up their minds in time to join the Arab cause.

Still, Wejh was taken, the coast was cleared of Turks, and the march had been a great advertisement. Abd el Kerim of the Juheina who had come to Lawrence a week before to beg for a mule to ride, and had been put off with the promise 'when Wejh is taken,' had said almost regretfully, 'We Arabs are a nation now'; the regret was for the good old days of tribal wars and raids which now were at an end. Feisal had very luckily stopped a private war between the Juheina and Billi just in time; the Juheina, seeing some camels grazing, had of old habit ridden out and driven them off. Feisal was furious and shouted to them to stop, but they were too excited to hear. He snatched his rifle and shot at the nearest man, who tumbled off his camel in fear; then the others checked their course. Feisal had the men up before him, beat the leaders with a camel-stick and restored the camels to the Billi. More than a nation the Arab army seemed to some of the tribesmen. 'The whole world is moving up to Wejh,' said one old man.

The success at Wejh stirred the British in Egypt to realize suddenly the value of the Revolt: the Commander-in-Chief remembered that there were more Turks fighting the Arabs than were fighting him. Gold, rifles, mules, more machine-guns and mountain-guns were promised: and in time sent, all except the mountain-guns, which were the most urgent need of all. Field-guns were no use because of the hilly road-less country of Western Arabia, but the British Army could, it seemed, spare no mountain-guns except a sort that fired only ten-pound shells, useless except against bows and arrows. It was maddening that the Turks should always be able to out-range the Arabs by three or four thousand yards. The French Colonel had some excellent mountain-guns at Suez with Alge-rian gunners, but would not send them unless an Allied bri-gade was landed at Rabegh to take over the conduct of the war from the Arabs. These guns were kept at Suez for a year; but then the French Colonel was recalled and his successor sent them; with their help the final victory was made possible. Meanwhile a great deal of harm was done to the reputation of the French, for every Arab officer passing through Suez on his way to Egypt or back saw these idle guns as a proof of French hostility to the Revolt.

But while the news of the taking of Wejh was still fresh, the French Colonel called on Lawrence at Cairo to congratulate him; he said that the success confirmed his opinion of Lawrence's military talent and encouraged him to expect help in extending the success. He wanted to occupy Akaba with an Anglo-French force and naval help. Akaba was the port at the very extreme point of the Red Sea on the opposite side of the Sinai peninsula from Suez, and a brigade landed there might advance eighty miles inland towards Maan. Maan was an important town on the pilgrims' railway about two hundred miles south of Damascus, and on the left flank of the Turkish army opposing the British on the borders of Palestine. Lawrence, who knew Akaba from his surveying days in the winter of 1913, told the Colonel that the scheme was impossible, because, though Akaba itself could be taken, the granite mountains behind it could be held by the Turks against any expedition trying to force the passes. The best thing was for Bedouin Arabs to take it from behind without naval help.

Lawrence suspected that the Colonel wanted to put this Anglo-French force in as a screen between the Arabs and Damascus, to keep them in Arabia wasting themselves in an attack on Medina. He himself, on the other hand, wanted to take them into Damascus and beyond. Both men knew what the other's intention was, but there was a natural concealment of the real issue. At last the Colonel, rather unwisely, told Lawrence that he was going to Wejh to talk to Feisal, and

Lawrence, who had not warned Feisal about French policy, decided to go too. By hurrying he was able to get there first and also to see and warn Newcombe.

When the Colonel arrived at Wejh eight days after Lawrence, he began by presenting Feisal with six Hotchkiss automatic guns complete with instructors. This was a noble gift, but Feisal asked for the quick-firing mountain-guns at Suez. The Frenchman put him off by saying that guns were no real use in Arabia; the thing to do was for the Arabs to climb about the country like goats and tear up the railway. Feisal was annoyed by the 'goats,' which is an insult in Arabic, and asked the Colonel if he had ever tried to 'goat' himself. The Colonel spoke of Akaba, and Feisal, who had had Lawrence's account of the geography of the place, told him that it was asking too much of the British to get them to risk heavy losses over such an expedition. The Colonel, annoyed by Lawrence's Oriental smile where he sat in a corner, pointedly asked Feisal to beg the British at least to spare the armoured cars which were at Suez. Lawrence smiled again and said that they had already started. Then the Colonel went away, defeated, and Lawrence returned to Cairo, where he begged the Commander-in-Chief not to send the brigade that was already waiting to be sent to Akaba. The Commander-in-Chief was delighted to find that this 'side-show,' too, was unnecessary.

Back again in Wejh a few days later Lawrence began hardening himself for his coming campaign, tramping barefoot over the coral or burning-hot sand. The Arabs wondered why he did not ride a horse, like every other important man. Feisal was busy with politics, winning over new tribes to the cause, keeping his father at Mecca in good humour, and his brothers in their places. He had to put down a small mutiny: the Ageyl had risen against their commander for fining and flogging them too heavily. They looted his tent and beat his servants, and then getting more excited remembered a grudge that they had against the Ateiba tribe and went off to do some killing. Feisal saw their torches and rushed to stop them, beating at them with the flat of his sword; his slaves followed. They subdued the Ageyl at last, but only by firing rockets from pistols among them, which set fire to their robes and frightened them. Only two men were killed; thirty were wounded. The commander of the Ageyl then resigned and there was no more trouble.

A wireless signalling set was mounted at Wejh by the Navy, and the two armoured cars from Suez arrived. They had just been released from the campaign in East Africa. The Arabs were delighted with the cars and with the motor-bicycles that were sent with them. They called the motor-bicycles 'devil horses,' the children of the cars, which were themselves the sons and daughters of the trains on the pilgrims' railway. About this time came Jaafar, a Mesopotamian Arab from Bagdad, whom Feisal at once made commander-in-chief of the regular Arab forces under him. Jaafar had been in the Turkish army and had fought well against the British. He had been chosen by Enver to organize the Senussi tribes in the desert west of Egypt, and going by submarine had made the wild men into a good fighting force. The British captured him at last and he was imprisoned at Cairo. He tried to escape one night from the Citadel there, slipping down a blanket rope, but fell, hurt his leg, and was recaptured. Later in hospital he read a newspaper account of the Sherif's Revolt and of the executions of Arab nationalists in Syria; he suddenly realized that he had been fighting on the wrong side.

Feisal's politics were going well. The Billi tribe and the Moahib joined him and the Howeitat and Beni Atiyeh beyond, so that he now had control of the whole country between the railway and the sea from a point a hundred and fifty miles north of Wejh right down to Mecca. Beyond the Howeitat and Beni Atiyeh, to the north, and spreading over the wide gravel and lava desert to the borders of Mesopotamia lived the powerful Ruwalla tribe, whose Emir Nuri was one of the four great Arabian princes, the others being Ibn Saud of Nejd in the central oases, the Emir of Jebel Shammar, and the Sherif of Mecca. Nuri was a hard old man whose word was law and who could not be either bullied or coaxed; he had won his supremacy by the murder of two brothers. Fortunately he had been on good terms with Feisal for years, and Feisal's messengers going to him to ask permission for the Arab army to pass through Ruwalla territory met Nuri's messengers already on the way with a valuable gift of baggage camels for Feisal. Nuri could not give armed help at present because if the Turks suspected him they would half-starve his tribesmen in three months; but Feisal could count on him, when the right time came, for armed help too. It was most important to have Nuri friendly because he controlled Sirhan, the one great chain of camping-grounds and water-holes across the northern desert to the Syrian border, where lived the famous tribe, the Howeitat. One Howeitat clan, the Abu Tayi, was ruled by Auda, the greatest fighting man in Northern Arabia; and to get in touch with Auda had been Feisal's and Lawrence's ambition for months. With Auda friendly it should be possible to win over all the tribes between Maan and Akaba, and then, after taking Akaba, to carry revolt farther north still behind the Turkish lines in Syria. And Auda did prove friendly; his cousin came in with presents on the seventeenth of February 1917, and the same day arrived a chief of another Howeitat clan that was settled near Maan. Further arrivals that day were Sherarat tribesmen from the desert between Wejh and the railway with a gift of ostrich eggs, Nuri's son with the gift of a mare, and the chief of another Howeitat clan from the coast south of Akaba. This last chief brought Feisal the spoils of the two Turkish posts on the Red Sea which he had just taken.

The roads to Wejh swarmed with messengers and volunteers and great sheikhs riding in to swear allegiance, and the Billi, who had hitherto only been lukewarm in the cause, caught the enthusiasm of the rest. Feisal's way of swearing in new converts was to hold the Koran between his hands, which they kissed and promised 'We shall wait while you wait and march when you march. We shall yield obedience to no Turk. We shall deal kindly with all who speak Arabic whether Arabians, Mesopotamians, Syrians or others. We shall put Arab independence above life, family or goods.' When the chiefs came to Feisal it happened sometimes that blood-enemies met in his presence, when he would gravely introduce them and later act as peacemaker, striking a balance of profit and loss between them. He would even help things on by contributing from his own purse for the benefit of the tribe that had suffered most loss. For two years this peace-making was Feisal's daily task, the combining of the thousands of hostile forces in Arabia against a common enemy. There was no feud left alive in the districts through which he passed, and no one ever questioned his justice. He was recognized as a power above tribal jealousies and quarrels, and finally gained authority over the Bedouin from Medina in the south to a point far beyond Damascus.

XII

Early in March information came to Lawrence from Egypt that Enver the Turkish Commander-in-Chief had ordered the Turks to leave Medina at once. The message had been intercepted on the pilgrims' railway, where Newcombe and Garland were already busy with Arab help blowing up bridges and tearing up the rails. The Turks were ordered to march out in mass along the line with railway trains enclosed in their columns; they were to go for four hundred miles north to a station (Tebuk) below Maan where they would form a strong left flank to the army facing the British. As the Turks in Medina were a whole Army-Corps of the best Anatolian troops with a great deal of artillery, the British were anxious to keep them away. So Feisal was therefore begged (and Lawrence instructed) either to take Medina at once or to destroy the garrison on its way up the line. Feisal replied that he would do his best, though the Turkish message was days old and the move was already timed to begin. Feisal's forces were, at the moment, all moving forward to harry the railway inland from Wejh along a length of a hundred and fifty miles; so that the second part of the demand from Egypt was being met. If it was not too late to catch the Turks coming out it might be possible to destroy the whole force. The Arabs would damage the railway line until it was too hopelessly broken for the store trains to pass, and the Turks would therefore be without supplies to take them farther. When they turned back they would find the line broken behind them too. Lawrence himself decided to go to Abdulla, who had now moved to a position just north-west of Medina, to find out whether it was possible, if the Turks were still in Medina, to attack them there.

When he started he was very weak with dysentery brought on by drinking the bad water at Wejh: he had a high temperature and also boils on his back which made camel-riding painful. With a party of thirteen men, of various tribes, including four Ageyl and a Moor, he set out at dawn through the granite mountains on his hundred and-fifty-mile ride. He had two fainting fits on the way and could hardly keep in the saddle. At one point on the journey the ill-assorted party began to quarrel and the Moor treacherously murdered one of the Ageyl. A hurried court-martial was held and the Moor was privately executed, with general consent, by a member of the party who had no kin for the other Moors in Feisal's army to start a blood-feud against.

One can well imagine Lawrence's loneliness on this ride. He was no longer merely a British officer; his enthusiasm for the Revolt on its own account had cut him off from that. Nor was he a genuine Arab, as his tribelessness reminded him only too strongly. He hovered somewhere midway between the one thing and the other like Mohammed's coffin in the fable. More immediately disturbing was the possibility of being too ill to ride further, and so of falling into the hands of desert tribesmen whose idea of medicine was to burn holes in the patient's body to let the evil spirits out: when the patient screamed they would say that it was the devil in him protesting. Eventually he reached Abdulla's camp just in time to stave off the collapse. He gave Abdulla Feisal's message and then went off to lie in a tent where his weakness kept him helpless for the next ten days.

This forced idleness had important results: though his body was weak, his brain cleared and he began to think about the Arab Revolt more carefully than he had yet done. It was something to do to keep his mind off his physical condition. Hitherto he had acted from instinct, never looking more than a step or two ahead at a time: now he could exercise his reason. He remembered the military writers whose works he had read at Oxford: he had not been required by his tutors to become acquainted with any campaigns later than Napoleon's, but he had, it seems, out of curiosity read most of the more modern military writers, such as the great Clausewitz, and von Moltke and the recent Frenchmen, including Foch (whose *Principes de la Guerre* had impressed him much until he found that Foch had, without acknowledgment, lifted many of his chief principles from an Austrian report on the 1866 campaign). He began by recalling the main principle on which all these writers agreed, that wars were won by destroying the enemy's main army in battle. But somehow it would not fit the Arab campaign; and this worried him.

He began to ask himself why they were bothering to attack Medina. What was the good of it to the Arabs if they captured it? It was no longer a threat as it had been when there were troops in it to spare for the attack on Mecca. It was no use as a base or a store-house. The Turks in it were powerless to harm the Arabs, and were now eating their own transport animals which they could no longer feed. Why not let them keep the town? Why do more than continue to blockade it? What of the railway, which used up a vast quantity of men in guard posts all down the line and yet was too long to be properly defended? Why not be content with frequent raids on it, between guard posts, blowing up trains and bridges, and yet allowing it to be just—only just—kept in working order, so that it would be a continual drain on the Turks to the north to keep it going and to feed the troops in Medina? To cut it permanently would be a mistake. The surrender of Medina would mean that the captured Turks would have to be fed, many of the troops guarding the railway would make their way back north, and the drain on the Turks of men and trains and food would stop. The Allied cause would, in fact, be best served by attracting and keeping as many Turkish troops as possible in this unimportant theatre of war, and by using as many Arabs as possible in the important theatre of war, which was Palestine.

When Lawrence got better, therefore, and left his stinking, fly-swarmed tent he did not urge Abdulla to attack Medina but suggested a series of pin-pricking raids against the railway, offering to set an example in these himself. Abdulla was more a politician than a man of action and more interested in field sports and practical joking than in generalship. However, he permitted Sherif Shakir, his picturesque half-Bedouin cousin, to make a raid against the nearest station on the railway, a hundred miles away, with a party of Ateiba tribesmen and one of the mountain-guns which the Egyptian gunners had left with Feisal and which Feisal had lately sent to Abdulla as a present. Lawrence, convalescent, went with Shakir, and, on the twenty- seventh of March, laid his first mine, an automatic one, on the railway. Because it was his first it was not very successful. He caught the front wheel of a train all right, but the charge was not big enough to do serious damage. Nor did Shakir succeed in his raid beyond killing a score of Turks, damaging the water-tower and station buildings with his gun, and setting a few wagons on fire; there was, that is to say, no looting. The chief dramatic interest of the raid seems to have centred round a shepherd boy who was captured by the Arabs and tied up while his sheep, Turkish property, were eaten before his unhappy eyes. However, Lawrence went again a day or two later with a party of Juheina to experiment further in automatic mines: he was fortunate enough to have a preliminary failure. A long train from Medina, full of women and children, 'useless mouths' whom the Turks could not feed and so were sending up to Syria, passed over the mine without exploding it. There had been a cloudburst the day before, in which Lawrence and his men had been caught, and the mechanism, owing probably to the slight sinking of the ground after the rain, was not in touch with the rails. He adjusted this when night came and, blowing up a few rails and a small bridge to explain plausibly to the Turks (who had seen them and were firing and blowing bugles all down the line) what he and the tribesmen were about, went away and left the mine behind. It caught the expected repair- train. Most of this story, the episodes of the two months, March and April 1917, which are left blank in *Revolt in the Desert*, are accessible, in greater detail, to inquisitive readers. The *World's Work* magazine published them as an article in America in 1921. The fees for this contribution and three others following went not to Lawrence but to keep a poet, who had lost money in an attempt to start a grocery-shop, from the bankruptcy court. Lawrence took great care, for some reason, not to let them appear in England;

and as I was the poet, and this book has the same text for England and America, the details will not be given by me now.

The fruits of Lawrence's visit to Abdulla, measured in action, were small. Abdulla did not have his brother Feisal's energy and military keenness, and had been allotted an unattractive part in the campaign, the blockade of Medina, which encouraged the inactive side of his character. (The siege of the city was never pressed and dragged on until after the Armistice in October 1918 when the commander, Fakhri Pasha, was given orders from Constantinople to hand Medina over to the Arab forces; and did so, compelled by a mutiny of his chief staff-officers.) But, apart from action, Lawrence's visit to Abdulla was of considerable importance; it marked a turning-point in the Arab campaign. His fortnight's solitary thinking in that tent gave him convictions: he decided on the tactics and strategy necessary if his party were to achieve that success in the north which he regarded as essential to justify the Arab Revolt. We find him acting hereafter with great deliberation and confidence, in striking contrast to his previous hesitating attitude as adviser to Feisal in the Yenbo and Wejh operations. He had been right before, but more or less by luck.

On April the tenth Lawrence returned to Wejh by leisurely stages. Abdulla had been very hospitable, but Lawrence preferred the atmosphere of Feisal's camp, where there was a more energetic spirit and a determination to win the war with as little Allied help as possible. A good way farther north on the railway than he had laid his mines there were now two parties doing demolitions (Garland's and Newcombe's, and Hornby's), but the Turks would find it just a shade less difficult to keep the railway going between Damascus and Medina than to arrange for the long and dangerous march-out of the

Medina garrison. At Wejh he found things going on well. More armoured cars had come from Egypt, and Yenbo and Rabegh had been emptied of their stores and men as a proof that the Revolt was now safe in the south and was moving north. The aeroplanes under Major Ross were here and also a new machine-gun company of amusing history. When Yenbo was abandoned there were left behind some heaps of broken weapons and two English armourer-sergeants. Also thirty sick and wounded Arabs. The armourer-sergeants, finding things boring, had dosed and healed the men and mended the machine-guns, and combined them into a company. The sergeants knew no Arabic but trained the men so well by dumb-show that they were as good as the best company in the Arab army.

XIII

Lawrence was about to withdraw from Feisal's tent at Wejh after the exchange of news and greetings, when there was a stir of excitement. A messenger came in and whispered to Feisal. Feisal turned to Lawrence with shining eyes, trying to be calm, and said: 'Auda is here.' The tent-flap was drawn back, and a deep voice boomed out salutations to 'Our Lord, the Commander of the Faithful,' then entered a tall strong figure, with a haggard face, passionate and tragic. It was Auda; and with him Mohammed, his only surviving son, a boy of eleven years old, already a fighting man. Feisal had sprung to his feet, an honour not due to Auda on account of his rank, for nobler chiefs had been received sitting, but because he was Auda, the greatest fighting man in Arabia. Auda caught Feisal's hand and kissed it; then they drew aside a pace or two and looked at each other, a splendidly unlike pair, Feisal the prophet, and Auda the warrior, each true to his type. They had an immediate understanding and liking for each other at this first meeting.

Auda was simply dressed in white cotton robes and a red headcloth. He looked over fifty and his black hair was streaked with white: yet he was straight and vigorous, and as active as a much younger man. His hospitality was such that only very hungry guests did not find it inconvenient; his generosity kept him poor in spite of the profits of a hundred raids. He had married twenty-eight times, and had been wounded thirteen times. He had killed seventy-five men with his own hand in battle and never a man except in battle. These were all Arabs; Turks he did not count and could not guess at the score. Nearly all his family and kin had been killed in the wars which he had provoked. He made a point of being at enmity with nearly all the tribes of the desert so that he might have proper scope for raids, which he made as often as possible. There was always an element of foresight in his maddest adventures, and his patience in battle was great. If he got angry his face would twitch uncontrollably and he would burst into a fit of shaking passion which could only be calmed by battle: at such times he was like a wild beast and men fled from his presence. Nothing on earth could make him change his mind or obey an order or do anything of which he disapproved. He saw life as an epic in which he took a leading part, though indeed he believed his ancestors even mightier men than himself. His mind was stored with old ballads of battle, and he was always singing them in his great voice to the nearest listener or to the empty air. He spoke of himself in the third person and was so sure of his fame that he would even shout out stories against himself. He had a demon of mischief worse even than Lawrence's and in public gatherings would say the most reckless or tactless things that he could find to say: more than that, he would invent and utter on oath dreadful tales of the private life of his hosts or guests. Yet even those whom he most embarrassed loved him warmly; for he was modest, simple as a child, honest, kind-hearted.

I heard the following story from a friend who was present at a state banquet given after the War at Maan in Transjordania when Sir Herbert Samuel, who had just been made High Commissioner of Palestine, was introduced to all the great chiefs of the district. Sir Herbert, somewhat shaken by an attempt that had just been made on his life, was glad of Lawrence's chance presence as interpreter. In his speech he trusted that the great chief Auda (turning towards him) was pleased with the settlement of the Turkish empire and hoped that a long reign of peace had begun in the East. Lawrence translated this into Arabic, and Auda burst out violently in answer, 'What peace so long as the French are in Syria, the English in Mesopotamia, and the Jews in Palestine?' Lawrence, with equal mischief, translated this literally into English, without turning a hair. Fortunately Sir Herbert was content to answer with a smile.

Auda had come down to Wejh chafing at the delay of the campaign, anxious only to spread the bounds of Arab freedom to his own desert lands. The weight of anxiety was off the minds of Feisal and Lawrence before even they sat down to supper. It was a cheerful meal but suddenly interrupted by Auda, who leaped up with a loud 'God forbid!' and ran from the tent. A loud hammering was heard outside and the rest of the company stared at each other. It was Auda pounding his false teeth to fragments on a stone. 'I had forgotten,' he explained, 'that Jemal Pasha' (the Turkish commander in Syria who had hanged so many of the Arab leaders) 'gave me these. I was eating my Lord Feisal's bread with Turkish teeth!' As a result Auda, having few teeth of his own, went about half-nourished for two months until a dentist was sent from Egypt to make him an Allied set.

AUDA

from a drawing by ERIC KENNINGTON

Auda and Lawrence liked each other at first sight. The irony of their friendship has never been properly appreciated. From his schooldays onward, the greater part of Lawrence's imaginative life seems to have been lived in the mediæval romances of Frankish and Norman chivalry. This was not a light passing romanticism, for Lawrence's Irish-Hebridean blood would not allow such a thing: light romanticism is an English trait. It was, as I have said, an incurable romanticism which is at times not to be distinguished from realism. An English schoolboy is content to play for awhile at being a knight of the Round Table out of the *Idylls of the King*, or a jousting baron out of *Ivanhoe*; but later to dismiss the game as a stupidity and take to football, cigarette-smoking and the appreciation of cinema-actresses. Lawrence did nothing of the sort. Instead he went behind Tennyson's Victorian sentimentality to the bolder and finer *Morte D'Arthur* of Malory; nor was he content to play at being a knight of the Holy Grail without binding himself, for the sake of personal efficiency, to the same rules of chastity and temperance and gentleness that Malory's Galahad had kept; he certainly kept and keeps a knightly sense of honour as strictly as a Geraint, or a Walter de Manny. He went behind Scott's false mediævalism in search of the real mediævalism; made an intense study of ancient armour and cathedrals and castles; read old French, studied the Crusades in the Holy Land itself. As an undergraduate he told a friend that in his opinion the world had virtually come to an end in 1500, destroyed by gunpowder and cheap printing. Lawrence so logically pursued his romantic career, which began by putting his nose between the pages of Scott and Tennyson, and then between those of Morris and Malory, and then between those of the original mediæval French and Latin romances, that at last he forced his whole head and shoulders and body between the pages of an epic in the making, and in the first book met Feisal, and in the second Auda.

This would have been all very well if Lawrence's mediævalism had been natural as Auda's was, the Middle Ages being not yet over in Arabia when he was born. But in his struggle against the forces of false romanticism, to avoid becoming a second Don Quixote, Lawrence had to arm himself with a careful twentieth-century scepticism which he continually used in test of his behaviour; true mediævalism was often cynical, never sceptical. It is, therefore, interesting to note that he carried three books with him throughout the Arabian campaign. The first was Malory's *Morte D'Arthur;* but the second was the comedies of Aristophanes, whose laughing scepticism, especially in his anti-militaristic *Lysistrata*, provides a fine antidote to false romanticism.

His choice of a third book was equally interesting—the *Oxford Book of English Verse*, a collection which, in my opinion, gives the poetry it contains too strong an atmosphere of literary artistry. Perhaps I should have added to my portrait of Lawrence that his blind desire to be a literary artist is the more to be wondered at because he might well be something better than a mere artist. Artistic writing comes from a competitive literary atmosphere and should be the last thing on earth for Lawrence to aim at; the pursuit of 'style' is a social practice of the vulgarest sort. Lawrence may be excused for carrying this anthology (which is no worse than most other anthologies and weighs little when printed on India paper) if he chose it merely as a mixed potpourri of the English poets, faintly recalling the true smell of each individual. But I do not believe that this was the case; for a straining after literary artistry is one of his characteristics. The justification of the literary epic that came out of this adventure, his *Seven Pillars*, is that where the pursuit of style is forgotten in the excitement of story-telling there is clean and beautiful writing, and that where it is not forgotten one feels that Lawrence is admitting an unfortunate taint, the suppression of which would be a suppression of part of the truth about himself. He has, in fact, only been able to keep his integrity by confessing to an occasional weakness. But of this more later. The influence of the *Oxford Book of English Verse* on his feelings and actions during the campaign would be well worth studying. The copy survives with marginal annotations, many of these dated.

At all events, Auda accepted Lawrence as a fellow-mediævalist (the shadow of the Crusades happily not falling between them) and Lawrence was content in his company and went through the next book of the epical romance with only occasional critical doubts about himself. There was need for true epic action if Akaba was to be taken, for it was a feat beyond the scope of unheroic twentieth-century soldiering. So the two took counsel together for a journey northward to catch Auda's Howeitat in their spring pastures of the Syrian desert: they would raise a camel-corps there and take Akaba by surprise from the east without guns or machine-guns. This would mean an encircling march of six hundred miles to capture a position which was within gun-fire of the British Fleet—which indeed was raiding the port at the moment. Yet the longest way was the only way; for Akaba was so strongly protected by the hills, elaborately fortified for miles back, that if a landing were attempted from the sea a small Turkish force could hold up a whole Allied division in the defiles. On the other hand, the Turks had never thought of facing their fortifications east against attack from inland. Auda's men could probably rush them easily with help of neighbouring clans of Howeitat from the coast and in the hills. The importance of Akaba was great. It was a constant threat to the British Army which had now reached the Gaza-Beersheba line and therefore left it behind the right flank: a small Turkish force from Akaba could do great damage and might even strike at Suez. But Lawrence saw that the Arabs needed Akaba as much and more than the British. If they took it, they could link up with the British Army at Beersheba, and show by their presence that they were a real national army, one to be reckoned with. Nothing but actual contact could ever convince the British that the Arabs were really worth considering as allies, and once the contact was made, there would be no more difficulty about guns, money and equipment: the Arab campaign would no longer be a side-show but part of the main battle, and the British would feed it properly.

Lawrence discussed with the British officers at Wejh, Feisal's advisers, the tactics that had occurred to him while he was lying sick in Abdulla's camp. It must always be remembered that Lawrence, though the Englishman most respected by the Arabs, was not the only one fighting in Arabia, and, more than that, was not even a senior officer. On this occasion his views were disregarded. It had been decided some weeks before, chiefly on Lawrence's impulse, to march the whole force inland from Wejh and occupy a large stretch of the pilgrims' railway with mixed Egyptian and Arab troops; all arrangements had been made and it was hoped that Medina would soon surrender. But Lawrence had changed his mind: he now argued, against this scheme, that it had been found bad policy to mix Egyptians and Arabs, that the Arabs could

not be trusted to attack or defend a line or a point against
regular troops, that the country which they proposed to hold
was barren, and that to force the Turks to waste men and arms
and food in holding Medina and the railway line would harm
them more than any military defeat that could be inflicted
on them. However, plans were already too far advanced, and
Lawrence could do nothing to sidetrack the expedition. He
decided to go off on his own to take Akaba and to ask his
seniors for no help in arms or stores that would in any way
weaken their own expedition.

Feisal was his stand-by (Feisal thought and planned and
worked for every one) and gave him twenty-two thousand
pounds in gold from his own purse to pay the wages of the
party and of all the new men enrolled during the journey. Sherif
Nasir, usual leader of forlorn hopes, was in command. Seventeen Ageyl went as escort, and to deal with the Syrian Arab
converts in the north came Zeki and Nesib, both important
men of Damascus. The gold was shared out between Nasir,
Auda, Nesib and Zeki. The party started on May the ninth;
every man carried a forty-five-pound bag of flour with him
as his rations for six weeks. There were a few spare rifles for
presents, and six camel-loads of blasting gelatine for blowing
up rails, trains or bridges in the north. It seemed a small force
to go out to win a new province, and so thought the French
representative with Feisal, who rode up to take a farewell pho-
tograph. Auda was worth photographing; he was dressed in
finery that he had bought at Wejh—a mouse-coloured great-
coat of broadcloth with a velvet collar, and yellow elastic-sided
boots. Nasir was the guide and knew this country almost as well
as his own; after two years of fighting and preaching always
beyond the front line of Feisal's armies he was very weary and

sunken in spirit. He talked sorrowfully to Lawrence of his beautiful home in Medina, the great cool house and its gardens planted with every sort of fruit-tree, the shady avenues, the vine-trellised swimming tank, the deep well with its wheel turned by oxen, the many fountains. Now, he said, the blight of the Turks was on the place: his fruit-trees were wasted, his palms chopped down. Even the great well, which had sounded with the creak of the wheel for six hundred years, had fallen silent; the garden, cracked with heat, was becoming as waste as the hills over which he now rode.

The baggage-camels went slowly, weak with the mange that was the curse of Wejh, grazing all the way. The riders were tempted to hurry them but Auda said no; because of the long ride before them they must go slowly and spare their beasts. This was a country of white sand which dazzled the eyes cruelly, and they were glad when they came to a small oasis in a valley where an old man, his wife and daughters, the only inhabitants, had a garden among the palm-trees. They grew tobacco, beans, melons, cucumbers, egg-plants, and worked day and night without much thought of the world outside. The old man laughed at his visitors, asking what more to eat and drink all this fighting and suffering would bring; he could not understand their talk of Arab liberty. He only lived for his garden. Every new year he sold his tobacco and bought a shirt for himself, and one each for his household; his felt cap, his only other garment, had been his grandfather's a century before.

At this place they met Rasim, Feisal's chief gunner, Maulud his A.D.C., and others, who said that Sherif Sharraf, Feisal's cousin, whom they were to meet at the next stopping-place, was away raiding. So they all rested for a day or two. The old

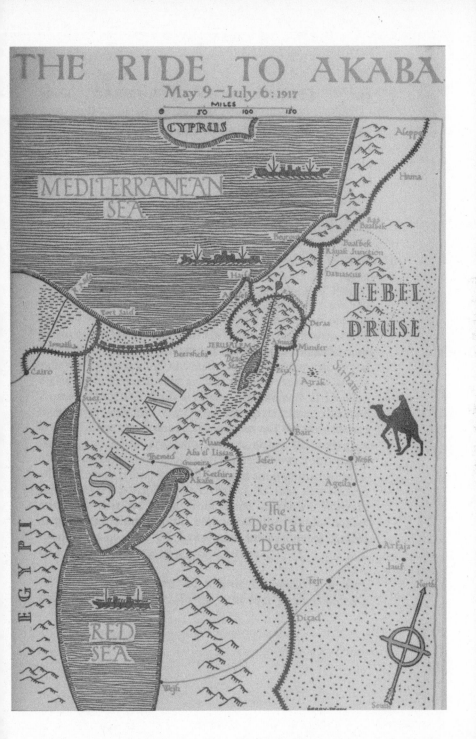

THE RIDE TO AKABA
May 9 — July 6 : 1917

MILES
0   50   100   150

CYPRUS

MEDITERRANEAN SEA

Aleppo

Hama

Beyrout

Ras Baalbek

Baalbek
Kiyak Junction

Haifa

Damascus

JEBEL DRUSE

Port Said

JERUSALEM
Beersheba
Dead Sea

Deraa

Azrak

Ajun

Mizher

Bair

Sirhan

Ismailia

Cairo

Suez

SINAI

Maan
Themed
Aba el Lissan
Guweira
Kethira
Akaba

Jefer

Nebk

Aquta

EGYPT

RED SEA

Wejh

The
Desolate
Desert

Arfaja

Jauf

Fejr

North

Digad

South

man sold them vegetables, Rasim and Maulud provided tinned meat, and they had music each evening round the camp-fire. This was not the monotonous roaring ballad-music of the desert, or the exciting melodies of the Central Oases which the Ageyl sang, but the falsetto quarter-tones and trills of Damascus love-songs given bashfully on guitars by Maulud's soldier-musicians. Nesib and Zeki, too, would sing passionate songs of Arab freedom, and all the camp would listen dead silent until each stanza ended, then give a sighing longing echo of the last note. The old man went on splashing out his water into the clay channels of his garden, laughing at such foolishness.

Auda hated the luxuriance of the garden and longed for the desert again. So on the second night they pushed forward again, Auda riding ahead and singing an endless ballad of the Howeitat. 'Ho! Ho! Ho!' he boomed on three bass-notes; and his voice guided the party through the dark valleys; Lawrence did not understand many words of the dialect, which was a very ancient form of Arabic. On this journey Nasir and Auda's cousin Mohammed el Dheilan took pains with Lawrence's Arabic, giving him alternate lessons in the classical Medina tongue and the vivid desert language. He had originally spoken, rather haltingly, the dialects of the country about Carchemish. Now, from mixing with so many tribes, he used a fluent ungrammatical mixture of every possible Arabic dialect, so that new-comers imagined that he came from some unknown illiterate district, the shot-rubbish ground of the whole Arabic speaking continent. Of Lawrence's knowledge of Arabic he has written to me in a recent letter:

'In Oxford I picked up a little colloquial grammar, before I first went out. In the next four years I added a considerable (4,000 word) vocabulary to this skeleton of grammar; words useful in archæological research mainly.

'Then for the first two years of the War I spoke hardly a word of it and as I had never learned the letters to read or write—and have not yet—naturally it almost all passed from me. So when I joined Feisal I had to take it all up again from the beginning in a fresh and very different dialect. As the campaign grew it carried me from dialect to dialect, so that I never settled down to learn one properly. Also I learned by ear (not knowing the written language) and therefore incorrectly; and my teachers were my servants who were too respectful to go on reporting my mistakes to me. They found it easier to learn my Arabic than to teach me theirs.

'In the end I had control of some 12,000 words; a good vocabulary for English, but not enough for Arabic, which is a very wide language; and I used to fit these words together with a grammar and syntax of my own invention. Feisal called my Arabic "a perpetual adventure" and used to provoke me to speak to him so that he might enjoy it. . . .

'I've never heard an Englishman speak Arabic well enough to be taken for a native of any part of the Arabic-speaking world, for five minutes.'

The march was difficult, over rocky country; at last the track became a goat-path zigzagging up a hill too steep to climb except on all fours. The party dismounted and led the camels. Soon they had great difficulty in coaxing them along, and had

to push and pull them, adjusting the loads to ease them. Two
of the weaker camels broke down and had to be killed: they
were at once cut up for meat and their loads repacked on the
others. Lawrence was glad when they came to a plateau at the
top: he was ill again with fever and boils. They rode over lava,
between red and black sandstone hills, and at last halted in a
deep dark gorge, wooded with tamarisk and oleander, where
they found the camp of Sharraf. He was still away and they
waited until he came three days later.

Sleeping here in a shepherd's fold Lawrence was awakened
by the voice of an Ageyl boy pleading to him for compassion.
His name was Daud and he had an inseparable friend called
Farraj. Farraj had burned their tent in a frolic and would be
beaten by the captain of the Ageyl who were with Sharraf.
Would Lawrence beg him off? Lawrence spoke to the captain,
who answered that the pair were always in trouble and had
lately been so outrageous in their tricks that he must make
an example of them. All that he could do was to let Daud
share Farraj's sentence. Daud jumped at the chance, kissed
Lawrence's hand and the captain's and ran up the valley. The
next day Farraj and Daud hobbled up to Lawrence, where he
was discussing the march with Auda and Nasir, and said that
they were for his service. Lawrence said that he wanted no
servants and that anyhow after their beating they could not
ride. Daud turned away defeated and angry, but Farraj went
to Nasir, knelt humbly and begged him to persuade Lawrence
to take them on: which he did.

Sharraf came and reassured them about water, which had
been an anxiety; there were pools of new fallen rainwater farther on their road. They set out then and had not gone far
before they met five riders coming from the railway. Lawrence

riding in front with Auda had the thrill 'Friend or enemy?' of meeting strangers in the desert, but soon they saw that the riders were friendly Arabs, and riding in front was a fair-haired, shaggy-bearded Englishman in tattered uniform. Lawrence knew that this must be Hornby, Newcombe's pupil who vied with him in smashing the railway. The persistent pair would cling for weeks to the railway with few helpers and often with no food, blowing up bridges and rails until they had exhausted their explosives or their camels and had to return for more. Newcombe was hard on his camels, whom he worked at the trot and who quickly wore out in that thirsty district; the men with him had either to leave him on the road—a lasting disgrace in the desert—or founder their own beasts. They used to complain: 'Newcombe is like fire, he burns friend and enemy.' Lawrence was told that Newcombe would not sleep except with his head on the rails, and that when there was no guncotton left, Hornby would worry the metals with his teeth. This was exaggerated, but gave a sense of their destructive energy which kept four Turkish labour battalions constantly busy patching up after them.

After greetings and exchange of news Hornby passed on and Lawrence's party continued the march over the lava desert. On this eighth day of their journey they camped in a damp valley full of thorny brushwood which was, however, too bitter for the camels to feed on. But they ran about tearing up the bushes and heaping them on a big bonfire, where they baked bread. When the fire was hot, out wriggled a large black snake which must have been gathered, torpid, with the twigs. The ninth day's journey was still over long miles of lava broken with sandstone, a dead, weary, ghostly land without pasture. The camels were nearly spent.

At last the lava ended and they came to an open plain of fine scrub and golden sand with green bushes scattered over it. There were a few water-holes scooped by someone after the rainstorm of three weeks before. By these they camped, and drove the unloaded camels out to feed. There was an alarm when a dozen mounted men rode up from the direction of the railway and began firing at the herdsmen, but the party at the camp ran at once to the nearest mounds and rocks, shouting, and began firing too. The raiders, whoever they were, galloped off in alarm. Auda thought that they were a patrol of the Shammar tribe. They rode on again over the plain through a fantastic valley in which were red sandstone pillars of all shapes and all sizes from ten to sixty feet in height, with narrow sand paths between, then over a plateau strewn with black basalt, and finally reached the water-pools of which Sharraf had spoken. Hornby and Newcombe had evidently camped here: there were empty sardine-tins lying about.

Daud and Farraj were proving good servants; they were brave and cheerful, rode well, worked willingly. They spent much time attending to Lawrence's camel which had the mange very badly on its face; having no proper ointment they rubbed in butter, which was a slight relief for the intolerable itch. This tenth day's journey brought the party to the railway which they had to cross near a station called Dizad. It ran in a long valley. They happened on a deserted stretch of line and were much relieved, because Sharraf had warned them of constant Turkish patrols of mule-mounted men, camel-corps and trolleys carrying machine-guns. There was good pasture on both sides of the line, and the riding-camels were allowed to graze for a few minutes while Lawrence and the Ageyl began fixing gun-cotton and gelatine charges to the rails. The camels

were then caught again and taken on to safety while the fuses
of the charges were lighted in proper order: the hollow valley
echoed with the bursts. This was Auda's first experience of
dynamite, and he improvised some verses in praise of its power
and glory. Then they cut three telegraph-wires, tied the free
ends to the saddles of six riding-camels and drove the astonished team far across the valley with the growing weight of
twanging wire and snapped poles dragging after them. When
the camels could pull no more, the tangle was cut loose. They
rode on in the growing dusk until the country, with its switch-
back of rock ridges, was too difficult to be crossed safely in the
dark by weak camels. They halted, but no fire was lit for fear
of alarming the Turks who, roused by the noise of the explosions, could be heard in the block-houses all along the line
shouting loudly and shooting at shadows.

The next morning they left the rocky country behind and
found themselves on a great plain: it was a country unknown
to Europeans, and old Auda told Lawrence the names of this
valley or that peak, bidding him mark them on his map. Lawrence said that he did not want to pander to the curiosity
of geographers in an unspoiled country. Auda was pleased
and began to give Lawrence instead personal notes and news
about the chiefs in the party or ahead on the line of march.
This whiled away dreary hours of slow march across this waste
of sand and rotten sandstone slabs. There were no signs of life
in this desert, which was named 'The Desolate,' no tracks of
gazelle, no lizards, rats or even birds. There was a hot wind
blowing with a furnace-taste and, as the day went on and the
sun rose, it blew stronger. By noon it was half a gale. The Arabs
drew their headcloths tightly across their faces to keep the
stinging sand from wearing open the sun-chapped skin into

painful wounds. Lawrence's throat was so dry that he could not eat for three days after without pain. By sunset they had gone fifty miles and came then to a valley full of scrub as dry as dead wood. The party dismounted wearily and gathered armfuls to build a great fire to show the rest of the party, from whom they had got separated the previous day after crossing the railway, where they were halting. When there was a fine heap gathered together they found that nobody had any matches. However, the main body came up an hour later, and that night they set sentries to watch because it was a district over which raiding parties frequently passed. They gave the camels the whole night for their grazing.

Noon of the twelfth day brought them to the place towards which they had been heading, an ancient stone well about thirty feet deep. The water was plentiful but rather brackish and soon grew foul when kept in a water-skin. On the thirteenth day out the sun was hotter than ever: at midday Auda and his nephew Zaal rode out hunting towards a green-looking stretch of country while the rest of the party rested in the shade under some cliffs. The hunters soon returned, each with a gazelle. Bread had been baked the day before at the well, and they had water in their skins, so they made a feast of it. On the fourteenth day they came in view of the great desert of sand-dunes called Nefudh which Wilfred Scawen Blunt, Gertrude Bell and other famous travellers had crossed. Lawrence wanted to cut across a corner of it but old Auda refused, saying that men went to Nefudh only out of necessity when raiding, and that the son of his father did not raid on a mangy, tottering camel. Their business was to reach the next place, Arfaja, alive.

They rode over monotonous glittering sand and over worse stretches of polished mud, often miles square and white as paper, which reflected back the sun until the eyes were tortured even through closed eyelids. It was not a steady pain but ebbed and flowed, piling up to an agony until the rider nearly swooned; then, falling away for a moment, gave him time to get a new capacity for suffering. That night they baked bread; Lawrence gave half his share to his camel which was very tired and hungry. She was a pedigree camel given to Feisal by his father who had her as a gift from the Emir Ibn Saud of the Central Oases. The best camels were she-camels: they were better tempered, less noisy and more comfortable to ride. They would go on marching long after they were worn out, indeed until they fell dead in their tracks of exhaustion: whereas the males when they grew tired would roar and fling themselves down, and die unnecessarily from sheer rage.

The fifteenth day was an anxious one: there was no water left, and another hot wind would delay them a third day in the desert. They had therefore started long before dawn over a huge plain strewn with brown flints which cut the camels' feet badly and soon set them limping. In the distance they saw puffs of dust. Auda said 'Ostriches,' and presently a man rode up with two great eggs. They decided to breakfast on these, but there was no more fuel than a wisp or two of grass. However, Lawrence opened a packet of blasting gelatine and shredded it carefully on the lighted grass, over which the eggs were propped on stones. Nasir and Nesib the Syrian stopped to scoff. Auda took his silver-hilted dagger and chipped the top of the first egg. A terrible stink arose and every one ran out of range. The second egg was fresh enough and hard as a stone. They dug out the meat with the dagger, using flints for plates. Even Nasir, who never before in his life had fallen so low as to eat eggs—eggs were counted as paupers' food in Arabia—was

AUDA AND HIS KINSMEN
(His son Mohammed is seated on the left)
Copyright American Colony Stores, Jerusalem

persuaded to take his share. Later oryx were seen, the rare Arabian deer, with long slender horns and white bellies, which are the origin of the unicorn legend. Auda's men stalked them: they ran a little but, being unaccustomed to man, stopped still out of curiosity, and only ran away again when it was too late.

The Ageyl were dismounted and leading their camels for fear that if the wind blew stronger some of them would be dead before evening. Lawrence suddenly noticed that one of his men, a yellow-faced fellow called Gasim from the town of Maan, who had fled to the desert after killing a Turkish tax-gatherer, was not with the rest. The Ageyl thought that he was with Auda's Howeitat, but when Lawrence went forward he found Gasim's camel riderless, with Gasim's rifle and food on it: it dawned on the party that Gasim was lost, probably miles back. He could not keep up with the caravan on foot, and the heat-mirage was so bad that the caravan was invisible two miles away, and the ground was so hard that it left no tracks. The Ageyl did not care much what happened to Gasim; he was a stranger and surly, lazy and ill-natured. Possibly someone in the party had owed him a grudge and paid it; or possibly he had dozed in the saddle and fallen off. His road-companion, a Syrian peasant called Mohammed, whose duty it was to look after him, had a foundered camel and knew nothing of the desert; it would be death for him to turn back. The Howeitat would have gone in search, but they were lost in the mirage, hunting or scouting. The Ageyl were so clannish that they would only put themselves out for each other. Lawrence had to go himself. If he shirked the duty it would make a bad impression on the men.

He turned his camel round and forced her grunting and moaning with unhappiness past the long line of her friends, into the emptiness behind. He was in no heroic temper; he was furious with his other servants for their indifference, and particularly with Gasim, a grumbling brutal fellow whose engagement he had much regretted. It seemed absurd to risk his life and all it meant to the Arab Revolt for a single worthless man. He had been keeping direction throughout the march with an oil-compass and hoped by its help to return nearly to that day's starting-place seventeen miles behind. He passed some shallow pits with sand in them and rode across these so that the camel tracks would show in them and mark the way for his return. After an hour and a half's ride he saw a figure, or a bush, or at least something black ahead of him in the mirage. He turned his camel's head towards it, and saw that it was Gasim. He called and Gasim stood confusedly, nearly blinded and silly, with his arms held out to Lawrence and his black mouth gaping. Lawrence gave him water, a gift of the Ageyl, the last that they had, and he spilled it madly over his face and breast in his haste to drink. He stopped babbling and began to wail out his sorrows. Lawrence sat him, pillion, on the camel's rump and turned about. The camel seemed relieved at the turn and moved forward well.

Lawrence went back by his compass course so accurately that he often found the old tracks that he had made in the pits. The camel began to stride forward freely, and he was glad at this sign of her reserve strength. Gasim was moaning about the pain and terror and thirst; Lawrence told him to stop, but he would not and sat huddled loosely so that at each step of the camel he bumped down on her hind-quarters. This and his crying spurred her to greater speed. Lawrence was afraid that she might founder, and again told him to stop, but Gasim only screamed the louder. Then Lawrence struck him and swore that if he made another sound he would be pushed off and abandoned. He kept quiet then. After four miles a black bubble appeared in the mirage, bouncing about. Later it broke into three and Lawrence wondered if they were enemies. A minute later he recognized Auda with two of Nasir's men, who had come back to look for him. Lawrence yelled jests and scoffs at them for abandoning a friend in the desert. Auda pulled at his beard and grumbled that had he been present Lawrence would never have gone back. Gasim was transferred to another rider's camel with insults. As they went forward Auda said, 'For that thing not worth the price of a camel. . . .' Lawrence interrupted: 'Not worth half a crown,' and Auda, laughing, rode up to Gasim, struck him sharply and made him, like a parrot, repeat his price. What had happened, apparently, was that Gasim had dismounted for something or other that morning, and sitting down had gone to sleep.

An hour later they caught up the caravan and towards evening they reached Sirhan, the chain of pastures and wells running up towards Syria. There among sand hills grown with tamarisk they halted. They had no water yet, but 'The Desolate' was crossed and they knew that they would get some the next day, so they rested the whole night and lit bonfires for the Emir of the Ruwalla's slave who had been with the caravan and had disappeared the same day. Nobody was anxious for him, for he had a camel and knew the country. He might be riding direct to Jauf, the capital of the Emir Nuri, to earn the reward of first news that the party was coming with gifts. However, he did not ride in that night or next day, and months afterwards the Emir told Lawrence that the man's dried body had lately been found lying beside his unplundered camel far out in the wilderness. He must have got lost in the mirage and wandered until his camel broke down, and there died of thirst and heat. Not a long death—the very strongest man would die on the second day in this summer season—but very painful. Fear and panic tore at the brain, and in an hour or two reduced the bravest man to a babbling lunatic; then the sun killed him. Lawrence himself learned to stand thirst as well as any of the Bedouin. He noticed that they did not drink on the march and learned to do as they did—to drink deeply at the wells and make it last, if need be, for two or three days. Only once in all his journeys did he get really ill from thirst.

The next day, the sixteenth of their journey, they came to the wells of Arfaja, grown about with a sweet-smelling bush after which the place was named. The water was creamy to the touch, with a strong smell and brackish taste: it soon went bad in the water-skins. There was plenty of grazing for the camels, so they stayed a day and sent scouts to the southern-most well of Sirhan to inquire for news of Auda's Howeitat, in search of whom they came. If they were not in that direction they would be to the north, and by marching up Sirhan the party could not fail to find them.

There was an alarm at the wells when a Shammar patrol of three men was seen hiding among the bushes. Mohammed el Dheilan, Auda's cousin and second man of the clan, went after them with a few men, but did not press the chase because of the weakness of his camels. He was about thirty-eight years old, tall, strong and active; richer because less generous than Auda, with landed property and a little house at Maan. Under his influence the Howeitat war-parties would ride out deli-cately with sunshades and bottles of mineral-water. He was the brain of the clan and directed its politics.

Lawrence was taking coffee that night, sitting at the camp-

fire with the Ageyl and Mohammed el Dheilan. While the cof-
fee-beans were being pounded in the mortar (with three grains
of cardamom seed for flavouring) and boiled and strained
through a palm-fibre mat, and they were talking about the
Revolt, suddenly a volley rang out and one of the Ageyl fell
screaming. Instantly Mohammed el Dheilan quenched the fire
with a kick of his foot that covered it with sand. The coffee
party scattered to collect rifles and shot back vigorously. The
raiders, a party of perhaps twenty, were surprised at the resistance and made off. The wounded man soon died. It was most
disheartening to be troubled by inter-Arab warfare when all
efforts should be concentrated on fighting the Turks.

The seventeenth and eighteenth days passed without
danger as they rode from oasis to oasis. Nesib and Zeki the
Syrians were planning works of plantation and reclamation
here for the Arab Government to undertake when it was at
last established. It was typical of Syrian townsmen to plan
wonderful schemes far ahead and leave present responsibilities to others. Some days before, Lawrence had said: 'Zeki,
your camel is mangy.' 'Alas,' he agreed, 'but in the evening
we shall make haste to dress her skin with ointment.' The
following day Lawrence mentioned mange again and Zeki
said that it had given him an idea. When Damascus was in
Arab hands, he would have a Government Veterinary Department for the care of camels, horses, donkeys, even sheep and
goats, with a staff of skilled surgeons. Central hospitals with
students learning the business would be founded in four districts. There would be travelling inspectors, research labora-
tories and so on. . . . But his camel had not been treated yet.

The next day the talk went back to mange and Lawrence
chaffed them about their schemes: but they began talking of

stud-farms for improving the breeds of animals. On the sixth day the camel died. Zeki said: 'Yes, because you did not dress her.' Auda, Nasir and the rest kept their beasts going by constant care: they might perhaps survive until they reached a tribe that had proper remedies.

On this eighteenth day they met a Howeitat herdsman who guided them to the camp of one of the chiefs. The first part of the journey was happily over and the gold and explosives were safe. A council was held and it was decided to present six thousand pounds to Nuri by whose permission the Howeitat were here in Sirhan; Nuri would probably allow them to stop a few days longer and enrol volunteers, and when they moved off would protect the Howeitat families and tents and herds. Auda decided to go to Nuri on this embassy, because he was a friend. Nuri was too near and too powerful a neighbour for Auda to quarrel with, however great his delight in war, and the two men bore with each other's oddities in patient friendliness. Auda would explain to Nuri what he, Nasir and Lawrence hoped to do, and say that Feisal wished him to make a public demonstration of goodwill towards the Turks. Only by these means could he cover the advance to Akaba while still keeping the Turks favourably disposed. Feisal knew that Nuri was at the Turks' mercy still; they could blockade his province from the north. So Auda went off with six bags of gold and said that he would rouse all his clan, the Abu Tayi Howeitat, on the way. He would be back soon.

Meanwhile the local families promised unlimited hospitality and Nasir, Lawrence, Nesib, Zeki and the rest were bound to accept it. Every morning they had to go to a different guest-tent and eat an enormous meal. About fifty men were present at each of these feasts and the food was always served on the same enormous copper dish, five feet across, which was lent from host to host and belonged really to Auda. It was always the same boiled mutton and rice, two or three whole sheep making a pyramid of meat in the middle with an embankment of rice all round, a foot wide and six inches deep, filled with legs and ribs of mutton. In the very centre were the boiled sheep's heads propped upright with flapping ears and jaws pulled open to show the teeth. Cauldrons of boiling fat, full of bits of liver, intestines, skin, odd scraps of meat, were poured over the great dish until it began to overflow on the ground; and at this sign the host called them all to eat. They would rise with good-mannered shyness and crowd about the bowl, twenty-two at a time, each man kneeling on one knee.

Taking their time from Nasir, the most honourable man of the company, they rolled up their right sleeves, said grace and dipped together with their fingers. Only the right hand might be used, for good manners. Lawrence always dipped cautiously; his fingers could hardly bear the hot fat. Nobody was allowed to talk, for it was an insult to the host not to appear to be very hungry indeed, eating at top speed. The host himself stood by and encouraged their appetites as they dipped, tore and gobbled. At last eating gradually slackened and each man crouched with his elbow on his knee, the hand hanging down from the wrist to drip over the edge of the tray. When all had finished Nasir cleared his throat for a signal and they rose together in haste, muttering, 'God requite it to you, host,' and then made room for the next twenty-two men. The more dainty eaters wiped the grease off their hands on a flap of the roof-cloth intended for this purpose. Then sighingly all sat down on carpets, while slaves splashed water over their hands and the tribal cake of soap went round. When the last man had eaten and coffee had been served, the guests remounted with a quiet blessing. Instantly the children would rush for what was left, and tear the gnawed bones from one another; some would escape with valuable pieces, to eat them safely behind a distant bush. The dogs yapping about finishing what was left. Nesib and Zeki soon broke down under this continual feeding, not being used to desert hospitality, so Nasir and Lawrence had to go out twice a day for a week and eat for the honour of Feisal.

On May the thirtieth they went forward again in company with the whole of the Abu Tayi; it was the first time that Lawrence had ever taken part in the march routine of a Bedouin tribe. There was no apparent order, but the caravan advanced simultaneously on a wide front, each family making a self-contained party. The men were on riding-camels; the black goat-hair tents and the howdahs in which the women were hidden were carried on the baggage-camels. Farraj and Daud were behaving with more than usual mischief in this care-free atmosphere. They rode about leaving a trail of practical jokes behind them. Particularly they made jokes about snakes. Sirhan was visited that summer by a plague of snakes— horned vipers, puff-adders, cobras and black snakes. By night movement was dangerous and at last the party learned to beat the bushes with sticks as they walked. It was dangerous to draw water after dark, for snakes swam in the pools or gathered in clusters on their brinks. Twice puff-adders invaded the coffee-hearth, twisting among the seated men.

Lawrence's party of fifty killed about twenty snakes daily. Seven men were bitten. Three died, four recovered after great fear and pain. The Howeitat treatment was to bind up the bite with snake-skin plaster and read chapters of the Koran to the patient until he died. They also pulled on thick blue-tas-selled red ankle-boots from Damascus over their feet when they went out at night. The snakes loved warmth and at night would lie beside the sleepers under or on the blankets: so great care was taken in getting up each morning. The constant danger was getting on everyone's nerves except Farraj's and Daud's. They thought it very witty to raise false alarms and give furious beatings to harmless twigs and roots: at last Law-rence at a noonday halt forbade them ever again to call out 'Snakes!' About an hour later, sitting on the sand, he noticed them smiling and nudging one another. His glance idly fol-lowed theirs to a bush close by where lay coiled a brown snake, about to strike at him.

He threw himself to one side and called out to another of his men, who jumped at the snake with a riding-cane and killed it. Lawrence then told him to give the boys half a dozen strokes with the cane to teach them not to take things too literally at his expense. Nasir, dozing beside Lawrence, woke up shouting: 'And six more from me!' Nesib and Zeki and the rest who had all suffered from the boys' bad sense of humour called out for more punishment still. However, Lawrence saved Farraj and Daud from the full weight of their compan-ions' anger; instead he proclaimed them moral outcasts and set them to gather sticks and draw water under the charge of the women, the greatest disgrace for sixteen-year-olds who counted themselves men.

The tribe moved on from well to well—the water always brackish—through a landscape of barren palms and bushes which were no use for grazing or firewood and only served to harbour snakes. At last they reached a place called Ageila where they came on a village of tents, and out rode Auda to meet them. He had a strong escort with him of Ruwalla horsemen, which showed that he had had success with Nuri. The Ruwalla, bareheaded and yelling, with brandished spears and wild firing of rifles and revolvers, welcomed the party to Nuri's empty house.

Here they stopped, pitched their tents, and received deputations from the clans and gifts of ostrich eggs, Damascus dainties, camels and scraggy horses. Three men were set to make coffee for the visitors, who came in to Nasir as Feisal's deputy and took the oath of allegiance to the Arab movement, promising to obey Nasir and follow him. Their presents included an unintentional one of lice; so that long before sunset Nasir and Lawrence were nearly mad with irritation. Auda had a stiff left arm due to an old wound, but experience had taught him how to poke a camel-stick up his left sleeve and turn it round and round against his ribs, which relieved the itch a good deal.

Nebk was the place decided upon for a rallying ground: it had plentiful water and some grazing. Here Nasir and Auda sat down for days to discuss together how to enrol the volunteers and prepare the road to Akaba, now about a hundred and eighty miles to the west. This left Nesib, Zeki and Lawrence at leisure. As usual the Syrians let their imagination run ahead of them. In their enthusiasm they forgot all about Akaba and their immediate purpose, and spoke of marching straight to Damascus, rousing the Druse and Shaalan Arabs on the way. The Turks would be taken by surprise and the final objective won without troubling about the steps between.

This was absurd. There was a Turkish army massing at Aleppo to recover Mesopotamia, which could be rushed down to Damascus. Feisal was still in Wejh. The British were held up on the wrong side of Gaza. If Damascus should be taken now by Nasir he would be left unsupported, without resources or organization, without even a line of communication with his friends. But Nesib was infatuated with his idea, and Lawrence could only stop him by intrigue. So he went to Auda and told him that if Damascus were made the new objective, the credit and spoils would go to Nuri and not him; he went to Nasir and used the friendship between them to keep him on the Akaba plan and also flattered Nasir's distinguished birth at the expense of Nesib's, a Damascene of doubtful ancestry. This was sordid but necessary. For Damascus, even if captured by surprise, could not be held six weeks; the British at Gaza could not attack at a moment's notice, nor would transport be available for a landing at Beyrout. And a set-back at Damascus would end the rebellion: rebellions that stand still or go back are always doomed. Akaba must be taken first.

Fortunately, Auda and Nasir listened to Lawrence but Nesib decided to go off with Zeki to the Druse mountains to prepare the way for his great Damascus scheme. The gold that Feisal had shared out to him was not enough for his purpose, so he asked Lawrence for a promise of more if he raised a separate movement in Syria under his own leadership. Lawrence knew that he could not do this, so promised Nesib that, if he now lent Nasir some of his gold to help him reach Akaba, funds would be got together there for the Syrian movement. He agreed, and Nasir was glad of two unexpected bags of gold for the payment of new volunteers. Nesib went off optimistically: Lawrence knew that he could do no harm with the little money that he had with him, and by talking too much might mislead the Turks into thinking that an immediate attack really was intended on Damascus.

XIV

What follows next is the brief and unsatisfactory story of what seems to have been the maddest and most dangerous adventure undertaken by any man in the whole course of the World War: a four-hundred-mile tour through the Turks' country with visits to their key-positions, without any disguise but the unbelievable folly of the journey. Lawrence decided to visit Damascus and the railway to the north of it. The exact account of it he has never given, even in his *Seven Pillars of Wisdom*, and I have been unable to piece it together accurately from the casual fragments which he has from time to time given his friends. But the motive of the journey seems clear, and the fact of it is beyond dispute. At Nebk Lawrence had time to think about his own part in the Revolt, and was not pleased with it. He began to see clearly things that he had been hitherto content to put into the background.

First of all, he was more or less an Englishman and bound to the hope of staving off his country's defeat. Successful war in the East, with the present deadlock in the West, might turn the scale and save further slaughter. Next, he was an Arab by adoption: the tribes trusted and loved him, and he was bound to do his honourable best for them. The Arabs could help the British to success while fighting their own war for freedom. So far, so good, but then came the difficulty. The Revolt had begun on false pretences. The British Government through the High Commissioner of Egypt had agreed to Sherif Hussein's demand for Arab freedom not only in Arabia but in parts of Syria and Mesopotamia, 'saving the interests of our ally France.' This clause concealed the secret Sykes-Picot treaty between England, France and Russia, in which it was agreed to annex some of the promised areas and establish 'spheres of influence' over the rest: in fact there was no genuine freedom possible. The High Commissioner had not been told beforehand of this treaty and so the Sherif did not know about it either. What apparently had happened was that the Foreign Office had two departments, each responsible for one of these agreements, and neither had taken the other into proper confidence. The High Commissioner, it may be noted, when instructed by the Government to make the agreement, had sent a strongly worded message of warning. He had said that in helping the Nationalist cause in Arabia a most dangerous thing was being done. Freedom for the Arabs might grow one day into a Frankenstein's monster; and he urged that great care should be taken to deal honourably with the Arab leaders; particularly he recommended that a single Government Department should be entrusted with all negotiations.

The Russian revolution took place in the spring of 1917, and the Bolsheviki published the secret treaty, copies of which the Turks sent about where they would do harm to England. Nuri had just had a copy sent him and confronted Lawrence with it; it was a great shock to Lawrence to be asked which of two contradictory pledges was to be believed. Lawrence did not know what to answer; he felt that the most honourable thing to do would be to send the Arabs home, and yet perhaps only by Arab help could the war in the East be won. So he said that England kept her word in letter and spirit, and that the later pledge cancelled the former treaty. This comforted Nuri, and the Arabs thereafter trusted Lawrence and fought finely with him: but instead of being proud he was bitterly ashamed of his deception. Later, he quieted his conscience as well as he might by telling Feisal all he knew and by refusing all decorations, rank and moneys that his part in the Revolt brought him personally. He would make the Revolt so well-armed a success that the Powers could not in honour or common sense rob the Arabs of what they had won: and he would fight another battle for the Arab Cause in the Council Chamber after the War ended.

But this was not all. He knew now that the War was entering another stage. In Syria the reputation of England was powerful and the reputation of the Bedouin leaders and of Mecca was low. He was the only man who, knowing the Syrians from before the War and having the confidence of the Arabians and being a representative of England, could carry the Revolt successfully north. All the responsibility fell on him. Was he strong enough to undertake it? He never had counted himself a man of action; books and maps were more in his line and he had left the Cairo office only under protest. And, again, towards what freedom was he leading the Arabs? A Confederation of Arab States, even if such could be founded against the wishes of France and England, would be necessarily the inheritor of the Turkish Empire. Town Syrians like Nesib and Zeki would run these states: their Governments might be more enterprising than the Turkish Government, but would be as corrupt; and the innocence and idealism of the desert Arabs on whose account alone he hoped for freedom would be infected by the filth of Damascus or Basra. Was the gift of freedom worth giving?

In this tangle of thought and shame he seems to have decided in Bedouin style to throw himself on the mercy of fate. He would go out on this mad ride and, so far from taking precautions, would expose himself to every possible danger. If the Turks were so foolish as to let him get back safely, they must pay the penalty of their folly, for he would carry the Revolt through to a finish with no more qualms. If they caught him, on the other hand, the Revolt would get no farther than the deserts of Arabia.

On June the third, 1917, in the fifth week of the journey from Wejh, he started off northward with a few of his body-guard and was away a fortnight. How he reached Damascus— he admits the visit—is not known, but it is possible that he went by way of the Druse mountains and the Lebanon, there visiting his friends the Christian Syrians, and that he turned south near Baalbek. He is said to have been convoyed by relays of local tribesmen, beginning with the Ruwalla, and changing them at each tribal boundary. Apparently none of his own men nor of Nasir's completed the journey with him. He is said to have been franked by private letters of Feisal's, but, as I say, nothing certain is known of his immediate purpose, his route or the results of his journey. At Ras Baalbek, south of Hama, considerably beyond Damascus and Baalbek, the far-thest points associated by rumour with his journey, there was an important bridge over which all the railway traffic between Constantinople and Syria passed. An intercepted enemy report of that month mentions the destruction of the bridge and one hesitates to regard this as a coincidence; yet its demo-lition must have meant the use of a great deal of explosive and Lawrence appears to have ridden light.

Of the Damascus visit little more than negative infor-mation can be given. Lawrence neither dined, lunched nor breakfasted with Ali Riza Pasha the Governor (as Mr. Lowell Thomas and others have stated), nor did he then or at any time since set eyes on Yasin, another Arab patriot. But it seems that he made arrangements with prominent members of the Freedom Committee in Damascus for the action to be taken when the Turks were finally expelled. There is a circumstantial story current that he rode into Damascus in English uniform on a camel and that seeing a notice pasted up offering a large reward for the capture alive or dead of 'El Orens, Destroyer of Railways,' with a portrait at the top, he decided to put the matter to a supreme test; he sat down to coffee under one of these notices: but, nobody connecting the man and the por-trait, after an hour or two he went on. That while he was in the city the men with him camped outside the walls in a cherry orchard: that there they were disturbed by some inquisitive Turkish policemen who, however, lie buried under the cherry trees. The poster story at least is untrue: none such were put up, nor was any camera-portrait of enlargeable size available. On the positive side, Lawrence has told me that he was never disguised during this ride, either as a woman or as anything else, but instead put off necessary visits to dangerous places until after darkness had set in. In the dark his figure could not be distinguished from that of any other Arab of the desert fringe. And the reference in *Seven Pillars of Wisdom* to his usu-ally wearing British uniform when visiting enemy camps may well refer to a practice begun on this ride. Whether or no he regarded Damascus as a 'dangerous place' I cannot say. Other picturesque incidents reported of this journey are as demonstrably untrue as the poster story. For instance, the Lowell Thomas account of his attempted visit to a military academy at Baalbek is disproved by there not having been a military academy there—only an infantry depot and a training camp. It is possible, though, that he visited these. Nor did he enter Rayak junction ('for the purpose of inspecting the railway repair shops'—another story) during the War. He seems, however, to have visited one or more of the bridges over the River Yarmuk, of which an account will be given in a later chapter, and to have been at Ziza, the headquarters of the Beni Sakhr tribe.

At all events, Lawrence's reticence about this ride is deliberate and based on private reasons, and it is my opinion that he has found mystification and perhaps statements deliberately misleading or contradictory the best way to hide the truth of what really happened, if anything of any serious importance did happen. His return journey was possibly by a Yarmuk bridge and across the Deraa-Amman railway to Azrak, and so to Nebk. I have marked the route, in the map, with dots to show my uncertainty.

XV

He returned on June the sixteenth and found Nasir and Auda still at Nebk; the final preparations for the march to Akaba had been made. Auda bought a small flock of sheep from a drover and gave a farewell feast, the greatest of the whole series. Hundreds of men were present and five fills of the great tray were eaten up as fast as they were cooked and carried in. After the feast the whole party lay round the coffee-hearth outside the tent in the starlight while Auda and others told stories. Lawrence happened to remark that he had looked for Mohammed el Dheilan in his tent that afternoon to thank him for the present of a milch camel, but had not found him. Auda began to laugh out loud until every one looked at him to know what the joke was. Auda pointed to Mohammed sitting gloomily beside the coffee-mortar and said to the company, 'Ho! shall I tell you why Mohammed has for fifteen days not slept in his tent?' To every one's delight he told how Mohammed had bought in the bazaar at Wejh a costly string of pearls and had not given it to any of his wives, so that they all began to quarrel and only agreed in one thing, to keep him out of the tent. This was Auda's usual mischievous invention and Mohammed, whose wives in the tent near by had come up close to the partition- curtain to listen, was much confused and appealed to Lawrence to witness that Auda lied.

Lawrence began his answer with the phrase that introduces a formal tale in Arabia. 'In the name of God the merciful, the loving-kind. We were six in Wejh. There were Auda and Mohammed and Zaal, Gasim, Mufaddhi and the poor man' (which meant Lawrence himself). 'And one night just before dawn Auda said, "Let us make a raid upon the market." And we said, "In the name of God." And we went; Auda in a white robe and a red headcloth, and

Kasim sandals of pieced leather. Mohammed in a silken tunic of "seven kings"* and barefoot.

Zaal . . . I forget Zaal. Gasim wore cotton and Mufaddhi was in silk of blue stripe with an embroidered headcloth. Your servant was as he now is.'

He paused, and the Howeitat sat dead-silent. Lawrence was mimicking Auda's epic style, also the wave of his hand, the booming voice and the accentuation of the points or what he thought were the points of his pointless stories. Parody was an unknown art among the Bedouin, and Lawrence's beginning had a tremendous effect on them. He went on to tell how they left the tents (giving a list of them) and walked down the village, describing all the passers-by and the ridges 'all bare of grazing, for by God, that country was barren. And we marched: and after we had marched the time of a smoked cigarette, we heard something, and Auda stopped and said, "Lads, I hear something." And Mohammed stopped and said, "Lads, I hear something." And Zaal said, "By God, you are

---

* See extracts from letters of Lawrence from Carchemish (page 27).

right." And we stopped to listen, and there was nothing, and the poor man said, "By God, I hear nothing." And Zaal said, "By God, I hear nothing," and Mohammed said, "By God, I hear nothing." And Auda said, "By God, you are right!" And we marched and marched and the land was barren and we heard nothing. And on our right came a man, a negro, on a donkey. The donkey was grey with black ears and one black foot and on its shoulder was a brand like this' (here Lawrence made a scribble in the air) 'and its tail moved and its legs. Auda saw it and said, "By God, a donkey." And Mohammed said, "By the very God, a donkey and a slave."'

Lawrence continued this Arab version of the 'Three Jovial Welshmen' with 'And we marched. And there was a ridge, not a great ridge but a ridge as great as from here to the what-do-you-call-it yonder; and we marched to the ridge and it was barren. The land was barren: barren: barren. And we marched; and beyond the what-do-you-call-it was a thing- um-bob as far as from this very place here to that actual spot there and afterwards a ridge; and we came to that ridge: it was barren, all that land was barren: and as we came up that ridge and were by the head of that ridge and came to the end of the head of that ridge, by God, by my God, by the very God, the sun rose upon us.'

This brought down the house. Every one knew the repetitions and linked phrases that Auda used to bring some sort of excitement into the dull story of a raid in which nothing happened, and they knew of old the terrible bathos of the sunrise which ended the story. But the walk to the market at Wejh was one also that many of them had taken. So they howled with laughter, rolling on the ground.

Auda laughed the loudest and longest, for he loved a joke

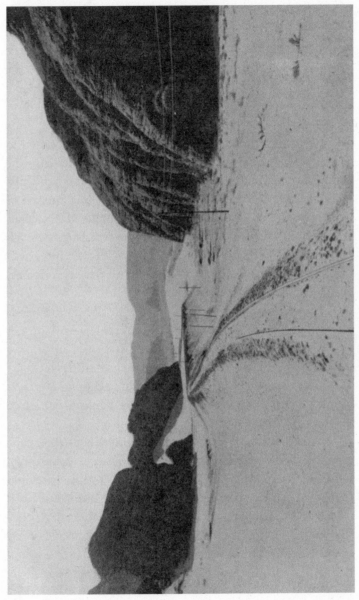

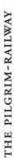

THE PILGRIM-RAILWAY

against himself, and Lawrence's parody had only proved to him how fine a story-teller he really was. So he went over to Mohammed, embraced him, and confessed that the necklace story was an invention. Mohammed in gratitude invited the whole camp to breakfast the next morning: they would have a sucking camel-calf boiled in sour milk.

The next day they rode off making for Bair, sixty miles away in the direction of Akaba. There were five hundred in the party now and every one was happy and confident. The country was limestone strewn with black flints, and in the distance were three white chalk hills. The leaders had a treat of rice that night, the chiefs of the Abu Tayi coming in to share it. At coffee-drinking Auda began provoking Lawrence with talk of the stars. 'Why are the Westerners always wanting everything?' he asked when Lawrence had said that astronomers every year make more and more powerful telescopes to map the heavens out more and more accurately, adding thousands to the number of known stars. 'Behind our few stars we can see God, who is not behind your millions,' said Auda. 'We want the World's End,' answered Lawrence. 'But that is God's,' said Zaal, half angry. Auda said that if the end of wisdom was to add star to star, the foolishness of the Arabs pleased him better.

He took Lawrence ahead next day: he wished to visit the grave of his favourite son, Annad, which was at Bair. Annad had been waylaid by his cousins of the Motalga tribe and fought them, one against five, until he was killed; Auda was bringing Lawrence to hear him mourn for the dead. As they rode down a slope to the grave, they were astonished to see smoke wreathing about the wells. They rode up carefully and found that the well-top had been shattered: looking down they found that the stone sides had been stripped and split and the shaft choked. Auda said, 'This is done by the Jazi.' They went to see another well beyond: it was also ruined. So was a third. There was a smell of dynamite in the air. It was clear that the Turks had got wind of their coming, and had possibly also raided the wells at Jefer where they had planned to concentrate before the attack. But in any case they could not reach Jefer without the Bair water. There was still, however, a fourth well some way off. They visited this rather hopelessly, and were delighted to find it undamaged. It was a well belonging to the Jazi tribe and that it had been spared seemed to prove that Auda was right. But one well was not enough for five hundred camels. So it was necessary to open the least damaged of the others. Lawrence went down in a bucket and found that a set of charges fixed lower in the shaft had not all been exploded: the Turkish engineers had evidently been surprised before they had time to finish their work. So he carefully unpacked the charges and took them up with him. Soon they had two fit wells and a clear profit of thirty pounds of Nobel dynamite.

They decided to stay a week at Bair and meanwhile sent off a party to buy flour in the villages near the Dead Sea—it would be back in five or six days—and a party to inquire about the wells at Jefer. If Jefer was not spoilt for them they would cross the railway below Maan and seize the great pass that led down from the plateau of Maan to the red sandstone plain of Guweira. To hold this pass they would have to capture Aba el Lissan, sixteen miles from Maan, where was a large spring of water; the garrison was small and they should be able to rush it. They could then hold the road to Akaba from Maan and the Turkish posts along it would have to surrender within a week for want of food; but before then the hill-tribes would probably have risen in sympathy and wiped them out.

It was important not to frighten the Turks at Maan before the attack began on Aba el Lissan, but the destruction of the Bair wells showed that the news of the Howeitat march had reached them. The only thing to do was to pretend that Akaba was not the place aimed at, but that they were driving farther north. Nuri had been misleading the Turks into thinking this and Newcombe had allowed some official papers to be stolen from him at Wejh in which was a plan for turning north at Jefer and attacking Damascus and Aleppo. Nesib was in Druse country preaching revolt and Lawrence in his Damascus ride had himself, it seems, hinted to the Druse tribes that they would soon have the Arab army there. The Turks were taken in by all this and made preparations to resist the northern advance by strengthening their garrisons.

To make the plan seem more likely still, Lawrence decided to raid the line about a hundred and twenty miles north near Deraa. He went with Zaal and a hundred and ten chosen men and they rode hard in six-hour spells with one- or two-hour intervals, day and night. It was a most eventful trip for Lawrence because the raid was carried out on the conventional lines of a tribal raid, the first in which he or possibly any Westerner had ever taken part. On the second afternoon they reached a Circassian village north of Amman in Transjordania; there was a big bridge not far from here, suitable to be destroyed. Lawrence and Zaal walked down in the evening to have a look at it and found the Turks there in force. They saw that four arches of the bridge had been washed away by the spring flood and the line was laid on a temporary structure while the Turks repaired the arches. It was useless to bother about a bridge already in ruins; so they decided to try to blow up a train instead. This would attract more attention than a bridge, and the Turks would think that the main body of the forces was at Azrak in Sirhan, fifty miles to the east. As they rode forward over a flat plain in the dark they heard a rumble and along came a train at great speed. If Lawrence had had two minutes warning he could have blown the engine to scrap-iron, but it rushed past and was gone. At dawn they found an ideal ambush, an amphitheatre of rock with pasture for the camels, hidden from the railway which curved round it, and crowned with a ruined Arab watch-tower from which Lawrence could get a fine view of the line. He decided to lay a mine that night. However, in the middle of the morning, a force of a hundred and fifty Turkish cavalry, regulars, were seen riding from the north directly towards the hill. The Arabs slipped out of sight just in time and the Turks went by. The place was called Minifer.

The Arabs went on to another hill, from where they saw a number of black hair-tents, summer quarters of a tribe of friendly Syrian peasants. Zaal sent messengers who brought back a gift of bread. Lawrence was glad of this, for their own flour had long been exhausted and they only carried parched corn with them, which they chewed. It was too hard for his teeth, so he had fasted for the last two days. The peasants promised to tell the Turks that the party had ridden off towards Azrak. After dark Lawrence and Zaal buried a big mine and waited for a train to pass. But none appeared that night or the next morning. Late in the afternoon a company of about two hundred mule-mounted Turks came up from the south. Zaal was for attacking them; a hundred men on camels suddenly charging down from higher ground could sweep double that number of lighter-mounted men off their feet. It would be a certain victory and they would capture not only the men but their valuable animals. Lawrence asked Zaal what the Arab casualties would be. Zaal thought five or six; Lawrence said that this was too many to lose. They had only one main object, the capture of Akaba; and they were here to mislead the Turks into thinking that the main body was at Azrak, not for loot. They could not afford to lose a man until Akaba had fallen. Zaal agreed, but the Howeitat were furious at having to let the Turks escape; they wanted the mules. To watch the company file unsuspecting by at point-blank range was too much for the patience of one boy, a cousin of Auda's, who sprang forward shouting to attract the Turks' attention and compel a battle. Zaal rushed after him, caught him, threw him down and began bludgeoning him until Lawrence feared that his now very different cries would arouse the Turks, after all. But they did not hear.

Now, if the Howeitat had had their battle, there would have been no keeping them on the Akaba plan. They would have driven home their captured mules in triumph to the tents by way of Azrak and not have come back again until too late. As for the prisoners Nasir could not have fed them, so that they would have had to be murdered, or else let go, in which case they would have revealed the raiding party's strength to the enemy. So the victory was let slip. But, what was even more disappointing, no train came for the rest of the day. So at night they returned to the line and blew up the most-curved rails they could find: these were chosen because the Turks would have to send all the way to Damascus for new ones. (This took the Turks three days and then the repair-train caught the mine that had been left behind and damaged its engine: so traffic stopped for three days more while the line was searched for traps. But of this they only learned later.)

They caught two Turkish deserters: one had been badly wounded while escaping and died soon afterwards; the other, though only wounded slightly, was very weak and feeble, his body so covered with bruises and weals, the cause of his desertion, that he dared only lie on his face. The Arabs gave him the last of their bread and water and did what they could for him; which was little. When they had to go away at midnight to water their camels some miles off they were forced to leave him behind on the hill. He could not walk or ride and they had no carriage for him. So Lawrence put a notice on the line in French and German to explain where the poor fellow was and to say that he had been captured wounded, after a hard fight. They hoped by this means to save him from being shot when the Turks found him, but coming back to Minifer six months later they saw his skeleton lying on their old camping-ground.

The next morning, many miles away on the return journey, they were watering their camels at the same cisterns that they had used on the way out, when a young Circassian came in sight driving three cows. This was dangerous, he might give an alarm. So Zaal sent off the men who had been most eager for a fight the day before, to stalk him. He was captured, unharmed but frightened. Circassians were swaggering fellows but cowards, and this fellow was in a cringing terror. To give him a chance of recovering his self-respect Zaal set him to fight at daggers with one of the party, a Sherari tribesman who had been caught stealing on the march: but after a scratch the man threw himself down weeping. He was a nuisance. They did not want to kill him, but if they let him go he would give the alarm and put the horsemen of his village on their trail. If they tied him up here he would die of hunger—they had no food to leave with him. And anyhow there was no rope to spare.

At last the Sherari said that he would settle it for them without murder. So he looped the man's wrist to his saddle and trotted him off with the rest of the party for the first hour: they were still near the railway but four miles from the village when the Sherari dismounted, stripped the Circassian of his outer garments and threw him down on his face. Lawrence wondered what was coming next; the Sherari then drew his dagger and cut the man deeply across the soles of his feet. The Circassian howled as if he were being killed. Then Lawrence understood. The man would be able to crawl to the railway on his hands and knees; it would take him about an hour, but his nakedness would keep him there in the shadow of the rocks until sunset. It was kinder than killing him, though he did not seem to be grateful.

Soon they came to a small station consisting of two stone buildings and crept within a hundred yards behind limestone rocks. They heard singing from one of the buildings, and a soldier drove out a flock of young sheep to pasture. The Arabs counted them hungrily, weary of a parched corn diet. The sheep settled the fate of the station. Zaal led a party of men round another side of the station and Lawrence saw him take very careful aim at the party of officers and officials sipping coffee in shaded chairs outside the ticket-office. He pressed the trigger; there was a crack and the fattest man slowly bowed in his chair and sank to the ground among his horrified friends. This was the signal for a volley and a rush. Zaal's men broke into the nearest building and began plundering; but the door of the other clanged to and rifles were fired from behind the steel shutters. Lawrence's party fired back, but soon saw that it was no good and stopped: so did the Turks and allowed the plundering to go on.

The sheep were driven off into the hills, where the camels were tied up, and the plundered building was splashed with paraffin and set on fire. Meanwhile the Ageyl were measuring out explosive and fixing charges; which were afterwards fired. A culvert, many rails and a quarter of a mile of telegraph-wire were destroyed. The explosions scared the sheep and the knee-haltered camels who shook off the rope-hitches and scattered in all directions. It took three hours to recapture them, but fortunately the Turks did not attempt anything in the interval, and the whole party reached Bair safely at dawn without losing a man. They had had a grand feast of mutton on the way; twenty-four sheep eaten at a sitting by a hundred and ten men. Nothing was left, for the riding-camels were trained to like cooked meat and finished off the scraps. The only difficulty had been the skinning, for there was a shortage of knives, but they had used flints instead.

At Bair they found that Nasir had bought a week's flour and were glad to think that they might well take Akaba before starving again. That day a messenger came post-haste from the Emir Nuri to say that four hundred Turkish cavalry had started from Deraa to Sirhan in search of them. He had sent his nephew as a guide to mislead them by devious routes, so that men and horses were suffering terribly from thirst. They were now near Nebk. The Turkish Government would believe that the expedition was still in Sirhan until the cavalry returned, and that would be some days. So the coast was clear, especially since the Turks thought that the Bair wells had been utterly destroyed and that therefore Maan was safe. The Jefer wells had been also destroyed, and that settled it. But Lawrence wondered whether the destruction of the wells at Jefer had not been bungled too. A Howeitat chief who had been present, and was one of those who had sworn allegiance at Wejh, sent secretly to say that the King's Well (Auda's family property and the biggest of the wells) had been dynamited from above; but that he had heard the upper stones clap together and key over the shaft. They hoped this was so and rode forward on June the twenty-eighth to find out, over a hard mud-plain blinding white with salt.

Jefer seemed hopeless; the seven wells were completely wrecked. However, they sounded around the King's Well and the ground rang hollow, so volunteers of the Ageyl began to dig away the earth outside. As they dug, the core of the well stood up in the hollow like a rough tower, and they carefully removed the stones until at last they knew that the report had been true; they could hear the mud fragments slipping between the stones and splashing many feet below. They worked hard, in relays, while the rest of the men sang to encourage them, promising rewards of gold when water was found. At sunset came a rush and rumble, followed by a splash and yells; the well was opened. The key of stones had given way and one of the Ageyl had fallen in and was swimming about trying not to drown. All night long they watered there, while a squad of Ageyl, singing in chorus, built up a new well-head. The earth was stamped in around this and the well was, in appearance at least, as good as ever. The Ageyl were rewarded by being feasted on a weak camel which had failed in the march that day.

From Jefer the next step was the pass of Aba el Lissan, where a Turkish block-house guarded the crest. A neighbouring clan of the Howeitat had promised to settle it, so picked men went from Jefer to help them. The Turks were not, however, taken by surprise; they manned their stone breastworks and drove the tribesmen off into cover. Thinking that this was only an ordinary tribal raid, they then sent a mounted party to take vengeance on the nearest Arab encampment. They found one old man, six women, and seven children there and cut their throats. The tribesmen only saw what was happening too late, but then furiously charged down from the hill across the return road of the murderers and cut them off almost to a man. They next attacked the now weakly-garrisoned block-house, carried it in their first angry rush and took no prisoners.

Hearing this news at Jefer the same day, Lawrence, Nasir, Auda and the rest went forward towards Aba el Lissan: striking the railway twenty miles south of Maan and blowing up a long stretch of it, including ten bridges. Lawrence had learned to destroy these at small expense by stuffing the drainage holes in the spandrels with five-pound charges of gelatine. The explosion brought down the arch, shattered the uprights, and stripped the side-walls. With short fuses it took only six minutes to finish each bridge. They continued their demolitions until all their explosive was gone and then struck westward towards Aba el Lissan, camping that evening about five miles from the railway on the Akaba side. Hardly had they finished baking their bread when three men galloped up to say that Aba el Lissan, the block-house, the pass and the command of the Akaba road were lost again. A large column of Turks, infantry and guns, had just arrived from Maan, and the Arabs at Aba el Lissan, disorganized as usual by victory, had run away. Lawrence learned later that this sudden move was an accident. A Turkish battalion from the Caucasus had arrived at Maan to relieve another that had been garrisoned there for some time; while it was still formed up at the station news arrived of fighting at Aba el Lissan and the battalion, with the addition of some mountain-guns carried on mules, was marched off at once to relieve the block-house. When the Turks climbed up to the pass they had found the place deserted, except for the vultures flying in slow uneasy rings above the block-house walls. The battalion commander was afraid that the sight would be too much for his troops, young conscripts who had never been on a battlefield before, and led them downhill again to the roadside spring, where they encamped all night.

The news was startling and unwelcome. The Arabs started off again at once, eating the hot bread as they rode. Auda was in front, singing, and the men joined in from time to time with the proud vigour of an army moving into battle. As they went, the camels in front kicked against the wormwood bushes and the scent hung in the air, making the road fragrant for those behind. They rode all night and came at dawn to the hill-crest overlooking the pass. Here the head-men of the tribe that had captured the block-house the day before were waiting for them, the blood still splashed on their anxious faces. It was decided to attack; unless the battalion were dislodged the dangers and trials of the last two months would go for nothing. And the Turks made this easy for them; they slept on in the valley while the Arabs surrounded them, seizing the crests of all the hills unobserved; and were caught in a trap.

At dawn the Arabs began sniping while Zaal and the horsemen rode to cut the Maan telegraph and telephone in the plain behind. The sniping went on all day. The Turks every now and then would make a sortie in one direction or another, but were soon driven back again to their position under some cliffs by the water spring. It was terribly hot on the hills, hotter than Lawrence had ever known it in Arabia, and the anxiety and constant moving made it worse. To make up for their small numbers they had to run behind the hill-crests from point to point to pretend to be more numerous than they really were. The sharp limestone ridges cut their naked feet, so that long before evening the more energetic men left a rusty print on the ground at every stride. Even some of the tough tribesmen broke down under the heat and had to be thrown under the shade of rocks to recover.

By noon the rifles had become so hot with shooting that they burned the Arabs' hands, and the rocks from behind which they aimed scorched their arms and breasts, from which later the skin peeled off in sheets. They were very thirsty but had little water and could not spare men to fetch more; so every one went without rather than that a few should drink. The only consolation was that the valley was far hotter, and the Turks less used to heat than themselves. The mountain-guns were being constantly fired, which made the Arabs laugh: the little shells burst far behind the hill-crests, though to the Turkish gunners they seem to be doing great damage.

Just after noon Lawrence himself broke down with something like a heat-stroke, and crawled into a hollow behind the ridge where there was a trickle of mud on the slope. He sucked up some moisture, making his sleeve a filter. Nasir joined him, panting, with cracked and bleeding lips, and then old Auda appeared striding along, his eyes bloodshot and staring, his face working with excitement. He grinned maliciously to see them lying there under the bank and croaked to Lawrence,

'Well, how is it with the Howeitat? All talk and no work?' Lawrence was angry with himself for his weakness and with every
one else. He spat back at Auda, 'By God, indeed they shoot a
lot and hit a little!' Auda, pale and trembling with rage, tore
his headcloth off and threw it on the ground. Then he ran
back up the hill like a madman shouting to the men in his
dreadful strained voice. They gathered together and scattered
downhill past Lawrence. Lawrence was afraid that things were
going wrong. He struggled up to Auda, who stood alone on
the hill-top glaring at the enemy, but all that Auda would say
was: 'Get your camel if you want to see the old man's work!'
Nasir and Lawrence mounted; the Howeitat were riding to
a lower part of the ridge, across the crest of which was an
easy slope down to the valley; it ran to a point rather below
the spring where the Turks were huddled. Behind the crest
they found four hundred camel-men massed, waiting. Lawrence asked where the horsemen were and was told: 'With
Auda yonder.' At that moment yells and shots poured up from
the valley. The Arabs kicked their camels to the crest and saw
the fifty horsemen galloping at full speed down another slope,
making straight for the Turks and shooting from the saddle.
Two or three went down, but the rest thundered forward. The
Turks hesitated, broke and ran.

'Come on!' Nasir screamed to Lawrence with his bloody
mouth, and away down over the crest plunged the four hundred camels, heading off the Turkish flight. The Turks did not
see them coming until too late: then they fired a few shots,
but for the most part only shrieked and ran faster. Lawrence's
racing camel stretched herself out and charged at such a speed
that she soon outdistanced the rest, and he found himself
alone among the Turks, firing wildly with his pistol. Suddenly

the camel tripped and fell headlong. Since she was going something like thirty miles an hour, Lawrence was torn from the saddle and went hurtling through the air for a great distance. He landed with a crash that drove all the power and feeling from his body and lay there waiting for the Turks to kill him, or the camels to trample him.

After a long time he sat up and saw that the battle was over. His camel's body behind him had divided the charge into two streams; he looked at it and saw that the heavy bullet of the fifth shot that he had fired from his revolver was embedded at the back of its skull!

A few of the enemy got away, the gunners on their mules and a few mounted men and officers. There were only a hundred and sixty prisoners taken, many of them wounded, for the Howeitat were avenging yesterday's murder of their women and children. Three hundred dead and dying were scattered in the valley. Auda came up on foot, his eyes mad with delight of battle, and the words bubbling incoherently from his mouth: 'Work, work, where are words? Work, bullets, Abu Tayi . . .' and he held up his shattered field-glasses, his pierced pistol-holster, and his leather sword-scabbard cut to ribbons. He had been the target of a volley which had killed his mare under him, but the six bullets through his clothes had not touched him. He told Lawrence later in confidence that thirteen years before he had bought a miniature Koran as an amulet. It had cost him one hundred and twenty pounds and he had never since been wounded. The book was a Glasgow photographic reproduction and was priced at eighteen-pence inside the cover; but nothing that the deadly Auda did might be laughed at. Least of all by Lawrence who, I think, envied Auda's natural mediæval style; he himself could only doubtfully and self-consciously use the materials of this scientific age in the mediæval setting. Mohammed al Dheilan was angry with Auda and Lawrence, calling them fools and saying that Lawrence was worse than Auda for insulting him and provoking the folly that might have killed them all. However, Lawrence could not regret his action, for the Arabs had only had two men killed and he would have been content to have lost many more. Time was of the greatest importance because of the food shortage, and this victory would frighten the little Turkish garrisons between Aba el Lissan and Akaba into quick surrender. As for Maan, prisoners told him that there were only two companies of Turks left in the town, not enough to defend it; much less to send reinforcements to Aba el Lissan.

The Howeitat then clamoured to be led to Maan, a magnificent place to loot, though the day's plunder should have satisfied them. However, Nasir and Auda helped Lawrence to restrain them; it would have been absurd to have gone there without supports, regulars, guns or communications, without gold even—for they were already issuing notes with promises to pay 'when Akaba is taken,' the first, notes ever passed current in Arabia—and no base nearer than Wejh, three hundred miles away. Yet it would be wise to alarm Maan further, so mounted men went north and captured two small garrison-villages between them and it; and news of this, and of the Aba el Lissan disaster, and of the capture of herds of convalescent army camels pasturing north of Maan by another of these raiding parties, all reached Maan together and caused a proper panic.

That night Lawrence experienced the shameful reaction after the victory: he went walking among the plundered dead with a sick mind; his thoughts were painful, emotional and shallow. Auda called him away at last; they must leave the battlefield. Partly this was a superstitious fear of the ghosts of the dead, partly a fear of Turkish reinforcements and of neighbouring clans, his blood-enemies, who might catch his force disorganized and pay off old grudges. So they moved on into the hills and camped in a hollow sheltered from the wind. While the tired men slept, Nasir and Auda dictated letters to the Howeitat near Akaba telling them of the victory and asking them to besiege the Turkish posts in their district until the force arrived. At the same time one of the captured officers to whom they had been kind wrote a letter for them to the garrisons at Guweira, Kethera and other posts on the way, advising surrender.

The food had been exhausted and water was scarce, so the expedition had to make haste forward. Fortunately the chief Howeitat sheikh of the hill tribes, an old fox who had been balancing in his mind which side to take, was impressed by the victory and captured the Guweira garrison of a hundred and twenty men. The next post on the Akaba road refused to surrender, so they decided to attack it, and in irony assigned the honour to the old fox and his less weary tribesmen, advising him to attack after dark. It was a strong post commanding the valley and looked costly to take. The sheikh shrank from the task and made difficulties, pleading the full moon. Lawrence promised that there would be no moon that night; by the greatest good luck he had noticed in his diary that an eclipse was due. So while the superstitious Turkish soldiers were firing rifles and clanging copper pots to frighten off the demon of darkness who was devouring their moon, the Arabs crept up and captured the place without loss.

They went on through the defiles and found post after post

deserted. News came that the defenders had all been with-drawn to trenches four miles from Akaba, a magnificent posi-tion for beating off a landing from the sea, though facing the wrong way for an attack from inland. They were, it was said, only three hundred men and had little food (the Arabs were in the same fix), but were prepared to resist strongly. This was found to be true. The Arabs sent a summons to surrender by white flag and by prisoners, but the Turks shot at both; at last a little Turkish conscript said that he could arrange it. He came back an hour later with a message that the Turks would sur-render in two days if help did not come from Maan. This was folly; the tribesmen could not be held back much longer and it might mean the massacre of every Turk and loss to the Arabs too. So the conscript was given a sovereign and Lawrence and one or two more walked down close to the trenches with him again, sending him in to fetch an officer to parley with them. After some hesitation one came and, when Lawrence explained that the Arab forces were growing and tempers were short, agreed to surrender next morning. The next morning fighting broke out again, hundreds of hill-men having come in that night knowing nothing of the arrangement; but Nasir stopped it and the surrender went off quietly after all. There were now no more Turks left between them and the sea.

When the Arabs rushed in to plunder Lawrence noticed an engineer in grey German uniform with a red beard and puzzled blue eyes; he was a well-borer and knew no Turkish. He begged Lawrence to explain what was happening and was astonished when he was told that this was a rebellion of the Arabs against the Turks. He wanted to know who the Arab leader was, and Lawrence answered: 'The Sherif of Mecca.' The German sup-posed that he would be sent to Mecca, but Lawrence told him,

'No, Egypt.' He inquired the price of sugar there and was glad to hear that it was cheap and plentiful. He was only sorry to leave the artesian well he had been boring, the pump of which was only half-finished. After quenching their thirst here with help of a sludge-bucket, Lawrence and his men raced on to Akaba in a driving sandstorm and splashed into the sea on July the sixth, exactly two months after setting out from Wejh.

XVI

Akaba was in ruins. Repeated bombardments by French and British warships had knocked the little town to pieces. To the Arabs it seemed hardly worth while taking at the cost of so much blood and pain and hunger. And hunger was still with them. They now had seven hundred Turkish prisoners to feed in addition to their original five hundred men and two thousand allies, no money (or any market to buy food in); and the last meal had been two days before. All that they had to eat was riding-camels, a most expensive form of food and a poor one. And dates. But this was July and the dates were still green. Raw, they tasted very nasty, and cooking made them no better. The only alternative to constant hunger was violent pains. The forty-two officer-prisoners were an intolerable nuisance. The colonel of the Turkish battalion at Aba el Lissan had been a difficulty ever since his capture, when Nasir had only just saved him from the fury of the tribesmen: the silly man was trying to restore the battle with a little pocket- pistol. Later he had grumbled at being given a quarter loaf of brown Turkish ration bread. Farraj and Daud had looted it for their master Lawrence, who divided it up among the four of them. The colonel asked was it a fit breakfast for a Turkish officer. Lawrence answered, certainly it was (he himself a British staff-officer had eaten his with relish), and he must expect to make it do for lunch and dinner as well and probably for to-morrow's breakfast, lunch and dinner too. The Turk also complained that one of the Arabs had insulted him with an obscene Turkish word: Lawrence answered that the man must have learned it from one of his Turkish masters and was rendering to Cæsar the things that were Cæsar's. At Akaba it was worse still: the officer-prisoners were disgusted when they found how unprovided their captors were: they thought it was only a fraud to annoy them and would not believe that Lawrence and Nasir had not all the delicacies of Cairo hidden somewhere in their saddle-bags.

In the evening, the first reaction after success having passed off, they thought of defence. Auda went back to Guweira and three other defensive posts were set in a semicircle about Akaba. Lawrence decided to go to Egypt at once with the great news and ask for food, money and arms to be sent at once by sea as reward. He chose eight men to go with him, mostly Howeitat, on the best camels of the force. A bad ride was ahead of them, and it was difficult to decide whether to go gently, sparing the animals, in which case they might fail with hunger; or whether to ride hard, when they might break down with exhaustion or sore feet in mid-desert. Lawrence decided in the end to keep at a walk; if they could hold out, they would reach Suez in fifty hours. But in such cases the test of endurance is harder for the man than for the camel, and Lawrence was near the end of his strength, having ridden an average of fifty miles a day for the last month, with very little food. To make halts for cooking unnecessary they carried lumps of boiled camel and cooked dates in a rag behind their saddles.

The camels were trembling for weariness early in the night, for the road wound up across the Sinai hills with a gradient of one in three and a half. When they reached the top one camel had to be sent back as unfit for further travel. The others were allowed to graze for an hour. About midnight they reached Themed, the only wells on the journey, watered the camels and drank themselves but did not stay many minutes. They rode all that night and when the sun rose gave the camels half an hour's grazing, then on again all day until sunset, when they halted for an hour. They rode all that second night at a mechanical walk, over hills, and when dawn came saw a melon-field sown in this no-man's-land between the armies by some adventurous Arab. They halted for an hour and cracked the unripe melons to cool their mouths, then again forward until Suez came in sight, or something that probably was Suez, a jumble of points bobbing about far away in the mirage. They reached great trench lines with forts and barbed wire, roads and railways; but they were all deserted and falling into decay; the war had long since moved on a hundred and fifty miles to the north-east. At last in the middle of the afternoon of the third day they arrived at the Suez Canal. They had ridden for forty-nine hours without sleep and with only four short halts and had come a hundred and sixty-eight miles. When it is remembered that they were tired men before they started, and that the camels were exhausted too, this must rank as a good ride, though Lawrence surpassed it himself later.

He found himself still on the wrong side of the Canal, and the garrison-post that he had aimed for was deserted—he did not know why, but learned later that there had been an outbreak of plague, so the troops were out camping in the uninfected desert. He found a telephone in a deserted hut

AKABA

and called up the Canal Headquarters. He was told that they were sorry but they couldn't take him across; there were no free boats; but next morning for sure they would send across and take him to the Quarantine Department (for he was now technically infectious). He tried again, explaining that he had urgent messages for Headquarters at Cairo, but he was rung off. Fortunately the telephone-exchange operator told him with friendly oaths that it was no use talking to the Canal people, and put him through to a Major, the Embarkation officer at Suez. He was an old friend of the Revolt, who would catch Red Sea warships as they entered the harbour and make them unwillingly pile their decks with stores for Wejh or Yenbo. The Major understood at once the urgency of the matter and sent his own launch from the harbour to take Lawrence across, making him swear not to tell the Canal authorities, until after the war, of this invasion of their sacred waters. The men and camels were sent up the Canal for ten miles to a rest-camp for animals; he arranged rations for them there by telephone.

At Suez where he arrived verminous and filthy, with his clothes sticking to his saddle-sores, he went to a hotel and had six iced drinks, a good dinner, a hot bath, and a comfortable bed. He appreciated this dull hotel-comfort after having in the last four desperate weeks, though not yet recovered from a severe illness, ridden fourteen hundred miles on camel-back through hostile country. They were weeks of little sleep, poor food, frequent fighting and never-ceasing anxiety at the hottest time of the year in one of the hottest countries of the world. Later he found that he weighed only seven stone, nine stone being his normal weight; though in his first year at the University he had carried eleven without being out of condition.

He went to Cairo by train on a permit-ticket given him by the Embarkation officer. A mixed party of Egyptian and British military police on the train was most suspicious of him. When he said that he was in the uniform of a staff-officer of the Sherif of Mecca they could not believe it. They looked at his bare feet, white silk robes, gold head-rope and dagger. 'What army, sir?' asked the sergeant. 'The Meccan army,' Lawrence answered. 'Never heard of it, don't know the uniform,' the sergeant said. 'Well,' said Lawrence, 'would you recognize the uniform of a Montenegrin dragoon?' This beat the sergeant. Any Allied troops in uniform might travel without permits, and the police, though expected to recognize all the uniforms of every army, were not even sure who all the Allies were. Mecca might be the name of some new country that had joined in without their knowledge. They wired up the line and a perspiring intelligence-officer boarded the train near Ismailia to check the statements of this possible spy; he was very angry to find that he had been sent on a fool's errand.

At Ismailia all changed and waited on the platform for the Port Said—Cairo express. Another train had also just arrived and from it stepped a tall determined-looking general in company with Admiral Wemyss, the Naval Commander-in-Chief, and two or three important staff-officers. They marched up and down the platform deep in talk. After awhile Lawrence caught the eye of a naval captain, who came over and spoke to him, wondering who he was. When the captain heard of the surprise capture of Akaba he was properly excited, promising to have a relief-ship sent there at once loaded with all the spare food in Suez. He would make immediate arrangements on his own responsibility so as not to disturb General Allenby. 'Allenby? what's he doing here?' asked Lawrence. 'Oh, he's

Commander-in-Chief now.' This was most important news. Allenby's predecessor, who at first had been against the Revolt, had gradually been brought to realize its value to him, and in his last dispatches to London had written in praise of the Arabs and particularly of Feisal. But after the second battle of Gaza, which had been forced on him by orders from London against his better judgment and ended in defeat, he had been recalled. Lawrence wondered whether he would have to spend months training Allenby in the same way to realize the importance of the Arabs. Allenby had been commanding divisions in France since the outbreak of war and was full of Western Front notions of gun-power and masses of men wearing down the enemy by sheer slaughter, ideas which did not apply at all well to war in the East. But he was a cavalry man and ready perhaps to go back to the old-fashioned idea of a war of movement and manœuvre.

Later at Cairo he sent for Lawrence, having got his report about Akaba. It was a comic interview. Lawrence was still in his Arab clothes, because when he went to the hotel to look out his old army uniform he found that insects had been at it. Allenby sat in his chair looking at Lawrence, very much puzzled at this haggard little man, with silk robes and a face burned brick red with the sun, explaining with a map a fantastic plan for raising the Eastern Syrians in revolt behind the enemy lines. He listened quietly, asking few questions and trying to make up his mind how far Lawrence was a charlatan and how far a real performer—a doubt that was also constantly in Lawrence's own mind. He asked what help he wanted. Lawrence said, stores and arms and a fund of two hundred thousand pounds in gold to convince and control his converts. Allenby put up his chin at last, a well-known deci-

sive gesture and said, 'Well, I will do for you what I can.' And
meant it. The meeting of Lawrence with Feisal had begun
a new successful phase of the war in Arabia, the meeting of
Lawrence with Allenby began an even more successful one.

Hitherto Lawrence had sent few and misleading reports
to Egypt—even these were, I am told, often doctored by
the Staff on the way to the Commander-in-Chief—because
he could not be sure how acceptable the truth would be, or
how well his secrets would be kept; he had not, for instance,
warned the Commander-in-Chief of his intended capture of
Akaba. But he learned to take Allenby more deeply into his
confidence and never afterwards regretted it. There was little
personal intimacy between the two then or afterwards—they
have not met since 1921—but great trust and liking. Allenby
is an extremely practical man and a first-class soldier: spiritual conflicts or philosophic doubts do not appear to touch
him and it is impossible to imagine him living among Bedouin
or doing any of the crazy things that were Lawrence's daily
life. Lawrence's methods and motives were a mystery and
remained a mystery to him, but he gratefully accepted him
as a fact and let the rest go by. Lawrence was simply to him,
as he told me recently, a first-class irregular leader and exactly
the man he wanted for the protection of the floating right
flank of his army. I asked whether in his opinion Lawrence
would have made a good general of regular forces too. 'A very
bad general,' said Allenby, 'but a good Commander-in-Chief,
yes. There is no show that I would believe him incapable of
running if he wanted to, but he would have to be given a free
hand.' I also asked Lawrence his opinion of Allenby. 'A great
man,' said Lawrence. 'For instance?' I asked. 'For instance,
when a Major-General of the Royal Army Medical Corps,

the surgeon-in-chief of Allenby's army, had to go, he chose to replace him with the Medical Officer of a Territorial unit, a mere lieutenant-colonel. And surely a man who can persuade armoured cars, cavalry, infantry, camel-corps, aeroplanes, warships and Bedouin irregulars to combine in a single military operation is a great man, isn't he?' When recently Lawrence published his book the one favourable opinion that he was really anxious to get was Allenby's, for the Field-Marshal is as strict on points of style—he loves Milton's *Comus*—as upon historical accuracy. Allenby approved both its style and accuracy; which satisfies Lawrence completely.

Meanwhile sixteen thousand pounds in English sovereigns were drawn from a Cairo bank to be sent to Nasir at once to enable him to pay his debts. It was important to redeem the notes that he had given out, which were army telegraph-forms pencilled with promises to pay gold at Akaba. The money went to Suez to join the flour that was being quickly loaded there, ready to be rushed to famished Akaba. These were the first things that mattered. After this the changed aspect of the war in Arabia had to be discussed with the Arab Bureau.

Lawrence began talking with authority. His capture of Akaba made him a person of very much greater importance than before and had given him confidence in himself. He told his seniors that the big operations about the railway near Medina were a mistake. The war had moved north now. He suggested that the base at Wejh should be closed down, as Yenbo had been closed before, and that the whole of Feisal's army should move up north and make its base at Akaba. Akaba was on Allenby's right flank, only a hundred miles from his centre, but eight hundred miles from Mecca. Once there at Akaba, it was logical that Feisal should no longer be tied

to his father at Mecca, the nominal Commander-in-Chief of
the Arabs, but should be made an army-corps commander
under direct control of Allenby. Lawrence had talked this over
with Feisal long before in Wejh and Feisal had been ready to
accept. The High Commissioner of Egypt who hitherto had
been the chief British partner did not mind the transference
being made; though Feisal's removal would weaken the forces
in Arabia. Abdulla, Ali and Zeid were strong enough to keep
the Turks in Medina from making another attempt on Mecca.
There was only one difficulty and that was Feisal's father, the
Sherif. Would he make any difficulty? Fortunately Colonel
Wilson, the High Commissioner's representative at Jiddah,
talked him over, and Feisal decided to move up to Akaba at
once. He sent his camel-corps up the coast and the remainder
of the army under Jaafar was transported by a warship. More
stores and ammunition were sent to Akaba, and British officers to distribute it properly at Feisal's orders.

Lawrence was at Jiddah with Wilson when two startling
telegrams arrived from the intelligence service in Egypt. The
first reported that the Howeitat at Akaba were carrying on a
treacherous correspondence with the Turks at Maan, the next
that Auda was connected with the plot. This was alarming, for
though Lawrence could not believe it of Auda, Mohammed
el Dheilan was quite capable of double play, and the old fox
who had captured Guweira was still less to be trusted. Three
days later Lawrence arrived by warship at Akaba, where Nasir
had no notion of anything wrong. He only told Nasir that he
wished to greet Auda, and asked for a swift camel and a guide.
At dawn he arrived at Guweira and found Auda, Mohammed
and Zaal in a tent together. They were confused at his sudden
appearance but said that all was well and they ate together

as friends. Other Howeitat chiefs came in and Lawrence distributed the Sherif's presents, telling them among other things that Nasir had at last got his month's leave to Mecca. The Sherif was enthusiastic for the Revolt and would not allow his officers leave from the front. Poor Nasir's banishment from his family had been a stock joke and it was said that he would certainly deserve a holiday when Akaba fell; but Nasir had not believed that it would be granted until he was handed Hussein's letter the day before. In gratitude Nasir sold Lawrence a famous pedigree camel, Ghazala, as the owner of which he had great honour among the Howeitat.

After lunch Lawrence took Auda and Mohammed for a walk and mentioned their correspondence with the Turks. Auda began to laugh, Mohammed looked disgusted. Then they explained, telling a farcical story of how Mohammed had wanted to get money from the Turks by a confidence trick and had therefore taken Auda's seal and written to the Governor of Maan offering to desert to the Turks if he were given money. A large sum was gladly sent on account, but Auda had waylaid the messenger, taken the spoils and was now denying Mohammed his share. Lawrence laughed with them over the story but knew that more lay behind it; the fact was, they had been angry that no guns or troops had yet arrived since Akaba had been taken a month before, and that no rewards had been given them for their part in it. Auda, feeling sorry for the Turks whom he had beaten so badly, was quite ready to fight on their side for a change: it was generosity rather than treachery with him. But both Auda and Mohammed were surprised at Lawrence's knowledge, wanting to know how he came by it and how much more he knew. He laughed at them, quoting, as if they were his own words, actual phrases of the letters that had been exchanged, and made them feel uncomfortable. Then he told them casually that Feisal's entire army was coming up, and that Allenby was sending rifles, guns, high-explosive, food and money. Finally he added that Auda's present expenses in hospitality must be great; would it help if something were advanced of the great gift that Feisal was bringing up to him? Auda agreed cheerfully to accept the advance and with it to keep the Howeitat well fed and cheerful. So Lawrence went back to Akaba, took ship back to Egypt and reported that there was no treachery at Guweira: everything was going on well there. But he did not explain the whole story; Headquarters would not have understood it.

XVII

While waiting for Feisal's army to come up Lawrence began getting his thoughts in order again. The war in Arabia was as good as over and Feisal's army, now under the wing of Allenby, was about to take part in the military deliverance of Syria. Syria Lawrence knew well. He had wandered up and down in it before the War, from city to city and tribe to tribe; he had even written a book about it. Syria was a fertile strip of land running between the eastern coast of the Mediterranean and the great Syrian desert, with a backbone of mountains dividing it. It had been for centuries a corridor between Arabia and Europe, Asia and Egypt, and held at one time or another by Turks, Greeks, Romans, Egyptians, Arabs, Persians, Assyrians and Hittites. It was naturally divided up into sections by the mountain spurs, and the constant passing to and fro of armies had filled the land with an extraordinary variety of peoples—to almost every valley a different population, each little colony kept separate from its neighbours by the spurs between. There were Circassians, Kurds, Turks, Greeks, Armenians, Persians, Algerians, Jews, Arabians, and many more, with as many varieties of religion among them as of race.

The six principal cities, Jerusalem, Beyrout, Damascus, Homs, Hama and Aleppo, were also each of them entirely different in character. The only possible bond between most of these pieces of the Syrian mosaic was the common language, Arabic, and though at this time there was much talk of Arab freedom, it was impossible to think of Syria as a national unity. Freedom to the Syrians meant local home-rule for each little community in its valley or city, but a freedom impossible in modern civilization where roads, railways, taxes, armies, a postal system, supplies have all to be maintained by a central government. And whatever central government might be imposed on Syria, even though Arabic were the official language, would be a foreign government; for there was no such thing as a true or typical Syrian. How to spread the Revolt up to Damascus over this chequer-board of communities each divided against its neighbour naturally by geography and history, and artificially by Turkish intrigue was a most baffling problem: which however Lawrence set himself to solve.

It was difficult to do anything on the Mediterranean side of the central mountain-range, where the mixed population was Europeanized and could probably not be converted to the idea of an Arab confederation with its headquarters in the ancient Arab capital of Damascus; it would prefer a French or English protectorate. But inland, between the mountains and the desert where the tribes were simpler and wilder, the national ideal might well be preached. Lawrence decided then to build up a ladder of friendly tribes in Eastern Syria beginning at the south with the Howeitat, for three hundred miles until Azrak was reached, half-way to Damascus. It was the method that had been used before in Arabia from Jiddah through Rabegh, Yenbo, Wejh to Akaba. Once they were at Azrak, the Arabs of the Hauran would probably rise in sympathy; the Hauran being a huge fertile land, just south of Damascus, populous with warlike self-reliant Arab peasantry. This rising should end the war.

Once more the tactics should be tip and run, not the regular advance of an organized army, and for this the eastern desert was most convenient. One might look on it as a sort of sea in which to manœuvre with camel-parties instead of ships. The railway, to cover it from the British Fleet, had been built down the eastern side of the central mountains and could be raided from the desert without fear of retaliation, for the Turks had no camel-corps worth anything, and in any case no important point to strike back against. From the war in the south Lawrence had learned that the best tactics were to use the smallest raiding parties on the fastest camels, and to strike at points widely separated with the most portable weapons of destruction. These weapons would be high-explosive for demolition work and light automatic guns, Hotchkiss or Lewis, which could be fired from the saddle of a camel running at eighteen miles an hour. Lawrence at once begged for quantities of these from Egypt.

The difficulty of the campaign was that, though all the tribes might join in the Revolt, their jealousies were such that no tribe could fight in a neighbour's territory and no tribal combinations were possible as they had been in Arabia. Feisal's authority in Syria was not great enough to heal the feuds. This meant that the brunt of the fighting had to be borne by a small force of Ageyl and others from the south, against whom, as distant strangers under the command of members of the Prophet's family, there was not so much prejudice. It was impossible for the Turks to foresee the strength and direction

LAWRENCE'S RIDES

October 1917 : January 1918

The Yarmuk Raid : The Mining at Minifer
The Spying in the Hauran : The Battle at Tafileh

MILES 5 — 100

Damascus

HAURAN

Mediterranean Sea

Haifa

Sheik Saad

JEBEL DRUSE

Tifau
Tel Shehab
Gadara
Mezerib
Remthe
Nisib

Arar
Deraa

Minifer
Abu Sawana

Amman
Hesban

Azrak

Jericho
Jerusalem

Amari

Sirhan

Gaza

El Arish

Beersheba

Kerak

Desert

Tafileh

Bair

SINAI

Petra

Maan

Jefer

Delagha
Wahetde
Aba el Lissan

Batra

Shedid

Guweira

Akaba

Ramm

of the attacks: the camels could, after a watering, travel two hundred and fifty miles in three days; and in an emergency could go a hundred and ten miles in twenty-four hours. (Twice Lawrence's famous Ghazala did one hundred and forty-three miles of a march alone with him.) This meant that it might not be impossible to strike at points near Maan on Monday, near Amman on Thursday, near Deraa on Saturday, and to get fresh tribesmen and camels from each district to join in the attack. Above all, the regular raiders must be self-supporting. From Akaba they could go out with six-weeks' flour-ration and ammunition, explosive and gold, and do without the compli-cated system of supply-trains and dumps which slows down the pace and shortens the fighting range of every regular army.

There must be no discipline in the ordinary sense of a chain of command going down from general to colonel, to captain, to lieutenant, to sergeant, to corporal, to private; every man must be his own commander-in-chief, ready, if need be, for single combat against the enemy without waiting for orders from above or co-operation from his fellows. And discipline could not in any case have been enforced: the Arabs were independent by nature and were serving voluntarily. Honour was the only contract and every man was free to draw his pay up to date and go home at any time he liked; only the Ageyl and the small regular army under Jaafar were serving for a definite term, so that the war when fought was fought with goodwill. There were no shameful incidents like those on the Western Front where the first dead man that I saw was an English suicide, and the last one also.

Mr. Herbert Read, by the way, has made a rather unfor-tunate critical condemnation of Lawrence's *Seven Pillars* as being an account of a campaign where men did not heroically suffer the machine-made boredom and agony of the Western trenches, and which therefore can hardly be taken seriously. This reads like a glorification of the more horrible sort of war at the expense of the less horrible, which cannot be what Mr. Read (an anti-militarist, and for good reason) intends. If he wishes to point out that all war is evil in itself, whatever its glamour, he should not complicate his argument by a false comparison of heroisms.

Six weeks had elapsed since the capture of Akaba, and the Arabs had had opportunity to strengthen themselves. Feisal and Jaafar had now arrived at Akaba with the army. Plentiful supplies were landed from Egypt and armoured cars and guns—though the long-range guns never arrived until the last month of the war—and Egyptian labourers to rebuild the town and turn round the fortifications to face inland. The defiles through the hills were strongly held. On the other hand, the Turks had also been busy and had the advice of the German general Falkenhayn who had been chiefly responsible for saving them two years before at the Dardanelles. They had sent down a whole division to Maan and fortified it until it was quite secure against attack except by the strong regular forces and heavy guns which the Arabs did not have. There was an aeroplane-station there now and great supply dumps.

It was probable that the Turks would try to retake Akaba by way of Aba el Lissan and Guweira. They had already pushed their way up to Aba el Lissan and fortified it while cavalry held the neighbouring hills. But Lawrence knew that Akaba was safe enough. He would even welcome a Turkish attempt on it, which could only end in great losses. There were Arab posts out north and south of the pass, and old Maulud with his mule-mounted regiment had taken up his position in the ancient ruins of Petra north of Maan and was encouraging the local tribes to raid the Turkish communications in competition with their rivals at Delagha, a few miles to their south. Raiding went on for weeks and the Turks got more and more irritated. To prick them into retaliation a long distance air-raid was made on Maan, from El Arish on the left of the British Army.

Thirty-two bombs were dropped about breakfast-time in and about the unprepared station: the aeroplanes flew dangerously low but returned safely the same morning to a temporary landing-ground thirty miles north of Akaba where the airmen patched up the shrapnel-torn wings of their machines. Two of their bombs had struck the barracks and killed a number of Turks, eight struck the engine-shed, doing great damage, one fell in the General's kitchen, four on the aerodrome. The next morning they visited Aba el Lissan, bombed the horse-lines and stampeded the animals, and then the tents and stampeded the Turks. The same afternoon they decided to look for the battery of guns that had troubled them that morning; there was just enough petrol and bombs. Skimming the hill-crest they came over Aba el Lissan at a height of only three hundred feet. They interrupted the Turks' usual midday sleep and took the place completely by surprise. They dropped thirty bombs, silenced the battery and were off again. The Turkish commander at Maan set his men digging bomb-proof shelters and dispersed his aeroplanes, when they had been repaired, for fear of a fresh attack on the aerodrome.

The next plan that Lawrence had for the Arabs was to reduce the troops that the Turks could spare for the Akaba attack by making frequent raids on the railway and so forcing them to defend it more strongly. The gloomy reaction after Aba el Lissan had long passed and left him adventurous as before and ready to kill without remorse. He thought out a series of demolitions for mid-September; it might be a good idea, too, to mine another train. He would try for one at a station called Mudowwara, eighty miles south of Maan, where a smashed train would greatly embarrass the enemy. Now, to make sure of the train new methods had to be found: the automatic mine was uncertain and might be set off by a trolley or by a train carrying civilian refugees which they would want to let pass; or, if the Turks put the engines to push instead of to pull the trains, might only explode under an unimportant wagon: and the train could then retire safely. What was wanted seemed to be a mine that could be exploded at will by electricity. The apparatus was sent to him from Egypt and explained by electricians on the guard-ship at Akaba. It consisted of a heavy white box, the exploder, and yards of heavy cable insulated with rubber. With the engine blown up and the train perhaps derailed, machine-guns and artillery would be needed to complete the destruction. For machine-guns, the Lewis guns would have to do, but artillery was a problem because to take along even the smallest mountain-guns meant slow travelling. Lawrence then thought of the Stokes trench-mortars which had lately been used successfully in France. They were simple guns, like small drain- pipes, tilted at an angle on a tripod. Down the mouth a heavy shell was allowed to slide, and when it struck the bottom a charge in its base was fired and it went flying two or three hundred yards and burst according to a time-fuse. This was not too short a range for a railway ambush and the Stokes shell was powerfully charged with ammonal.

Two sergeant-instructors were sent from Egypt to teach the Arabs at Akaba how to use these weapons. The one in charge of the Lewis guns was an Australian; reckless, talkative, tall and supple. The Stokes-mortar sergeant was an English countryman; slow, stocky, workmanlike and silent. Lawrence knew them as Lewis and Stokes, naming them after their guns. They were excellent instructors and though they knew no Arabic taught the tribesmen by dumb-show, until in a month's time they could use the guns reasonably well.

Lawrence decided that his raid might include an attack on Mudowwara station. It was not strongly held, and three hundred men might rush it at night and destroy the deep well there. Without its water, the only plentiful supply in the dry hot section below Maan, the trains would have to waste their wagon-space in carrying water-tanks. Lewis was anxious to join in the raid; he was sick of being a mere instructor at the base in Egypt and wanted to do some fighting. Stokes said that he would come too. Lawrence warned them what to expect, of hunger, heat and weariness, and explained that if anything happened to him it might go badly with them alone with the Arabs. This warning only excited Lewis and did not put off Stokes. Lawrence lent them two of his best camels.

So they started on September the seventh, riding up to Guweira where they collected some of Auda's Howeitat tribesmen. Lawrence was at first afraid that the heat would be too much for the sergeants. The granite walls of the valley down which they rode were burningly hot; a few days before in the cooler palm-gardens of Akaba beach the thermometer had shown a hundred and twenty degrees. It was now even hotter. As neither of the sergeants had ever been on a camel before he let them take the ride easily. He was amused at the way that they behaved with the Arabs. Lewis, the Australian, seemed at home from the first and behaved freely towards the

Arabs, but was astonished when they treated him as equals; he could not have imagined that they would forget the social difference between a white man and a brown. This race prejudice, however, would soon wear off: meanwhile the joke was that Lewis was burned a good deal browner than any of the Arabs. On the other hand, Stokes, the Englishman, remained insular and his shy correctness reminded the Arabs all the time that he was not one of them. They treated him with respect and called him 'sergeant,' whereas Lewis was merely 'the long fellow.' Lawrence found them typical of the two opposite kinds of Englishmen in the East: the kind that allowed themselves to be influenced by native customs and thought in order to be able the more easily to impose their will on the country; and the kind that became more English by reacting against native customs and thought. Lawrence being an extreme instance of the former type, to the point of identifying himself at times with the Arabs rather than with the English, seems to have felt a sneaking regard for the John Bull constancy of Sergeant Stokes.

When they came near Guweira a Turkish aeroplane droned over and the party at once rode off the open road into bushy country where the camels would not be seen. It was a daily aeroplane that never did much damage but provided the idle Guweira camp with excitement and conversation. They halted, still in the saddle, until the aeroplane had dropped its three bombs and returned to its own lines near Maan. Lawrence found the Howeitat all at odds. Auda who drew the wages for the whole tribe, only a clan of which he ruled personally, was using his power to compel the smaller clans to accept him as their leader. This they resented, threatening either to go home or to join the Turks. Feisal had sent up a sherif, a close kinsman, to settle the dispute, but Auda was obstinate, knowing how much the success of the Revolt depended on him. Now some of the clans from the south towards Mudowwara were about to desert the cause, and they were the very men on whom Lawrence was counting for help in his operations; but Auda would not give way. However, he told Lawrence to ride forward some miles with his twenty baggage-camels and halt to wait events.

They went, glad to leave behind the swarms of flies that plagued them at Guweira. Lawrence much admired the way that the sergeants stood the stifling heat, the worst that they had ever experienced; it was like a metal mask over the face. Not to lower themselves in the Arabs' estimation, they did not utter a word of complaint. They were, however, ignorant of Arabic or they would have known that the Arabs were themselves making a great fuss about it. Rumm, a place of springs, half-way to Mudowwara, should have been their first halt, but they went on by easy stages, stopping the night in a grove of rustling tamarisk under a tall red cliff. In the very early morning, while the stars were still shining, Lawrence was roused by the Arab commander of the expedition, one of the Harith, a poor member of the Prophet's family. He crept up shivering and said, 'Lord, I have gone blind.' Blindness for an Arab was a worse fate than for a European and the sherif must now look forward to a life of complete blankness. However, he would not go home; he could ride, he said, though he could not shoot, and he would make this his last adventure and, with God's help, would retire from active life at least with the consolation of a victory.

They rode for hours the next day through the valley of Rumm, a broad tamarisk-grown avenue two miles wide between colossal red sandstone cliffs. They rose a sheer thousand feet on either side, not in an unbroken wall, but seemed built in vertical sections like a row of skyscrapers. There were caverns high up like windows and others at the foot like doors. At the top were domes of a greyer rock. The pygmy caravan passing down this street for giants felt awed and kept quite silent. Towards sunset there was a break in the cliffs to the right, leading to the water. They turned in here and found themselves in a vast oval amphitheatre floored with damp sand and dark shrubs. The entrance was only three hundred yards wide, which made the place more impressive still. At the foot of the enclosing precipices were enormous fallen blocks of sandstone, bigger than houses, and along a ledge at one side grew trees. A little path zigzagged up to the ledge and there, three hundred feet above the level of the plain, jetted the water-springs. They watered their camels here and cooked rice to add to the bully beef which the sergeants had brought, with biscuits, as their ration.

Coffee was also prepared for visitors: they had heard Arab voices shouting in the distance at the other end of the place. The visitors soon arrived, head-men of the several Howeitat clans, all boiling with anger and jealousy against Auda. They suspected Lawrence of sympathizing with Auda's attempt to force them to offer him their allegiance; they refused to help Feisal further until he gave them assurance that they would be allowed complete independence as clans. Lawrence had to do the entertaining that night in place of the blinded sherif; the awkwardness of the occasion made his task doubly difficult. One of the head-men, by name Gasim abu Dumeik, a fine horseman who had led the hill-men at Aba el Lissan, was particularly furious in his denouncement of Auda. Lawrence singled him out for a verbal battle and finally silenced him. The other head-men, for shame, gradually veered round to Lawrence's side and spoke of riding with him the next day to Mudowwara. Lawrence then said that Zaal would arrive the next day and that the two of them would accept help from all the clans except Gasim abu Dumeik's. And that the good services of this clan would be wiped from Feisal's book because of Gasim's words and it would forfeit all the honour and rewards that it had earned. Gasim withdrew from the fireside, swearing to go over to the Turks at once. The cautious others tried in vain to stop his mouth. Next morning he was there with his men ready to join or oppose the expedition as the whim went. While he hesitated Zaal arrived and the pair had a violent quarrel. Lawrence and one or two more got between them and stopped the fight: the other chiefs then came quietly up in two's and three's as volunteers, begging Lawrence to assure Feisal of their loyalty.

He decided to go to Feisal at once to explain matters and, commending the sergeants to Zaal, who answered for their lives with his own, rode off hurriedly with a single attendant to Akaba. He found a short cut and reached Akaba in six hours. Feisal was alarmed to see him back so soon, but the affair was soon explained and Feisal at once appointed a distinguished member of his family to go to Rumm as mediator. The sherif rode back to Rumm with Lawrence and there, gathering together the Arabs, including Gasim, began to smooth over their difficulties and persuade them to peace. Gasim, no longer defiant but sulky, would not make any public statement, so about a hundred men of the smaller clans dared defy him by promising to join the raid. This was better than nothing, but Lawrence had hoped for at least a force of three hundred to deal successfully with the station. And there was no suitable leader now that the sherif was blinded. Gasim would have done, had he been willing. Zaal was the only other possible choice, but he was too closely related to Auda not to be suspected; and he was too sharp-tongued and sneering for even his good advice to be taken willingly. On the sixteenth of September, therefore, the party started out, without a leader.

At Rumm one curious incident had occurred which, though it had nothing to do with the war, made a profound impression on Lawrence. He was bathing in a little rock-pool, under one of the lesser springs—his first freshwater bathe for many weeks—lying in the clear water and letting the stream wash away the dirt and sweat of travel. His clothes were in the sun on the rock-ledge, put there for the heat to chase out the vermin. An old grey-bearded ragged man suddenly appeared, with a face of great power and weariness, and sat down upon Lawrence's clothes, not seeming to notice them or him. At last he spoke and said: 'The love is from God; and of God; and towards God.' It was the strangest thing that Lawrence had ever heard in Arabia. The connection of God with Love was an idea quite foreign to the country. God was Justice, or God was Power or Fear, but never Love. Christianity was not a wholly Semitic creed, but a grafting of Greek idealism upon the hard Law of Moses, the typical Semite. It was this Greek element that had enabled it to sweep over non-Semitic Europe. Galilee, where Christianity originated, was half-Greek: at Gadara (of the swine) there was a Greek university of which St. James seems to have been a student, and with whose doctrines his Master was almost certainly familiar. But the old man at Rumm was a puzzle; he was a tribesman, a true Arab, and his brief sentence seemed to contradict all that

seemed eternally fixed in the Semite nature. Lawrence afterwards invited the old man to the evening meal, hoping that he
would utter doctrine, but he would only groan and mutter,
and the riddle remained unsolved. The

Arabs said that he was always so. All his life long he had
wandered about, moaning strange things, not troubling himself for food or work or shelter. He was given charity by the
tribes in pity of his poverty and madness, but never answered
a word or talked aloud except when out by himself or alone
among the sheep and goats.

The ride from Rumm began unpropitiously; though half
an hour after starting some shamefaced men of Gasim's clan
rode out to join them, unable to endure the sight of others
raiding without them. There was no common feeling between
the different little parties that made up the force. Zaal was
admittedly the most experienced fighter among them and yet
the other sullen chiefs would not even allow him to settle the
order of the march. Lawrence spent all his time riding up and
down the column from one chief to the other trying to draw
them together for the common purpose. He was treated by
them with some respect, both as Feisal's deputy and as the
owner of Ghazala, though Ghazala was that day matched with
the only other camel in Northern Arabia better than herself,
a beast called El Jedha, ridden by one Motlog, her old owner.
El Jedha had been a year or two before the sole occasion of a
big tribal war.

XVIII

I t fell on Lawrence then to be the leader, a task to which he was opposed on principle. He had from the first made a point of letting the Arabs run their own campaign as far as possible by themselves: he was merely their technical adviser and assistant. But he now constantly found himself forced into leadership, not only because of his obvious qualities as a desert fighter and outwitter of the Turks, but because of his freedom from tribal complications, his hole-hearted zeal for the Revolt, his disregard of loot and distinctions, his generosity and tact. Yet, again, he was a most unsuitable commander of a Bedouin raid. It meant his deciding such difficult questions as food-halts, pasturage, road-direction, pay, disputes, division of spoil, feuds and march-order. To be an efficient leader in this sense would mean a lifetime's training. However, he managed that day without mishap and was rewarded at night by seeing the party sit down at only three camp-fires. Around one were Lawrence's own men, including three Syrian peasants of the Hauran, from whom he intended to learn on the road such things as would be useful to him later when the Revolt was carried up to their country. At the second fire was Zaal with his twenty-five famous camel-riders. At the third were the other jealous clansmen from Rumm. Late at night, when hot bread and gazelle-meat had made tempers better, it was possible for Lawrence to gather all the chiefs together at his own neutral hearth to discuss the next day's fighting. It was decided to water the next evening at a well in a covered valley two or three miles the near side of Mudowwara station; and from there go forward to see whether it could be taken with the few men that they had.

Next day, then, they reached the well, an open pool a few yards square. It looked uninviting. There was a green slime over the water with queer bladder-like islands on it, fatty-pink. The Arabs explained that the Turks had thrown dead camels into the well to make the water foul; but time had passed and the effect was wearing off. They filled their water-skins; it was all the drink that they could hope for unless they took Mudowwara. One of Zaal's men slipped in by mistake and when he struggled out again, leaving a black hole in the green scum, the disturbed water stank horribly of old dead camel. At dusk Zaal, Lawrence, the sergeants and one or two more crept forward quietly to a Turkish trench-position on a ridge four or five hundred yards from the station. It was deserted. The station lay below with its lighted doors and windows, and its tent-camp. Zaal and Lawrence decided to creep nearer. They went on until they could hear the soldiers talking in the tents. A young, sickly-looking officer sauntered out towards them; they could see his features in the light of a match with which he lit a cigarette, and were ready to spring up and gag him; but he happened to turn back. At the ridge they held a whispered council of war. The garrison was perhaps two hundred men—Lawrence had counted the tents—but the station buildings seemed too solid for the Stokes shells, which were time-fused, not bursting on percussion; and the hundred and sixteen Arabs, though they had the advantage of surprise, could not yet be trusted to fight honourably together. So Lawrence voted against the attack, which was put off until a better day. They went away then, deciding at least to make sure of a train. Mudowwara was not taken for another eleven months.

Some miles south of the station they found an ideal place for their mine and ambush. There was a low ridge of hills under cover of which they could ride quite close to the railway, and where the ridge ended was a curve such as Lawrence always chose for his mines because of the difficulty of replacing curved rails. This curve was within range of the ridge, which was fifty feet above the level of the rails; and a raised embankment across a hollow seemed exactly the right spot for the mine, for in the middle there was a two-arched bridge which allowed for the passage of flood-water in the rainy season. Whatever the effect of the mine might be on the engine, the bridge would certainly go and the coaches behind would be derailed. From behind the ridge, which was on the outside, not the inside of the curve, Lewis could sweep the lines in either direction and Stokes could use his trench-mortar unobserved. Lawrence was glad to have his two chief responsibilities posted where they had a safe retreat, especially as Stokes was weak with dysentery from the Mudowwara water, and Lewis unwell too.

The camels were hobbled out of sight and Feisal's negro freedmen, who were in charge of the baggage-camels, carried their loads to the chosen place—the two Stokes guns with their shells, the two Lewis guns, the electric mine apparatus and the gelatine. Lawrence went to the bridge to dig a bed between the ends of two steel sleepers in which to bury his sandbag-full of gelatine, a fifty-pound shaking jelly. It took

him two hours to do this properly because he had to remove
the ballast which he had dug out, carrying it in a fold of his
cloak, and dump it where it would not show. Also he had been
forced to cross a sandbank and the tracks of his feet had to
be covered. Then the two heavy wires, each two hundred
yards long, had to be unrolled, connected with the charge
and carried over the ridge where the exploder was to be put
under cover. The wires were stiff and would not lie flat unless
weighed down with stones, and it took three hours more to
hide the marks made in burying them. Lawrence finally finished off the job with a pair of bellows and long brushings
of his cloak to imitate a smooth wind-swept surface. It was
well done; nobody could see where the mine was, or how the
wires ran. The man who fired the exploder, however, being
out of sight of the bridge, had to be given the signal from a
point fifty yards ahead of him; so Lawrence decided to give
the signal rather than work the exploder himself. Feisal's favourite freedman Salem was given that honour and was taught on
the disconnected exploder to bang down the handle exactly
as Lawrence raised his hand for an imaginary engine on the
bridge. Meanwhile the rest of the men, who had been left with
the camels, had got tired of the valley and were perched upon
the skyline with the sunset flaming behind them (the ambush
was west of the line), in full view of a small Turkish hill-post
four miles to the south and also of Mudowwara somewhat
farther to the north. Lawrence and Zaal threw them off the
ridge, but it was too late; the Turks had seen them and began
to let off rifles at the lengthening shadows for fear of a surprise
attack. However, Lawrence hoped that the Turks might think
them gone if the place looked deserted in the morning; so they
stayed in the valley, baked bread and settled down comfort-

ably for the night. The party was now united and, ashamed of their folly on the skyline, the jealous Howeitat tribesmen chose Zaal for their leader.

The next day, the nineteenth of September, Zaal and his cousin Howeimil managed with difficulty to keep the fidgeting Arabs in the hollow, but perhaps after all the Turks saw something, for at nine o'clock a party of forty men came out from the southern post, advancing in open order. If they were left alone they would discover the ambush in an hour's time; if they were opposed the railway would be alarmed and traffic held up. The only thing to do was to send a small party to snipe at them and, if possible, draw them away in pursuit behind another ridge of hills out of sight. This would hide the main position and reassure the Turks as to the size and intention of the force they had seen. The trick worked well; they could hear by the shots gradually sounding fainter in the distance that the Turks were being drawn off.

An ordinary patrol of eight men and a stout corporal then came up the line from the south in search of mines or obstructions. Lawrence could see the corporal mopping his forehead, for it was now eleven o'clock and really hot. They walked over the mine without noticing anything, but a mile or two farther on halted under a culvert, lay down, drank from their water-bottles and at last went to sleep. It seemed that the Turks were quite satisfied that the ridge was deserted, but about noon Lawrence through his field-glasses saw a force of about a hundred soldiers coming up towards them from Mudowwara, about six or seven miles away. They were marching very slowly and no doubt unwillingly at the thought of losing their accustomed midday sleep, but it could not be more than two hours before they arrived. Lawrence decided to pack up and move off, trusting to luck that the mine would not be noticed and that he might come back later and try again. They sent a messenger south to their drawing-off party to arrange a meeting-place behind some rocks a mile or two away. But a minute later the watchman reported smoke from the south. There was evidently a train in the next station and, as they watched, it came puffing out towards them. A wild scramble followed as the Arabs got into position behind the ridge. Stokes and Lewis forgot their dysentery and raced to their guns.

The train rushed on at full speed and Lawrence saw that there were two engines in front, not one, which rather upset his calculations: but he decided to fire the mine under the second. If he mined the first, the second might uncouple and steam away with the wagons. He was glad that it was not an automatic mine. The Arabs with their rifles were only a hundred and fifty yards from the bridge, and the Stokes and Lewis guns three hundred; the exploder was in between, on the same ridge. On came the train at full speed and opened random fire into the desert where the Arabs had been reported. The firing sounded heavy and Lawrence wondered if his eighty men were enough for the battle. There were ten coaches with rifle-muzzles crowded at the windows and sandbag nests on the roofs, filled with sharpshooters. The whistles screamed round the curve, and Salem was dancing round the exploder on his knees, calling on God to make him fruitful. As the front wheels touched the bridge Lawrence raised his hand in the signal to Salem.

There was a terrific roar and the line vanished behind a column of black dust and smoke a hundred feet high and wide, while fragments of steel and iron struck clanging all about. An engine-wheel went whirling over the ridge and fell heavily in the desert behind. There followed a deathly silence. Lawrence ran to join the sergeants while Salem picked up a rifle and charged into the smoke. As Lawrence ran he heard shots, and the Bedouin could be seen leaping forward towards the track. The train was stationary and the Turks were tumbling out of the doors on the other side to shelter behind the railway embankment beyond. Then the Lewis gun opened fire straight down the train, and the long row of Turks on the roofs was swept off by the furious spray of bullets. When Lawrence reached Stokes and Lewis, the Turks behind the eleven-foot high embankment, in the middle of which the bridge had been, were firing point-blank at the Arabs between the wheels of the train. The Lewis gun could not reach them, protected by the train and by the curve of the embankment, but the Stokes mortar could. Its second shell dropped among them in the hollow and made a shambles of the place. The survivors ran in a panic across the desert, throwing away their rifles and equipment. This was the turn of Lewis again, who, with his assistant, a Sherari boy, mowed down the Turks as they ran. That ended the battle. The Sherari dropped the Lewis gun and rushed down to join the others in the plundering. The whole affair had taken ten minutes. Lawrence looked north and saw the hundred men from Mudowwara breaking back uncertainly to the railway to meet the train-fugitives running up the line. He looked south and saw the other thirty Arabs racing each other to share in the spoil. The Turks with whom they had been fighting, were coming slowly after them firing volleys. Evidently the plunderers would be safe for half an hour more.

Lawrence ran down from the ridge to see what effect the mine had had. The bridge was gone and into the gap had fallen the front wagon, which had been filled with sick. The smash had killed all but three or four and rolled dead and dying in a bleeding heap at one end. One of those still alive called out the word 'typhus' in delirium. So Lawrence wedged the door shut, and left them until their friends should come. He was feeling pretty sick. The wagons following were derailed and smashed; the frames of some were buckled beyond repair. The second engine was a blanched pile of smoking iron. The first engine had come off better; though it was derailed and lying half over with the cab smashed, its driving gear was intact and the steam still at pressure. The destruction of locomotives was the chief object of the campaign against the railway, so Lawrence had kept a box of gun-cotton with fuse and detonator ready for this very emergency. He put it on the cylinder, lit the fuse and drove the plunderers back a little way. In half a minute the charge burst, destroying the cylinder and the axle too. The engine would not run again.

The Arabs had gone raving mad. They were running about at top speed, bareheaded, half-naked, screaming, shooting in the air, clawing at each other, as they burst open trucks and staggered off with immense bales which they ripped open by the side of the railway, smashing what they did not want. The train had been packed with refugees, sick men, volunteers for boat-service on the Euphrates, and families of Turkish officers returning to Damascus. To one side of the wreck stood thirty or forty hysterical women, unveiled, tearing their clothe? and hair, shrieking together. The Arabs paid no attention to them, busy looting their absolute fill for the first time in their lives. Never was such a litter of household goods—carpets, mattresses, blankets, clothes for men and women, clocks, cooking-pots, food, ornaments and weapons. Camels became common property: each man loaded the nearest with what it would carry and shooed it westward into the desert while he turned to his next fancy. The women, seeing Lawrence unemployed, rushed and caught at him, howling for mercy. He comforted them that there was no danger, but they would not let him go until they were knocked away by their husbands, who in turn grovelled at Lawrence's feet in an agony of terror, pleading for their lives. He kicked them off with his bare feet and broke free. Next a group of Austrian officers and non-commissioned officers, artillery instructors to the Turks, quietly appealed to him in Turkish for quarter: he answered in German. Then one of them, mortally wounded, asked in English for a doctor. There was none, but Lawrence said that the Turks would soon be there to care for him. The man was dead before that, and so were most of the others, for a dispute broke out between them and the Arabs; an Austrian foolishly fired at one of Lawrence's Syrians, and before Lawrence could interfere all but two or three were cut down.

Among the passengers were five Egyptian soldiers captured by the Turks in a night-raid of Davenport's two hundred miles down the line. They knew Lawrence and told him of Davenport's efforts in Abdulla's sector where he was constantly pegging away without much encouragement from the Arabs and forced to rely mostly on imported Egyptians like these. Lawrence set the five to march off the prisoners to the appointed rallying-place behind the hills westward. Lewis and Stokes had come down to help Lawrence, who was a little anxious about them. The Arabs in their madness were as ready to attack friend as enemy. Three times Lawrence had to defend himself when they pretended not to know him and snatched at his things. Lewis went across the railway to count

the thirty men he had killed and to find Turkish gold and trophies in their haversacks. Stokes went into the hollow behind
the embankment, where he saw the effect of his second shell
and turned back hurriedly. One of Lawrence's Syrians came
up with his arms full of booty and shouted to Lawrence that
an old woman in the last wagon but one wished to see him.
Lawrence told the man to put down the booty and go at once
for Ghazala and some baggage-camels to remove the guns; for
the Turks were coming close and the Arabs were escaping one
by one towards the hills, driving their staggering camels before
them. Lawrence was annoyed with himself for not having
thought of moving the guns earlier. Meanwhile he went to the
last wagon but one, found a trembling old invalid, the Lady
Ayesha by name, a friend and hostess of Feisal's, who wanted
to know what was happening. Lawrence reassured her that no
harm would come to her and found the old negress, her servant, whom he sent to bring a drink from the leaking tender
of the first engine. The grateful Lady Ayesha later sent him
secretly from Damascus a charming letter and a little Baluchi
carpet as a remembrance of their odd meeting. Later still—as
I hear from an indirect but trustworthy source—Lawrence,
who made it his principle to get no spoils of any sort from the
War, sent the carpet with an equally charming letter to Lady
Allenby, who now has it in her bedroom.

The Syrian never brought the camels. All of Lawrence's servants, overcome with greed, had escaped with the Bedouin.
No one was now left but the three Englishmen. They began to
fear that they must abandon the guns and run for their lives,
but just then saw two camels cantering back. It was Zaal and
Howeimil, who had missed Lawrence and returned to find
him. Lawrence and the sergeants were rolling up the cable,

their only piece. Zaal dismounted and told Lawrence to climb up, but he loaded the camel with the wire and exploder instead; Zaal laughed at the quaint booty. Howeimil was lame from an old wound on the knee and could not walk, but couched his camel while the Lewis guns were hoisted across behind him, tied butt to butt and looking like scissors. There remained the mortars, but Stokes appeared unskilfully leading a stray bag-gage-camel which he had caught. Stokes was too weak to run, so he was given Zaal's camel with the mining apparatus; the trench-mortars were put on the baggage- camel, and Howeimil went off in charge of them. Meanwhile Lawrence, Lewis and Zaal, in a sheltered hollow behind the old gun-position, made a fire of cartridge-boxes, petrol and wreckage, banked the Lewis-gun drums and spare rifle ammunition round it, and gingerly laid some Stokes shells on top. Then they ran. As the flames reached the cordite and ammonal there was a colossal burst of fire, thousands of cartridges exploded in series like machine-guns, and the shells roared off in columns of dust and smoke. Both parties of Turks were impressed by this noise, and decided that the Arabs were posted strongly. They halted and began to send out flanking parties according to rule. Through the gap between the main body of the northern party and their flankers working round on the western side, the three men ran panting away into concealment among the farther ridges.

At the rallying-place Lawrence found his missing camels and the Syrian servants with them. In his soft deadly voice he told the Syrians what he thought of them for their desertion. They pleaded that camels had become common property and that someone else had gone off with the right ones. But this did not excuse them for having found others for themselves and loaded them up with plunder. Lawrence asked if anyone was hurt and was told that a boy had been killed in the first Arab rush; three others were slightly wounded. The rush had not been ordered and was a mistake; the Lewis and Stokes guns could have managed the killing without Arab help, and Lawrence felt that he was not responsible for the boy's death. Then one of Feisal's freedmen said that Salem was missing, and others that he had been last seen lying wounded just beyond the engine. Lawrence had not been told and was angry, for Salem was under his charge. For the second time he had been put by Arab carelessness in the position of leaving a friend behind. He called for volunteers to rescue the negro. Zaal and twelve of his men said that they would try, but when they came near the train they saw that they were too late. A hundred and fifty Turks were swarming over the wreck and by now Salem would be dead, and not only dead but tortured and mutilated as the Turkish habit was. (The Arabs made a practice now of mercifully killing their own badly wounded to prevent them falling alive into Turkish hands.)

They had to go back without Salem, but took the opportunity of recovering some of the baggage, including the sergeants' kits, which had been left at the camping-ground. The Turks caught them at this and opened fire with a machine-gun. Others ran to cut them off. Zaal, a dead shot, stopped with five others at a ridge-top and fired back, calling to the remainder of the party to escape while he held the Turks up. So they retired from ridge to ridge, hitting at least thirteen or fourteen Turks at the cost of four of their camels wounded. The Turks gave up the pursuit.

Victory always undid an Arab force: this was now no longer a raiding party but a stumbling baggage-caravan loaded to breaking-point with enough household goods to make an Arab tribe rich for years. Of the ninety prisoners, ten were friendly Arab women on the way to Damascus from Medina who had now decided to go instead to Mecca by way of Akaba. These and thirty-four wounded Turks were mounted in pairs on the spare camels that had been used for carrying the explosives and ammunition. The sergeants asked Lawrence to give them a sword each as a souvenir; and he was going down the column to look for something for them when suddenly he met Feisal's freedmen and to his astonishment saw, strapped on the crupper behind one of them, the missing Salem. He was unconscious and soaked with blood from a wound through his back near the spine. Apparently he had been hit in his rush downhill and left for dead near the engine; where the tribesmen stripped him of his cloak, dagger, rifle, and headgear. One of his fellows had found him alive and carried him off home without, as he should have done, telling Lawrence. Salem soon recovered but ever afterwards bore Lawrence an undeserved grudge for abandoning him when wounded and under his charge.

They had to water again at the evil-smelling well—the prisoners had drunk all their water—and its nearness to Mudowwara made this dangerous. However, they made what haste they could and found it unoccupied. So back safely to Rumm by the same long avenue; in the dark this time, which made the cliffs more terrifying still, for they were invisible except as a jagged skyline high overhead on either side. From Rumm to Akaba, entering in glory laden with spoil, and boasting that the trains were now at their mercy. The two sergeants hurriedly returned to Egypt, having had the adventure they wanted. They had won a battle single-handed, had dysentery,

DEMOLITIONS ON THE RAILWAY

lived on camel-milk, learned to ride a camel fifty miles a day without pain. They were awarded medals by Allenby.

The success excited the camp at Akaba. Everybody wanted to try this new and profitable sport of train-mining. The French captain of the Algerian company of gunners at Akaba, by name Pisani, was the first volunteer, an active and ambitious officer on the look-out for decorations. Feisal provided three young noblemen of Damascus who were eager to lead tribal raids, and on the twenty-sixth of September the party rode to Rumm in search of tribesmen volunteers. Lawrence said that the next raid was especially intended for Gasim's clan. This was heaping coals of fire on the adversary's head, but the adversary was too greedy to refuse the chance. The difficulty indeed was to keep down the numbers. They took a hundred and fifty men and a huge train of baggage-camels for the spoils.

This time they worked in the direction of Maan, riding over the Syrian border into the high hills by Batra where the keen air of the northern desert came blowing at them through a pass at the top. From Batra they turned west and struck the railway, marching along it until they came to a convenient bridge in an embankment, as at Mudowwara. Here, between midnight and dawn, they buried an automatic mine of a new and wonderful lyddite type. They lay in ambush a thousand yards away among the wormwood thickets, but no train came that day or the following night. Lawrence found the waiting intolerable. The Arabs paid no attention to the leaders appointed by Feisal and would listen to no one but Lawrence, whose success was now beginning to have results very unwelcome to him. He was asked to act as judge and had to consent. With Feisal's example and his own pre-war experience at Carchemish to help him out, he settled during that six days' ride twelve cases of armed assault, four camel-thefts, a marriage, two ordinary thefts, a divorce, fourteen feuds, two cases of evil eye and a bewitchment.

The evil eyes he cured by staring at their possessors with his own for ten minutes ('horrible blue eyes,' as an old Arab woman once told him, 'like bits of sky through the eye-holes of a skull'), the bewitchment by casting a mock-spell of his own over the wizard. Then he began to realize what he was doing—probably Pisani's presence reminded him that he was only an Englishman playing at being an Arab. He went off on a long train of shameful thought about himself and the fraud that he was playing on the Arabs. Again Pisani's presence reminded him that he was leading them into this war of freedom knowing well enough that the chances were heavily against their being allowed to keep the freedom if ever they won it. The agony of his mind's conflict at Nebk returned to him in double force. The stings of a scorpion on his left hand kept him awake that night with an arm so swollen that at least he was distracted by the pain from further thinking, but by next morning his position began troubling him again, and he decided to renounce his leadership. He called up the sheikhs to tell them of his decision. But at that moment a train was reported, and as always happened with Lawrence, who was another Hamlet, sudden enforced action cleared away his philosophic doubts and hesitations. He jumped up to watch the success of the mine.

However, the train with its cargo of water-tanks passed over without accident. The Arabs, who wanted something better than water, thanked him as if he had intended this failure. He had then to go down to lay an electric mine over the other;

the electric mine would set the first one off. The Turks did not catch him at work, for it was their hour of midday sleep. There were three bridges in the embankment and the southern one had been chosen for the ambush. Under the arch of the middle bridge Lawrence hid the exploder. The Lewis guns were put under the northern one to rake the far side of the train when the mine went off. On the near side was a convenient cross-channel in the valley, three hundred yards from the railway, where the Arabs could line up behind the wormwood bushes. No train came that day; enemy patrols went constantly up and down the rails, but without finding the mine. The next morning, the sixth of October, a train came out of Maan, but ahead of the train a patrol was walking, and there was an anxious wait to see which arrived first. If the patrol won the race it would give warning to the train; however, Lawrence calculated that it would be beaten by two or three hundred yards, so the Arabs took up their position. The train came on panting up the gradient. It was a heavy train with twelve loaded wagons.

Lawrence sat by a bush where he could see the mine, a hundred yards away, and the exploder and the Lewis guns. He gave the signal when the engine was exactly over the arch and the history of Mudowwara was repeated. There was the same roar and cloud, but a green one this time, because lyddite was being used instead of gelatine, and then the Lewis gun rattled and the Arabs charged. Lawrence smiled sourly to see Pisani running excitedly at their head singing the Marseillaise, as if this was a battle for French freedom. A Turk on the buffers of the fourth wagon from the end uncoupled the tail of the train and let it slip downhill. Lawrence ran to stop it by putting a stone underneath a wheel, but was amused at the trucks sliding off on their own to safety; his effort was half-hearted. And he had reached a point of such carelessness about his own safety that he only laughed at a Turkish colonel in the run-away wagons who fired point-blank at him from a window with his pistol. The Western military idea of trying to end the War by reducing the enemy's man-power seemed comic in the desert. And the bullet only grazed his hip.

The train had been derailed, the engine ruined and the tender and front wagon telescoped. Twenty Turks were killed, the others taken prisoners, including four officers who stood in tears begging for their lives, which, however, the Arabs never intended to take. The wagons contained seventy tons of food-stuffs urgently needed down the line, as they learned from the captured way-bill. For a joke Lawrence receipted this and left it in the van, sending the duplicate to Feisal as detailed report of the success. What could not be taken was destroyed under the direction of Pisani. As before, the Arabs became merely camel-drivers, walking behind a long string of loaded animals. This time Lawrence was not deserted; Farraj held the camel, while Sheikh Salem (Gasim's brother) and another of the leading Arabs helped with the exploder and the heavy wire. But rescue parties of the Turks were four hundred yards away by the time they got off. There were no Arabs killed or wounded.

Lawrence's pupils afterwards practised the art of mining by themselves and rumours of their success spread through the tribes, not always intelligently. The Beni Atiyeh tribe wrote to Feisal: 'Send us a *lurens* and we will blow up trains with it.' Feisal sent them one of the Ageyl who helped them to ambush a most important train. On board were the Turkish colonel who had left his garrison in the lurch at Wejh, twenty thousand pounds in gold, and precious trophies. The Ageyl repeated history by only saving the wire and exploder for his share. During the next four months seventeen engines were destroyed and much plunder taken. Travelling became a great terror for the Turks. People paid extra for the back seats in trains. The engine- drivers went on strike. Civilian traffic nearly ceased. The threat was extended to Aleppo merely by having a notice posted in Damascus to say that all good Arabs would henceforward travel on the Syrian railway at their own risk. The Turks felt the loss severely; not only could they not any longer think of marching out of Medina, but they were short of engines in Palestine too, just when Allenby's threat began to trouble them.

Meanwhile, in the middle of September, Allenby calling Lawrence to Egypt asked him what exactly his aims were. Was this blowing up of the railway more than a melodramatic advertisement for Feisal's cause? Lawrence explained his policy, unchanged since he framed it in Abdulla's camp six months before. He was hoping to keep the line to Medina working, but only just working: the garrison was helpless to do the Arabs harm and cost less to feed than it would in a prisoners' camp in Egypt if it surrendered. And while the mining was going on, the Arab regulars were being properly trained for a move into Syria. Allenby asked about the pass to Akaba north of Aba el Lissan where he knew from spies that the Turks intended a big attack. Lawrence explained that he and the Arabs had been working for months to provoke the Turks to come forward, and at last were about to be rewarded. The Turks had been hesitating because they had no idea of the strength of the Arabs, who being mostly irregulars went about in parties, not in stiff formation; so that neither aeroplanes nor spies could count them. On the other hand, Lawrence and Feisal always knew exactly what the Turkish forces were because they were regular troops and the Arab intelligence service was excellent. So the Arabs could always decide in time whether to fight or avoid fight.

Allenby understood then. And when at last the big attack was made from Maan on Akaba by way of the northern pass, Maulud with his regulars let the Turks into a trap from which few of them escaped. They never made another attempt on Akaba.

XIX

In October, 1917, Allenby, who was fast reorganizing the British Army on the borders of Palestine, had decided on an attack of the Gaza-Beersheba line, to begin on the last day of the month. He had resolved that this time the attempt must not fail as before for want of artillery and troops, but since the Gaza end of the line (nearest the sea) was very strongly entrenched—its very strength seemed to have tempted the former disastrous British attacks—the scheme was to try south at the Beersheba end. Elaborate care was taken to deceive the Turks with false secret documents which they were allowed to capture, into thinking that the Beersheba attack was a mere feint and that the main attack was coming from Gaza.

It was for Lawrence to decide how much help the Arabs could afford to give Allenby. He was in the unfortunate position of serving two masters. And he did not 'hate the one and love the other, cling to the one and despise the other.' He admired and had the confidence of both, yet found himself unable to explain the whole Arab situation to Allenby, or the whole British plan to Feisal. Allenby expected much from Lawrence as one of his officers. But Feisal trusted him implicitly and this trust made him perhaps more careful on the Arab behalf than he might otherwise have been: and Feisal's was the weaker cause, always attractive to Lawrence. Now, the country immediately behind the Turkish lines was peopled with tribes friendly to Feisal and a sudden rising there might have an enormous effect on the War. If Allenby was given a month's fine weather to make possible the advance of his cumbrous artillery and supplies he ought to be able to take not only Jerusalem, which he was aiming at, but Haifa too. In that case it would be a chance for the Arabs to strike from behind at the all-important junction of Deraa, the nerve-centre of the Turkish army in Palestine, where the Medina-Damascus railway joined the railway that ran to Haifa and to Jerusalem. Near Deraa were great untouched reserves of Arab fighting men, secretly taught and armed by Feisal from his base at Akaba. Four main Bedouin tribes could be used there and, better still, the peasants of the Hauran plain to the north, and the Druses, a settled mountain folk from the east.

The attack on Beersheba had not yet begun, so Lawrence was in doubt whether or not to call up all these helpers at once, to rush Deraa at the same time as Allenby attacked Gaza and Beersheba, smash all the railway lines, and even go on to surprise Damascus. He could count on at least twelve thousand men, and success would put the Turks facing Allenby into a desperate condition. He was greatly tempted to stake everything on immediate action but could not quite make up his mind. As a British officer he should have taken the risk, as a leader of the Arab Revolt he should not have. The Arabs in Syria were imploring him to come. Tallal, the great fighter who led the tribes about Deraa, sent repeated messages that, given only a few of Feisal's men in proof of support, he could take Deraa. This would have been all very well for Allenby, but Feisal could not decently accept Tallal's offer unless he was sure that Deraa could be held once it was taken. If anything went wrong with the British advance and the Turks sent rein-forcements down from Aleppo and Damascus, Deraa would be recaptured and a general massacre would follow of all the splendid peasantry of the district. The Syrians could only rise once and when they did there must be no mistake. The English troops were brave fighters, but Lawrence could not yet trust Allenby, or rather the commanders under him who were, he thought, quite capable of ruining a perfectly sound scheme, as at the Suvla landing in the Dardanelles campaign, by not prof-iting from their first sudden gains. And there was the weather. So he decided to postpone the rising until the following year. It is difficult to say now whether he was right. Allenby's army fought excellently, but was later held up by the rains.

He had to do something less than raising a general revolt, in return for Allenby's supplies and arms. So he decided that it would have to be a big raid made by a Bedouin tribe without disturbing the settled peoples, and something that would help Allenby in his pursuit of the enemy. The best plan was to blow up one of the bridges crossing the deep river-gorge of the Yarmuk just west of Deraa on the line leading to Jerusalem. This would temporarily cut off the Turkish army in Palestine from its base at Damascus, and make it less able to resist or escape from Allenby's advance. It would be a fortnight before either of the two biggest bridges could be rebuilt. To reach the Yarmuk would mean a ride of about four hundred and twenty miles from Akaba by way of Azrak. The Turks thought the danger of an attempt on the bridges so slight that they did not guard them at all strongly. So Lawrence put the scheme before

Allenby, who asked him to carry it out on November the fifth or one of the three days following. If the attempt succeeded and the weather held for the British advance, the chances were that few of the Turkish army would get back to Damascus. The Arabs would then have the opportunity of carrying on the wave of the attack from a half-way point where the British, because of transport difficulties, must stop exhausted. They should be able to sweep on to Damascus.

In that case some important Arab was needed to lead the raid from Azrak. Nasir, the usual pioneer who had led the Akaba expedition, was away. But Ali ibn el Hussein was available, the young Harith chief whom Lawrence had met disguised in his first ride to see Feisal a year before, and who had lately been active in raids on the railway down the line just above Davenport's section. Ali knew Syria, for he had been, with Feisal, the forced guest of the Turkish general Jemal at Damascus. Besides, his courage, resource and energy were proved, and no adventure had ever been too great or disaster too deep but Ali had faced it with his high yell of a laugh. He was so strong that he would kneel down, resting his forearms palm upwards on the ground, and rise to his feet with a man standing on each hand. He could also outstrip a trotting camel running with bare feet, keep his speed for a quarter of a mile, and then leap into the saddle. He was headstrong and conceited, reckless in word and deed, and the most admired fighter in the Arab forces. Ali would win over the tribe of Beni Sakhr, who were half-peasants, half-Bedouin, on the southern border of Syria. There were good hopes also of securing the Serahin, the tribe about Azrak, and there were others farther north on whom they might count for help.

Lawrence's plan was to rush from Azrak to the Yarmuk vil-

ALI IBN EL HUSSEIN
from a drawing by Eric Kennington

lage which was the ancient Gadara; it commanded the most westerly of the two most important bridges, a huge steel erection guarded by a force of sixty men quartered in a railway station close by. No more than half a dozen sentries were, however, stationed actually on the girders and abutments of the bridge itself, as Lawrence had learned on his previous ride to Damascus through this country. He hoped to take some of Auda's tough Abu Tayi Howeitat with him under Zaal. They would make certain the actual storming of the bridge. To prevent enemy reinforcements coming up, machine-guns would sweep the approaches to the bridge; the men to handle these were a party of Mohammedan Indian cavalrymen, now mounted on camels, under command of Jemadar Hassan Shah, a firm and experienced man. They had been up-country from Wejh for months, destroying rails, and might be assumed to be by now expert camel-riders. The destruction of the great steel girders with only small weights of explosive was a problem. Lawrence decided to fix the charges in place with canvas strips and buckles and fire them electrically. But this was a dangerous task under fire, so Wood, an engineer officer at Akaba, came as a substitute in case Lawrence might be hit. Wood had been condemned as unfit for active service on the Western front after a bullet through the head.

They were making their last preparations when an unexpected ally arrived, the chief Abd el Kader. He was an Algerian of a family that had been living in Damascus since his grandfather, the defender of Algiers against the French, had been deported from there thirty years before. Abd el Kader, quarrelsome, deaf and boorish, was a religious fanatic who, being recently sent by the Turks on secret political business to Mecca, had paid a dutiful call instead on Sherif Hussein and come away with a crimson banner and noble gifts, half-persuaded of the right of the Arab cause. Now he offered Feisal the help of his Algerian villagers, exiles like himself, living on the north bank of the Yarmuk, half-way between the two important bridges but close to others whose destruction might answer nearly as well. This seemed excellent. As the Algerians did not mix with their Arab neighbours, the destruction of the bridge or bridges could be arranged quietly without exciting the whole peasant countryside into revolt.

Suddenly a telegram came from the French Colonel to say that Abd el Kader was a spy in Turkish pay. This was disconcerting, but there was no proof, and the Colonel was not greatly liked himself since his letter to Abdulla about the English and his earlier intrigues at Jiddah. Probably he was annoyed at Abd el Kader's private and public denunciations of the French. So Feisal asked Abd el Kader to ride with Lawrence and Ali ibn el Hussein, telling Lawrence privately: 'I know he is mad, I think he is honest. Guard your heads and use him.' He joined the party. Whether or not he was a spy, he was a great annoyance to the party: being a religious fanatic he resented Lawrence's undisguised Christianity, and being ridiculously vain, resented being sent along with Ali whom the tribes treated as greater, and with Lawrence whom they treated as better than himself. Also his deafness was most inconvenient.

For his body-guard Lawrence took six Syrian recruits, chosen largely for their knowledge of the various districts through which he had to pass, with two Biasha tribesmen and the inseparable Farraj and Daud. These two were busy as usual at practical jokes and on the morning of October the twenty-fourth, the day of departure from Akaba, they completely disappeared. At noon came a message from fat Sheikh Yusuf, the Governor, to say that they were in prison and would Lawrence come and talk about it? Lawrence found Yusuf shaking between laughter and rage. His new cream-coloured riding-camel had strayed into the palm-garden where Lawrence's Ageyl were encamped. Farraj and Daud, not suspecting that the camel was the Governor's, had painted its body bright-red with henna and its legs blue with indigo before turning it loose. The camel caused an uproar in Akaba and when Yusuf with difficulty recognized the circus-like animal as his own, he hurried out his police to find the criminals. Farraj and Daud were found stained to their elbows with dye and though swearing innocence were soundly beaten and sent to prison in irons for a week. Lawrence arranged their release by lending the Governor a camel of his own until the dye had worn off the other, and promising that the Governor should beat the boys again after the expedition. So they joined the caravan singing, though they had to walk mile after mile because of a new kind of saddle- soreness which they called 'Yusufitis.'

The expedition went by way of Rumm, crossing the railway line near Shedia, but it was not a compact or happy family. Abd el Kader was continually quarrelling with Alt ibn el Hussein, who prayed God to deliver him from the man's bad manners, deafness, conceit. Wood was ill and the Indians, who proved to be very bad at loading and leading the baggage-camels, had to be helped with them by Lawrence's body-guard, and lagged far behind: Lawrence was not much troubled by these difficulties, because on the first stage of the journey he had for companion Lloyd (now British High Commissioner in Egypt), who had originally come out with him from England. It was a great thing to have someone European-minded and well-read to talk to again after months with the Arabs. Lawrence's Bedouin self wore off as he rode ahead with Lloyd, so engrossed in talk that they nearly lost touch with the Indians behind and, losing direction too, nearly ran into Shedia station. They turned in time and crossed the railway line in safety between two block-houses; contenting themselves merely with cutting the telegraph-wires. Ali and Abd el Kader were crossing the line farther north and soon came a rattle of machine-gun and rifle-fire: evidently they had not been lucky in their crossing. It turned out later that they had two men killed.

Lawrence's first stop was Jefer, where he had been before on the ride to Akaba and had repaired the damaged well: he took his party safely across the silver plain of polished mud and salt, and near Jefer found Auda encamped with a few of his tribesmen, including Zaal and Mohammed el Dheilan. The old man was having a violent dispute over the distribution of wages which he drew in bulk for the whole tribe, and was ashamed to be found in such difficulties. However, Lawrence did what he could to smooth them over and by giving the Arabs something else to think about, made them smile; which was half the battle. He then went to Zaal and explained his plan to destroy the Yarmuk bridges. Zaal disliked it very much. He had been most successful that summer in his fighting with the Turks, and wealth made life precious to him. And the train-ambush at Mudowwara from which he had barely escaped with his life had tried his nerve; so now he said that he would only come if Lawrence insisted. Lawrence did not insist. Lloyd having to go home at this point, he was left despondent among the Arabs to unending talk of war and tribes and camels.

The first thing was to help Auda to settle the money dis-

putes and to light again in the Howeitat the flame of enthusiasm now nearly extinct after months of hardship. At dark
Lawrence sat by Auda's camp-fire, an Arab once more,
talking in the hot persuasive tones that he had caught from
Feisal, gradually kindling them to remember their oath, their
promise to put the war with the Turks before all disputes and
jealousy. He won them over, man by man, addressing them
by name, reminding them of their ancestral glories, of their
own brave deeds, of Feisal's bounty, of the baseness and the
approaching collapse of the Turks. He was still at work near
midnight when Auda held up his camel-stick for silence. They
listened, wondering what the danger was, and after a while
heard a rumble, a muttering like a very distant thunderstorm.
Auda said: 'The English guns.' Allenby, a hundred miles north
across the hills, was beginning the preparatory bombardment
for his next day's successful attack on Beersheba, with Gaza
to fall five days later. This sound closed the argument. The
Arabs were always convinced by heavy artillery. When Lawrence and his party left the camp the next day in a happier
atmosphere than they had found it, Auda gratefully came up
and embraced Lawrence with 'Peace be with you.' But he also
took the opportunity of the embrace to whisper windily, while
his rough beard brushed Lawrence's ear: 'Beware of Abd el
Kader.' He could not say more; there were too many people
about.

They continued that day, the thirty-first of October,
towards Bair. The winter was approaching; it was now a time
of peaceful weather with misty dawns, mild sunlight and an
evening chill. The Indians were such bad camel-masters that
they could manage no more than thirty-five miles a day—fifty
was the least that an Arab would think of doing on a long

march—and had to stop to eat three meals a day. The midday
halt brought an alarm. Men on horses and camels were seen
riding up from the north and west and closing in on the
party. Rifles were snatched up and the Indians ran to their
machine-guns. In thirty seconds the defence was ready; Ali
ibn el Hussein cried out, 'Hold the fire until they come close.'
Then one of Lawrence's body-guard, belonging to a despised
clan of serfs, the Sherarat, but a devoted servant and brave
fighter, sprang up laughing and waved his sleeve in the air as
a signal of friendship. They fired at him, or perhaps over him.
He lay down and fired back, one shot only over the head of
the nearest man; that perplexed them, but after awhile they
waved back in answer. Then he went forward, protected by the
rifles of his party, to meet a man of the enemy, also advancing
alone; it was a raiding party of Arabs of the Beni Sakhr tribe
who pretended to be much surprised on hearing whom they
had been about to attack, and rode in to apologize.

Ali ibn el Hussein was furious with the Beni Sakhr for their
treacherous attack: they answered sullenly that it was their
custom to shoot over the heads of strangers in the desert.
'A good custom,' said Ali, 'for the desert. But to come on us
suddenly from three sides at once seems to me more like a
carefully prepared ambush.' Border Arabs like the Beni Sakhr
were always dangerous, being not villagers enough to have
forgotten the Bedouin love of raiding, not Bedouin enough
to keep the strict desert code of honour. (There is a Scottish
proverb that I learned from Lawrence's mother, who speaking
of another Border, quoted: 'The selvage is aye the warst part
o' the web.') The Beni Sakhr raiders, ashamed, went forward
to Bair to give warning of the approach of the party. Their
chief thought it best to make up for the bad reception that

such important men as Ali ibn el Hussein and Lawrence had been given, by preparing a great feast for them. First there was a public reception, every man and horse in the tribe turned out, and there were wild cheers of welcome, volleys in the air, gallopings and curvetings: and clouds of dust. 'God give victory to our Sherif,' they shouted to Ali, and to Lawrence, 'Welcome, Aurans, forerunner of fighting!'

Abd el Kader grew jealous. He began to show off, climbing up on the high Moorish saddle of his mare, and with his seven Algerian servants behind him in a file began the same prancing and curveting, shouting out 'Houp! Houp!' and firing a pistol unsteadily in the air. The Beni Sakhr chief came up to Ali and Lawrence, saying, 'Lords, please call off your servant. He cannot either shoot or ride, and if he hits someone, he will destroy our good luck of to-day.' The chief did not know Abd el Kader's family reputation for 'accidental' shootings in Damascus. His brother Mohammed Said had had three successive fatal accidents among his friends, so that Ali Riza, the Governor of Damascus and a secret pro-Arab, once said: 'Three things are notably impossible. The first, that Turkey should win this war. The second, that the Mediterranean should become champagne. The third, that I should be found in the same room with Mohammed Said, and he to be armed.'

Ali had a little business to settle before dinner. A party of negro workmen had been sent by Feisal to re-line the blasted well from which Lawrence and Nasir had picked the gelignite on the way to Akaba. They had been here for months, living on the forced hospitality of the Beni Sakhr and doing no work. Feisal had asked Ali to see what was happening. Ali hurriedly held a court, tried them, found them guilty and had them beaten, out of sight, by his own negroes. They returned stiffly, kissed hands to show repentance and respect, and soon the whole party, including the masons, were kneeling down at the feast.

The Beni Sakhr hospitality was even richer than that of the Howeitat. Lawrence, Ali and the rest ate ravenously, for good manners, at mutton and rice which was soused in so much liquid butter that they splashed their clothes and greased their faces in their first polite haste. The pace was slackening somewhat, though the meal was far from its end, when Abd el Kader grunted, rose to his feet, wiped his hands on a handkerchief and sat back on the carpets by the tent wall. Lawrence and the rest did not know whether to rise too, for the custom was for all to rise together. They looked to Ali their leader, but he merely grunted 'the boor!' and the eating went on until everyone was full and had begun licking his fingers. Then Ali cleared his throat as the usual signal, and they went back to the carpets, while the next relay fed and then the children. Lawrence watched one little five-year-old in a filthy smock stuffing with both hands until at the end, with swollen stomach and shining face, it could manage no more. Then it staggered off speechlessly, a huge unpicked mutton-rib hugged to its breast. In the corner the chief's slave was eating his customary portion, the sheep's head; splitting the skull and sucking the brain. In front of the tent the dogs crunched their bones.

As for Abd el Kader, he had not been behaving badly according to his own standards or indeed those of the border, which allowed the full-fed man to go off at his own time. But Ali was a sherif and a hero and therefore the good manners of the central desert ruled for that feast. So Abd el Kader was ashamed. He tried to carry it off by worse behaviour. He sat spitting, grunting and picking his teeth, and to show his grandeur further, sent a servant for his medicine chest and poured himself out a dose, grumbling that such tough meat gave him indigestion. This was abominable. Lawrence had once met a chief with a scar right across his cheek which he had come by in this way: he had been politely gulping food at a feast when he had begun to choke; unable to speak but anxious to explain that this was not meant as an insult, he had slit his mouth to the ear with his dagger to show that it was only a piece of meat stuck behind his back teeth.

As the party sat about the tribal coffee-hearth, all but Abd el Kader who had gone off to a fire of his own, they heard the guns again thudding away in preparation for the second day's bombardment of Gaza. It was a good moment for telling the chief why they had come. Lawrence said that they proposed a raid near Deraa and asked him for help. He did not mention the bridge, after his failure to get Zaal and his men; it might seem too forlorn a hope. However, the chief agreed to come himself and chose out fifteen of his best men and his own son Turki, a brave boy of seventeen, though ambitious and greedy like his father. He was an old friend of Ali's. Lawrence gave Turki a new silk robe, and he strutted among the tents in it, without his cloak, crying shame on any man who held back from the adventure.

That night they rode out from Bair, in company with the Beni Sakhr men. Their chief had first to pay his respects to his dead ancestor whose grave was near that of Auda's son. He decided that, as there was great danger ahead, he would make a propitiatory offering of a head-cord to add to the ragged collection looped round the gravestone. And as the raid was Lawrence's idea, he thought he might ask Lawrence to provide one. Lawrence handed over a rich red silk and silver ornament, remarking with a smile that the virtue of the offering lay with the giver. The thrifty chief man pressed a halfpenny on Lawrence to make a pretence of purchase and get the virtue for himself. A few weeks later Lawrence passed by again and noticed that the head-cord was gone. The chief cursed loudly in his hearing at the sacrilege. Some godless Sherari, he said, had robbed his ancestor: but Lawrence could guess where it really was.

Lawrence nearly succumbed to the idleness that the weather invited the next day. But he had *to* be busy learning to recognize the tribal dialect of the Beni Sakhr, and making mental notes of the bits of family-history that the tribesmen gave him in casual conversation. Family- history and tribal custom were to these desert people in place of books. Nothing was so wearing, and yet nothing so important as the detailed memory that Lawrence had in good manners to cultivate, whenever he met a new tribe, for relationships and feuds and ancestry and the ownership of camels and similar matters. When they halted that night the noise of Allenby's guns was very loud and clear, possibly because the hollows of the Dead Sea sent the noise echoing up to their high plateau. The Arabs whispered, 'They are nearer. The English are advancing. God deliver the men under that rain!' They were thinking of the Turks, so long their weak and corrupt oppressors whom now they loved more, in their moment of defeat, than the strong foreigner with his blind unswerving justice, their victor.

The next day they went forward over ridges of sun-browned flints so closely grown over with a tiny saffron plant that the whole view was golden with it; and about noon saw from the top of a ridge a party of trotting camels coming fast towards them. Turki cantered forward, with carbine ready cocked, to see who the strangers were, but while they were still a mile off the Beni Sakhr chief recognized his kinsmen Fahad and Adhub, famous fighters, the war-leaders of the clan. They had heard the news of the raid and ridden at once to join it. Lawrence was glad of them. The next halt was Ammari in Sirhan where there were water-pools among the salty hummocks. They were mostly too bitter to drink, though there was one which was thought very good by contrast. It lay in a limestone hollow and the water, which tasted of mixed brine and ammonia, was of a deep yellow colour. Into this pool, for a joke, Daud pushed Farraj fully dressed; he sank out of view and then rose quietly to the surface at the side of the pool under an overhanging rock-ledge and lay hid: Daud waited for him to rise, but when there was no sign of him, got into an agony of anxiety about his friend and, tearing off his cloak, jumped in after him. There was Farraj smiling under the ledge. They were fine swimmers, having once been pearl-divers in the Persian Gulf. Afterwards they began scuffling in the sand beside the water-pool. They returned to Lawrence's camp-fire, dripping wet, in rags, bleeding and covered with mud and thorns, most unlike their usual foppish selves. They then had the impudence to say that they had tripped over a bush while dancing, and that it would be like Lawrence's generosity if he gave them new clothes. He did nothing of the kind, but sent them off at once to clean themselves up.

The next day there was another alarm, which again proved a false one. It was only a party of a hundred Serahin tribesmen on their way to offer allegiance to Feisal. Now that they could give the oath to Ali ibn el Hussein instead and be spared the long dangerous journey through the territory of other tribes and across the Turkish railway, they turned about with joy. They came back singing to their tents the same day as they had started out, and there was a great welcome for the combined party. After more mutton and bread and some sleepless hours on the verminous rugs offered them, which they could not politely refuse, Lawrence and Ali ibn el Hussein roused the old chief and his lieutenant, and explained the intentions of the raid. They listened gravely but said that the western bridge at Gadara was impossible because the Turks had just filled the woods about it with hundreds of military wood-cutters; the bridges in the middle they would not like to visit under the guidance of Abd el Kader whom they mistrusted and who would be among his own villagers there; the eastern bridge by Tell el Shehab was in the country of their blood-enemies who might take the opportunity to attack them in the rear. Also, if it rained the camels would not be able to trot over the muddy plains on the farther side of the line between Azrak and the bridges, and the whole party might be cut off and killed.

This was very bad. The Serahin were Lawrence's last hope and, if they refused to come, it would be impossible to destroy the bridge by the day that Allenby asked for it to be destroyed. So Ali ibn el Hussein and Lawrence collected the better men of the tribe and set them round the camp-fire with the chief of the Beni Sakhr and Fahad and Adhub to break cold prudence down with desperate talk. Though duty to Allenby provided the occasion, Lawrence was true Arab now, preaching with a prophetic eloquence the gospel of revolt. Its glory, he urged, lay in bitterness and suffering, and the sacrifice of the body to the spirit. Failure was even more glorious than success; it was better to defy a hostile Fate by choosing out the sure road to death, proudly throwing away the poor resources of physical life and prosperity and so making Fate ashamed at the poorness of its victory. To honourable men the forlorn hope was the only goal, and if by chance they escaped alive, then the next forlorn hope. They must believe that there was no final victory except at last after innumerable hazards to go down to death, still fighting. The Serahin listened entranced; their worldliness vanished and before daylight came they were swearing to ride with Lawrence anywhere.

Now, Lawrence was as sincere as he ever had been in his life, and this speech struck out in an hour of need gives the clue to much of his strange history. His has been the romantic love of failure, of self-humiliation, of poverty. A habit of mind caught from the desert: though perhaps latent in his blood, of which the Spanish strain—and Spanish is half-Arab—shows in the severity of his jaw and the cruel flash of his rare and quickly appeased anger. And yet with all his love of failure Lawrence has been queerly dogged with success. As Miss Gertrude Bell said of him once, 'Everything that he touches flowers.' His forlorn hopes all come off, he casts his bread magnificently upon the waters and is peevish to find it again (much swollen) after many days. The more deeply he abases himself the higher he finds himself exalted. So hostile Fate revenges itself neatly by refusing to take his sacrifices; and provokes him to a philosophic bitterness which is hourly contradicted by his natural impulse towards gentleness and affection.

They called Abd el Kader and taking him aside among the thickets shouted into his ear that the Serahin were coming with the party and would be guided by him to the bridges near his home. He grunted that it was well, but Lawrence and Ali ibn el Hussein swore never again, if they survived, would they take a deaf man as a conspirator with them. Exhausted, they rested for an hour or so, but soon had to rise to review the Serahin. They looked wild and dashing, but blustered rather too much to be quite convincing. And they had no real leader; the chief's lieutenant was more a politician than a soldier. How-

AZRAK

ever, they were better than nothing, so the increased party went forward to Azrak.

Azrak was a place of ancient legends; like Rumm and the vast ruins of Petra, most strangely haunted. It had been the home of ancient shepherd kings with musical names whose chivalrous memory lived in the Arab epics, and before that of a garrison of unhappy Roman legionaries. There was a great fort on a rock above rich meadows and palms and water-pools. Ali from the ridge that overlooked the place yelled out 'Grass!', leaped off his camel and flung himself down among the harsh green stems that were so exciting to him after the salt and stony desert. Then with his Harith war-cry he raced along the marsh, his skirts girded up and his feet splashing among the reeds.

Soon they noticed that Abd el Kader had vanished. They looked for him in the castle, among the palms, everywhere. At last they heard that he had ridden off northward not long after the start from the Serahin camp, making for the Druse mountains. The tribesmen had not known what the plans were, and, hating the man, had been glad to let him go without saying anything. But it was bad news. They must now give up the thought of destroying the middle bridges, and if Gadara was impossible because of the wood-cutters, the only bridge left for attack was Tell el Shehab. But Abd el Kader had certainly gone to the enemy with information of their plans and strength, and surely the Turks would trap them at the bridge. They took counsel with Fahad, who advised going on with the plan, trusting to the usual incompetence of the Turks. But the decision was not confidently taken.

XX

The next day, the fourth of November, they were off again, through rich pasture valleys where gazelle were shot. The flesh was toasted on ramrods over the fire until the outside of the lumps was charred but the inside was juicy and sweet. At this midday halt two of Lawrence's bodyguard quarrelled. One shot off the head-rope of the other, who fired back, putting a bullet through the assailant's cloak. Lawrence sprang between them and knocked their weapons up, ordering in a loud voice that the right thumb and forefinger of each should be cut off. This had the desired effect; they violently embraced and their companions offered to answer with their own lives that the quarrel was ended. Lawrence called Ali ibn el Hussein in as judge and he bound them over to good behaviour. But first they must seal their promise by the curious old penance of striking their own heads sharply with the edge of a heavy dagger until the blood trickled down to the waist. The wounds were not dangerous but ached for some time as a reminder of the promise given.

At Abu Sawana they found a long pool of delicious rainwater where they filled their water-skins. In the distance they saw a retreating party of Circassian horsemen sent by the Turks to see if this water was occupied—the two parties had missed each other by five minutes; which was lucky for both. On the fifth of November they reached the railway and, Lawrence and Fahad scouting ahead, crossed at dusk without interruption and rode five miles beyond. They camped in a hollow fifteen feet deep where there was grazing for the camels, but it was inconveniently near the railway, and they had to keep a close watch on the camels to prevent them from straying into view, and on the tribesmen to make them keep their heads down when patrols passed along the line.

At sunset, Lawrence and Ali ibn el Hussein decided that they would have to reach Tell el Shehab, blow up the bridge and get back east of the railway by the next dawn. This meant a ride of eighty miles in the thirteen hours of darkness with an elaborate mining operation thrown in. It was too much for the Indians, whose camels were tired out by bad handling—the fault of the Indians' cavalry training. So Lawrence only took the six best riders on the six best camels and Hassan Shah, their admirable officer, with a single machine-gun. The Serahin were doubtful fighters, so Ali and Lawrence decided, when the time came, to use them to guard the camels while a storming party of the Beni Sakhr, who could be trusted, went forward with the blasting gelatine to settle the bridge. The fighting force then consisted of Fahad and twenty Beni Sakhr, the seven Indians, forty Serahin, Ali ibn el Hussein with six slaves, Wood, and Lawrence with eight of his own men. The other two of Lawrence's men developed sudden illnesses which prevented them coming: Lawrence excused them for the night and afterwards of all duties whatsoever. They and the rest of the party to be left behind were told to ride to Abu Sawana and wait there for news.

It was a nervous ride. First they stumbled on a terrified pedlar with two wives, two donkeys and a load of raisins, flour and cloaks on the way to the nearest Turkish railway station. One of the Serahin had to be left behind to guard them in case they gave the alarm. He was to release them at dawn and then escape over the line to Abu Sawana. Next a shepherd heard the party coming and fired shot after shot into the middle of them, but without hitting anybody. Then a dog barked. Then a camel loomed up suddenly on the track—but it was a stray and riderless. Then, in a hollow, they came on a woman, probably a gipsy, who ran off shrieking. They passed a village and were fired on while yet distant. These incidents delayed them and in any case the Indians, riding woodenly like cavalrymen, were going much too slowly. Lawrence and Ali rode behind urging on the lagging animals with camel-sticks.

Then it began to rain and the fertile soil of the plain grew slippery. A camel of the Serahin fell, then one of the Beni Sakhr, but the men had them up in a moment and trotted forward. One of Ali ibn el Hussein's servants halted and dismounted. Ali hissed him on and, when the man mumbled, cut him across the head with his cane. The camel plunged forward and the man, snatching at the hinder girth, managed to swing himself into the saddle; Ali pursued him with the cane. At last the rain stopped and their pace increased as they trotted downhill. They heard a vague rushing sound in the distance; it would be Tell el Shehab waterfall. So they pressed forward confidently. A few minutes later they stopped on a grassy platform by a cairn of stones. Below them, in the darkness, lay the Yarmuk River in its deep gorge. The bridge would be on the right. They unloaded. The moon was not yet over Mount Hermon, which stood before them, but the sky was bright

FAHAD OF THE BENI SAKHR
from a drawing by Eric Kennington

with its rising. Lawrence served out the gelatine—four hundred and fifty pounds in thirty-pound bags—to the Serahin porters. They then started down.

First went the Beni Sakhr, scouting under Adhub. The ravine was slippery with the rain and two or three men fell heavily. When they were at the worst part of the descent, there was a clanking, screaming noise, and white puffs of steam came up from below. The Serahin hung back, but Wood drove them on. It was only a train from Galilee, low down in the ravine on the same side of the river. Lawrence, in the light of the engine furnace, could see open trucks in which were men in khaki—probably British prisoners being taken to Aleppo. They worked down to the right and at last saw the black shape of the bridge, and at the farther end a flicker of light, the fire by the sentries' guard tent. Wood stayed here with the Indians, who mounted their machine-gun ready to fire at the tent. Ali ibn el Hussein, Fahad, Lawrence, the Beni Sakhr chief, and the rest crept on downwards in single file until they reached the railway where it began to curve to the bridge. There the party halted while Lawrence and Fahad stole forward. They reached the bridge and slowly crawled along the abutment in the shadow of the rails until they reached a point where the girders began. They could see the sentry walking up and down before his fire, sixty yards away, without setting foot on the bridge itself. They wished him either much nearer or much farther. Fahad shuffled back and Lawrence followed, to bring the gelatine-porters along. He was going to attack the girders and risk the sentry.

Before he reached them there was a loud clatter and bump. Someone had fallen and dropped his rifle. The sentry started and stared up. He saw something moving high up in the light of the now risen moon; it was the machine-gunners climbing down to a new position so as to keep in the retreating shadow. He challenged them loudly, lifted his rifle and fired, yelling to the guard in the tent to turn out. Instantly, there was confusion and uproar. The Beni Sakhr blazed back at random. The Indians, caught on the move, were not able to use their machine-gun against the tent in time. The guard rushed out into its prepared trench and opened rapid fire at the flashes of the Beni Sakhr rifles. The Serahin porters had been told that gelatine would explode if hit, so they threw their sacks far down into the ravine and ran.

Lawrence and Fahad were left at the end of the bridge. It was hopeless now to climb down the ravine in search of the gelatine with no porters to help and sixty Turks firing from just across the bridge; so they ran back up the hill and told Wood and the Indians that it was all over. They reached the cairn where the Serahin were scrambling on their camels and did the same, trotting off at full speed. The whole countryside was roused. Lights sparkled everywhere over the plain, and rifle fire began from all the neighbouring villages. They ran into a party of peasants returning from Deraa, and the Serahin, smarting under Lawrence's sarcasm about their fighting qualities, fell on them and robbed them bare. The victims ran off screaming for help; the village of Remthe heard them, and mounted men poured out to cut off the raiders' retreat. The Serahin lagged behind, encumbered with their booty, while Lawrence and Ali hurried forward to safety with the rest, driving the slower camels along, as before, with their sticks. The ground was still muddy and many camels fell; but the noise behind spurred them on again.

At dawn, the tired party reached the railway in safety on

the way back to Abu Sawana. Wood, Ali ibn el Hussein and the chiefs amused themselves by cutting the telegraph wires to Medina. This, after their proud intention of the night before! Allenby's guns still drumming away on the right were a bitter reminder of failure. It began raining again, and when they reached the long pool at Abu Sawana they had to explain to the men left behind there the causes of their failure. Not a glorious failure even, thought Lawrence, remembering his speech of five days before, but a silly shameful one. Every one was equally to blame, but that made it no better. The two body-guardsmen began to fight again; another of them refused to cook rice and Farraj and Daud knocked him about till he cried; Ali had two of his servants beaten—and nobody cared a bit. The party had come nearly a hundred miles, over bad country in bad conditions between sunrise and sunset, without halt or food.

They took counsel in the cold rain as to what must be done next. The Beni Sakhr wanted honour and the Serahin wanted to wipe out their disgrace. They still had the electric-mine apparatus and a thirty-pound bag of gelatine; so Ali ibn el Hussein said: 'Let's blow up a train.' Every one looked at Lawrence. He would have liked to encourage them, but there were difficulties. They would have no food left after that night and, though the Arabs were accustomed to starving, the Indian machine-gunners were of no use unless well fed. And to mine a train properly the machine-guns were needed. The Indians could not even be given camel-flesh to eat; it was against their principles, though they were Mohammedans like the Arabs.

Lawrence explained this to Ali ibn el Hussein, who said: 'Only blow up the train and we Arabs will manage the wreck without the machine-guns.' The others agreed; so they sat down to make out a definite plan. The Indians miserably moved off towards Azrak but, to make their departure honourable, Lawrence asked Wood to go with them. He consented, and wisely, for he was showing signs of pneumonia. The remaining sixty Arabs, with Lawrence as guide, went towards Minifer, to the camp behind the hill under the ruined watch-tower, where he had been in the spring.

At dusk they went down to lay a mine at the rebuilt culvert that he had blown up before. They had hardly got there when a train passed. This was annoying. It was still more annoying later when, after spending all night burying the gelatine under a sleeper on the arch of the bridge and hiding the wires—it was the mud that made him take so long—Lawrence was signalled at dawn to run back under cover while a patrol went by; for, in that interval, a train, seen too late through the mists, steamed past at full speed.

Ali ibn el Hussein said that bad luck was with the expedition. For fear that someone would next be accused of having the evil eye, Lawrence suggested putting out new watching posts, north and south, and gave as a task to the remainder to pretend not to be hungry. Waiting in cold wind and rain, without food, was bad; the only half-consolation was that Allenby was being held up by the bad weather too, and the Arabs would be partners with him next year when the Revolt was riper.

At last a train was signalled; an enormously long train, the report was, coming very slowly. Lawrence had only a sixty-yard length of wire and so had to put the exploder quite near the line behind a small bush, where he waited in suspense for half an hour wondering why the train did not appear. The engine was apparently out of order and the long gradient made it

go very slowly on its wood fuel. At last it appeared. The first
ten trucks were open ones, full of troops, but it was too late
to choose; so when the engine was over the mine, Lawrence
pushed down the handle.

Nothing happened. He sawed it up and down four times.
Still nothing happened, and he realized that the exploder was
out of order and that he was kneeling behind a bush only a
foot high with a Turkish troop-train crawling past fifty yards
away. The Arabs were under cover two hundred yards behind
him, wondering what he was at; but he could not dash back
to them or the Turks would jump off the train and finish off
the whole lot. So he sat still, pretending to be a casual Arab
shepherd and, to steady himself, counting the trucks as they
went by. There were eighteen open trucks, three box-wagons
and three officers' coaches. The engine panted slower and
slower and he thought every moment that it would break
down. The troops took no particular notice of him, but the
officers came out on the little platforms at the ends of the
carriages, pointing and staring.

He was not dressed like a shepherd, with his gold circlet
and white silk robes, but he was wet and mud-stained, and
the Turks were ignorant about Arab costume. He waved innocently to them and the train slowly went on and disappeared
into a cutting farther north. Lawrence picked up the exploder
and ran. He was hardly in safety when the train finally stuck;
and while it waited for nearly an hour to get up steam again,
an officers' party came back and very carefully searched the
ground by the bush. However, the wires were well hidden;
they found nothing and, the engine picking up again, away
the whole lot went.

The Arabs were most unhappy. Bad luck was certainly with

them, grumbled the Serahin. Lawrence was sarcastic at their expense and a fight nearly started between the Serahin and the Beni Sakhr, who took Lawrence's part. Ali ibn el Hussein came running up. He was blue with cold and shaking with fever. He gasped that his ancestor, the Prophet, had given sherifs the faculty of second sight, and he knew that the luck was turning. That comforted them and the luck certainly began when, with no tool but his dagger, Lawrence forced the box of the exploder open and coaxed the electric gear into working order. All that day they waited, and still no train. It was too wet to light a fire and nobody wanted to eat raw camel; so they went hungry again. It was another cold, wet night: Lawrence spent it lying sleeplessly by the exploder, which he had re-connected with the wires.

Ali awoke next morning feeling better and cheered the party up. They killed a camel then and were about to light a fire with some half-dry sticks, warmed under a cloak all night, and shavings of the gelatine, when a train was signalled from the north. They left the fire and dashed to their positions. The train was racing downhill with two engines and twelve passenger-coaches. Lawrence arrived at the exploder just in time to catch the driving-wheel of the first engine. The explosion was terrific. He was sent spinning backwards. He righted himself and found that his left arm was badly gashed and his shirt ripped to the shoulder. Between his knees lay the exploder, crushed under a sooty piece of iron; close by was the horribly mangled body of the engine-driver. He hobbled back, half-conscious, with a broken toe, saying weakly in English: 'Oh, I wish this hadn't happened.' The Turks opened fire, and Lawrence fell. Ali ran forward to him with Turki and some servants and Beni Sakhr tribesmen. The Turks had the range

and hit seven of the rescuers in a few seconds; the rest picked
Lawrence up and hurried him into shelter. He secretly felt
himself all over and found that, besides the bruises and cuts
from flying boiler-plate, he had five different bullet wounds;
none were serious, but all uncomfortable. His clothes were
ripped to pieces.

The train was a wreck; both engines had fallen through
the broken bridge and were beyond repair. Three coaches had
telescoped, the rest were derailed. One was decorated with
flags—the saloon of the Turkish General commanding the
Eighth Army Corps. There had been four hundred troops on
board and the survivors, now recovered from the shock, were
under shelter and shooting hard under the eye of their Corps
Commander. The Beni Sakhr had grabbed some loot from the
train in the first rush—rifles, bags, boxes and some loose military medals from the saloon, but soon had to draw off. If
only there had been a machine-gun posted not a Turk would
have escaped. Adhub inquired for Fahad, and one of the Serahin said that he had been killed in the first rush; he showed
Fahad's belt and rifle in proof that he was dead and that he
and his friends had tried to save him. Adhub said nothing, but
ran to the rescue right among the Turks, and, by a miracle,
came back safely dragging Fahad, who was badly wounded
in the face but alive. The Turks began to attack then and the
Arabs, after giving them a volley which killed twenty men and
drove the rest back, drew off, firing as they went. Lawrence
could only go very slowly because of his hurts, but pretended
to Ali that he was interested in the Turks and studying them.
Turki, who was giving protecting fire from the ridges as they
went, got four bullets through his headcloth.

At last they reached their camels—now forty men instead

of sixty—and galloped eastward out of range. After five miles they met a friendly caravan with flour and raisins, and, halting under a barren fig tree, cooked their first meal for three days. There was camel meat, too, for one of the body-guard, Rahail, had remembered to bring a haunch along from their previous interrupted meal. There, Fahad and the other wounded men were attended to. The next day they went on to Azrak, showing their booty of rifles and medals and pretending that it was a victorious return and that they had done all that they had intended to do.

XXI

The weather had broken now finally and the Turks in Palestine were safe until the following year. Lawrence remained at Azrak with Ali ibn el Hussein and the Indians, and sent to Feisal for a caravan of winter supplies. It was a good place for preaching the Revolt and comfortable for the winter, once the ruined fort had been cleaned out and in part re-roofed. The Indian, Hassan Shah, took charge of the defence of the fort, mounting machine-guns in the towers and placing a sentry, an unheard-of thing in Arabia, at the postern gate. They settled down here with coffee-fires and story-telling, and Ali and Lawrence daily entertained the many visitors who came in to swear loyalty to the Revolt— Arab deserters from the Turks, Bedouin chiefs, head-men of peasant villages, Syrian-Arab politicians, Armenian refugees. There were also traders from Damascus with presents of sweetmeats, sesame, caramel, apricot paste, nuts, silk clothes, brocade cloaks, headcloths, sheepskins, patterned rugs and Persian carpets. In return the traders were given coffee, sugar, rice and rolls of cotton-sheeting, necessities of which the war had deprived them. The tale of plenty at Azrak would have a good political effect on Syria.

During this wet weather an opportunity came to Lawrence for having a look at the Hauran and in particular the Deraa district, the inevitable scene of the next Arab advance. For Tallal, the head-man of Tafas, a village in the Hauran, rode in one morning and consented to act as his guide. Tallal was a famous fighter, outlawed by the Turks, of whom he had killed twenty-three with his own hands. There was a price on his head but he was so powerful that he rode about as he pleased. He carried richly ornamented arms and wore a green cloth coat with silk frogs and a lining of Angora sheepskin. His other clothes were silk, his saddle was silver-mounted and he wore high boots. Under such guidance Lawrence had a safe and interesting trip round the vital railway junction which was to be the scene of heavy fighting in September, 1918. He seems, though, to have got into trouble on the return journey, after he had parted with Tallal, for he records his arrest by the Turks (who took him for a deserter from their army) and his punishment in custody for his refusal to obey an order given him by the military governor, a Turkish major. This incident, apparently, did permanent damage to his nerve, coming as it did after the grave disappointments of the bridge and train failures and the exhaustion of the last few months.

Back at Azrak, he heard the story of Abd el Kader. The mad fellow, after his desertion of the Yarmuk party, had gone in triumph to his villages, flying the Arab flag, his men firing joy shots behind him. The people were astonished and Jemal, the Turkish governor, went to him protesting against the insult. Abd el Kader received Jemal in pomp, remarking that the whole country was now under the rule of the Sherif of Mecca, who graciously, however, confirmed all the existing Turkish officials in their appointments! Next morning he made a second progress through the district. Jemal complained again and Abd el Kader drew his gold-mounted Meccan sword and swore to cut off his head. The Turks saw that he was quite mad and so disbelieved his story that a raid was intended that night on the Yarmuk bridge. Later they employed him again, as before his ride to Mecca, to have secret dealings with the Syrian Arab nationalists and then to betray them.

The weather was now worse than ever, with sleet, snow and continual gales. It was obvious that there was nothing but talking to be done in Azrak. Lawrence felt himself a fraud, teaching and preaching armed revolt to this foreign people while knowing the whole time that it was unlikely that they would ever benefit by their strongest efforts. And he disliked the Syrian townsmen with their compliments and servility as they came 'craving an audience' with their 'Prince and Lord and Deliverer.' He preferred the simple desert manners of men who would come bluntly up to him with their requests, shouting: 'Ho, Aurans! Do this for me.' He decided to go off again to see if he could do anything active against the Turks on the Dead Sea, He handed over his remaining money and the care of the Indians to Ali ibn el Hussein. They took an affectionate farewell, exchanging clothes in sign of intimate friendship, and on November twenty-third Lawrence rode off south, alone except for Rahail, the strongest of his followers.

He was making by night for Akaba across the wet plain and the going was fearful. The camels were continually falling with their riders until, after some hours, Lawrence halted in despair and they lay down in the mud and slept till dawn. They rode on the next day, caked with mud. About noon, to the north of Bair, they were suddenly fired at by four men who rushed shouting from ambush. They asked Lawrence's name, saying that they were Jazi tribesmen. It was a plain lie, for Lawrence saw that their camel-brands were of the Faiz tribe. They covered Lawrence and Rahail with their rifles at four yards' range and, jumping off their own camels, told them to do the same. It was to be murder, but Lawrence kept his head. He just laughed in their faces and remained in the saddle. This puzzled them. Then he asked the man who appeared to be their leader whether he knew his name. The Arab stared, thinking Lawrence mad, but came nearer, his finger on the trigger. Lawrence, covering him with a pistol under his cloak, bent down and whispered: 'It must be *Teras*' (that is, Seller of Women), 'for no other tradesman could be so rude.' It was an insult which in the desert meant instant death for the man who uttered it, but the Arab was too astonished to shoot. He took a step back, looking round to see if Lawrence had a large armed party near; for otherwise he could never have dared so to provoke an armed man. Then Lawrence turned slowly, calling to Rahail to follow, and rode off. The Arabs stood and watched them go and only recovered their senses when they were a hundred yards away. Then they fired and charged in pursuit, but Lawrence and Rahail were well mounted and escaped. The Faiz were a very shifty tribe. On one of Lawrence's rides in the previous summer—I believe the Damascus ride—he had been given hospitality by their chief, a prominent member of the secret freedom society. Asleep on the rich rugs of the guest-tent, he had been roused by a whispered warning under the tent-flap. It was one of the chief's brothers, telling him that messengers had been sent by his host to the nearest Turkish garrison. Lawrence only just escaped in time: the traitor died shortly afterwards, probably murdered by his own people for disgracing them.

They passed Bair the next night and reached Jefer at dawn, having come a hundred and thirty miles in thirty hours over bad country. Lawrence had fever heavy on him and kept going at this pace because he wanted to reach Akaba before a caravan, that had gone there from Azrak to bring back stores, started back again. He had long ceased caring what happened to his own body and was resolved to humble Rahail, who had for months been aggressively boasting of his strength and endurance, by riding him to a standstill. Before they passed Bair Rahail was begging for a halt; before they reached Jefer he was crying with self-pity, but softly lest Lawrence should hear him. Beyond Jefer they came on Auda's tents, stopping only for a greeting and a few dates, and then on again. Rahail was past protest and riding white-faced and

silent. They continued all that day and all the next night on their weary camels, crossing the railway. Lawrence's fever was dying down now and he fell into a trance in which he saw himself divided into different persons, one riding the camel, the others hovering in the air and discussing him. Rahail roused him at dawn, shouting that they had lost direction and were riding towards the Turkish lines at Aba el Lissan. They changed direction and reached Akaba by way of Rumm the following midnight.

To him at Akaba came urgent message from Allenby who had beaten the Turks in a series of battles, capturing Jaffa and the outskirts of Jerusalem, to report to him at once. Lawrence went by air, and arrived just in time to hear of the fall of Jerusalem. Allenby was too busy with news of victories to wish to hear details of the failure at the Yarmuk bridge, or to mind very much; a simple statement was enough. He kindly invited Lawrence to take part in the official ceremony of entry into

Jerusalem and Lawrence accepted, with a quick-change into British staff-officer's uniform with brass-bound hat and red tabs.

For the Akaba success, by the way, Lawrence had been made a major and gazetted a Companion of the Bath, but steadfastly refused to wear the ribbons and has never accepted these or any other decorations. He was recommended by the High Commissioner of Egypt for the Victoria Cross, instead, but the recommendation was, much to Lawrence's relief, refused. The Victoria Cross is not given for good staff-work or brainy leadership but for courage of the fighting sort. This courage was of course not admitted by Lawrence in his official report—he has never admitted it since—and the Victoria Cross could not in any case have been awarded, on technical grounds: 'No senior officer was present as witness.' The nearest senior officer was several hundreds of miles away on the right side of the Turkish lines. Lawrence's lieutenant-colonelcy came early in 1918, to put him on the same level as Lieutenant-Colonel Joyce who was graded as General Staff Officer, First Class, for liaison with the Arab Regular Army; Lawrence was General Staff Officer, First Class, for liaison with the Bedouin Arabs. It would not be correct to say that Lawrence accepted this rank; he just went on working, whatever they called him. The Distinguished Service Order to which he was gazetted was a present for the Tafileh battle of which an account is given a few pages ahead. His full-colonelcy Lawrence applied for himself (just after the capture of Damascus), much to the surprise of General Headquarters where his indifference to rank and awards was a standing joke. But he explained that he wanted the rank (special, temporary, acting and with all other possible qualifications) merely to secure for himself a berth on the staff-train through Italy which accepted no officers of lower rank than full colonels. He got his way. He called it his 'Taranto rank.'

So far as I know, he only once used the privileges of his rank for other than travelling. Once at a rest-camp he stopped to watch a bullying officer bawling at two wretched privates, battle- wearied men, who were passing on the far side of the barrack square: 'Come here, you two loungers! Take your hands out of your pockets! Why the hell didn't you salute me? Don't you know I'm a Major?' The poor fellows mumbled something. 'Now stand over there,' said the major, 'and let me see you march past and salute.' They obeyed and were walking off hurriedly when the major recalled them. 'Now come back and do it again properly.' They did it again. 'One moment, Major,' said a voice behind him; 'there is something you have forgotten.' The major wheeled round and saw a rather haggard-looking bareheaded boy in a tunic starred and crowned, on the shoulders, with badges of rank: Lawrence. The major saluted in confusion; the soldiers, happier now, were shuffling off, but Lawrence beckoned them to stop.

'The thing that you have forgotten, Major,' Lawrence went on gently, 'is that in this army the salute is paid not to the man but to the rank, and the officer saluted is ordered by the King, whom he represents, to return the salute. But of course you know that.' The major was speechless. 'You will therefore salute those men,' said Lawrence, 'whose salutes just now you failed to return.' The major saluted, choking with rage. But the merciless Lawrence continued: 'Major, those private soldiers saluted you twice. You will therefore return their salutes a second time.' And the Major had to obey. . . . This story recalls another: Lawrence, shortly after the War ended, was in Oxford Street, London, one night, walking head-down in the drizzling rain. He was pulled up by a lieutenant-colonel for not saluting him. The lieutenant-colonel was accompanied by a woman, obviously a new acquaintance. Lawrence slowly peeled off the badgeless rain-coat that he was wearing and showed his rank. The lieutenant-colonel grew red in the face. Lawrence said, 'You can go away.' . . . The woman went a third way.

To return. Allenby and Lawrence exchanged news and plans together. Allenby would be kept inactive until February, when he intended to push down to Jericho, which lies just north of the Dead Sea. Lawrence said that the Arab army could link up with him there if the daily fifty tons of supplies that were usually landed at Akaba were sent to Jericho instead. Akaba could be abandoned as a base now that there was no more danger from the Turks in that quarter (they had soon to withdraw from Aba el Lissan to trenches just outside Maan). Allenby agreed gladly. It was important for the Arabs to move up to Jericho, for on the way they could stop the food that was reaching the Turkish army from villages south of the Dead Sea, being taken up to the north end in boats from a little below Kerak in the south.

Back in Akaba with a month to wait before the move could begin, Lawrence decided to try the armoured cars in an experimental raid on the railway. They were now in Guweira, to which a motor-road had been built from Akaba by Egyptian labourers and the cars' crews; from thence it was an easy run across dry mud-flats to the railway near Mudowwara. The trip was a holiday for Lawrence; there was little danger because the cars were proof against machine-guns and rifles and went very fast. The expedition consisted of three armoured Ford cars mounted with machine guns, a half-battery of two ten-

pounder guns carried by three more cars, Talbots, and open
Rolls-Royces for scouting. The crews were all British and there
was bully-beef, biscuit and tea, with two warm blankets for
each man at night. Lawrence, with no Arabs about, was content to be as English as ever he had been and enjoyed for once
being present at a fight in which he had not to take the leading
part; he could stand on a hill watching through field-glasses.
It was these friendly outings with the Armoured Car and Air
Force fellows that persuaded him, even then, that his best
future, if he survived the War, was to enlist. The cars came up
close to a Turkish post at the station next above Mudowwara
and shelled and machine-gunned the trenches, but since the
Turks did not surrender and there was no Arab force handy
for charging, went off again to do the same at another station higher up. Lawrence only wanted to test the possibility
of using the cars against the railway and as they were clearly a
success came home to Guweira the same day.

The siege of Medina was still maintained in Central Arabia
by Feisal's brothers, Abdulla and Ali; Yenbo was being used
again as a base. Lawrence could not persuade the British
advisers there, who were still under the High Commissioner
of Egypt and not, like him, under Allenby, that there was no
point in making Medina surrender. And when they asked him
to cut the railway permanently at Maan because it was difficult for them to cut it where they were, he had to pretend
that the troops with him were too cowardly to attempt the
operation.

XXII

At Akaba Lawrence began increasing his body-guard, which had started with Farraj, Daud and the Syrians. (It may be as well to point out here that the names of most of the *subsidiary* characters in Lawrence's account, such as Farraj, Daud, Sergeants Lewis and Stokes and so on, are disguised. The names of the more important people such as Auda, Tallal, Colonel Wilson, are not.) It was advisable to do this because the price put on his head by the Turks—as also on Ali ibn el Hussein's—had risen to twenty thousand pounds. He chose followers who could live hard and ride hard, men proud of themselves and of good family. Two or three of these had joined him already and set a standard by which to judge new candidates. One day Lawrence was reading* in his tent when one of the Ageyl noiselessly entered. He was thin, dark, short, but most gorgeously dressed, with three black plaited love-locks hanging on each side of his face. On his shoulder he carried a very beautiful, many-coloured saddlebag. Greeting Lawrence

---

* It has been said that besides Malory, Aristophanes and *The Oxford Book of English Verse* he also carried Doughty's *Arabia Deserta*, but this is untrue, though his memories of the book were most helpful to him, in the absence of maps, for the first part of the campaign.

with respect, he threw the saddlebag on the carpet, saying: 'Yours,' and disappeared as-suddenly as he had come. The next day he brought a camel saddle with its long brass horns exquisitely engraved. 'Yours,' he said again. The third day he came empty-handed in a poor cotton shirt, to show his humility, and sank down as a suppliant, asking to enter Lawrence's service. Lawrence asked him his name. 'Abdulla the Robber,' he answered (the nickname was, he said, inherited from his honoured father), and told his story sadly. He had been born in a town of the Central Oases and when quite young had been imprisoned for impiety. Later he had left home in a hurry, owing to an unlucky scandal about a married woman, and taken service with the local Emir, Ibn Saud, the present ruler of Mecca. For hard swearing in this puritanical service, he had suffered punishment and deserted to the service of another Emir. Unfortunately, he had then come to dislike his officer so much that he struck him in public with a camel-stick. After recovering in prison from the terrible beating that he got for this, he had taken a job on the pilgrims' railway which was then being built. A Turkish contractor docked his wages for sleeping at midday and he retaliated by docking the Turk of his head. He was put into prison at Medina, escaped through a window, came to Mecca, and for his proved integrity and camel-manship was made carrier of the post between Mecca and Jiddah Here he settled down, setting his parents up in a shop at Mecca with the bribe-money that he alternately got from merchants and robbers. After a year's prosperity, he was waylaid and lost his camel and its consignment. His shop was seized in compensation. He joined the Sherif's camel police and rose to be a sergeant, but for his hard swearing and dagger-fighting was reduced again. On this occasion he accused a tribesman of the

Ateiba of bringing about his downfall through jealousy and stabbed the man in court in front of Feisal's cousin, Sharraf, who was trying the case. He nearly died of that beating. Then he entered Sharraf's service. When war broke out he became orderly to the captain of the Ageyl, but after the mutiny at Wejh, when the captain resigned and became an ambassador, the Robber missed the companionship of the ranks and now applied to enter Lawrence's service. He had a letter of recommendation from the captain. Lawrence read it. It said that Abdulla the Robber had been two years faithful but most disrespectful; that he was the most experienced of the Ageyl, having served every Prince in Arabia and having always been dismissed after stripes and prison for offences of too great individuality; that he was the best rider of the Ageyl, next to the writer of this letter, a great judge of camels and as brave as any son of Adam. Lawrence engaged him at once as captain of half the body-guard and never regretted it. This was only informal rank: his pay was the same as the rest.

Abdulla the Robber and Abdulla el Zaagi, the captain of the other half, a man of more normal officer type, examined all candidates for service between them, and a gang of desperate-looking villains grew about Lawrence: the British at Akaba called them cut-throats, but they only cut throats at Lawrence's order. Most of them were Ageyl, wonderful camel- masters who would call their beasts by name from a hundred yards away and make them stand guard over the baggage. Lawrence paid them six pounds a month and provided them also with their camels and rations; whereas the ordinary Arab in Feisal's ranks had to provide his camel out of the same pay. So Lawrence had the pick of the countryside at his disposal. They spent their wages chiefly in buying clothes of every possible colour—only they did not presume to wear white, which was what Lawrence himself always wore. They fought like devils with Turks and outsiders, but not among themselves. The Robber and El Zaagi kept them in order with punishments so severe that they would have been monstrous had not the men, who were at liberty to resign whenever they liked, taken a perverse pride in them. They had for Lawrence a blind, half-superstitious devotion, and in his service nearly sixty of them died. The bravest individual deed of the war was performed by one of them who twice swam up the subterranean water-conduit into Medina and returned with a full report of the besieged town. Lawrence had to live up to their standard of hardness. He had learned to keep himself fit by breaking all civilized habits, eating much at one time, then going without food for as many as four days and afterwards over-eating. The same with sleep—doing without it for days except for drowsy naps taken while still riding, and riding carefully, on long night journeys. The men with him suffered less than he did from the heat, but he less than they in the frost and snow of the short winter that they passed in the mountains. In physical endurance there was equality between them, but in spirit and energy he outdid them. Throughout the campaign, it goes almost without saying, Lawrence had a secret personal motive, stronger than patriotism, religion, personal ambition, love of adventure or of justice, in the light of which alone his extraordinary feats become intelligible. But shortly before the capture of Damascus this motive was, it seems, removed, and this is one explanation, I believe, of his coming so quickly away from the scene of his triumph, leaving the work of consolidating the Arab achievement to other hands; and of much that has happened to him since.

ABDULLA EL ZAAGI

from a drawing by Eric Kennington

On the eleventh of January, 1918, Nasir, the usual pioneer leader for Feisal, made an attack on Jurf, the nearest railway station to Tafileh, the group of villages commanding the south end of the Dead Sea. He took with him some Beni Sakhr tribesmen, some Arab regulars under Nuri Said (the chief-of-staff to General Jaafar, Feisal's commander-in-chief of the regular forces), a mountain-gun, and some machine-guns. They had luck in capturing the station, which the tribesmen camel-charged before Nuri Said intended them to, with a loss of only two killed. Two engines, the water-tower, the pump and the railway points were then blown up by the engineers. They took two hundred prisoners with seven officers and much booty, including weapons, mules and seven trucks of Damascus delicacies intended for the officers' messes at Medina. The regulars, mostly Syrians, then tasted olives, sesame paste, dried apricot and other sweets and pickles for the first time since they had left home three or four years before. There was also a whole truck of tobacco. When Feisal heard that the Medina garrison was now quite without anything to smoke, he was so sorry for the Turks, being a confirmed smoker himself, that he sent a number of pack-camels loaded with cheap cigarettes straying into their lines, with his compliments.

Lawrence was glad to see how well the army could manage without his personal direction. This was a raid merely, but Nasir and Lawrence soon followed it up by marching from Jefer to Tafileh with Auda and his tribesmen. Nasir appeared at dawn on a cliff above the valley, threatening to bombard the place if it did not surrender. It was only a bluff, because Nuri Said with the guns had gone back to the base, and the Turkish garrison may have known this. Supported by most of the villagers, they began to fire at the Howeitat, who spread out along the cliff and fired back. All except Auda. He rode in anger alone down the cliff-path, and reining in close to the houses bellowed out: 'Dogs, do you not know Auda?' When they heard the terrible name of Auda, the villagers' hearts failed them and they compelled the Turks to surrender.

Tafileh was a great anxiety to Feisal's brother Zeid, whom Feisal now sent up, with more guns and machine-guns, to take charge of the Dead Sea operations. Auda's Abu Tayi were in occupation alongside their former blood-enemies, another clan of Howeitat, the Motalga. The Motalga were twice as numerous as the Abu Tayi. Among them were two boys of good birth whose father had been killed by Auda's son, Annad. Auda pretended a great magnanimity towards these boys, forgiving them for Annad's death at the hands of their uncles. But they had not forgotten their dead father and muttered of further vengeance. Auda laughed at the boys and threatened to whip them round the market-place; so to stop further mischief Zeid thanked him for his services and paid him a large sum in gold; and Auda went back to his tents for a while. Things then quieted down in Tafileh, for Zeid had plenty of money to pay for the food he bought for the men, and the villagers, who had only sided with the Turks because some of their hated neighbours had sided with Feisal, consented to join in the Revolt.

Suddenly on the twenty-fourth of January came the news that the Turks were advancing from Kerak to retake the village. Lawrence was astonished and annoyed. Tafileh was no possible use to the Turks: their only hope of holding Palestine against Allenby was to keep every possible man for the defence of the River Jordan. Apparently the chance of surprising the Arabs for a change, instead of being surprised by them, was a temptation that

made them forget common-sense strategy. And it was a real surprise. The Turkish General in command of the Amman garrison
was in charge; he had with him about nine hundred infantry,
a hundred cavalry, twenty-seven machine-guns and two mountain howitzers. Their cavalry drove in the Arab mounted posts
guarding Tafileh on the north and by dusk were only about a
mile off. Zeid decided to give the village to the Turks and defend
the cliffs on the south side of the deep valley in which Tafileh lay.
Lawrence objected strongly. To give up the village meant antago-
nizing the villagers and, in any case, the southern cliffs were dangerous to defend because a Turkish force could slip round from
the railway on the east and cut off the defenders. Zeid listened to
Lawrence's advice and decided to hold the northern cliffs of the
valley, but not before most of the villagers had cleared out with
their movable goods in a midnight panic.

Tafileh was about four thousand feet above sea-level, and
it was freezing and blowing hard; Lawrence, who was up all
night seeing to things, was in a furious temper at the disturbance. He decided that the Turks should pay for their greedi-
ness and stupidity. He would give them the pitched battle that
they were so eager for and obligingly kill them all. This was the
one occasion in the War that Lawrence abandoned his principles of irregular mobility and fought a real battle, as a sort of
bad joke, on the ordinary easy textbook lines. Zeid, who was
a very cool young man and had learned much since his defeat
by the Turks before Rabegh fourteen months previously, let
Lawrence have his way.

There had been firing all night to the north. The local peasants were strongly resisting the Turks on the other side of the
northern cliffs, and Lawrence had sent the young Motalga chiefs
with whom Auda had quarrelled, to tell them to hang on, for

help was coming. The boys galloped off at once on their mares, with an uncle and about twenty relations, the most that could be rallied in the confusion, and the Turkish cavalry were held up till the morning. Then Lawrence started his battle in earnest.

First he sent forward Abdulla, a Mesopotamian machine-gun officer of Feisal's, with two automatic guns to test the strength and disposition of the enemy. He then found some of his body-guard turning over the goods lying in the street after the night's panic and helping themselves to whatever they fancied. He told them at once to get their camels and ride to the top of the northern cliffs by the long, winding road, and to bring another automatic gun. He took a short cut himself, climbing barefoot straight up the northern cliffs to the plateau at the top. There he found a convenient ridge about forty feet high which would do well for a defence position if he could find any troops to put there. At present he had nobody. But very soon he saw twenty of Zeid's Ageyl body-guard sitting in a hollow and by violent words managed to get them to arrange themselves on the ridge-top as if they were look-outs of a big force behind. He gave them his signet-ring to use as a token and told them to collect as many new men as they could, including the rest of his bodyguard.

Abdulla's arrival had encouraged the Motalga and the peasants; together they had pushed the Turkish cavalry from the ridge across the corner of a two-mile-wide plain, triangular in shape, with the ridge as its base, and over the nearer end of another low ridge that made the left-hand side of the triangle. At this second ridge the Arabs stopped and took up a defensive position, behind a rocky bank. Lawrence, who, from climbing up the cliff, was warmer than he had been, went forward towards them, across the plain, until he came under shell-fire. The Turkish main body, were shelling the ridge where the Arabs were, but the shrapnel that they were using was bursting far beyond in the plain. He met Abdulla on his way back to Zeid with news. Abdulla had lost five men and an automatic gun from shell-fire and had used up all his ammunition. He would ask Zeid to come forward with all the available troops. Lawrence was delighted and went on to the ridge.

When he reached it, the Turks had shortened the range and the shrapnel was bursting accurately overhead. Obviously some of the enemy must have come forward where they could get observation and signal back to the guns. He looked about and saw that the Turks were working round on the right of the ridge and would soon turn them out. There were about sixty Arabs at the ridge: the Motalga, dismounted, firing from the top, at the bottom sixty peasants on foot, blown and miserable, with all their ammunition gone, crying to Lawrence that the battle was lost. He answered gaily that it was only just beginning and pointed to the men on the reserve ridge, saying that the army was there in support. He told the peasants to run back, refill their cartridge belts and hold on to the reserve ridge for good.

The Motalga held the forward ridge for another ten minutes and had nobody hurt, but then had to leave in a hurry. They overtook Lawrence, who had started back before them since he had no horse, and one of the young chiefs lent him a stirrup to hold as he ran. Lawrence was counting his steps (it was a distraction from the pain of running with bare feet over sharp sticks and stones) to discover the exact range from the part of the ridge that they had just left to the reserve ridge. Here he found eighty men, and new ones were constantly arriving. The rest of his body-guard turned up with their automatic gun, and a hundred more Ageyl and two more guns. The Turks were occupying the ridge that the Motalga had just left, and to delay their attack Lawrence ordered the three automatic rifles to fire occasional shots. They were to fire short, so as to disturb the enemy, though not too much, and so make them delay their attack. It was just noon and Lawrence went to sleep for an hour or two, knowing that the Turks would do nothing for a while. In the middle of the afternoon Zeid arrived with the rest of the army—twenty men on mules, thirty Motalga horsemen, two hundred villagers, five more automatic guns, four machine-guns and an Egyptian Army mountain-gun which had been right through the campaign since the battle of the date-palms. Lawrence woke up to welcome them. He had all day long been making jokes about military tactics, quoting tags from the textbooks. At the ridge with the Motalga he had told the young chief that the great Clausewitz had laid it down that a rear-guard effects its purpose more by being than by doing. But the joke would have been lost on the boy, even had twenty Turkish machine-guns not been in action against the top of the ridge and distracted his attention. Now he had Turk-trained Arab regular officers to try his wit upon: he sent Rasim, Feisal's chief gunner but a cavalry leader for this occasion, to envelop the enemy's left wing, adding mock instructions to 'attack them upon a point, not a line. By going far enough along any finite wing, it will be found eventually reduced to a point consisting of a single man.' Rasim liked the joke and promised to bring back that man. With Rasim were five automatic guns and all the mounted troops, the Motalga horse, the mule-men and Lawrence's men on camels. The senior Motalga chief drew his sword and made a heroic speech to it, addressing it by name (every good sword in Arabia has a name, as in the

MAHMAS

from a drawing by Eric Kennington

days of European chivalry). They rode off under cover round the right-hand side of the triangular plain, where there was another ridge corresponding with the one that the Turks were occupying. They would take a few minutes to get round and meanwhile a hundred peasants arrived who were the herdsmen of this district: they had quarrelled with Zeid the day before about war-wages, but hearing of the fighting had generously sunk old differences and come up to help.

General Foch had somewhere advised attack only from one flank, but Lawrence decided to improve on him. He sent the herdsmen to work round on the left with three automatic guns. Knowing well every ridge and hollow, they managed to crawl unseen to within three hundred yards of the extreme Turkish right. The Turks had arranged their machine-guns in line right along the crest of the ridge with no post set out on either flank and no supports; it was lunacy. Lawrence, knowing the range, set four machine-guns to fire along the Turkish ridge-crest and keep the enemy busy. The crest was rocky and the flying chips of stone were as alarming as the bullets that scattered them.

It would soon be sunset and the Turks were losing heart at the unexpected resistance. 'Never have I seen rebels fight like this in my forty years of service,' said their general. 'The force must advance.' But he spoke too late. Rasim on the right and the herdsmen on the left attacked simultaneously and wiped out the crews of the machine-guns on each Turkish flank with a burst of fire from their automatics. That was the signal for the main body of the Arabs They charged forward, headed by Zeid's chief steward on a camel, his robes billowing in the wind, and the crimson standard of the Ageyl flapping over his head. Lawrence stayed behind with Zeid, who was clapping his hands for joy to see the Turkish centre collapse and stream back towards Kerak. Behind the Arabs followed a body of Armenian villagers, deported here some years before after the Turkish massacres; they were armed with long knives and howling for vengeance on the Turks.

Then Lawrence realized just what he had done: to avenge a personal spite against the Turks and to parody the usual farce of a regular battle, he had caused a wanton and useless massacre. And, worse, he had carelessly thrown away the lives of many of his Arab friends. It would have been quite possible to have refused battle, even without yielding the village, and by manœuvring about to have drawn the Turks into a trap from which they would have escaped with some loss and great irritation. But this was ghastly. The Turkish survivors were pouring down a steep defile back towards Kerak, with the whole force of Arabs in pursuit. It was too late now for Lawrence to run after and call the Arabs off, and he was too tired to try. In the end, only fifty exhausted Turks of the whole brigade got safely back. For though the Arab army did not pursue the broken enemy for more than a mile or two, the peasants farther along the Kerak road shot them down one by one as they ran.

The Arabs had captured the two mountain howitzers (very useful to them afterwards), the twenty-seven machine-guns, two hundred horses and mules, two hundred and fifty prisoners. But twenty or thirty dead Arabs were carried back across the cliff to Tafileh and the sight filled Lawrence with shame. Then it began to snow and the wind blew to a blizzard. Only very late and with great difficulty they got in their own wounded; the Turkish wounded had to lie out and were all dead the next day. The blizzard continued and Lawrence was unable to follow up his success. He amused himself by writing a report of the battle, in his boyish handwriting, to the

British Army Headquarters in Palestine. It was a parody, like the battle itself, and full of all the usual military catchwords used in official despatches. It was taken quite seriously. Lawrence was thought to be a brilliant young amateur doing his best to imitate the great models and the bad joke was turned against him by the offer of another military decoration, the Distinguished Service Order this time.

He partly regained his self-respect three days later by a far more important piece of work, which was the stopping of the transport of food up the Dead Sea, which Allenby had asked him to undertake. He had arranged with a chief of the Beersheba Bedouin, encamped near by, to raid the Turkish ships that were at anchor in a little port below Kerak at the southeast end of the Dead Sea. This was one of the two occasions in British military history when mounted men have fought and sunk a fleet. The Bedouin, in a sudden charge at dawn, surprised the sailors asleep on the beach, then scuttled the launches and lighters in deep water and looted the port. They took sixty prisoners, burned the storehouse, and came away without any loss to themselves.

Lawrence in making his report ironically countered the award of the military D.S.O. by recommending himself for a naval D.S.O., which has a different coloured ribbon. But this time Headquarters saw the joke; which he hammered away at later in a further ridiculous self-recommendation.

At Tafileh it was colder than ever and though there was food enough Lawrence could not stand the squalor of crowding with his twenty-seven men in two tiny rooms. It was the fleas and the painful smoke of green wood on the open fire, and the dripping mud roof. And his men's tempers. One of the Syrians who had given trouble before on the ride to the Yarmuk bridge had a dagger fight with Mahmas, a camel-driver. In Europe, Mahmas would have been called a homicidal maniac, so possibly it was not the guardsman's fault. If Mahmas was worsted in argument or laughed at, or even for a mere fancy, he would lean forward with his little dagger and rip the other man up. Three men at least he had killed so; once Lawrence had the unpleasant task of disarming him when he was running amok. After the War when Eric Kennington, who has edited the illustrations of this book, was in Transjordania drawing portraits of Arabs, one of the men he chose out, without knowing his history, was Mahmas. As he was working on the portrait he noticed the whites of Mahmas's eyes turning up queerly and his face going insane; and suddenly he was on Kennington with his dagger raised. Kennington pretended to pay no attention but stooped carelessly to pick up a piece of chalk. This saved his life. The madness died and Mahmas was as friendly as he had been before the attack. Kennington sketched in the dagger as a comment on the occasion.

For his fight—quarrelling in the guard was an unforgivable offence—Mahmas was heavily whipped by El Zaagi, his captain, so was the other contestant. Lawrence, in the next room, could not endure the noise of the blows after his Deraa experience and stopped El Zaagi before he had gone very far. Mahmas was weeping before the punishment started and when it was over was in disgrace as a coward. To the Syrian, who had endured without complaint, Lawrence gave an embroidered silk headcloth next morning for his faithful services; but did not tell the man the real reason of the gift. After this, Lawrence decided to scatter his body-guard among the other houses. The men were too high-spirited to be shut up together in two small rooms with nothing to do. He went off himself on a journey to get the gold that Zeid would need, when the fine weather came, for enrolling the new tribesmen through whose territory the Arabs were to advance.

On the fourth of February, 1918, Lawrence started towards Akaba with five men, on camels, across the hills; a most painful ride in bitter cold and whirling snow. At a night halt in the shelter of the rock the four men with him, lying on the frozen ground beside their camels, resigned themselves to death. They would not speak or move when he called to them and he could only rouse them by pulling one of them up by the love-locks, which startled him painfully to life, and the others then woke up too. From Feisal in Akaba he got thirty thousand pounds in gold, two attendants of the Ateiba tribe and a party of twenty men under a sheikh to carry the gold. The gold was in £1,000 bags, each bag weighing about twenty-two pounds. Two were enough weight for each camel, swung on either side of the saddle. They had hardly started before the sheikh stopped for hospitality at the tent of a friend and said that perhaps he and his men might come on with Lawrence the next day, if the weather improved. Lawrence knew what delay this would mean and decided that the best way to get the party moving for sure the next day was to ride on ahead and shame them into following. So he went forward with his own attendants. The wind blew so bitter, that the men, who, being from Central Arabia, had never experienced cold like this before and now saw snow for the first time in their lives, thought from the pains in their lungs that they were strangling. The party rode behind the hill where old Maulud and his regulars were besieging the Turks at Maan: for Lawrence wanted to spare his men the unhappiness of passing a friendly camp without a halt.

Maulud's men had been here for two solid months in dug-outs on the side of the hill. Their only fuel was wet worm-wood, on which they with difficulty baked bread every other day. They had no clothes but khaki drill uniform; and when Feisal's supply officer had applied on their behalf to Egypt for ordinary khaki serge the answer had been that Arabia was a tropical country and that therefore only tropical kit could be issued. Nor could he get them sufficient army boots. (The reg-ulars got boots, most of them. The irregulars did not, though their need was as great.) They slept in wet verminous pits on empty flour sacks, six or eight huddled together in a bunch to make their few blankets go as far as possible. More than half of them died or were broken in health by the cold and wet. But Maulud, by his great heart, somehow kept the survivors in their places, daily exchanging shots with the Turks. Their camp was four thousand feet above sea-level.

Lawrence's journey grew worse, with frequent falls and a wind so violent that they could do no more than a mile an hour against it. They had frequently to dismount and pull the camels up mud-banks and through icy streams. After many hours the men flung themselves, weeping, on the ground and refused to go farther, so they camped there for the night in the slush between their camels. The next day, coming on a Howeitat camp, the two Ateiba tribesmen refused to go far-ther with Lawrence. They said that it would be death. Law-rence called them cowards and swore that he would go the rest of the journey alone with their four bags of gold, in addition to his own two. He had a very fine cream-coloured camel, by name Wodheiha, who saved his life that day: she refused to take a short cut over some frozen mud-flats, but, when he fell through the cat-ice and got bogged to the waist, came

close so that he could pull himself out by grabbing at her fet-
lock. He did ten miles that afternoon, travelling all the time,
and stopping the night at an old Crusaders' castle where a
friendly chief was encamped. The old man was hospitable but
mentioned, as he blessed the meal, that the next day his two
hundred men must starve or rob, for they had neither food
nor money and his messengers to Feisal were held up by the
snow. Lawrence immediately gave him five hundred pounds
on account until his subsidy came.

In the morning he rode out again on the last stage of his
journey to Tafileh. With him came two men from the castle
as escort, but they soon deserted him and he went on alone.
That afternoon, climbing uphill through snowdrifts that completely hid the path, Wodheiha grew very tired, missed her
footing and slipped eighteen feet, with Lawrence, down the
steep hill-side into a frozen snowdrift. After the fall she rose
trembling and stood still. He was afraid that she had come to
the end of her strength and vainly tried to tow her out, up to
his neck in snow. Then he hit her from behind but could not
budge her. He mounted her and she sat down. He jumped off
and heaved her up, wondering if the drift was too deep for
her. With his bare hands and feet he scooped her a road. The
crust was sharp and cut his wrists and bare ankles till they bled
over the snow, but he carried the little road back to the path,
mounted Wodheiha again and rushed her successfully up the
hill-side. They went on cautiously, Lawrence sounding the path
with his stick or digging new roads through the deeper drifts.
In three hours they were on the mountain-ridge overlooking
the valley of the Dead Sea. Thousands of feet below he could
see village-gardens green and happy in their summer-like
weather. Towards evening Wodheiha balked at a snow-bank

and he was afraid that she would not manage it this time and would have to be left there to die. So he led her back a hundred yards and charged her over at a canter. The other side of the bank was slippery, having been exposed to the sun all the afternoon. Wodheiha lost her footing and went slithering down on her tail, with locked legs, for about a hundred feet; Lawrence still in the saddle. There were stones under the snow and she sprang up in rage, lashing her tail, then ran forward at ten miles an hour, sliding and plunging down the path towards the nearest mountain-village. Lawrence was clinging to the saddle, in terror of broken bones. Some men of Zeid's were weather-bound at this village, and came out much amused at the distinguished entry. Lawrence made the last eight miles to Tafileh in safety, gave Zeid some money and his letters and went gladly to bed.

He went forward the next day to plan out the Arab advance to Kerak and so along the eastern side of the Dead Sea. The weather was improving and he was reassured that the steps of the advance would be easy. Jericho was still in Turkish hands, but would soon fall, and it would be as well to go forward at once to threaten the Turkish left flank on the eastern bank of the Jordan. He came back and told Zeid of his plans. But the Tafileh district had seen too many changes in the fortune of the Arab Revolt to decide on any more risks on its behalf. Zeid had to confess that to arrange a further advance was beyond his powers.

This was a facer for Lawrence, who had promised Allenby to fulfil a certain programme by certain dates and had drawn special credits for the operation. His scheme was now breaking down, not for military reasons, but because of a defect in propaganda, for the purpose of which Lawrence was attached to Feisal's head-quarters. It therefore reflected personally upon him.

There was nothing for Lawrence to do but go at once to Allenby at his Headquarters at Beersheba, confess to failure and resign. He started late the same afternoon with four men, cutting straight across country, first down five thousand feet from the Tafileh hills and then up three thousand feet into Palestine. At Beersheba he met his old friend, Hogarth, and explained the whole business to him. That his breakdown should have been with Zeid, a little man whom he liked, put a finishing touch to his general feeling of exhaustion. Lawrence went on to complain that never since he landed in Arabia had he been given an order, never anything more than requests and options. He was tired to death of free-will and responsibility, all he wanted now was to resign and be given a job in which he was not compelled to think or act for himself; any routine job would do. Also he had for the last year and a half ridden something like a thousand miles a month on camels, not to mention thousands of miles more in crazy aeroplanes and jolting cars. In each of his last five fights he had been wounded and he now so dreaded further pain that he had to force himself to go under fire. He had generally been hungry, and lately always cold. Frost and dirt had poisoned his wounds to a mass of festering sores. And the guilt of the fraud on the Arabs and of the deed of Tafileh was heavy on his mind.

However, it was not to be. Hogarth took him to the head of the Arab Bureau, who refused to let him resign. The Imperial War Cabinet was counting on Allenby to end the deadlock in the West by winning the war in the East. If Allenby could take Damascus and possibly Aleppo, Turkey would be forced to surrender and that might encourage Austria and Bulgaria to follow suit; the Germans could not then hold out longer. But Allenby could not win his war without a protected right flank and Lawrence was the only man with enough control of the Arabs to give him this. The matter of a few paltry thousand pounds was not going to stand in the way of victory. So he was actually ordered this time to take up the task, and quietly accepted the inevitable.

Allenby wanted to know whether Lawrence could still link up with him at Jericho, which had just been taken, and so continue the advance north to Amman. Lawrence said that he could not manage at present without a great deal of help. The first trouble was Maan, which was holding up the Arab Army. Maan must be taken and, now that the time had come, the pilgrims' railway must be permanently cut. The Arab Army could do it but would want seven hundred baggage camels for transport, also money, more guns, more machine-guns and protection from a counter-attack from Amman. Allenby promised all this, and Lawrence promised in return that when Maan fell the Arab Army would move up to Jericho and join in Allenby's great advance on Damascus from the Mediterranean Coast to the Dead Sea.

He went to Feisal at Akaba and explained that the Arabs would now soon be driven out of Tafileh by the Turks, but that Tafileh did not matter. Amman and Maan were the only important points from now on and a Turkish force in Tafileh would actually waste the Turkish strength. Feisal, anxious for Arab honour, sent a warning message to Zeid, but without avail; for six days later the Turks drove him out of the place.

XXIII

Spring had come and the war was starting again in earnest. The Arab army was now very well provided with transport and everything else it wanted except enough guns; it had a special branch of Allenby's staff to look after its interests, under Colonel Dawnay. He was the only British officer, Lawrence writes, who ever learned to understand the difference between national revolt, with the irregular fighting it entailed, and modern warfare between large regular armies, and to keep the two going together without confusion.

The plan that was worked out for the taking of Maan was for the armoured cars to go to Mudowwara and permanently cut the railway there while the Arab regulars seized the railway, a day's march north of Maan, and compelled the Turkish garrison to come out to fight if they would not starve. The Arab regulars were now easily a match for the Turks and would have the help of irregulars on their flanks. Feisal and Jaafar liked the plan but, unfortunately, the other officers wanted to make a direct assault on the town and old Maulud wrote to Feisal protesting against British interference with Arab liberty. Then, though the supplies, arms, pay and transport were all now being supplied by the British, Lawrence and Dawnay saw that it would be wise to give the Arabs their way even if it was a foolish way. The Arabs were volunteers in a far truer sense than the British Army, in which enlistment by every able-bodied man had now for some months, though 'deemed voluntary,' been in fact compulsory; (for, as Lord Carson said with perhaps unconscious humour, 'the necessary supply of heroes must be maintained at all costs'). Arab service was literally voluntary, for any man was at perfect liberty to return home whenever he liked.

A large number of the Arab irregulars were going to Atara, seventy miles due north of Bair, there to wait for news of Allenby's attack on Amman, fifty miles to the north-west. Lawrence went, too, with his body-guard. On the fourth of April the army started with its train of two thousand baggage camels and reached Atara four days later without loss. At the crossing of the railway, Lawrence happened to be ahead of his body-guard. It was near sunset and everything seemed peaceful enough; but as he rode up the embankment the camel's feet scrambled in the loose ballast and out of the long shadow of a culvert on the left, where no doubt he had slept all day, rose a Turkish soldier. He looked wildly at Lawrence, who had a pistol in his hand, and then with sadness at his own rifle yards away out of reach. Lawrence stared at him and said softly, 'God is merciful.' The Turk knew the sense of the Arabic phrase and a look of incredulous joy came over his fat, sleepy face. However, he made no answer. Lawrence pressed the camel's shoulder with his foot; she went carefully over the metals and down the bank on the other side. The Turk had enough good feeling not to shoot him in the back, and he rode away with the warmth of heart that a man always has towards a life he has saved. When, at a safe distance, he looked back, the

Turk had his thumb to his nose and was twinkling his fingers in farewell.

At Atara everything was green and fresh with spring, and the camels were enjoying themselves greatly. News came that Amman was taken; the Arabs were making an immediate move farther north to join them, but further reports said that the British had been driven out again with heavy losses. Lawrence, who had lately impressed on the Arabs that the British never failed in their attacks, refused to believe the story, but it was true. Major Buxton's battalion of English camel-corps had taken the town, but the Australian cavalry, who were to have attacked on his right, had their animals so wearied after the fighting at the Jordan- crossing and a long march over the central mountain range, that they were forced to leave Buxton to carry on the battle on his own. He was driven out with a loss of over half his force and a second attack the next day had to be called off; other British troops that came up to help him had, as one of their officers has informed me, been drinking too much ration-rum on empty stomachs.

This meant no advance for the Arabs. They turned south. But first Lawrence went spying into Amman in company with three gipsy women and Farraj disguised, like himself, as one of them. He had a good look round and decided that the place should be left alone as too strong for Arab attack. As they were returning some Turkish soldiers stopped them and made love to them; they only escaped by running away at top speed. Lawrence decided in future to use British khaki uniform again as the best disguise because too brazen to be suspected. Farraj was a changed person. Daud had died of the cold and wet that terrible winter, and Farraj went about heavy-eyed and restless, alone. He took greater care than ever of Lawrence's camel, saddles and clothes, and of the coffee-making, but never made another joke and began praying regularly three times a day. A week after this Amman visit he was himself dead, being mortally wounded in a mounted raid against a Turkish railway-patrol.

They then rode down towards Maan to see how the attack there was getting on. The Arabs had done well; under Jaafar they had cut the line north of Maan, destroying a station and three thousand rails; and south of Maan Nuri Said had accounted for another station and five thousand rails. They were making an attack now on Maan itself. Lawrence came upon old Maulud badly wounded, his thigh-bone splintered above the knee; but he called to Lawrence in a weak voice from the litter, 'Thanks be to God, it is nothing. We have taken Semna.' 'I am going there,' said Lawrence. Semna was the crescent-shaped hill overlooking Maan from the west, and Maulud, though hardly able to see or speak for exhaustion, craned over the side of the litter to point backwards to the hill and explain the best way of defending the place against counter-attack. Two days later, when Auda's Abu Tayi had taken two Turkish posts on the farther side of the station and Jaafar, now in command, had massed his guns on the south, Nuri Said led an attack on the railway station. They captured it, but unfortunately the ammunition of the artillery covering their advance gave out and the station was retaken. This was disappointing, but the Arab troops had behaved so well under machine-gun fire and made such good use of ground, that it was clear that they could be used safely in future without a stiffening of British troops. This discovery was something to set off against defeat.

The next move was against the eighty miles of railway north

of Mudowwara. Colonel Dawnay was in charge of the attack which was to be made by the armoured cars, with aeroplanes to drop bombs and Egyptians and Arab tribesmen to do the hand-to-hand fighting. He issued formal typewritten opera- tion-orders with map references and an accurate programme of times and objectives. This rather amused Lawrence, whose fighting hitherto had all been of the careless verbal sort, ('Let's attack that place over there; you go round this way and I'll go round the other, and afterwards we'll blow something up if we can'), and who did not regard the present operations as on a big enough scale to justify the use of the typewriter.

As Dawnay knew no Arabic, Lawrence came along as interpreter to look after the tribesmen and the Egyptians. He knew that one misunderstanding would spoil the delicate balance of the Arab Front and that such misunderstandings would be bound to occur unless somebody responsible was continually on the watch. As he was himself about the only man intimate enough with the Arabs to be ceaselessly with them without boring them into sulks, he tried to god-father every mixed expedition. The programme worked out exactly except that the Turks at the post north of the first station to be attacked surrendered ten minutes too soon and that the Arab tribesmen who took the south post did not advance in alternate rushes with covering fire, as they were expected, but made a camel-charge, steeple-chasing across the Turkish breastworks and trenches. Then the station itself surrendered and the Arabs enjoyed the maddest looting of their history. Lawrence himself broke his no-looting rule by taking off the brass station-bell (which, after the War, I once heard him ring out of his window in the quadrangle of All Souls College at Oxford, to wake up someone he wanted in the place). He was called in to settle a dangerous dispute about loot between the Arabs and the Egyptians. However, this was arranged, for nearly all the Arabs were, for once, completely satisfied with what they had got. They moved off home; only a few faithful ones were left behind for the attack on the next station. These few were rewarded. There was no fighting—the Turks had run away—and plenty of loot; so they praised themselves loudly for their loyalty. Mudowwara itself was the next objective, but there was a troop-train in the station and the Turks opened on the armoured cars with accurate gun-fire at four miles' range, so the attack was not pressed. Meanwhile, Lawrence and Hornby in Rolls-Royces were running up and down the line, blowing up bridges and rails. They used two tons of gun-cotton. Lawrence visited the place south of Mudowwara where he had mined his first train, and destroyed the long bridge under which the Turkish patrol had slept on that adventurous day in the previous September.

Mohammed el Dheilan (the victim of Auda's pearl-necklace story) and the Abu Tayi tribesmen then took five more stations between Maan and Mudowwara and so eighty miles of line were cut beyond repair. That settled the fate of Medina, four hundred miles to the south.

Early in May Lawrence went up to Palestine to discuss the future with Allenby, leaving the Arabs and English to make another eighty-mile break north of Maan. On arrival he found to his disgust that Allenby's chief of staff had decided on a raid against Salt, with the help of Beni Sakhr tribesmen. This was trespassing on Lawrence's ground, and clumsy trespassing. He asked who was to lead the Arab forces and was told: 'Fahad, at the head of twenty thousand tribesmen.' It was ridiculous. Fahad was never able to raise more than four hundred of his own clan and, in any case, he had now moved south to help the new operations just above Maan. Some of his greedy relations must have ridden over to Jerusalem to screw money out of the English by giving these impossible promises. Of course no Beni Sakhr appeared and the raid miscarried with heavy losses; the survivors only just escaped being cut off and captured.

The Arabs now found that there were disadvantages as well as advantages in being tied to the English. Allenby could not make his intended great attack because the Germans had begun their last big offensive and his best troops were being taken from him and hurried to France to save a breakthrough. The Arabs had to wait, too, until new troops reached Allenby from India and his army was reorganized—a delay of perhaps four or five months. Meanwhile Allenby was lucky if he could hang on to his Jerusalem-Jaffa line. He told Lawrence so on May the fifth, the very day chosen for the great joint advance north. It was bad news for the Arabs besieging Maan with forces only half the size of the garrison. Maan was well supplied with stores and ammunition—the Turks had sent down a supply column of pack animals—and now that the pressure from the English was relaxed, big forces of Turks would probably come down from Amman, raise the siege and push the Arabs out of Aba el Lissan.

However, Allenby said that he would do his very best for Lawrence in helping the Arab army in every way but with men. He promised repeated aeroplane raids on the railway and these turned out most useful in hindering the Turks in their advance. As Allenby was giving Lawrence tea that day, he happened to remark that he was sorry that he had been forced to abolish the Imperial Camel Brigade, which was in

MULE TRANSPORT NEAR ABA EL LISSAN
Copyright French Army Photo. Dept.

Sinai, but men were short and he had to use them as cavalry up at Jerusalem. Lawrence asked what was going to be done with the camels. Allenby told him to ask the Quartermaster-General. So Lawrence left the tea-table and went to the Quartermaster-General's office with the question. The Quartermaster-General, who was very Scotch, answered firmly that the camels were needed as transport for one of the new divisions which were on their way from India. Lawrence explained that he wanted two thousand of them. The Quartermaster-General answered briefly that he might go on wanting. So Lawrence went back and said aloud at the tea-table that there were for disposal two thousand two hundred riding camels and thirteen hundred baggage camels. All, he said, were earmarked for transport, but of course *riding camels were riding camels!* The staff whistled and looked wise, as if they doubted whether riding camels could carry baggage. Lawrence had known that a technicality might be useful, even a sham one, for every British officer had to pretend that he understood animals, as a point of honour. So he was not surprised that night at dinner to find himself on one side of Allenby, with the Quartermaster-General on the other.

With the soup, Allenby began to talk of camels, and the Quartermaster-General immediately said how lucky it was that the Indian Division's transport would now be brought up to strength by the disbanding of the Camel Brigade. It was a bad move; Allenby cared nothing for strengths. He turned to Lawrence and said with a twinkle: 'And what do you want them for?' Lawrence answered hotly: 'To put a thousand men into Deraa any day you please.' Now Deraa junction (the secret of whose weakness against surprise Lawrence had bought at great cost to himself) was the nerve-centre of the

Turkish army. Its destruction would cut off, from Damascus and Aleppo, both the line south to Amman and Maan and the line east to Haifa and Northern Palestine. So Allenby turned to the Quartermaster-General again and smilingly said: 'Q, you lose.'

It was a princely gift, for now the Arab army could move about freely far from its base and could win its war when and where it pleased. Lawrence hurried back to Feisal, who was at Aba el Lissan, and teased him by first talking at length about histories, tribes, migrations, the spring rains, pasture, and so on. At last casually he mentioned the gift of two thousand camels. Feisal gasped with delight and sent his slave running for Auda, Zaal, Fahad, and the rest of his chiefs. They came in anxiously asking: 'Please God, is it good?' He answered with shining eyes: 'Praise God!' The chiefs heard the news with astonishment and looked at Lawrence, who said: 'The bounty of Allenby.' Zaal spoke for them all: 'God keep his life and yours.' Lawrence replied: 'We have been made victorious.' The chiefs were as delighted as Feisal.

But before the camels could be used against Deraa the nearer danger must be settled. There was a big Turkish force gathering at Amman for the relief of Maan. Nasir was asked to delay it by another big breach of the railway at Hesa, half-way between the two towns. He succeeded by the old method of blowing up bridges north and south, the night before, and at dawn bombarding the station, with a camel-charge to follow. As usual, there were no losses at all. Hornby and others with explosives then hurriedly demolished fourteen miles of railway.

This was excellent: the Turks would be delayed at least a month and it would be the end of August before they could patch up the railway just north of Maan and be ready to attack Aba el Lissan. By that time, for it was now early June, Allenby would be nearly ready to advance again and the Turks might not dare to make the attempt. The Arab forces could then be divided into three main parties: a thousand cam-el-men to take Deraa, and two or three thousand infantry to join up with Allenby at Jericho, the remainder to continue to keep watch above Maan. Lawrence decided to get Sherif Hussein, as nominal commander-in-chief of the Arab armies, to send Feisal all the regular troops besieging Medina under his brothers, Abdulla and Ali. Medina was in a pitiful state now, with short rations and scurvy, cut off from Damascus by the railway-breach between Maan and Mudowwara, and needed no more harrying; while the Arab troops were urgently needed for the advance north. But the old man was jealous of Feisal's success and made difficulties. Lawrence went down to Jiddah to talk him over, bringing letters from Feisal, Allenby and the High Commissioner of Egypt, the Sherif's paymaster. But the Sherif, pleading the fast of Ramadan, retired to Mecca, a holy place where Lawrence could not follow him. The Sherif consented to talk over the telephone, but sheltered himself behind the incompetence of the Mecca exchange whenever he did not like the conversation. Lawrence, in no mood for farce, rang off and came away.

Allenby was going to begin his attack on September the nineteenth and, to make sure that the Turks did not begin their move on Aba el Lissan before it started, something new was needed. Dawnay was then inspired to remember the sur-viving battalion of the Imperial Camel Corps, the one that had been in the Amman raid, three hundred men under their capable officer, Major Buxton. Allenby's chief-of-staff agreed to lend this battalion to the Arabs for a month, on two conditions: the first that a scheme of operations should be provided, the second—a quaint one—that there should be no casualties. The actual operation-orders made out by Dawnay and Lawrence are, as a matter of interest, to be found in an appendix at the end of this book.

Buxton's march was to be the diversion; three weeks later the real blow was to be struck at Deraa. Lawrence calculated that the two thousand new camels would supply the necessary transport for five hundred Arab mule-mounted regulars, the battery of French quick-firing mountain-guns that had at last been sent from Suez, machine-guns, two armoured cars, engineers, camel-scouts and two aeroplanes. They would strike at Deraa, destroying the junction and paralysing the Turkish communications three days before Allenby launched his attack. Allenby had said that he would be content if 'three men and a boy with pistols' were before Deraa on September the sixteenth. This expedition was a liberal interpretation of the phrase. The arrangements for equipping this force would be made by the British officers at Akaba, while Lawrence went off with Buxton.

Of the part played by Lawrence in relation to these British officers, one of them, Major Young, has written clearly enough:

> 'The British officers who were helping the Arabs were at first all under political control, but as soon as the revolt took definite military shape a special liaison staff was formed at Allenby's Headquarters to deal with what were known as the Hejaz operations and a number of officers were attached to the Arab forces. Dawnay was officially the chief staff officer of

the Hejaz liaison staff (the telegraphic name for which was "Hedge- hog"), just as Joyce was officially the senior British officer with Feisal's army. But Lawrence really counted more than either of them with Allenby and Feisal. He used to flit backwards and forwards between the two as the spirit moved him.

'Besides being helped with munitions and rations Feisal was lent five armoured cars, a flight of aeroplanes, two 10-pounder guns mounted on Talbot cars, a detachment of twenty Indian machine-gunners, a section of French Algerian gunners armed with four "65" mountain-guns, an Egyptian Army battalion for guard duties at Akaba, and later on a detachment of the Egyptian Camel Corps and a company of the Egyptian Camel Transport to help him with his transport. All these were under the command of Joyce . . . whose staff consisted of a chief staff-officer, a base-commandant for Akaba, a combined supply and ordnance officer, two medical officers and a works officer. Others drifted in and out helping with demolitions, ciphering and deciphering telegrams, landing stores, pegging down wire roads in the sand and doing a hundred other odd jobs.

'Mr. [Lowell Thomas]'s cinema pictures were a triumph of journalistic composition. But they depicted only the earlier Lawrence of the heroic period and wrongly credited him with doing single-handed the whole of the later work of "Hedge-hog" and of Joyce and the British staff. I came too late, so that I practically never saw the real Elizabethan Lawrence who characteristically drew back into his shell during that

long period of preparation after the taking of Akaba.
Like the Bedouin with whom he rode he held aloof
from regular soldiers and everything that they did. At
the same time it is bare justice to give him the chief
credit for the whole series of Arab operations which
ended in the setting up of Arab rule in Damascus.'

To this account it should be added that Colonel Joyce,
the senior British adviser to Feisal since Newcombe had
been captured on a raid in Southern Palestine, was officially
Lawrence's superior officer throughout the campaign. He
acted as commandant at Akaba until the work at the port
became too heavy to be combined with his front-line duties,
when he appointed a major from Egypt, Scott, to take on
the duty. The Arab affair was run with great economy of
British helpers; it was Lawrence's policy to let it be managed
with only one-twentieth of the staff that a more formal side-
show would have expected. It was Joyce who decided on the
main policy of the Revolt when Lawrence was off on raids
or making plans for advances. Lawrence acted as his chief
source of intelligence.

The supply and ordnance officer was Captain Goslett (who
took one or two of the photographs in this book). His view of
the Arab campaign was a very different one from Lawrence's.
The supply-question covered all Feisal's supporters for hundreds of miles around, and was enormous. There were also
huge trade-imports at Akaba, not directly concerned with
the campaign, for the carriage and regulation of which he
was responsible. Goslett was (and is again) a London busi-
ness-man, whose organizing ability and patience were put to
a most severe test. There were some hundreds of English at

Akaba, but except for the Armoured-Car men they were not there for fighting. They suffered no casualties, except for the death of a corporal who was accidentally killed while doing amateur police-work on his own.

To encourage the regular Arab officers by recognizing their great services in the fighting about Maan and against the railway, Allenby distributed decorations. Jaafar, the commander- in-chief, was given a C.M.G., and Allenby delighted him by providing, as a guard of honour for the ceremony, the same troop of Dorset Yeomanry that had gained great credit two years before by galloping him down in the Senussi desert and taking him prisoner. Jaafar had also won the German Iron Cross in 1915. This double event in a single war is possibly a unique performance.

During these months of planning, Lawrence had not (in spite of Major Young's account) interrupted his active adventures. One strange ride in July took him to Kerak, Themed and Amman, all held by Turkish troops. He was inspecting the ground for the coming Arab advance to Jericho. At Kerak, where he arrived at midnight with a party of camel-men, the Turks were terrified and locked themselves into their barracks, expecting the worst. But nothing happened. The sheikh with Lawrence merely swore that he was hungry and had a sheep killed and cooked for him by the villagers. Later, in the pitch-dark, they stumbled over some Turkish cavalry watering at a stream, and were fired on. Lawrence protested with fluent Turkish curses and the Turks replying bad-temperedly with a few more shots drew off.

Everywhere he went there was Arab hospitality, guestings and coffee-fires at which he preached revolt, until he had made sure of all the clans in the ladder of his advance. On the way back, the party was mistaken for Turks by some British aeroplanes which, swooping low, emptied drum after drum of Lewis-gun ammunition at them. Fortunately, the shooting was bad. (Later, in reporting the affair to Air Vice-Marshal Sir Geoffrey Salmond, Lawrence ironically recommended himself for the Distinguished Flying Cross, 'for presence of mind in not shooting down two Bristol Fighters which were attempting to machine-gun my party from the air.' He had made the regulation signal agreed upon for such cases; and had twenty automatic rifles in the party.) As soon as the aeroplanes had disappeared, a party of Turkish policemen tried to chase them.

Next day, near Jurf, where Lawrence was going to inspect the ground for an attack by Arab regulars—Jurf was the only water-supply for the Turks on that part of the line—much worse happened. A party of mixed horse and foot from the railway cut off his retreat and more troops appeared in front. There was no escape and the Arabs with Lawrence, taking cover, resolved to hold out to the last. Lawrence, half-glad, saw that all was over. He decided to imitate Farraj and end it quickly. He rode alone against the enemy. The mounted Turks came forward to meet him, finger on trigger, calling out 'Testify!' He answered: 'There is no god but God; and Jesus is a prophet of God'—a queer statement which no Mohammedan could make, and yet no Christian could make either; the sort of tactless thing that a nervous man might blurt out by mistake. They did not shoot; they gasped, stared and cried out: 'Aurans!' They were friends, a party of Arab regulars, raiding the railway, but dressed in the uniforms of slain Turks and mounted on captured horses. Their rifles, too, were Turkish. They had never seen Lawrence before and had mistaken his party for members of an unfriendly Arab tribe with whom they had just been fighting.

The following letter was written by Lawrence from Cairo on the fifteenth of July, 1918, to his Oxford friend Mr. V. Richards, whose eyesight had hitherto debarred him from active service. The hastiness of its style would probably make Lawrence repudiate it; but the contents are valuable as contemporary evidence of his state of mind at this critical point in the campaign.

'15. 7. 18.

'Well, it was wonderful to see your writing again, and very difficult to read it: also pleasant to have a letter which doesn't begin "Reference your G.S. 102487b of the 45th." Army prose is bad, and I have so much of it that it makes me fear contamination in my own.

'I cannot write toanyone just now. Your letter came tome in Aba el Lissan, a little hill-fort on the plateau of Arabia S.E. of the Dead Sea, and I carried it with me down to Akaba, to Jidda, and then here to answer. Yet with all that I have had it only a month, and you wrote it three months ago. This letter will be submarined, and then it is all over for another three years.

'It always seemed to me that your eyes would prevent all service for you, and that in consequence you might preserve your continuity. For myself, I have been so violently uprooted, and plunged so deeply into a job too big for me, that everything feels unreal. I have dropped everything I ever did, and live only as a thief of opportunity, snatching chances of the moment when and where I see them. My people have probably told you that the job is to foment an Arab rebellion against Turkey, and for that I have to try to hide my Frankish exterior, and be as little out of the Arab picture as I can. So it's a kind of foreign stage, on which one plays day and night, in fancy dress, in a strange language, with the price of failure on one's head if the part is not well filled.

'You guessed rightly that the Arab appealed to my imagination. It is the old old civilization, which has refined itself clear of household gods, and half the trappings which ours hastens to assume. The gospel of bareness in materials is a good one, and it involves apparently a sort of moral bareness too. Arabs think for the moment, and endeavour to slip through life without turning corners or climbing hills. In part it is a mental and moral fatigue, a race trained out, and to avoid difficulties they have to jettison so much that we think honourable and brave: and yet without in any way sharing their point of view, I think I can understand it enough to look at myself and other foreigners from their direction, and without condemning it. I know I'm a stranger to them, and always will be: but I cannot believe them worse, any more than I could change to their ways.

'This is a very long porch to explain why I'm always trying to blow up railway trains and bridges instead of looking for the well at the world's end. Anyway, these years of detachment have cured me of any desire ever to do anything for myself. When

they untie my bonds I will not find in me any spur
to action. However, actually one never thinks of
afterwards: the time from the beginning is like one
of those dreams which seems to last for æons, and
then you wake up with a start, and find that it has
left nothing in your mind. Only the different thing
about this dream is that so many people do not wake
up in this life again.

'I cannot imagine what my people can have told
you.* Until now we have only been preparing the
groundwork and bases of our revolt, and do not yet
stand on the brink of action. Whether we are going
to win or lose, when we do strike, I cannot ever persuade myself. The whole thing is such a play, and one
cannot put conviction into one's day dreams. If we
succeed I will have done well with the materials given
me, and that disposes of your "lime light." If we fail,
and they have patience, then I suppose we will go on
digging foundations. Achievement, if it comes, will
have a great disillusionment, but not great enough to
wake me up.

'Your mind has evidently moved far since 1914. That
is a privilege you have won by being kept out of the
mist for so long. You'll find the rest of us aged under-
graduates, possibly still unconscious of our unfitting
grey hair. For that reason I cannot follow or return
your steps. A house with no action entailed, quiet,

---

* Mrs. Lawrence had written: 'Ned has been in the Hejaz fighting with the Arabs
against the Turks for the last year and more. He has been doing wonderful things,
blowing up trains, bridges, etc., and killing Turks by the hundred. He has had all sorts
of decorations, which he ignores. He says that if any private letters are sent giving his
rank and honours he will return them unopened.' . . .

and liberty to think and abstain as one wills—yes, I think abstention, the leaving everything alone and watching the others still going past, is what I would choose to-day, if things ceased driving me. This may be only the reaction from four years' opportunism, and is not worth trying to resolve into terms of geography and employment.

'Of course the ideal is that of the "lords who are" still "certainly expected,"* but the certainty is not for us, I'm afraid. Also for very few would the joy be so perfect as to be silent. Those words peace, silence, rest, and the others take on a vividness in the midst of noise and worry and weariness like a lighted window in the dark. Yet what on earth is the good of a lighted window? and perhaps it is only because one is over-borne and tired. You know when one marches across an interminable plain a hill (which is still the worst hill on earth) is a banquet, and after searing heat cold water takes on a quality (what would they have said without this word before?) impossible in the eyes of a fen-farmer. Probably I'm only a sensitized film, turned black or white by the objects projected on me: and if so what hope is there that next week or year, or to-morrow, can be prepared for today?

'This is an idiot letter, and amounts to nothing except a cry for a further change, which is idiocy, for I change my abode every day, and my job every

* A reference to a previous letter of his own from Cairo in 1915: 'You know Coleridge's description of the heavenly bodies in *The Ancient Mariner.* "Lords that are certainly expected . . ." etc. I don't want to be a lord or a heavenly body, but I think that one end of my orbit should be in a printing-shed with you. Shall we begin by printing Apuleius' *Golden Ass*, my present stand-by?'

two days, and my language every three days, and still
remain always unsatisfied. I hate being in front, and
I hate being back and I don't like responsibility, and
I don't obey orders. Altogether no good just now. A
long quiet like a purge and then a contemplation and
decision of future roads, that is what is to look forward to.

'You want apparently some vivid colouring of an
Arab costume, or of a flying Turk, and we have it all,
for that is part of the mise-en-scène of the successful
raider, and hitherto I am that. My bodyguard of fifty
Arab tribesmen, picked riders from the young men
of the deserts, are more splendid than a tulip garden,
and we ride like lunatics and with our Beduin pounce
on unsuspecting Turks and destroy them in heaps:
and it is all very gory and nasty after we close grips. I
love the preparation, and the journey, and loathe the
physical fighting. Disguises, and prices on one's head,
and fancy exploits are all part of the pose: how to reconcile it with the Oxford pose I know not. Were we
flamboyant there?

'If you reply—you will perceive I have matting of
the brain—and your thoughts are in control, please
tell me of B—, and if possible W—. The latter was
the man for all these things, because he would take a
baresark beery pleasure in physical outputs. . . .

'L.'

XXIV

The plan that Lawrence had in mind for Buxton's camel-corps was this: it would start from the Suez Canal, across Sinai to Akaba, arriving on the second of August. The next step was from Akaba through the passes to Rumm. From Rumm it would make a raid on Mudowwara which was still holding out after having been threatened for over a year, and destroy the Turkish water-supply, thereby completing the strangle-hold on Medina. From Mudowwara it would go by the old Jefer and Bair route to Kissir on the railway, three miles south of Amman, to destroy the big bridge and tunnel which the British cavalry and camel raid had left undamaged: this would delay the Turkish relief of Maan for three weeks, by which time Allenby's offensive would be beginning. The camel-corps would then be back on Allenby's front by way of Tafileh and Beersheba on August the thirtieth.

Besides the Englishmen Lawrence would take his own body-guard and pick up sponsors from other Arab tribes as he went. The ride was a great responsibility for him. To take a large body of Christian troops in khaki through Arab tribal territory was at least as dangerous an adventure as the fighting that had to be done against the Turks. He asked Buxton's leave

THE CAMPAIGN IN THE NORTH

Miles
0   50   100

to address the men, without their officers, before they started. I have had from one of them an account of his speech, and the extraordinary impression it made on him and his comrades. At first sight they had not trusted Lawrence in the least, disliking his Bedouin dress and Bedouin gestures; whispering that he was a spy and would betray them. But once he began to talk: 'We are about to start on a trip so long and difficult that the Staff believe we won't manage it . . . ,' he captured their imaginations. He knew the value of the appeal to personal vanity. He told them that they had to ride a thousand miles in thirty days, nearly twice the set daily march of their brigade, through desert country, on short rations for man and beast, with two difficult night-attacks on Turkish posts thrown in. Any delay in the march would mean thirst or starvation, probably both, and if they wore out their camels by careless riding they would be stranded in the desert and would probably never return. He asked them to be very patient with the excitable Arabs, particularly at the wells.

Buxton's first impression of Lawrence can be given in a quotation from a private letter that he wrote home on the fourth of August. He was at Rumm watering the camels at the springs in the great amphitheatre; with great difficulty, for the Beni Atiyeh tribe were there too, watering a thousand camels a day, and jealousy for first turn might lead to disturbance and bloodshed:

'*August 4th*, 1918. *4th Anniversary of War.*
'RUMM,

'I am sitting between two rocks with a waterproof sheet overhead, somewhere in the middle of Arabia, between Akaba and the Euphrates. It is a place with rocky mountains on each side of me which last night in the evening light became a most wonderful rosy red colour growing purple as the shadow fell across them. The wells are about three hundred yards up a stiff cliff, and the difficulties of watering camels are terrific. We have been watering camels the last thirty-six hours continuously day and night, and I hope to get off with my column this evening. We are here very much under sufferance of the Sherif, and none of the inhabitants and Arabs here like us at all, and rifles which reverberate like a battle are continuously going off. Lawrence and his odd-looking cut-throat band have just left us to rejoin the Sherif near Maan, and we have now Nasir, a relation of the Sherif, who acts as intermediary between us and the Arabs.

'Our first night attack against the Turks will take place about forty miles from here, two nights ahead. To-morrow about daybreak I go on with Nasir and two or three of my officers dressed as Arabs, or rather with Arab head-gear and coat, to give the proper "silhouette" effect, and we do a personal reconnaissance of the places to be attacked about sunset and then rejoin the column on the march after making plans for the attack.

'Lawrence has started all this Arab movement. He is only a boy to look at, has a very quiet, sedate manner, a fine head but insignificant body. He is known to every Arab in this country for his personal bravery and train-wrecking exploits. I don't know whether it is his intrepidity, disinterestedness and mysteriousness which appeal to the Arab most, or his success in finding them rich trains to blow up and loot. After a train success he tells me the army is like Barnum's show and gradually disintegrates. At any rate it is wonderful what he has accomplished with the poor tools at his disposal. His influence is astounding not only on the misbeguided natives, but also I think on his brother officers and seniors. Out here he lives entirely with the Arabs, wears their clothes, eats only their food, and bears all the burdens that the lowliest of them does. He always travels in spotless white, and in fact reminds one of a Prince of Mecca more than anything. He will join us again later, I hope, as his presence is very stimulating to us all and one has the feeling that things cannot go wrong while he is there. . . .'

Lawrence had ridden off not to Maan, as Buxton's letter says, but to Akaba where he collected his body-guard, sixty strong, and rode with them to Guweira. El Zaagi had sorted them out in Ageyl fashion to ride in a long line with a poet to right and a poet to left, each among the best singers. Lawrence was on Ghazala, whose calf had recently died and left her in great grief. Abdulla the Robber, riding next to Lawrence, carried the calf's dried pelt behind his saddle. Ghazala in the middle of the singing began to tread uneasily, remembering her grief, and stopped, gently moaning. Abdulla leaped off his camel and spread the pelt before her. She stopped crying and sniffed at it three or four times, then whimpering went on again. This happened several times that day but in the end she forgot her grief. At Guweira he left his body-guard to wait. An aeroplane took him to Jefer—to Feisal who was there with

Nuri, the Emir of the Ruwalla. It was Nuri who had given Lawrence and Auda leave a year before to ride through his territory on the way to Akaba. He had now to be asked a far greater favour, the passage through his country of British troops and armoured cars. If he consented it would mean war with the Turks toward whom, at Feisal's request, he had so far kept up a show of friendship. Nuri was a hard, short-spoken old man of seventy, and it was with great relief that Feisal and Lawrence heard his plain 'Yes.' It came at the end of a great conference of all the Ruwalla chiefs where Feisal and Lawrence in the tent at twilight sat preaching revolt. The combination was irresistible; their method perfected after two years was to say just enough to set the Ruwalla imagination on fire so that the tribesmen almost believed themselves the inventors of the idea and began spurring Feisal and Lawrence to greater enthusiasm and more desperate action.

Lawrence's short stay at Rumm with Buxton's men had made him home-sick for England. (It was an ideal England which he loved with a perverse Anglo-Irish sentiment which was quite compatible with being out of sympathy with most Englishmen.) So here at Jefer he accused himself of play-acting, of continuing his cruel fraud on the Arabs for the sake of England's victory.

But then Nuri once more came to him with documents. The English Government had been working with its foreign departments still at odds together. Besides the original pledges to the Sherif promising Arab independence and the later Sykes-Picot treaty partitioning up the Arab area between England, France and Russia, there were now two more statements: a promise made to seven prominent Arabs at Cairo that the Arabs should keep such territory as they conquered

BUXTON'S MEN BLOWING UP
MUDOWWARA STATION

from the Turks during the war, and a promise to the Zionists for a Jewish National Home in Palestine. Which of all these was Nuri to believe? Once more Lawrence smiled and said, 'The latest in date.' Nuri took it good-humouredly and ever afterwards helped Lawrence well, yet warned him with a smile: 'But if ever henceforth I fail to keep a promise,' said Nuri, 'it will be because I have superseded it with a later intention.'

Lawrence's loyalty was further tried by his discovery that negotiations had been begun between the British Government and the Conservative Turks about the terms of Turkey's surrender. The news did not come to him officially but privately through friends in Turkey, and the Arabs had not been first consulted. This was most unfortunate because the Conservatives, unlike their powerful opponents the Nationalists (headed by Kemal, the present head of the Turkish Republic), were most unwilling to allow Arab governments to be set up in Syria. The British proposals would have been fatal to many of the Arabs already in arms for freedom. Lawrence therefore encouraged Feisal to begin a correspondence with the Kemalists, so that in case Allenby's thrust failed and a separate peace were made by the British with the Conservative Turks, there might still be a chance of winning and holding Damascus by alliance with the Turkish Nationalists against the Conservatives.

It seems that after all this Lawrence did not quite know where he was, and the only relief as usual for his distress of mind was violent action and a longing for death to end his shame. Yet from actual suicide he shrank. That would be to take death far too seriously; it would not be cowardice but a flippancy unworthy of a serious person like himself. The most that he could allow himself was a constant exposure to danger, leaving himself only the narrowest margin of safety and always hoping for an accident. Accidents, however, though numerous were never fatal; he was too scrupulous about keeping the honourable margin. If he had not been so much in love with the idea of death, he would have been killed a hundred times over.

Nuri's young nephew Bender begged Lawrence before all the chiefs to give him a place in the body-guard. He had heard wild tales of its excessive joys and sorrows from Rahail, his foster-brother, with whom Lawrence had made the ride from Azrak. Lawrence did not want Bender; a luxurious young man who was too much of a responsibility. But Lawrence could not shame him in front of the chiefs, so he turned the request by asking, 'Am I a king to have Ruwalla princes as my servants?' Nuri's eye met Lawrence's in silent approval.

From this meeting with Nuri he flew back to Guweira, and from there decided to go forward with the armoured cars as far as Azrak to prepare Buxton's road. They crossed the railway safely and at Bair met Buxton coming up with his camel-corps from the attack on Mudowwara. He had captured the place and its garrison of about a hundred and forty men with a loss of four killed and ten wounded; destroyed the wells, the engine pumps and the great water-tower, and more than a mile of rails. The only trouble was that the supply-column that accompanied him had left the last stop, Jefer, half-mutinous with fear of the desert and had lost, stolen or sold a third of the rations which the baggage camels were carrying. So the force had to be reduced by fifty of Buxton's least needed men, a hundred camels, and one of the two armoured cars. There was great delay at Bair, watering at the only two wells. At one of these there were six hundred camels of the Howeitat and Beni Sakhr, and at the other a mob of a thousand Druses, Syrian refugees,

Damascus merchants and Armenians, all on their way to Akaba. Lawrence helped Buxton with the watering: the Howeitat were astonished at the English, never having imagined that there were so many of that tribe in the world.

It was Lawrence's thirtieth birthday and he made it the occasion for a long self-examination, an inquiry into his personality, and his desire to understand his personality, and the difficulties and deceits arising from his desire to understand his personality by testing its effect on others. His desire to be liked and his ambition to be famous, and his cautious or shamefaced restraint of both these impulses. His refusal to believe good of himself or his works; his actual dislike of as much of himself as he could see and hear and feel.

At this point he was roused by shouts and shots. He was afraid that a quarrel had broken out between Buxton's men and the tribesmen, but it was only an appeal for help against the Shammar who some miles away had driven off eighty Howeitat camels. By the time that he had sent in pursuit four or five relatives of the men robbed, his train of thought was broken. They went forward then. Lawrence's body-guard were, for this ride, set to lead or drive the baggage camels carrying the six thousand pounds of gun-cotton for the blowing up of the bridge. They were disgusted at this unexciting and menial task, particularly as their charges were very slow Somali camels which could do no more than three miles an hour. El Zaagi urged them on, taunting them with being coolies and drovers, offering to buy their goods when they came to market, and made them laugh in spite of themselves. They kept up by lengthening the marches into the night and stealing time from the breakfast and midday halts.

They brought the caravan through without the loss of a

single beast, a fine performance for such gilded gentlemen; but then, they were the best camel-masters for hire in all Arabia.

Lawrence was delighted with the Imperial Camel-Corps. Buxton had revised all the hard-and-fast rules of march discipline. His men no longer rode in line but in irregular clumps, each man picking his easiest way over the bad ground. He had reduced and re-hung the loads, and broken the old clock-work system of halting once every hour. Each march his men became more workmanlike, more at home on their animals, tougher, leaner, faster. If only the Indian camel-men had learned to accommodate themselves in the same way to irregular fighting, the Yarmuk bridge raid of the previous autumn might have ended successfully.

However, Kissir bridge and tunnel escaped too. On August the twentieth they came within sight of the railway and hid in the ruins of a Roman temple some miles off. Lawrence sent forward members of his body-guard who were peasants of the district to scout in the three villages between them and the bridge. They returned to say that by bad luck Turkish tax-gatherers were in the villages that night, measuring out the heaps of corn on the threshing- floors under guard of troops of mounted infantry. Three such troops were in the three villages nearest the great bridge, villages close to which they would have to pass on their way to blow it up. And a Turkish aeroplane had come over their column that morning and probably seen them. They took counsel. Lawrence had no doubt that Buxton's men could deal with the Turkish bridge-guard and blow up the bridge. The only question was whether the business was worth its cost in British lives. The plan was to dismount nearly a mile from the bridge and advance on foot. The blowing up of the bridge with three tons of gun-cotton would wake up the whole district and Turkish patrols might stumble on the camel-park, which would be a disaster. Buxton's men could not, like Arabs, scatter like a swarm of birds after the explosion, to find their own way back. In night-fighting some of them would be sure to be cut off. They might lose altogether fifty men. This was too expensive. The destruction of the bridge, anyhow, was only to frighten and disturb the Turks so that they would leave Maan alone until August the thirtieth, when the great attack on Deraa was to be made from Azrak. This was already the twentieth. The danger seemed nearly over now, for the Turks had wasted the last month, doing nothing.

Buxton's men were most disappointed when they heard that the raid was off, but Lawrence reassured them that the chief object of their coming would be gained. He sent men down to the villages to spread reports of a coming great attack on Amman, of which this was the advance guard. It was what the Turks dreaded most; patrols were sent up at once to report on the truth of the villagers' wild reports, and found the hill-top, where the raiders had been, littered with empty meat tins, and the valley slopes cut up by the tracks of enormous cars. Very many tracks there were; as Lawrence, with his single car, had taken care that there should be. This alarm checked them for a week; the destruction of the bridge would only have added a few days more. The expedition returned by way of Azrak, where the Englishmen bathed in the pools, and to Bair (shouting 'Are we well fed? No! Do we see life? Yes!'), where they found a few more 'iron rations' dumped for them from Akaba. Then Buxton took them back to Palestine. Lawrence returned with the armoured cars to Akaba.

XXV

At Akaba preparations for the grand expedition of all arms to cut the railways at Deraa were complete—so complete that Dawnay and Joyce were both for the moment on holiday. Lawrence was glad to be there to cope with a most unexpected and absurd situation. The Sherif, Hussein, had issued a Royal Gazette from Mecca with a proclamation to the effect that fools were calling Jaafar Pasha the General Officer Commanding the Arab Northern Army, whereas there was no such rank, indeed no rank higher than captain in the Arab Army, in which Sheikh Jaafar, like many another, was doing his duty. Hussein had heard of Jaafar's C.M.G. and had published this proclamation in jealousy without warning Feisal. He intended by it to spite the Syrian and Mesopotamian Arabs in Feisal's army. They were fighting, he knew, to free their own countries for self-government, but he was aiming at a regular Arab Empire which he was ambitious to rule from Mecca, with the spiritual leadership of the Mohammedan world thrown in. Jaafar and all the Arab officers at once resigned. Feisal refused the resignations, pointing out that their commissions as officers were issued by himself and he alone was disgraced by the proclamation. He telegraphed to Mecca resigning command. Hussein appointed Zeid in his place. Zeid promptly refused to take command. Hussein sent threatening messages by cable and all military life was at an end from Akaba to Aba el Lissan.

Lawrence had to do something. The first alternative was to put pressure on Hussein to withdraw his statement; the second to ignore the humours of this narrow-minded old man of seventy, and carry on; the third, to set up Feisal in independence of his father and, when Damascus fell, try to give him a throne there. But the difficulty was that the expedition had to start in three days' time if it was to reach Deraa before Allenby began his advance. The first course was best, to avoid the appearance of dissension among the Arabs, but might take weeks. So Allenby and the High Commissioner of Egypt (who provided Hussein's subsidy) were at once set to work on the Sherif, whose answers to Feisal through them were cabled across to Akaba in cipher. Lawrence, remembering Hussein's trick on the telephone, saw to it that the cable-station at Akaba only accepted the desirable parts of the messages and made a hopeless jumble of the others, notifying these to Mecca as 'corrupt.' Fortunately Hussein instead of repeating the censored passages, toned them down until at last there came a long message, the first half a lame apology and withdrawal of the proclamation, the other a renewal of the offence in a new form.

Lawrence suppressed this second half and took the first to Feisal marked 'very urgent.' The secretary decoded it and Feisal read it aloud to the staff about him, concealing his surprise at the meek words of his usually obstinate and tyrannical old father. At the end he said, 'The telegraph has saved all our honour.' Without Feisal the great expedition to Deraa, which it was hoped might mean also Damascus, would have been incomplete and Lawrence had pressed him to come in spite of his father; Feisal having resigned his command had offered very nobly to come under Lawrence's. So now he bent towards Lawrence, adding in an undertone: 'I mean the honour of nearly all of us.' Lawrence said demurely, 'I do not understand what you mean.' Feisal answered, 'I offered to serve for this last march under your orders, why was that not enough?' 'Because it would not go with your honour,' said Lawrence. 'You always prefer mine before your own,' Feisal murmured, then sprang up energetically to his feet saying, 'Now, sirs, praise God and work!'

The expedition started only a day late. Lawrence first had to suppress a mutiny among the Arab regular soldiers who knew something bad was happening, but had heard only the false rumour that Feisal had deserted. He had not been seen out of his tent for a week. The gunners thought that their officers were betraying them and ran to turn the guns on their tents. However, Rasim had foreseen this and, secretly collecting the breech-blocks in his own tent, had outwitted them. At this ludicrous moment Lawrence came smiling along and talked to the men, telling as a great joke the whole story of Hussein's proclamation and the resignations; they laughed like schoolboys at the private quarrels of their leaders. Feisal then appeared, driving through the lines in his Vauxhall car which was painted with the holy green colour of the Prophet's family; and the situation was saved.

Lawrence went by armoured car to Azrak and at Bair heard the news that the Turks at Hesa had moved suddenly to Tafileh and were advancing south to the relief of Maan. The chief of the Beni Sakhr who brought the news thought Lawrence mad when he laughed aloud. But, now that the expedition had started, the Turks might relieve Maan and take Aba el Lissan, Guweira, Akaba itself for all he cared. The news meant that the Turks believed in the pretended threat to Amman and were making a counter-stroke. Every man that they sent south was a man, or rather ten men lost. Deraa was all that mattered now. To complete the deception Lawrence had sent thousands of his 'horsemen of St. George' (British sovereigns) to the Beni Sakhr tribe to purchase all the barley on their threshing-floors for a force that would be shortly coming along from Azrak, through their villages, towards Amman. The Turks got the news soon, as was intended. Hornby was going in charge of the other expedition to join up with Allenby at Jericho, so that if the Deraa plan failed the combined parties could make the feint on Amman a reality. But the Turkish advance on Tafileh checked him and he had instead to defend Shobek against them.

The Deraa expedition was now assembling at Azrak and on the twelfth of September was complete. First arrived Lawrence's body-guard, jolly on their well-fed camels, then two aeroplanes, then the rest of the armoured cars and a great baggage train. Feisal brought the Arab regular army, a thousand camel-men on Allenby's gift-camels; with the French Algerian gunners under Pisani. Nuri appeared with the Ruwalla tribesmen; and Auda with Mohammed el Dheilan and the Abu Tayi; and Fahad and Adhub with their Beni Sakhr; and the chief of the Serahin; and many more Bedouin, Druses and town-Syrians flocking from all directions. And the great outlaw Tallal arrived, who had taken Lawrence spying in the Hauran the winter before.

First of all it was necessary to cut off Deraa from Amman.

For this purpose a detachment of Indian Gurkhas on camels under their British officer were sent to raid a block-house on the railway just north of Amman, while a party of Egyptian camel-corps blew up near-by bridges and rails. Two armoured cars went with them, and local guides. The rest of the army moved up to Umtaiye, a great rainwater-pit fifteen miles below Deraa, and waited there for news.

Unfortunately this demolition did not come off; the Arabs between the raiders and the line disliked the Indians, despised the Egyptians and would not let them pass. So Lawrence went himself the next day from Umtaiye with two armoured cars and a hundred and fifty pounds of gun-cotton to the nearest point on the line, where there were two good bridges to destroy and easy going for the cars. Joyce came with him. While Joyce's car kept the neighbouring block-house busy, Lawrence's ran to the biggest bridge, whose guard-garrison of eight men made a first brave defence but then surrendered—as also did the block-house garrison. Joyce and Lawrence then hurriedly set about the bridge, destroying it scientifically so that the four arches were smashed but the skeleton left tottering. The Turks would first have the difficult task of destroying it completely before they could begin rebuilding.

The cars then bumped off, because a large body of Turks was seen coming up in the distance. Lawrence's car bumped too carelessly; at the first watercourse there was a crash and it stuck. They hurriedly inspected the damage and found that the front bracket of the near back-spring had broken; a hopeless break which only a workshop could mend. The driver, Rolls, was nearly in tears over this mishap, the first structural damage in a team of nine cars driven for eighteen months over the maddest country. But he realized that the fate of the whole

AT GUWEIRA

party rested on him and said that there was just one hope. They might jack up the fallen end of the spring and wedge it, by balks upon the running-board, into nearly its old position. With the help of ropes the thin angle-irons of the running-board might carry the additional weight.

There was in each car a length of timber to help the double car-tires over muddy places; three blocks of this would do for the proper height. But there was no saw, so they used machine-gun bullets instead, and soon had their three blocks. The Turks heard the machine-gun firing and halted cautiously. Joyce's car also heard and came back to help; the repair was hurriedly made, only just in time. When they got back to Umtaiye they strengthened it with telegraph-wire and it lasted until they reached Damascus. The loss of this bridge would keep the Turks from reinforcing Deraa from Amman and also help Zeid and Jaafar with the Arab army at Aba el Lissan, and Hornby at Shobek, for the Turks massing at Tafileh were delayed until the line was mended behind them.

Meanwhile the Arab expedition moved to Tell Arar, four miles north of Deraa, where they were to cut the northern railway to Damascus. Lawrence and Joyce hurrying to join them in the armoured cars arrived late because of bad going over heavy plough-land. They watched the battle from a hill: Ruwalla horsemen dashing towards the line over the liquorice-grown bed of a watercourse, and a Ford car, with machine-guns, bouncing after. A Turkish guard-post opened fire, but Pisani's guns silenced it and the Ruwalla took it with only one man killed. Ten miles of railway were won in only an hour's fighting and the Egyptians, after a halt for breakfast, began steady demolition-work from south to north while the Arab army swarmed over the plain. Lawrence could hardly realize the good fortune. It was September the seventeenth, two days before Allenby could throw forward his full power. In two days the Turks might decide to change their dispositions to meet this new danger from the Arabs at Deraa, but they could not do so before Allenby struck. Lawrence had cut the one railway that connected the Turks in Amman, Maan, Medina, Nazareth, Nablus, the Jordan valley, with their base in Damascus and with Aleppo, Constantinople, Germany.

The Egyptians used 'tulips,' which were thirty-ounce charges of gun-cotton planted beneath the centre of the central sleeper of each ten-yard section of the track. The sleepers were hollow steel and the explosion made them hump bud-like two feet in the air. The lift pulled the rails three inches up, the drag pulled them six inches together, and the chairs were inwardly warped. This threefold distortion put them beyond repair. And it was quick work; six hundred such charges could be laid and fired in two or three hours and would take the Turks a week to mend. While they were busy, eight Turkish aeroplanes flew out from Deraa and began dropping bombs. They did not seem to notice the Egyptians on the railway but came diving down with machine-gun fire among the Arabs. There was no overhead cover on the plain at all, so the only thing was to scatter and present the thinnest possible target, while Nuri Said's automatic guns rattled back at the aeroplanes and Pisani's mountain-guns fired shrapnel and made them fly too high to bomb accurately.

The question now was how to get at the Yarmuk railway-bridge which Lawrence had failed to blow up the year before. Its destruction would top off the cutting of the other two lines from Deraa. The enemy aeroplanes were, however, making movement impossible. There had been two British aeroplanes with the expedition, but the only useful one, a Bristol Fighter, had been damaged in an air-fight the day before and had flown back for repairs to Jerusalem; there remained only an antiquated and almost useless B.E.12 machine. But Junor, the pilot, had heard at Azrak from the pilot of the returning Bristol Fighter that enemy aeroplanes were active at Deraa and most bravely decided to take his place. When things were at their worst at Tell Arar he suddenly sailed in and rattled away at the eight Turkish aeroplanes with his two guns. They scattered for a careful look and he flew westward drawing them after him: he knew that the chance of an air-fight usually makes aeroplanes forget their ground-target. It was deliberate self-sacrifice on Junor's part, for his machine was utterly useless for air-fighting. Nuri Said hurriedly collected three hundred and fifty regulars and marched them in small parties across the rails. He was making for Mezerib, seven miles west from Deraa, the key to the Yarmuk bridge. The returning aeroplanes would probably not notice that his men were gone. Armed peasants were sent on after Nuri Said, and half an hour later Lawrence called up his body-guard, to follow himself.

As he did so, he heard a droning in the air and to his astonishment Junor appeared, still alive, though surrounded by three enemy aeroplanes, faster than his own, spitting bullets at him. He was twisting and side-slipping splendidly, firing back. But the fight could only end in one way. In a faint hope that he might get down alive Lawrence rushed with his men and another British officer, Young, to clear a landing-place by the railway. Junor was being driven lower; he threw out a message to say that his petrol was finished. The body-guard worked feverishly, rolling away boulders, and Lawrence put out a land-

ing-signal. Junor dived: the machine took the ground beauti-
fully but a flaw of wind then overturned it and he was thrown
out. He was up in a moment with only a cut chin, and rescued
his Lewis-gun and machine-gun and ammunition just before
one of the Turkish aeroplanes dived and dropped a bomb by
the wreck. Five minutes later he was asking for another job.
Joyce gave him a Ford car and he ran boldly down the hill
until near Deraa and blew a gap in the rails there before the
Turks saw him. They fired at him with artillery but he bumped
off in the Ford, still unhurt.

Lawrence hurried forward to Mezerib with his bodyguard,
but an aeroplane saw them and began dropping bombs: one,
two, three misses, the fourth fell right among them. Two camels
fell, terribly wounded, but the riders escaped unhurt and
scrambled up behind two of their friends. Another machine
came by and dropped more bombs. A shock spun Lawrence's
camel round and nearly knocked him out of the saddle with a
numbing pain in his right arm. He felt that he was hard hit and
tears came to his eyes with the pain and the disappointment
of being put out of action so soon before the triumphant end.
Blood was running down his arm. Perhaps, if he did not look
at it, he might carry on as if he were unhurt. The aeroplane
was machine-gunning them now and his camel swung round.
He clutched at the pommel and realized that his damaged arm
was there, still in working order. He had judged it blown off.
He felt for the wound, and found a very small very hot splinter
of metal sticking into his arm. He realized how bad his nerves
were. This was, by the way, the first time that he had been hit
from the air, of all his twenty or more wounds.

Mezerib surrendered after a bombardment by Pisani's
guns and twenty machine-guns. (Tallal had previously gone

forward demanding a bloodless surrender—he knew the sta-
tionmaster—but the Turks had fired a volley at him and at
Lawrence, who came with him, from point-blank range: they
had crawled back painfully through a field of thistles, Tallal
swearing.) The station was looted by hundreds of Hauran
peasantry. Men, women and children in a frenzy fought like
dogs over every object; even doors and windows, door-frames
and window-frames, steps of the stairs, were carried off.
Others smashed and looted the wagons in the siding. Lawrence and Young cut the telegraph, the Palestine army's main
link with home. They cut it slowly to draw out the indignation
of the German-Turkish staff at Nazareth. The Turks' hopeless
lack of initiative made their army a directed one, so that by
destroying the telegraph Lawrence went far towards turning
them into a leaderless mob. The points were then blown
in and tulips planted all over the station track. Among the
captures were two lorries crammed with delicacies for some
German canteen. Nuri Said found an Arab prising open a tin
of bottled asparagus and cried out: 'Pigs' bones!' The peasant
spat in horror and threw them down. Nuri Said picked them
up and later shared them with Lawrence, Joyce and Young.
The trucks were splashed with petrol and set on fire and the
blaze that evening acted as a beacon for hundreds and hundreds of Arab peasant rebels who came on camel, on horse, on
foot, in great enthusiasm, hoping that this was the final release
of their country.

Visitors were welcome. Lawrence's business was to let each
one tell him all the news he wanted to tell; afterwards re-ar-
ranging it in his mind and getting a clear picture of the whole
enemy situation. Even the magistrates of Deraa itself came
offering to open the town, but Lawrence put them off, to their

disappointment. Though he knew that the town controlled the local water-supply, the possession of which must force the railway-station to surrender too, he would not risk accepting the gift. If Allenby did not completely break the Turks, Deraa might be retaken and a merciless massacre of the Hauran peasants would follow.

The next step was to blow up Tell el Shehab bridge. There had arrived the boy-chief of Tell el Shehab village, which crowned the cliff above the bridge: he described the position of the large Turkish guard at the bridge. Lawrence thought that he was probably lying, but he went off and soon returned with his friend the commander of the Turkish bridge-guard, an Armenian captain, who confirmed the story. The Armenian was anxious to betray his charge; he suggested an ambush in his own room at the village to which he would in turn call all his lieutenants, sergeants and corporals—hated Turks—to be trussed up by three or four waiting Arabs. The rest of the force would be ready then to rush the leaderless guard. Lawrence agreed and at eleven o'clock he and Nasir were close to the village with camel-men and the body-guard bringing bags of gelatine. Lawrence knew the bridge well since his attempt on it with Ali ibn el Hussein and Fahad from the other side of the ravine. It was pitch-dark and the damp air came up from the river, wetting their woollen coats. Waiting for the Armenian to come and fetch the trussers-up they could hear the occasional cries of the sentry challenging passers-by on the bridge far below, and the constant roar of the waterfall, and then the noise of a train, with the squealing of brakes as it stopped in the station close by the bridge. After awhile the boy-chief came up holding his brown cloak open to show his white shirt like a flag. He whispered that the plan had failed. The train in

AN ARMOURED FORD IN THE DESERT
Copyright Imperial War Museum

the ravine had been sent up with German and Turk reserves from Afuleh under a German colonel to rescue panic-stricken Deraa. They had arrested the Armenian captain for being absent from his post. There were dozens of machine-guns and dozens of sentries patrolling up and down.

Nuri Said offered to take the place by main force. Surprise and numbers were on the Arab side, but Lawrence was at his old game of reckoning the cost and as usual found it too dear. They said good night to the chief, thanked him, and turned back. Lawrence, Nasir and Nuri Said sat with rifles ready on the cliff edge, waiting for their men to get back out of danger. Lawrence's rifle was a famous one, a British Lee-Enfield captured at the Dardanelles and given by Enver, the Turkish commander-in-chief, as a present to Feisal, with an inscription on a gold plate; Feisal had given it to Lawrence. It was a great temptation sitting there to fire a rocket pistol into the station and scare the Germans into all-night terror. Nasir, Nuri and Lawrence all had the same childish idea at the same moment, but managed to restrain each other from carrying it out. Instead, some of the body-guard were sent to blow up rails in the ravine a mile or two beyond the bridge, Tallal providing guides. The echoing explosions gave the Germans a bad night. Then the rest of the army moved from Mezerib towards Nisib on their way back to Umtaiye. Before leaving they lit a long time-fuse to a mine under the water-tower. When the Germans came forward from Tell el Shehab—they heard that Mezerib was empty—the mine exploded with a tremendous noise and they cautiously retired again.

Nisib was ten miles south of Deraa. Pisani's guns shelled the station at two thousand yards' range and the machine-guns supported him. But the Turks would not surrender, returning a hot fire from the trenches. This did not matter much, for the real objective was not the station but a great bridge a few hundred yards to the north, protected by a Turkish post which Nuri Said now began to bombard. Lawrence's men were tired out, like their camels, and when he asked them to come forward with him against the bridge they refused. They knew that one bullet in the gelatine that they were carrying would blow them sky-high.

It was the first time that they had flinched. Lawrence tried to get them forward by making jokes, but it was hopeless. At last he cast them off and standing on the crest with bullets cracking round him called by name the youngest and most timid of them all to come with him to the bridge. He shook like a man in a sick dream but obeyed quietly. They rode over the crest towards the bridge. Lawrence then sent the young Arab back to tell the men that he would hurt them worse than bullets if they did not join him. He intended to go forward to see whether the guard-post was holding out after the bombardment. While the bodyguard hesitated, up came El Zaagi with Abdulla the Robber: they were men who feared nothing. Mad with fury that Lawrence had been betrayed these two dashed at the shrinkers and chased them over the ridge-top, with no more harm than six bullet-grazes. The post was indeed abandoned, so Lawrence dismounted and signalled to Nuri Said to cease fire. He and his body-guard crept up on foot to the bridge and piling eight hundred pounds of explosive against the piers, which were about five feet thick and twenty-five feet high, blew it to pieces. This was Lawrence's last bridge, the seventy-ninth since he started and a most important one, for the Arab army was to wait close by at Umtaiye until Allenby's troops came up to join it.

The Turkish aeroplanes were a pest. Umtaiye was only twelve miles from their aerodrome near Deraa and they kept coming over and dropping bombs on the Arab camp. The irregulars would soon lose their nerve and go off home unless something was done; so Lawrence and Junor went off in two armoured cars to raid the aerodrome. They got quite close by silencing the cars and found three aeroplanes on the ground. One they shot to pieces; the two others escaping flew to Deraa and returned to chase the cars with bombs. The first dropped its four bombs all together from a height and missed badly, but the other flew low, placing one bomb at a time with great care. Lawrence and Junor drove slowly on over rocky ground, quite defenceless. One bomb sent a shower of stones through the driving slit of Lawrence's car but only cut his knuckles. Another tore off a front tire and nearly overturned them. But they returned safely to Umtaiye.

Two days later a news-aeroplane was due at Azrak, so Lawrence decided to go back in it to Palestine and beg Allenby to send along some Bristol Fighters. He rode towards Azrak with his body-guard, intending on the way to smash another bridge. But he noticed that his men were red-eyed and trembling and obeyed orders with hesitation: evidently El Zaagi and The Robber had mercilessly gone through the list of those who had flinched at Nisib. He decided that they were not in form that night, so sent the Egyptians and Gurkhas (on the first stage of their journey back to help Zeid at Aba el Lissan) to do the raid instead. He followed them in an armoured car and Junor came, too, in his Ford. Lawrence, who was guiding, lost the way in the darkness; his wits were wandering after five sleepless nights in succession. But the Egyptians fired their thirty tulips all right, while Lawrence and Junor overtook a train and machine- gunned it. Junor let fly a green shower of tracer-bullets which probably did little harm but made the Turks howl with terror.

At Azrak they found the aeroplane waiting with the first amazing news of Allenby's victory. He had burst through at every point and the Turkish army was in rout. Lawrence sent the news to Feisal, advising him to proclaim the general revolt at last, and flew off to Palestine. An hour or two later he was with Allenby who was very calm in spite of the magnitude of his victory and was allowing the Turks no rest. He was making three new thrusts: with the New Zealanders to Amman, with the Indians to Deraa, with the Australians to Kuneitra in the Hauran. The New Zealanders would stop at Amman but the other two divisions would later converge on Damascus. Allenby asked Lawrence to assist all three advances with his Arabs but not to push on to Damascus until the Indians and Australians were in line with him. Lawrence in return asked for aeroplanes, and was given them: two Bristol Fighters, with an enormous Handley-Page and a D.H.9 to carry petrol and spare parts.

Back with the Arabs the next day Lawrence told them that Nablus was taken and Afuleh and Haifa and Baisan. The news ran like fire through the camp. Tallal began boasting, the Ruwalla shouted for instant march on Damascus, even the still smarting body-guard cheered up. That day, the twenty-second of September, Lawrence was breakfasting near Umtaiye with the airmen: there were sausages frying. Suddenly a watcher called out: 'Aeroplane up.' The pilots of the Bristol Fighters jumped into their machines, and the pilot of the D.H.9 looked hard at Lawrence, silently asking him to come up with him to handle the machine-guns. Lawrence pretended not to understand. He had learned the theory of air-fighting all right, but it was knowledge not yet become instinctive action. No, he would not go up. The pilot looked reproachfully at him while the air-fight began without them. Five minutes later the Bristols were back, having driven down a two-seater and scattered three scout-aeroplanes. The sausages were still hot. They ate them and drank some tea and were starting on some grapes, a present from the Druse country, when again the watcher cried 'Aeroplane' and up the pilots jumped and soon brought it down in flames.

Later with Feisal (whom he had gone by air to fetch with his staff from Azrak) and Nuri, the Emir of the Ruwalla, Lawrence went off north in Feisal's green Vauxhall to see the Handley-Page alight. Twenty miles from the landing-ground they met a single Arab tribesman running southward like the prophet Elijah with grey hair and grey beard flying in the wind and his clothes girded about his loins. He yelled out to the car, waving his bony arms, 'The biggest aeroplane in the world' and rushed on to spread his great news among the tents. They found the Handley-Page surrounded by Arabs who cried out, 'Indeed and at last they have sent us THE aeroplane, of which these others were foals.' Before night the news had spread all over the Hauran and across the Druse mountains and every one knew by this token that the Arabs were on the winning side. The great machine unloaded a ton of petrol, oil and spare parts for the Bristol Fighters, and rations for the men; then sailed off for night-bombing at Deraa.

The task that Allenby had set the Arab army was to harass the Turkish Fourth Army until the New Zealanders forced it out of Amman, its headquarters, and afterwards to cut it up on its retreat north. Feisal's force now consisted of four thousand men, of whom three thousand were irregulars. But these irregulars were nearly all under the sovereignty of the Emir Nuri, whose word nobody dared disobey, so Feisal could count on them. The old man led a charge of Ruwalla horsemen in a further raid on the railway and under his eye the tribe showed unusual valour; armoured cars came along too and the line was now permanently broken between Amman and Deraa. It only remained to wait for the fugitives streaming up from Amman in flight from the New Zealanders.

A body of hostile cavalry was reported to be coming north towards them. The Emir Nuri with his Ruwalla horse and Tallal with his Hauran horse went to meet it. Armoured cars joined them. But it was only a mob of fugitives looking for a short cut home, so hundreds of prisoners were taken and much transport. A panic spread down the line and troops miles away from the Arabs threw away all they had, even their rifles, making a mad rush towards supposed safety in Deraa.

XXVI

Lawrence suggested at a midnight council that the whole Arab force should move up to Sheikh Saad, north of Deraa, astride the line of retreat of the main Turkish forces. The British staff- officer appointed by Joyce as senior military adviser for the expedition objected. He said that Allenby had set the Arabs as watchmen merely of the Fourth Army; they had seen its disorderly flight and their duty was over. They might now honourably fall back twenty miles out of the way to the east and there join forces with the Druses under their leader, Lawrence's foolish friend Nesib.

Lawrence would not hear of this. He was most anxious for the Arabs to be first in Damascus and to do their full share of the fighting. To thrust behind Deraa into Sheikh Saad would put more pressure on the Turks than any British unit was in a position to put. They could be prevented from making another stand this side of Damascus, and the capture of Damascus meant the end of the War in the East, and probably the end of the European War too. So for every reason the Arabs should go forward. The staff-officer would not be convinced. He argued and tried to drag Nuri Said into the debate. Finally he insisted that he was the senior military adviser and must reluctantly point out that as a regular officer he knew his business. It was not the first time that Lawrence had been slighted for not being a regular. He merely sighed, and said that he must sleep now, because he was getting up early to cross the line with his body-guard and the Bedouin, whatever the regulars did. However, Nuri Said decided to come with Lawrence and so did Pisani, and so did the rest of the British officers. And Tallal and the Emir Nuri and old Auda were already pressing forward.

Tallal and Auda undertook attacks on Ezraa and Ghazale, towns on the Damascus railway. The Emir Nuri would sweep towards Deraa in search of escaping Turkish parties. Lawrence himself went to Sheikh Saad with his body-guard, arriving there at dawn on the twenty-seventh of September. There was nearly a serious accident here, for they were invited to guest at the tent of one of the Emir Nuri's blood-enemies. Fortunately, the man himself was absent, so Lawrence's party accepted: Nuri, when he arrived, would find himself temporary host of his enemy's family and have to obey the rules. It was a great relief. Throughout the campaign they had been bothered with these same blood-feuds, barely suspended by Feisal's authority. It was a constant strain keeping enemies apart, trying to keep the hostile clans in friendly rivalry on separate ventures, making them camp always with a neutral clan between, and avoiding any suspicion of favouritism. As Lawrence comments, the campaign in France would have been harder to control if each division, almost each brigade, of the British Army had hated every other one with a deadly hatred and had fought at every chance meeting. However, Feisal, Nasir and he had managed successfully for two years and the end was only a few days off.

Auda returned boasting, having taken Ghazale by storm and captured a train, guns and two hundred men. Tallal had taken Ezraa, held by none other than Abd el Kader, the mad Algerian. When Tallal came the townsmen joined him and Abd el Kader had to escape to Damascus. Tallal's horsemen were too heavy with booty to catch him. The Emir Nuri captured four hundred Turks with mules and machine-guns: these prisoners were farmed out to remote villages as labourers to earn their keep. The rest of the army now arrived under Nuri Said and the peasants came shyly up to look at it. Feisal's army had hitherto been only a legendary thing. When no Turks were about, the peasants had spoken in whispers the famous names of its leaders—Tallal, Nasir, Nuri, Auda, 'Aurans'; whom now they saw in the flesh.

Lawrence and five or six others went up a hill for a look south to see if anything was moving. To their astonishment a company of regulars in uniform—Turks, Austrians, Germans—was coming slowly towards them with eight machine-guns mounted on pack-animals. They were marching up from Galilee towards Damascus after their defeat by Allenby, thinking themselves fifty miles from any war. Some of the Ruwalla nobles were at once sent to ambush them in a narrow lane: the officers showed fight and were instantly killed, the men threw down their arms and in five minutes had been searched and robbed and were being led off to the prisoners' camp in a cattle-pound. Next, Zaal and the Howeitat were sent against three or four other parties seen moving in the distance, and soon returned, each man leading a mule or a pack-horse. Zaal disdained to take such broken men prisoners. 'We gave them to the girls and boys of the village for servants,' he sneered.

The whole of the Hauran had now risen and in two days' time sixty thousand armed men would be waiting to cut up the Turkish retreat. A British aeroplane hovered over and dropped word that Bulgaria had surrendered. Evidently the whole war would soon be at an end as well as this Eastern campaign. The Germans were burning storehouses and aeroplanes at Deraa and another aeroplane dropped word that a Turkish column of four thousand men was retiring north from the town towards Sheikh Saad, and another column of two thousand from Mezerib. The smaller column seemed a safer size to attack, so the bigger, which later proved to be more like seven thousand strong, was let go by, with merely the Ruwalla horse and some Hauran peasants to harry it and cut off stragglers.

Tallal was anxious about the Mezerib Turks, because their path would lie through his own village of Tafas. He hurried there as fast as he could, determined to hold a ridge south of it. Lawrence galloped ahead of him, hoping to delay the Turks until the rest of the army came up. Unfortunately the camels and horses were tired out. On their way they met mounted Arabs herding a drove of Turkish prisoners stripped to the waist, beating them on with sticks. The Arabs shouted that these were the remnants of the police battalion at Deraa. Their record of monstrous cruelty towards the peasants Lawrence knew well and he made no appeal for mercy.

At Tafas he arrived too late. The Governor of Syria's own lancer regiment had already taken it and was burning the houses after massacring the inhabitants. Lawrence and the Arabs lay in ambush on a ridge to the north as the Turks marched out in good order with the lancers in front and rear, infantry in a central column, a flank-guard of machine-guns, guns and transport in the centre. When the head of the long column showed itself beyond the houses the Arabs opened fire with machine-guns. The Turks replied with field-guns, but as usual the shrapnel was badly ranged and burst far behind the ridge. Then up came Nuri Said and Pisani with mountain-guns, and Auda, and Tallal, nearly frantic with the news of the massacre of his people. The Arabs lined the northern ridge and opened rapid fire with mountain-guns, rifles and machine-guns. Tallal, Sheikh Abd el Aziz and Lawrence with their attendants slipped round behind the Turkish column, the last parties of which were just leaving the smoking village. There seemed to be no soul left alive in the ruins. But then from a heap of corpses a child tottered out, three or four years old, her dirty smock stained red with blood from a lance thrust where neck and shoulder joined. She ran a few steps, then stood and cried in a voice that sounded very loud in the ghastly silence, 'Don't hit me, Baba.' Abd el Aziz choked out something: it was his village as well as Tallal's. He flung himself off his camel and stumbled to the child. His suddenness frightened her, for she threw up her arms and tried to scream, but instead dropped in a little heap; the blood rushed out again and she died.

They saw four more dead babies and scores of corpses, men and women obscenely mutilated. El Zaagi broke out in peals of hysterical laughter: Lawrence said, 'The best of you are those who bring me the most Turkish dead.' They rode after the Turks, killing stragglers and wounded without mercy. Tallal had seen all. He gave one moan, then rode to the upper ground and sat awhile on his mare, shivering and staring at the retreating Turks. Lawrence moved near to speak to him, but Auda restrained him with a hand on his reins.

Very slowly Tallal drew his headcloth about his face, then

LAWRENCE AND HIS BODYGUARD AT AKABA

Summer, 1918

seemed to take hold of himself and galloped headlong, bending low and swaying in the saddle, right at the main body of the enemy. It was a long ride down a gentle slope and across a hollow. Both armies waited for him. Firing had stopped on both sides and the noise of his hooves sounded unnaturally loud as he rushed on. Only a few lengths from the enemy he sat up in the saddle and shouted his war-cry, 'Tallal, Tallal!' twice in a tremendous voice. Instantly the Turkish rifles and machine-guns crashed out and he and his mare fell riddled through and through among the lance-points.

Auda looked cold and grim. 'God give him mercy,' he said, 'we will take his price.' Then he slowly moved after the enemy. He took command of the Arabs, sending out parties of peasants this way and that and at last by a skilful turn drove the Turks into bad ground and split their force into three parts. The pursuit continued. The smallest section, consisting chiefly of German and Austrian machine-gunners grouped round three motor-cars, fought magnificently. The Arabs were like devils; hatred and revenge so shook them that they could hardly hold their rifles straight to fire. At last this section was left behind while Lawrence and his men galloped after the other two which were fleeing in panic. By sunset all but a few were destroyed. For the first time in the war Lawrence gave the order: 'No prisoners.' The peasants flocked to join in the attack. At first only one man in six had a weapon, but gradually they armed themselves from the fallen Turks until at nightfall every man had a rifle and a captured horse.

Just one group of Arabs who had not heard of the horror of Tafas took prisoners the last two hundred men. Lawrence went up to inquire why their lives had been spared, not unwilling to leave them alive as witnesses of Tallal's price. But a man on the ground screamed out something to the Arabs and they turned to see who it was. It was one of their own men, his thigh shattered, left to die. But even so he had not been spared. In the manner of Tafas he had been further tormented with bayonets hammered through his shoulder and other leg, pinning him to the ground like a collector's specimen. He was still conscious. They asked him, 'Hassan, who did it?' For answer he looked towards the prisoners huddled together near him. The Arabs shot them down in a heap and they were all dead before Hassan too died.

The killing and capturing of the retreating Turks went on all night. Each village, as the fight rolled towards it, took up the work. The main body of seven thousand men had tried to halt at sunset, but the Ruwalla had forced them on in a stumbling scattered mob through the cold and darkness. The Arabs, too, were scattered and nearly as uncertain and the confusion was indescribable. The only detachments that held together were the Germans. Lawrence for the first time felt proud of the enemy that had killed his two younger brothers. They went firmly ahead, proud and silent, steering like armoured ships through the wrack of Turks and Arabs. When attacked they halted, took position, fired at the word of command. It was glorious. They were two thousand miles from home, without hope and without guides, footsore, starving, sleepless: yet on they went, their numbers slowly lessening.

The Ruwalla took Deraa in a mounted charge that night; the garrison had been holding up the Indians at Remthe. Lawrence rode to Deraa to take charge of things, with his body-guard and Nuri Said. He was riding his grand racing-camel, Baha, so called from the bleat that she had from a bullet wound in her throat. He gave her liberty to stretch herself out, drawing ahead of the tired body-guard, so that he arrived alone at Deraa in the full dawn. Nasir was already there arranging for a military governor and police. Lawrence helped him by putting guards over the pumps and engine-sheds and what remained of the looted repair-shops and stores. Then he explained to Nasir what course had to be taken if the Arabs were not to lose hold of what they had won. Nasir, who now for the first time heard that there would be difficulty in persuading the English to take the Arabs seriously, was bewildered. But he soon grasped the point.

General Barrow, commanding the Indians, was advancing now to attack the town, not knowing that it was already captured. Some of his men began firing on the Arabs and Lawrence rode out with El Zaagi to stop them. A party of Indian machine-gunners was proud to capture such finely-dressed prisoners, but Lawrence explained himself to an officer and was allowed to hurry off to find General Barrow. His troops were already encircling the town and his aeroplanes bombed Nuri Said's men as they entered from the north. Barrow seemed annoyed that the Arabs had got there first, but Lawrence was not sorry for him; particularly since he had delayed a day and a night watering at the poor wells at Remthe, though his map had showed the lake and river of Mezerib close ahead on the road by which the enemy was escaping. Barrow said that his orders were to take Deraa and he was going there anyhow, whoever was in possession. He asked Lawrence to ride beside him. But Baha's smell disturbed the horses, so Lawrence had to take the centre of the road while the General and his staff rode their bucking horses in the ditch. Barrow said that he must put sentries in Deraa to keep the populace in order. Lawrence explained gently that the Arabs had appointed a military gov-

ernor. When they reached the wells the General said that his
engineers must inspect the pumps. Lawrence answered that
he would welcome their assistance, but that the Arabs had
already lit the furnaces and hoped to begin watering his horses
in an hour's time. Barrow snorted that Lawrence seemed to be
at home; so he would only take charge of the railway station.
Lawrence pointed to an engine moving out towards Mezerib
and asked Barrow to instruct his sentries not to interfere with
the proper working of the line by the Arabs.

Barrow had no orders as to the status of the Arabs and had
come in thinking of them as a conquered people; Lawrence
wondered how to prevent him from doing anything foolish
to antagonize them. He had read a military article, written
by Barrow years before, in which the General had insisted
that Fear was the people's main incentive to action in war
and peace; and knew what he was up against. Then Barrow
remarked that he was short of forage and food-stuffs, and
Lawrence, kindly offering to provide these, persuaded him
that he was the guest of the Arabs. Barrow was sufficiently
convinced to salute Nasir's little silk flag propped on the bal-
cony of the Government office, with a sentry beneath it. The
Arabs thrilled with pleasure at the compliment and were ready
to listen to Lawrence's instructions that these Indians must be
given all hospitality as guests. Later, General Allenby's Chief
Political Officer assured Barrow that Lawrence's attitude
was politically right, so all was well. There had been no dis-
turbances, though the Indians pilfered freely from the Arabs,
and the Bedouin were horrified at the manner of the British
officers towards their men. They had never seen such personal
inequality before.

Thousands of prisoners had meanwhile been taken by

the Arabs. Most were boarded out in the villages, some were handed over to the British, who counted them again as their own captures. Feisal drove up in his green car from Azrak the next day, September the twenty- ninth, with the armoured cars behind him. General Barrow, now watered and fed, was due to meet Chauvel, the general commanding the Australians, for a joint entry into Damascus. He told Lawrence to ask Feisal to take the right flank. That suited Lawrence, for there along the railway was Nasir still hanging on to the main Turkish retreat (the column seven thousand strong which the Ruwalla had harried on the night of the Tafas massacre), reducing its numbers by continuous attack night and day. He stayed another day at Deraa, having much to attend to, but his memories of the place were too horrible, and he camped outside the town with his body-guard.

He could not sleep that night, so before dawn he went off in the Rolls-Royce towards Damascus. The roads were blocked with the Indians' transport; he took a cut across country and along the railway. He overtook Barrow, who asked him where he was going to stop that night. 'At Damascus,' Lawrence answered, and Barrow's face fell. Barrow was advancing very cautiously, sending out scouts and cavalry-screens through friendly country already cleared of Turks by the Arabs. Lawrence's Rolls-Royce continued along the railway till he came on Nasir, the Emir Nuri, and Auda with the tribes, still fighting. The seven thousand Turks had melted to two in three days' ceaseless battle. Lawrence could see the survivors in ragged groups halting now and then to fire their mountain-guns. Nasir rode up to greet Lawrence on his liver-coloured Arab stallion (the splendid creature was still spirited after a hundred miles of running flight). With him were old Emir Nuri and about thirty of his servants. They asked whether help was coming at last. Lawrence told them that the Indians were just behind. If they could only check the enemy for just an hour. . . . Nasir saw a walled farm-house ahead guarding the track and he and Nuri galloped forward to hold it against the Turks.

Lawrence drove back to the Indian cavalry and told a surly old colonel what a gift the Arabs had waiting for him. The colonel hardly seemed grateful, but at last sent a squadron out across the plain. The Turks turned their little guns at it. One or two shells fell near and to Lawrence's disgust the colonel ordered a retirement. Lawrence and the staff-officer in the car with him dashed back and begged the colonel not to be afraid of the wretched little ten-pound shells, hardly more dangerous than rocket-pistols. But the old man would not budge, so the Rolls-Royce had to rush back farther until Lawrence found a general of Barrow's staff and got him to send some Middlesex Yeomanry and Royal Horse Artillery forward. That night the remaining Turks broke, abandoning their guns and transport, and went streaming off across the eastern hills into what they thought was empty land beyond. But Auda was waiting there in ambush, and all that night, in his last battle, the old man killed and killed, plundered and captured until, when dawn came, he found that all was over. So passed the Turkish Fourth Army.

It may be interesting to note the record of these operations in the official handbook, *A Brief Record of the Advance of the Egyptian Expeditionary Force*:

'The Fourth Mounted Division (General Barrow's) coming up from the south with the Arab forces on its right entered Deraa unopposed on September 28th, and next day got in touch with the retreating

Turks in the Dilli area. For two days the enemy was pressed and harassed, his columns were fired upon and broken up, and on September 30th the division got into touch with the other divisions of the Desert Mounted Corps and reached Zerakiye late that night.'

Other references to the Arabs' services are similarly reticent. (There are, however, plentiful references to the way that the Beni Sakhr tribe *failed* the Amman raiders some months previously.) This withholding of credit where due was, I think, principally Lawrence's fault; he did not send detailed reports to General Headquarters. He was, of course, far too busy. What really mattered to him was not that the Arabs should be given homage in Allenby's despatches—they would not for the most part have been particularly gratified—but that they should set up a government in Damascus before somebody else did.

XXVII

The war was over. Lawrence went on to Kiswe, where the Australians were waiting for Barrow to join them. He did not stop long, for Allenby had allowed him and Feisal a single night in which to restore order in Damascus before the British entry. The Ruwalla horse was sent in at dusk to find Ali Riza, the governor, and to ask him to take charge of things. Ali Riza who, as chairman of the committee of freedom, had long been prepared to form an Arab government when the Turks finally left, was away, put by the Turks in command of the army retreating from Galilee. But Shukri, his assistant, was there and with unexpected help, as will be related, set up the Arab flag on the Town Hall as the last Turkish and German troops marched out. It is said that the hindmost general saluted it ironically.

Four thousand Ruwalla tribesmen were sent in to help Shukri keep order. All that night huge explosions were heard from the town, and showers of flame shot up. Lawrence thought that Damascus was being destroyed. But dawn showed him the beautiful city still standing: it had only been the Germans blowing up the ammunition dumps and stores. A horseman galloped out with a bunch of yellow grapes, a token from Shukri, crying: 'Good news: Damascus salutes you.' Lawrence, who was in the Rolls-Royce, gave Nasir the tidings. Nasir's fifty battles since the Revolt began in Medina two and a half years back had earned him the right of first entry. So Lawrence gave him a fair start with the Emir Nuri while he stopped to wash and shave at a wayside brook. Some Indian troopers again mistook him and his party for Turks and tried to take them prisoners. When delivered from arrest Lawrence drove on up the long central street to the Government buildings.

The way was packed with people crowded solid on either side of the car, at the windows, on the balconies and housetops. Many were crying, some cheered faintly, a few bolder ones cried out greetings. But for the most part, there came little more than a whisper like a long sigh from the gate of the city to the city's heart. At the Town Hall there was greater liveliness. The steps and stairs were packed with a swaying mob yelling, embracing, dancing, singing. They recognized Lawrence and crushed back to let him pass.

In the antechamber he found Nasir and the Emir Nuri seated. On either side of these stood—Lawrence was dumb with amazement at the sight—his old enemy the Algerian Abd el Kader who had betrayed him on the Yarmuk raid, and Mohammed Said, the assassin, his brother. Mohammed Said leaped forward and said that he and his brother, grandsons of the famous Abd el Kader, Emir of Algiers, had, with Shukri, formed the government the previous afternoon and proclaimed Hussein 'Emperor of the Arabs' in the ears of the humbled Turks and Germans. Lawrence turned inquiringly to Shukri, an honest man beloved in Damascus and almost a martyr in the people's eyes for what he had suffered at Jemal's hands. Shukri told how these two alone of all Damascus had stood by the Turks until they saw them running. Then with their Algerian retainers they had burst in on Shukri's committee where it sat in secret and brutally assumed control.

Lawrence determined with Nasir's help to check their impudence at once. But a diversion interrupted him. The yelling crowd was parted as if by a battering ram; men went flying right and left among ruined chairs and tables while a familiar voice roared them to silence. It was Auda, in a dog-fight with the chief of the Druses. Lawrence and Mohammed el Dheilan sprang forward and broke the two apart. They forced Auda back while somebody else hustled the Druse chief into a side room. Auda, with bleeding face and his long hair streaming over his eyes, was too blind with rage to know what was happening. They held him down in a gilt chair in the great pompous state-hall, where he shouted till his voice cracked. His body was twitching and jerking, his hands reached wildly for any weapon within reach. The Druse had hit him first and he swore to wipe out the insult in blood. Zaal and one or two more came in to help. It was an hour before they could calm Auda down and get him to promise to pospone his vengeance for three days.

Lawrence went out and had the Druse chief secretly and speedily removed from the city. When he returned Nasir and Abd el Kader had gone off. There remained Shukri. Lawrence took him out in the Rolls-Royce to show him off as acting-Governor to the delighted city. The streets were more crowded than ever. Damascus went mad with joy. The men tossed up their red felt hats, the women tore off their veils. Householders threw flowers, hangings, carpets into the road before the car. Their wives leaned out, screaming with laughter, through the harem- lattices, splashing Lawrence and Shukri with bath-dippers of scent. Dervishes ran before and behind, howling and cutting themselves with frenzy, while a measured chant rose from the men of the crowd: 'Feisal, Nasir, Shukri, Aurans,' rolling in waves round the city. Chauvel, like Barrow, had no instructions as to what to do with the captured city and was relieved when Lawrence told him that an Arab government was appointed. But Lawrence begged him to keep his Australians out of Damascus that night, because there would be such a carnival as the city had not seen for six hundred years and Arab hospitality might pervert the troops' discipline. Chauvel agreed, and asked if it would be convenient to make a formal entry the next day. Lawrence said: 'Certainly.'

While they were discussing ceremonial antics there was enormously more important work waiting inside and outside the city for both of them. Lawrence felt ashamed to be spoiling Chauvel's entry in this rather low-down way, but the political importance of winning the game of grab justified everything. Now he hurried off to the Town Hall to find Abd el Kader and his brother, but they had not returned, and when he sent a messenger to their house he received only a curt reply that they were sleeping. So should Lawrence have been, but instead he was eating a snatch meal with the Emir Nuri, Shukri and others, seated on gold chairs at a gold table in the gaudy banquet-hall. He told the messenger that the Algerians must come at once or they would be fetched: the messenger ran off hurriedly.

The old Emir asked quietly what Lawrence meant to do. He answered that he would dismiss Abd el Kader and his brother. The Emir asked whether he would call in English troops. Lawrence answered that he might have to do so, but the trouble was that afterwards they might not go. The Emir thought a moment and said, 'You shall have the Ruwalla to do all you want to do, and at once.' He ran out to muster his tribe. The Algerians came to the Town Hall with their body-guards, murder in their eyes, but on the way met the Ruwalla tribesmen massed under their Emir; and Nuri Said with his Arab regulars in the Square; and in the Town Hall itself Law-rence's reckless body-guard lounging in the antechamber. They saw that the game was up; but it was a stormy meeting.

Lawrence speaking as Feisal's deputy pronounced their gov-ernment abolished. He named Shukri as acting Military Gov-ernor until Ali Riza's return. Nuri Said was to be Commandant of Troops, and he appointed also a Chief of Public Security and an Adjutant-General. Mohammed Said in a bitter reply denounced Lawrence as a Christian and an Englishman; he called on Nasir, whom he and his brother had been enter-taining and who knew nothing of Abd el Kader's treacheries, to assert himself. Nasir did not understand this falling out of his friends: he could only sit and look miserable. Abd el Kader leaped up and cursed Lawrence, working himself up to a fanatic passion. Lawrence paid no attention at all. This maddened Abd el Kader even more. Suddenly he went for Lawrence with a drawn dagger.

Like a flash old Auda was on him, still boiling with fury from the morning's insult and longing for a fight. Lawrence he loved and trusted as much as he loathed the traitor Abd el Kader. It would have been heaven for the old man to have torn the Algerian limb from limb with his great hands. Again he was pulled away. Abd el Kader was frightened, and the Emir Nuri closed the debate in his short dry way by saying that the Ruwalla were at Lawrence's service, and no questions asked.

The Algerians rose and angrily swept out of the hall. Lawrence was convinced that they should be seized and shot, but he did not want to set the Arabs a bad example of political murder on the first day of their government.

He set about helping Shukri and the rest to organize the government of the city and province. He knew that the change from war to peace was an ungracious one; rebels, especially successful rebels, were necessarily bad subjects and worse governors. Feisal's unhappy duty would be to rid himself of most of his war-friends and replace them by the officials who had been most useful to the Turkish Government. These were the solid steady people who had been too unimaginative to rebel and who would work for an Arab government as solidly and steadily as they had for the Turks. Nasir did not realize this, but Nuri Said and the Emir Nuri knew it well.

Quickly they collected a staff and began to take the necessary administrative steps. A police force. The water-supply (for the city-conduit was foul with dead men and animals). The electric light supply; most important, for to have the street-lights working again would be the most obvious sign that peace had come at last—it was successfully working that night. Sanitation; the streets and squares were full of the strewn relics of the Turkish retreat, broken carts, baggage, dead animals, typhus and dysentery corpses. Nuri Said appointed scavengers to clear up and distributed his few doctors among the hospitals, promising drugs and stores next day if any were to be had. A fire-brigade; the local fire-engines had been smashed by the Germans and the storehouses were still on fire, but volunteers were sent to blow up houses around the fires to keep the flames from spreading farther. The prisons; warders and prisoners had vanished together, so

Shukri proclaimed a general amnesty. Civil disturbance; they must gradually disarm the citizens or at least persuade them not to carry rifles in the street. Relief-work; the destitute had been half-starved for days, so the damaged food rescued from the burning storehouses was distributed among them.

The general food-supply; there were no food-stocks in Damascus and starvation would follow in two days if steps were not taken at once. It would be easy to get temporary supplies from the near villages if confidence were restored, the roads safeguarded and the transport animals (carried off by the Turks) replaced by others from the general pool of captures. The British refused to share out, so the Arab army had to give the city all its own transport animals. The railway; for the future food-supply. Pointsmen, drivers, firemen, shopmen, traffic-staff had to be found and re-engaged immediately. The telegraph-system; the lines had to be repaired and directors appointed. Finance; the Australians had looted millions of pounds in Turkish notes, the only currency in use, and reduced it to no value by throwing it about. One trooper had given a boy a five-hundred pound note for holding his horse for three minutes. What was left of the British gold from Akaba was used to stabilize the currency at a low rate of exchange; but new prices then had to be fixed and this meant setting up a printing press.

Then a newspaper was demanded, to restore public confidence. Then Chauvel demanded forage for his forty thousand horses. He had to be given it, for otherwise he would be compelled to seize what he needed by main force. The Arabs could expect little mercy from Chauvel and the fate of Syria's freedom depended on his being satisfied. Three Arabic- speaking British officers who had been on the Akaba

expedition with Lawrence helped him and Shukri and the rest
with all this hasty organization. Lawrence's aim had been to
run up a façade rather than a whole well-fitted building, but
so furiously well had the work of that evening been done that
when he left Damascus three days later the Syrians had a government which endured for two years without foreign advice,
in an occupied country wasted by war, and against the will of
at least one of the occupying Allies.

Lawrence writes then:

> 'Later I was sitting alone in my room working and
> thinking out as firm a way as the turbulent memo-
> ries of the day allowed, when the muezzins began to
> send their call of last prayer through the moist night
> over the illuminations of the feasting city. One, with
> a ringing voice of special sweetness, cried into my
> window from a near mosque. I found myself invol-
> untarily distinguishing his words: "God alone is
> great: I testify that there are no gods but God: and
> Mohammed is his Prophet. Come to prayer: come
> to security. God alone is great: there is no god—but
> God."
>
> 'At the close he dropped his voice two tones, almost
> to speaking level, and softly added: "And He is very
> good to us this day, O people of Damascus." The
> clamour hushed, as every one seemed to obey the call
> to prayer on this their first night of perfect freedom.'

It is with this passage that Lawrence closes the popular
abridged version of his great *Seven Pillars of Wisdom*. But
almost dishonestly, for there followed this further sentence:

'While my fancy, in the overwhelming pause, showed me my loneliness and lack of reason in their movement: since only for me, of all the hearers, was the event sorrowful and the phrase meaningless.'

He is referring, I think, both to the extinction of that strong personal motive that kept him alive through the almost incredible hardships of his task, and to the shame he felt for deceiving the Arabs with what still seemed the hollowest of frauds.

XXVIII

He went to sleep, for the first time for days, but was almost immediately aroused by news that Abd el Kader was making rebellion. He sent word across to Nuri Said, glad that the mad fellow was digging his own grave. Abd el Kader had summoned his retainers, told them that the members of the new government were merely the tools of the English and called on them to strike a blow for religion while there was yet time. The simple Algerians had taken his word that it was so and run to arms. They were joined by the Druses, who were angry that Lawrence had sharply refused to reward them for their services; they had joined the Revolt too late to be of any real use. Algerians and Druses together began to burst open shops and to riot.

Lawrence and Nuri Said waited until dawn, then moved men to the upper suburbs and swept the rioters towards the river-districts of the centre of the city. Here machine-guns kept a constant barrage of fire along the river-front, aimed merely at blank walls but impossible to pass. Mohammed Said was captured and gaoled; Abd el Kader fled back to his Yarmuk village. The Druses were expelled from the city, leaving horses and rifles in the hands of the Damascus citizens enrolled for the emergency as civic guards. By noon everything was quiet and the street traffic became normal again with the pedlars hawking, as before, sweetmeats, iced drinks, flowers and little crimson Arab flags.

When the fighting began Lawrence had called up Chauvel on the telephone and he had at once offered troops. Lawrence thanked him and asked for a second company of horse to be added to the company already stationed at the principal Turkish Barracks; to stand by in case of need. But they were not needed. The only startling effect was on the war-correspondents. They were in a hotel, the blank wall of which was the stop-block of one of the barrages, and began telegraphing home without sufficient caution the wild stories that were flying about.

Allenby, still in the neighbourhood of Jerusalem, asked Lawrence to confirm their reports of wholesale massacre. He sent back a death-roll naming the five victims and the hurts of the ten wounded.

He returned to the organization of public services. The Spanish Consul called officially; he was representing the interests of seventeen nationalities and had been vainly searching for some responsible governing body with which to deal. Lawrence was glad of the opportunity of using such international channels for spreading the authority of a Government which he had audaciously appointed on his own initiative. At midday an Australian doctor appeared, imploring Lawrence for the sake of humanity to take notice of the Turkish hospital. Lawrence ran over in his mind the three hospitals in Arab charge, the military, the civil, the missionary, and told him that they were as well cared for as they could be. The Arabs could not invent drugs and Chauvel could not let them have any of his. The doctor went on to describe a huge range of filthy buildings without a single medical officer or orderly, packed with dead and dying; mainly dysentery cases, but at least some typhoid; and it was to be hoped, no typhus or cholera.

Lawrence wondered if he could mean the Turkish barracks where the two Australian companies were stationed. He asked whether there were sentries at the gates. 'Yes, that's the place,' said the doctor, 'but it's full of Turkish sick.' Lawrence walked there at once and parleyed with the Australian guard. At last his English accent got him past the little lodge, and a garden filled with two hundred wretched prisoners in exhaustion and despair. He stood at the great door of the barrack and called up the dusty echoing corridors.

Nobody answered. The guard had told him that thousands of prisoners had yesterday gone from here to a camp beyond the city. Since then no one had come in or out. He walked over to a shuttered lobby and stepped in. There was a sickening stench and a heap of dead bodies laid out on the stone floor, some in uniform, some naked. A few were corpses of no more than a day or two old; some had been there for days. Beyond was a great ward from which he thought he heard a groan. He walked down the room between the beds, lifting his white silk skirts off the filthy floor. It seemed that every bed held a dead man; but as he went forward there was a stir as several tried to raise their hands. Not one of them had strength to speak, but the dry whisper 'Pity, pity' came in unison.

Lawrence ran into the garden where the Australians had picketed their horses and asked for a working party. They could not help him. Kirkbride, the young English officer who had been with Lawrence since Tafileh and had been foremost in suppressing the Abd el Kader rebellion, came to help. He

FEISAL JUST AFTER HIS MEETING WITH ALLENBY
Copyright Imperial War Museum

had heard that Turkish doctors were upstairs. He burst open a door and found seven men in nightgowns sitting on unmade beds in a great room, boiling toffee. Lawrence impressed on these Turks that the dead must be at once sorted from the living and a list of the numbers presented to him in half an hour's time. Kirkbride, a tall fellow with heavy boots and a ready revolver, was a suitable overseer of this duty.

Lawrence then found Ali Riza, now back again from the Turks and appointed Governor, asking him to detail one of the four Arab Army doctors to take charge of the place. When the doctor arrived the fifty fittest prisoners of the lodge were pressed to act as a labour party and set in the backyard to dig a common grave. It was cruelty to work men so tired and ill, but haste gave Lawrence no choice. The doctor reported fifty-six dead, two hundred dying, seven hundred not dangerously ill. A stretcher party was formed, but before the work was done two of their bodies were added to the heap of dead men in the pit. The Australians protested that it was no fit place for a grave; the smell might drive them from their garden. . . . Lawrence found quicklime to cover the bodies. Before the work was finished it was midnight, and Lawrence went off to his hotel, leaving Kirkbride to finish the burying and close the pit.

Lawrence then slept—for four days he had only allowed himself three hours' sleep—and in the morning everything in Damascus seemed to have cleared up wonderfully. The tram-cars were running, the shops open, grain and vegetables and fruit were coming in well from outside. The streets were being watered to lay the terrible dust, though no surface treatment would remedy the damage of three years' heavy lorry traffic. Lawrence was particularly glad to see numbers of British troops sightseeing unarmed in the city. The telegraph was restored with Palestine and Beyrout. He was sorry to hear that the Arabs had seized Beyrout the night before, for as long ago as the Wejh operations he had warned them, when they took Damascus, to leave Beyrout and the Lebanon to the French, but to take the port of Tripoli, fifty miles north, instead. Still, he was glad to think that they felt themselves grown-up enough to disobey him.

Even the hospital was better. The fifty prisoners, now called 'orderlies,' had cleaned up the litter and rubbish. Others had gone through the wards, lifting and washing each patient. One ward had been cleared of beds, brushed out and sprinkled with disinfectant, and the less serious cases were about to be transferred here for their ward to be cleaned in turn. At this rate three days would have seen the place in fairly good order.

Lawrence was arranging other improvements when an Army Medical Corps major strode up and asked him shortly whether he spoke English. 'Yes,' said Lawrence. The Major looked with disgust at his skirts and sandals and asked: 'You're in charge?' 'In a way I am,' Lawrence answered. 'Scandalous, disgraceful, outrageous, ought to be shot . . .' the major bellowed. At this sudden attack Lawrence, whose nerves were very ragged, began to laugh hysterically; he had been so proud of himself for having bettered what was apparently past hope. The major had not seen the charnel-house of the day before, nor smelt it, nor helped in the burying of the putrefying corpses. He smacked Lawrence in the face and stalked off.

When Lawrence returned to the hotel he saw large crowds round a familiar grey Rolls-Royce: he ran in and found Allenby. Allenby welcomed him and approved the steps that he had taken for setting up Arab governments at Deraa and Damascus. He confirmed Ali Riza's appointment as his mili-

tary governor and regulated the spheres of interest for Feisal
and Chauvel. He agreed to take over the barracks-hospital
and the railway. In ten minutes all difficulties had slipped
away: Allenby's confidence and decision and kindliness were
like a pleasant dream.

Then Feisal's train arrived from Deraa and the rolling
cheers as he came riding up could be heard louder and louder
through the windows. He was coming to call on Allenby, and
Lawrence was happy to be the interpreter between his two
masters at their first meeting. Allenby gave Lawrence, for
Feisal, a telegram just received from the British Government
'recognizing to the Arabs their status as belligerents.' But
nobody knew what it meant in English, let alone in Arabic,
so Feisal, smiling but still with tears in his eyes from his welcome by the crowd, put it aside to satisfy the ambition of
a year—he thanked Allenby for the trust which had helped
his Revolt to victory. 'They were a strange contrast,' writes
Lawrence—'Feisal large-eyed, colourless and worn, like a fine
dagger; Allenby gigantic and red and merry, fit representative
of the Power which had thrown a girdle of humour and strong
dealing around the world.'

The interview lasted only a few minutes and when Feisal
had gone Lawrence made Allenby the first and last request
that he had ever made for himself—leave to go away. For a
while Allenby would not give it, but Lawrence pointed out
how much easier the change from war to peace conditions
would be for the Arabs if his influence were removed. Allenby
understood and gave his permission and then Lawrence at
once realized how sorry he was to be going.

He took leave of his Arab friends. Among those others who
came to say good-bye was Chauvel, who thanked Lawrence

warmly for all he had done for him. He went off then in a
Rolls-Royce. For more than a year after there were groups
of his friends hanging about the aerodromes in hope of his
return. It rather annoyed the Air Force officers when they
landed from a flight that each time a small mob came pressing
about the machine, to draw back always disappointed, crying:
'No Aurans!'

XXIX

He returned to England, arriving in London, after four years' absence, on Armistice Day, November 11th, 1918. Feisal arrived a few weeks later and Lawrence, after first escorting him round England, accompanied him to Paris for the Peace Conference. Lawrence had been appointed by the British Foreign Office as a member of the British Delegation, and he now used the same extraordinary energy that had gone towards winning the war in the Desert for winning the war in the Council Chamber. But he knew well that it was a losing one.

The French had made things difficult for a start by refusing to recognize Feisal as the ruler of Damascus and of the other Syrian cities that they wanted for themselves. And Feisal's position was not at all a secure one. His only right to take part in the Peace Conference was as representing the 'ally' Sherif Hussein, his father, whose claim to call himself King of the Hejaz (the Holy Province and the Red Sea coast as far as Akaba) was alone recognized. All official business had to be transacted in Hussein's name, though actually no Hejaz business came before the Peace Conference. All discussion was limited to Syria and Mesopotamia, about which Hussein's right to treat was not admitted by the French. If Hussein and Feisal had been in agreement it would have been easier, but the ambitious narrow-minded old man was most jealous of his son. He wanted to rule a great religious Empire consisting of all the Arabic- speaking parts of the old Turkish Empire, and to make Mecca his capital.

While the war lasted it was advisable not to oppose him too strongly, since unity was necessary in the Arab movement; but when the Armistice came Lawrence set about putting him quietly in his place. Mecca was the worst city in the whole Arabic-speaking world, a hot-bed of religious fanaticism (and also of vice) and, because of its sanctity and its distance from Syria and Mesopotamia, impossible as the capital of any enlightened State. Also the Desert (for Mecca was the Desert) could never rule the settled lands: the settled lands were passing into modern civilization and the Desert would always remain barbarous and primitive.

Sir Henry McMahon, who as High Commissioner of Egypt had concluded the first treaty with Hussein that made him enter the war on the side of the Allies, has told me about Lawrence at Paris. 'I was appointed,' he said, 'as British member of the delegation to Syria, Palestine and Mesopotamia to report on the feeling of the peoples concerned as to what governments would be most welcome to them and on the possibility of gratifying their wishes. When I got to Paris nobody seemed to know anything about what was happening; I could not even find out who my colleagues were. The only person who seemed to know every one and everything and to have access to all the Big Three—Clemenceau, Lloyd George and Woodrow Wilson—was Lawrence. I don't know how he did it, but he was in and out of their private rooms all the time and, as he was about the only man who knew the whole Eastern geographical and racial question inside out, they were probably glad of his advice. He found me my colleagues at once, all except the French delegate: but, possibly, the French never intended the delegation to go, for the Frenchman was never appointed and never will be, and nothing ever came of the business.'

Lawrence took Lloyd George into his confidence, a man in whom he found a sympathy for small or oppressed nations that matched his own, and explained to him simply what the problem was. Arab independence had begun in the Desert; as was to be expected, for the Desert is the starting-off point of all great Arab movements. But as soon as it reached the settled countries of Syria and Mesopotamia it had to be stabilized there; the Desert has always made sudden magnificent efforts that in the end tail off into nothing. He wanted Damascus as the settled home of this new Arab independence and he wanted Feisal as the first ruler of the new Syrian state with Damascus as his capital. The French, in exact accordance with the terms of the Sykes-Picot treaty, might be satisfied with having Beyrout and the Lebanon and the north Syrian coast for their own, and with the privilege of assisting the Damascus State with what advice its administrators needed.

Mesopotamia would form another Arab State, or perhaps two, even, and eventually some generations hence when communications by road, rail and air had drawn together the more civilized Arab provinces, there might be a United States of Arabia. Lawrence advised that nothing should now be done to promote early confederation; but that, particularly, nothing should be done to hinder it. The Desert should be left alone to look after itself in the old way without interference from the settled lands of Arabia, or from the rest of the world.

Lloyd George might have agreed to this, but unfortunately the Sykes-Picot Treaty had put Mosul into the sphere of French influence. This did not distress Lawrence, but it threatened ruin to the military occupation of Mesopotamia which the Imperial Government, Bagdad having been won at such cost, intended to turn into a British administered province. So when the case came up before the Council of Ten—present, Clemenceau and Pichon (France), Lloyd George (England), Montagu (Indian Government), Sonnino (Italy) and others—the French were allowed to take the same equivocal attitude towards Syria as the British were taking towards Mesopotamia. Lawrence was present as Feisal's interpreter at this most eventful meeting and spoke in Arabic, French and English. An amusing incident was Pichon's speech quoting St. Louis and France's claims on Syria during the Crusades. Feisal, a successor of Saladin, replied, 'But pardon me, M. Pichon, which of us won the Crusades?'

The various contradictory pledges which Lawrence had first been shown by the Emir Nuri were then discussed, and finally, after months of intrigue, Feisal and Clemenceau appear to have come to a secret working agreement. Feisal was, with French help, to rule the greater part of inland Syria, from Damascus; the French took Beyrout and the Syrian coast. The Jews were given a home in Palestine, under British protection. But the British kept Mesopotamia and discouraged all agitation there towards Arab independence. Nothing of this agreement, if it was an agreement, was made public during the life of the Peace Conference: but Feisal returned to Syria and the working arrangement began to show itself.

Lord Riddell has kindly given me the following story: 'After the final debate at Versailles I had a talk with Feisal and Lawrence. The latter ascribed to Feisal the following observation: "In the desert, overtaking a long caravan of camels, you find each camel tied by his nose-rope to the tail of the camel in front of him; but when you reach the head of the string after a long walk you find that it is led by a little donkey!" The implication was of course that the stately ones were dull and lacking in brains, and that the leaders were artful but not profound.'

This was how matters stood at the close of the Peace Conference and Lawrence was not at all satisfied with them: as he clearly showed in his letter to *The Times* in 1920, printed in Appendix B. In England, at his first coming, he had refused to accept his British decorations. According to an account that he gave me a few months later, he explained personally to his Sovereign that the part he had played in the Arab Revolt was dishonourable to himself and to his country and government. He had, by order, fed the Arabs with false hopes and would now be obliged if he might be quietly relieved of the obligation to accept honours for succeeding in his fraud. He said respectfully as a subject, but firmly as an individual, that he intended to fight by straight means or crooked until His Majesty's ministers had conceded to the Arabs a fair settlement of their claims. According to this account, to which Lawrence had nothing to add when I submitted my version of it to him recently, for verification, His Majesty, though unwilling to believe that Ministers of the Crown were capable of double-dealing, respected Lawrence's scruples, permitting him to forgo his decorations. Lawrence expressed his gratitude, and thereupon also returned his foreign decorations to their donors with an account of the circumstances.

Lord Stamfordham, His Majesty's Private Secretary, to whom I wrote for permission to print this paragraph, has been good enough to get His Majesty's own recollections of the interview: 'His Majesty does not remember that Colonel Lawrence's statement was what you have recorded: but that, in asking permission to decline the proffered decorations, Colonel Lawrence explained in a few words that he had made certain promises to King Feisal: that these promises had not been fulfilled, and consequently, it was quite possible that he might find himself fighting against the British Forces, in which case it would be obviously impossible and wrong to be wearing British Decorations. The King has no recollection of Colonel Lawrence's saying that the part he had played in the Arab Revolt was dishonourable to himself and to his Country and Government.'

He returned to Cairo during the tail-end of the Peace Conference to collect his diaries and photographs of the war-period and on his way by Handley-Page was in a bad crash at Rome. Both the pilots were killed and Lawrence had three ribs and a collar-bone broken, with other injuries. It was at Paris that he began writing his book *Seven Pillars of Wisdom*, of which the next chapter will treat. In July 1919 he was demobilized and at the conclusion of the Peace Conference returned to London and lived there until November 1919, when he was elected to a seven-year research fellowship at All Souls' College, Oxford. 1920 he again spent in London. Meanwhile things were developing politically. After Clemenceau retired, the French Government's attitude to Syria became stiffer, and the working agreement that had apparently existed was replaced by a veiled state of war. This soon gave an excuse for open hostilities, and Feisal, not himself resisting, was turned out of Damascus. He withdrew to Palestine and thence to Italy and England, where he pleaded to the British Government for help. Nothing could be done for him and he returned to Mecca. Here he lived for some while until he received an invitation, through his father, from influential elements in Bagdad to visit Mesopotamia as their nominee for the now vacant throne of that country. He obtained assurances from the British Government that his acceptance of the throne would be welcome to it; and was duly crowned in Bagdad with the assistance of Sir Percy Cox, the British High Commissioner.

It had seemed after Feisal's expulsion from Damascus that Lawrence's worst fears were realized, that having duped the Arabs with false hopes he had been unable even to win them a small degree of independence. But he did not give up hope. Finally, in February 1921, the crisis in Mesopotamia became so acute that Middle Eastern affairs were transferred to the sphere of the Colonial Office and the appointment was made of Mr. Winston Churchill as Colonial Minister. He sent for Lawrence and offered him the post of adviser to himself, with the promise of a fair deal if he would help to put things straight in the East. Lawrence consented on one condition, that the war-time pledges given to the Arabs should at last be honoured. His 'straight means or crooked' are plainly given in the following letter which he wrote to me in reply to certain queries of mine as to his motives and intentions during this very obscure period:

'Events in Mecca had changed much between June 1919, when I found the Coalition Ministry very reluctant to take a liberal line in the Middle East, and

March 1921, when Mr. Winston Churchill took over.
The slump had come in the City. The Press, with help
from many quarters, including mine, was attacking
the expense of our war-time commitments in Asia.
Lord Curzon's lack of suppleness and subtlety had
enflamed a situation already made difficult by revolt
in Mesopotamia, bad feeling in Palestine, disorder
in Egypt and the continuing break with Nationalist
Turkey. So the Cabinet was half persuaded to make a
clean cut of our Middle East responsibilities; to evac-
uate Mesopotamia, "Milnerize Egypt," and perhaps
give Palestine to a third party. Mr. Churchill was
determined to find ways and means of avoiding so
complete a reversal of the traditional British attitude.
I was at one with him in this attitude: indeed I fancy I
went beyond him in my desire to see as many "brown"
dominions in the British Empire as there are "white."
It will be a sorry day when our estate stops growing.'

(The Lawrence who wrote that last sentence is difficult to reconcile with the nihilistic Lawrence without
national predilections, but both are Lawrence—or
rather Shaw—and you can take your choice.)

The War Office (under Sir Henry Wilson) was a strong
advocate of Mesopotamian withdrawal, since the minimum
cost of military occupation was twenty million pounds a
year. Winston Churchill persuaded Sir Hugh Trenchard, the
Air Chief of Staff, to undertake military responsibility there
for less than a quarter that cost. The Royal Air Force was to
be used instead of troops and the Senior Air Officer would

command all forces in Irak. This was a new departure in Air history: but Sir Hugh Trenchard was confident in the quality of the men and officers under his command. And Lawrence, who advocated the change with all his powers, believed that such early responsibility would be the making of the young Service. (Lawrence again in a purposeful mood!)

But this policy would only be practicable if it were joined with a liberal measure of Arab self-government controlled by a treaty between Irak (the Arabic name for Mesopotamia) and Great Britain, instead of a Mandate. The Cabinet agreed after an eventful discussion and the new policy brought peace.

> 'British and native casualties in the five years since the treaty was made with Irak have only been a few tens, whereas before the treaty they had run to thousands. The Arab Government in Irak, while not wholly free from the diseases of childhood, is steadily improving in competence and self-confidence. There is a progressive reduction in the British personnel there. The country has financial independence in sight. Our aim is its early admission to the responsibility of membership of the League of Nations. Our hope is that it will continue its treaty relations with Great Britain in return for the manifest advantages of intimate connection with so large a firm as the British Empire.
>
> 'I told Lloyd George at Paris that the centre of Arab Independence will eventually be Bagdad, not Damascus, since the future of Mesopotamia is great and the possible development of Syria is small. Syria now has 5,000,000 inhabitants, Irak only 3,000,000. Syria will only have 7,000,000 when Irak has 40,000,000. But I envisaged

Damascus as the capital of an Arab State for perhaps twenty years. When the French took it after two years, we had to transfer the focus of Arab nationalism at once to Bagdad; which was difficult, since during the war and armistice period British local policy had been sternly repressive of all nationalist feeling.

'I take to myself credit for some of Mr. Churchill's pacification of the Middle East, for while he was carrying it out he had the help of such knowledge and energy as I possess. His was the imagination and courage to take a fresh departure and enough skill and knowledge of political procedure to put his political revolution into operation in the Middle East, and in London, peacefully. When it was in working order, in March 1922, I felt that I had gained every point I wanted. The Arabs had their chance and it was up to them, if they were good enough, to make their own mistakes and profit by them. My object with the Arabs was always to make them stand on their own feet. The period of leading-strings could now come to an end. That's why I was at last able to abandon politics and enlist. My job was done, as I wrote to Winston Churchill at the time, when leaving an employer who had been for me so considerate as sometimes to seem more like a senior partner than a master. The work I did constructively for him in 1921 and 1922 seems to me, in retrospect, the best I ever did. It somewhat redresses, to my mind, the immoral and unwarrantable risks I took with others' lives and happiness in 1917–1918.

'Of course Irak was the main point, since there

could not be more than one centre of Arab national feeling; or rather need not be: and it was fit that it should be in the British and not in the French area. But during those years we also decided to stop the subsidies to the Arabian chiefs and put a ring-wall around Arabia, a country which must be reserved as an area of Arabic individualism. So long as our fleet keeps its coasts, Arabia should be at leisure to fight out its own complex and fatal destiny.

'Incidentally, of course, we sealed the doom of King Hussein. I offered him a treaty in the summer of 1921 which would have saved him the Hejaz had he renounced his pretensions to hegemony over all other Arabic areas: but he clung to his self-assumed title of 'King of the Arabic Countries.' So Ibn Saud of Nejd outed him and rules in Hejaz. Ibn Saud is not a system but a despot, ruling by virtue of a dogma. Therefore I approve of him, as I would approve of anything in Arabia which was individualistic, unorganized, unsystematic.

'Mr. Churchill took a moderate line in Palestine to obtain peace while the Zionist experiment is tried. And in Transjordania he kept our promises to the Arab Revolt and assisted the home-rulers to form a buffer-principality, under the nominal presidency of Feisal's brother Abdulla, between Palestine and the Desert.

'So as I say, I got all I wanted (for other people)— the Churchill solution exceeded my one-time hopes— and quitted the game. Whether the Arab national spirit is permanent and dour enough to make itself into a modern state in Irak I don't know. I think it may, at least. We were in honour bound to give it a sporting chance. Its success would involve the people of Syria in a similar experiment. Arabia will always, I hope, stand out of the movements of the settled parts, as will Palestine too if the Zionists make good. Their problem is the problem of the third generation. Zionist success would enormously reinforce the material development of Arab Syria and Irak.

'I want you to make it quite clear in your book, if you use all this letter, how from 1916 onwards and especially in Paris I worked against the idea of an Arab Confederation being formed politically before it had become a reality commercially, economically and geographically by the slow pressure of many generations; how I worked to give the Arabs a chance to set up their provincial governments whether in Syria or in Irak; and how in my opinion Winston Churchill's settlement has honourably fulfilled our war-obligations and my hopes.'

There is little to add to this account. The French have had great trouble in Syria since Feisal left and their repressive methods have involved them in war with the Druses and a destructive bombardment of Damascus; and in heavy expenses in running the province.

Feisal, ruling securely in Bagdad, has sent his son to an English Public School, so that when he succeeds his father relations between England and Irak may continue cordial. Zeid was not too old to become an undergraduate at Balliol College, Oxford. He rowed in the '2nd Torpids' boat, and the next

LAWRENCE AT VERSAILLES

term wired apologies to the Master of Balliol for coming back late: Feisal was ill and Zeid thought that it was his duty to act as Regent in Irak until he recovered. Abdulla in Transjordania, the country east of the Jordan and south of the Yarmuk, with an opening to the Red Sea at Akaba, still enjoys his practical joking and blindman's buff; he manages his kingdom well enough (his first prime minister was Ali Riza), though the townsmen and villagers complain that he is too lenient to the semi-nomadic tribes in letting them off taxes. However, it is not want of firmness on Abdulla's part: when old Auda, from the edge of his dominions, refused to pay his taxes, sending an insolent message, Abdulla caught him and put him into gaol at Amman. Of course Auda, being Auda, escaped, but the old man then thought better of it and paid the taxes. Auda died this year of cancer; his amulet protected him to the end from death in battle; and, as Lawrence once prophesied, the Middle Ages of the Desert Border have died with him.

Abdulla originally came to Transjordania with the idea of making war on the French to avenge his brother's expulsion, but has suspended his hostile intentions. An amusing incident occurred in 1921 when he found two French Catholic priests stirring up anti-British propaganda. He dismissed them from his kingdom and put in their places two American Presbyterian missionaries. When a furious protest came from the Vatican, Abdulla replied innocently, pleading his ignorance of the difference between the various Christian sects; however, as Lawrence happened to be with him at the time, we may doubt this.

Certainly the extraordinary disappearance of a steamroller, from the Palestine Border, which later after much useful work in road-making across in Transjordania was found again abandoned near the border, may be safely put down to Lawrence's magic; and perhaps also Abdulla's official letter to the Palestine Government, saying that among their hosts of steam- rollers the Transjordanians have great difficulty in identifying any deserting machines from Palestine, suggests Lawrence's style.

Abdulla's most dangerous neighbour is Ibn Saud, who now rules practically the whole of the Arabian peninsula. Ibn Saud has the support of a puritan sect of Arabs known as the Brothers, founded over a hundred years ago by a prophet called Wahab; hence they are sometimes called the Wahabis. Arabia under him is going through a period not unlike the Commonwealth in England under Cromwell, except that Ibn Saud is far more strict than Cromwell in keeping religious virtue among his followers. Smoking a cigarette, even, is an abominable offence. He has stopped inter-tribal raiding throughout his dominions, but permits raiding across the borders. He has spread his influence as far north as Jauf, from which he has expelled the Ruwalla—old Nuri the Emir is dead—and across Sirhan.

The worst thing about the Brethren is that they have learned Turkish methods of war and employ them even against Arabs who are not Brethren. A body of about a thousand of these fanatics came marching up in 1922 from the Central Oases in an eight-hundred-mile raid on Amman. They surprised a little village close to the railway, twenty miles south of Amman, and massacred every man, woman and child. The chief of the Faiz Beni Sakhr, however, caught them a day or two later and few escaped back to Arabia to tell the tale: no prisoners were taken. The Faiz victory was accidentally helped by a British aeroplane which happened to be flying over: the Brethren thought that it was going to bomb them and threw down their arms.

Against further inroads Abdulla has an efficient defence force with British advisers. It is unlikely that the Wahabi faith will spread to the settled country from the desert. The new prosperity in the north of the Arabic-speaking area since the departure of the Turks will discourage this. The railway south from Damascus is working again, but only as far as Maan and not very busily; a branch-line is, however, planned to Akaba.

Of Lawrence during this political period there are many stories which one day will be collected, true and false together, in a full-length 'Life and Letters' which this book does not, of course, pretend to be. I can, however, vouch for the truth of two or three typical ones. Lawrence went to Jiddah in June 1921 and tried to make the treaty with Hussein to which he refers in the letter that I have quoted. Hussein kept him arguing for two months in the heat, hoping to break down British opposition to his claim for a paramount position above other Arab princes, and finally put him off altogether, suggesting that he should continue the negotiations with his son Abdulla in Amman. Lawrence sent a cipher cable to Lord Curzon, the Foreign Minister. 'Can do nothing with Hussein. Are you fed up or shall I carry on with Abdulla?' Curzon, who was a stickler for the diplomatic phrasing of official despatches, asked his secretary: 'Pray, what does this term *fed up* signify?' The secretary, who had a sense of humour, replied, 'I believe, my lord, that it is equivalent to "disgruntled."' 'Ah,' said Curzon, 'I suppose that it is a term in use among the middle classes.' When 'carry on' had also been explained, Curzon gave consent to the Abdulla negotiations and Lawrence carried them on. Meanwhile the secretary, a friend, had told him in a private letter of the 'fed-up' episode. So Lawrence, having successfully concluded his negotiations

with Abdulla, again cabled to Curzon in cipher: 'Have wan-
gled things with Abdulla. Details follow by letter. Note, the
necessary verb "wangle" is absent from the diplomatic cipher.
I submit that a letter-group be allotted to it to save spelling it
each time.' The word is now in the cipher book.

A late member of the Foreign Office staff, who wishes
to remain anonymous, has told me an even odder story of
Lawrence and Lord Curzon. 'It was at the first meeting of
the British Cabinet held to discuss the Middle-Eastern situation. Curzon made a well-turned speech in Lawrence's
praise, introducing him. I could see Lawrence squirming at
the praise, which he seemed to think was misplaced, and at
the patronage. Lawrence already knew most of the ministers
present. It was a very long speech and when it ended Curzon
turned to Lawrence and asked him if he wished to say anything. Lawrence answered sharply, "Yes, let's get to business.
You people" (imagine Curzon addressed as "you people"!)
"don't understand yet the hole you have put us all into!"
Then a remarkable thing happened. Curzon burst into
tears, great drops running down his cheeks, to an accompani-
ment of slow sobs.

'It was horribly like a mediæval miracle, the weeping of
a church image. I felt dreadful; probably Lawrence did too.
However, Lord Robert Cecil, who seemed to be hardened to
such scenes, of which hitherto I only knew by hearsay, inter-
posed roughly: "Now, old man, none of that!" Curzon wiped
his eyes, blew his nose in a silk pocket-handkerchief, and
dried up. And business proceeded.'

At Paris Lawrence had several rows with politicians and
soldiers. The most sensational was in the hall of the Hotel
Majestic, the headquarters of the British delegation. A

major-general began treating him as an interfering young fellow who had no business to be poking his nose into matters that did not concern him. Lawrence retorted warmly. The general barked out, 'Don't dare to speak to me in that tone. You're not a professional soldier.' This stirred Lawrence. 'No,' said he, 'perhaps I'm not; but if you had a division and I had a division, I know which of us would be taken prisoner.'

Throughout these years Lawrence lived in great retirement. The advertising of his Arabian adventure both by the Press and by Mr. Lowell Thomas's cinema lecture-tour proved most unwelcome to him. He received an enormous mail, including, it is said, over fifty offers of marriage from unknown women, and was relentlessly and unsuccessfully pursued by lion-hunting hostesses. Most of the time that he was not writing his book or engaged in politics he spent reading, catching up with modern literature after a four years' break, and looking at pictures and sculpture.

In his visit to the East in 1921, treaty-making, he did return by air as had been prophesied, and found a crowd still waiting at the aerodrome to greet him with 'Aurans at last!' A friend of mine was talking to him shortly afterwards, at Jerusalem, when an Arab came up and saluted. It was a member of the body-guard, 'an awful-looking scoundrel with love-locks and a sash-full of weapons.' Lawrence asked if he was doing anything important now. The man, trembling with pleasure at seeing Lawrence, answered, 'No, lord, nothing important.' 'Then you must go to Basra and enrol in the service of Lord Feisal, who will want your services and the services of the rest.'

Lawrence met Foch at Paris. It is related that Foch remarked in a friendly way to Lawrence, 'I suppose now that there will soon be war in Syria between my country and your Arabs?

Will you be leading their armies?' 'No,' Lawrence answered, 'unless you promise to lead the French armies in person. Then I should enjoy it.' The old Marshal wagged his finger at Lawrence. 'My young friend, if you think that I am going to sacrifice the reputation that I have so carefully compiled on the Western Front by fighting you on your own ground and under conditions imposed by yourself, you are very much mistaken.' Asked whether this story was true, Lawrence has replied that 'the event has faded from my retentive memory,' which can mean anything that anyone likes it to mean.

One more story (out of its place but recalled by this discussion of international affairs):

When Lawrence was working up from Akaba into Syria he once took a mobile hospital with him on a raid. All the stretcher-camels were, for economy of transport, loaded up with dynamite. The Royal Army Medical Corps Headquarters in Palestine got to hear of this and telegraphed expecting that the Arab Army would in future observe the Geneva Convention which insists that the transport devoted to fighting shall be kept distinct from that devoted to medical work. Lawrence on his next raid therefore left both hospital *and doctor* behind. The Medical Headquarters again protested, and Lawrence replied that transport could not be wasted on non-combatants. This enraged the Surgeon-General, who tried to catch Lawrence by wiring a peremptory request to know how Lawrence proposed, in the absence of his medical officer, to dispose of his wounded. Lawrence then replied tersely, 'Will shoot all cases too hurt to ride off.' This closed the argument.

XXX

Lawrence wrote his great history of the Arab Revolt, *Seven Pillars of Wisdom*, or seven out of ten books of it, between February and June, 1919, in Paris. He did the present beginning of the introduction in six hours in the Handley-Page aeroplane, on his way from Paris to collect his belongings in Cairo: the rhythm of it is affected, he says, by the slow 'munch, munch, munch' of the great Rolls-Royce engines. In London he wrote an eighth book, but had all the eight stolen from him about Christmas 1919 while changing trains at Reading. Only the introduction and the drafts of two books remained.

He has never imagined a political motive for the theft, but his friends have. They even whisper darkly that one day the lost text may reappear in certain official archives. Lawrence himself hopes it will not: he had destroyed most of his war-time notes as he went along and when he began again the weary task of rewriting the quarter of a million words he could not quite trust his memory. However, Colonel Dawnay, who saw both texts, tells me that one chapter at least that he read more carefully than others in the original seems to be the same, word for word and almost comma for comma, in the second version. Lawrence still had two skeleton-diaries and some rough route-sheets, but little else.

This second writing was done in less than three months at the rate of some four to five thousand words a day. But Lawrence, immoderate as usual, did not keep to a daily ration. He did it in long sittings and probably set up a world's literary record by writing Book VI in twenty-four hours between sunrise and sunrise without a pause. Book VI was about 34,000 words in length! 'Naturally the style was careless,' he says. But it served as a basis for a careful literary rewriting; which is the *Seven Pillars* as it was finally published. He wrote it in London, Jiddah and Amman in 1921, again in London in 1922, in the Royal Tank Corps near Dorchester in 1923 and 1924, and in the Royal Air Force at Cranwell in 1925 and 1926. He checked the historical accuracy with the help of all available official documents and his British friends who had served with the Arab army.

Lawrence does nothing by halves and not only set about making the book a history of the Arab Revolt which the Arabs themselves would never write, but one that he would not be ashamed of as literature. For this last ambition he secured the advice of two of the best-known English writers and taught himself with their help to write professionally.

Seven Pillars of Wisdom is, beyond dispute, a great book; though there is such a thing as a book being too well written, too much a part of literature. Lawrence himself realizes this and was once, indeed, on the point of throwing it into the Thames at Hammersmith. It should somehow, one feels, have been a little more casual, for the nervous strain of its ideal of faultlessness is oppressive. Lawrence charges himself with 'literary priggishness,' but that is unfair. His aim was, all the time, simplicity of style and statement and this he achieved in the most expert way. He has, somewhere, confessed to a general mistrust of experts and it may be that he should have carried it further, and dispensed with expert advice in literary matters too. (Possibly, though, in actual practice he did; he was always a difficult pupil.) On the whole I prefer the earliest surviving version, the so-called Oxford text, to the final printed book which was the version that I first read consecutively. This is a physical rather than a critical reaction. The earlier version is 330,000 words long instead of 280,000 and the greater looseness of the writing makes it easier to read. From a critical point of view no doubt the revised version is better. It is impossible that a man like Lawrence would spend four years on polishing the text without improving it, but the nervous rigor that the revised book gave me has seemingly dulled my critical judgment. I may add that Lawrence had foreseen the effect that the book would have on me and refrained for many years from letting me see it.

Lawrence was anxious to make the book as solid as possible, so he employed the best artists that he could find to do drawings for it under the art-editorship of Eric Kennington.

He published something more than a hundred copies for subscribers at thirty guineas apiece and gave away half as many more to friends. But he was so keen to do things well that he actually spent £13,000 on the edition—the reproduction of the pictures alone cost more than the subscriptions— leaving himself £10,000 out of pocket. It was to pay this debt to his backers (for he has no private means) that the abridgment *Revolt in the Desert* was undertaken for public sale. He made it in two nights, at Cranwell Camp, with the help of two other airmen, Miller and Knowles. The *Seven Pillars* was never intended for publication: it was to be a private record for Lawrence and a few friends. *Revolt in the Desert* was only published by the accident of the £10,000 debt. It is a series of incidents loosely strung together and purged of the more personal material. Single copies of the *Seven Pillars* now sell at extraordinary prices.

Lawrence has not made a penny himself from either of these books. He was scrupulous to arrange that when the debt of the *Seven Pillars* was paid off the extra money made by *Revolt in the Desert* should not go to him. It has been a set determination of his to make nothing out of the Arab war directly or indirectly. His army pay went towards the expenses of the campaign. His salary from Winston Churchill for the year at the Colonial Office he did not spend on himself either, but used it for official purposes. (On the other hand, Lawrence's friends have much benefited by his generosity. The gift of a *Seven Pillars* with the note 'please sell when read' has been worth as much as £500.)

The success of *Revolt in the Desert* called for a French translation, but when an application for the rights came from a Paris publisher Lawrence offered permission on one condition—that the book must bear on its jacket the inscription: 'The profits of this book will be devoted to a fund for the victims of French cruelty in Syria.' So there could be no French translation so long as he controlled the book rights.

I have never yet met with an explanation of the meaning *Seven Pillars of Wisdom* in all that has been written about the book. It is reminiscence from a chapter in the *Book of Proverbs*, part of which runs as follows:

'Wisdom hath builded a house: she hath hewn out her seven pillars. She crieth upon the highest places of the city, "Whoso is simple let him turn in hither . . . If thou be wise, thou shalt be wise for thyself.'"

The idea is, I believe, further elaborated in later Jewish theological writings. This title was all that Lawrence rescued from an earlier book of travel written in 1913 and destroyed in 1914; it compared the seven cities of Cairo, Smyrna, Constantinople, Beyrout, Aleppo, Damascus and Medina.

The Seven Pillars of Wisdom will not be reprinted in Lawrence's lifetime. It is not a book, people agree on Lawrence's behalf, that should be published for a popular audience. (A simple member of the public, an electrician, was shown the most painful chapter while proofs were being passed. Then he could do no work for a week, but walked up and down the pavement outside his house, unable to rid his mind of the horror of it. The chapter about the Turkish hospital is almost as painful.) Also popular publication might, they say, involve Lawrence in a series of libel actions: he seems to spare nobody in his desire to tell the whole story faithfully (least of all himself). Again, the censor might, it is suggested, ban as obscene some of the more painfully accurate accounts of Turkish methods of warfare. But in any case Lawrence never intended publishing the book, except privately, so these remarks are really irrelevant. The book was first written as a full-length and unrestrained picture of himself, his tastes, ideas and actions. He could not have deliberately confessed to so much had there been any chance of the book coming out. Yet to tell the whole story was the only justification for writing anything at all. And once written a strictly limited publication of the book promised to remove the need of even thinking about that part of his life again.

The historical accuracy of Lawrence's account has been jealously questioned by some overseas reviewers of *Revolt in the Desert*: he has been accused of self-interested exaggeration. However, as there were forty or fifty British officers, besides Arabs, as witnesses of his activities and as no one of them has challenged the accuracy of his statements, this criticism hardly calls for answer. Moreover, all the documents of the Arab Revolt are in the archives of the Foreign Office and will soon be available to students, who will be able to cross-check Lawrence's account and are likely to find that his chief fault has been telling rather less than the truth.

It has been suggested that Lawrence's part in the Eastern War was devoid of serious military significance. Part of a letter protesting against this point of view may be reprinted from a London weekly. I know the writer as an expert in these matters:

'SIR,—

'Your reviewer of *Revolt in the Desert* denies the Arab Army any "serious military significance," and suggests that Allenby's advance on Damascus would have been successful had it never existed. As one who took part in the Palestine campaign, and was for a considerable time entrusted with the preparation of the "Enemy Order of Battle," may I affirm the contrary? The revolt of 1916 isolated the Assir Division of six battalions, destroyed two-thirds of the Hejaz. Division of nine battalions and brought a new division (58th) from Syria to Medina. In the autumn of 1917 when Lord Allenby struck his first blow the equivalent of twenty-four battalions was strung out on the line from Deraa to Medina. I include mounted infantry and camel corps. Some artillery was also engaged. Had the Arabs sat still two-thirds of this force, which included good Anatolian units such as the 42nd and 55th Regiments, would have been available for the Gaza-Beersheba front. In 1918 the British threat to Transjordania only became possible because of the growing strength of the revolt and the increasing sympathy of the local Arab population for Arab success. Lord Allenby's demonstrations and the activity of the Arabs tied up more and more Turks and some German units, and by September, 1918, rein-forcements from Rumania (part of the 25th Division) and the Caucasian front (48th Division) liberated by the Russo-Rumanian collapse, had been used up east of Jordan instead of on the Palestine front. Without going into details of military organization and the dis-location of troops, dull reading to any but the pro-fessional military historian, I can confidently assert that the Arab Army of 4,000 fighting men and an uncertain number of occasional pillagers was worth an Army Corps to the British Army on the Palestine front, not only on account of the Turks, whom it kept busy in the wrong place, but on account of the strain it put on Turkish transport and supply.

'Finally, may I remark that Lawrence and his Arabs saw a good deal more at Tafas than one mutilated Arab woman, and the wonder to me is not that they saw red then, but that they generally showed such astonishing restraint against an enemy who habitually shot his Arab prisoners, tortured Arab wounded with obscene ingenuity, and often indulged in gross brutal-ities, at the expense of non-combatants, women and children.

'Yours, etc.,

'B.'

The humour of the controversy lies in the siding of Lawrence himself with the critics of whom 'B.' disposes so crushingly. What is called 'serious military significance' is part of the whole modern theory of War, the seeking out and destroying by one side of the organized military forces of another—a theory which he rejected as futile and barbarous almost from the start. What Lawrence wanted, rather, was to achieve serious *political* significance for the Revolt by whatever means lay readiest to his hand. Actual fighting, as opposed to pin-pricking raids and demolitions, was a luxury that he indulged the Arabs in merely to save their self-respect. They could not have thought freedom honourably won without it. The capture of Akaba is a clear instance of an operation that, though it affected the more conventional war at Gaza and Beersheba, had in itself serious political rather than serious military significance. It was only by an accident that the Turkish battalion happened to bar the way at Aba el Lissan and invite destruction. The rest of the operation was more like a chess problem; white to play and mate in three moves.

This is not the place, and it probably is not the time to weigh up Lawrence's strategy and tactics during the Arab Revolt. Of the strategy he makes no secret whatever. It lies in *Revolt in the Desert* open for anyone who can use a map intelligently. The *Seven Pillars* gives yet fuller details; the first number of the *Army Quarterly* (1920) contains a long article by him on the subject of irregular war—a summary of the results of his sick-bed theorizing in Emir Abdulla's camp in March 1917. The obvious comment to be made on his strategy is that it enabled the Arab Revolt in the sphere of politics, as in the sphere of war, to assume a much larger share of influence and attention than its material importance justified. B.'s letter just quoted, had it compared the Arabs' resources in arms and equipment, as well as in men, with those of the Turkish forces opposed to them, would have made the point still clearer. Lawrence would probably take this judgment as the highest praise, for we find him throughout insisting, with a repetition that conveys the painfulness of his problem, upon the extreme economy of means necessary. The material and military assistance that the Arabs could themselves provide, with all the goodwill in the world, was small. Nor might it be helped out by large borrowing of material and military resources from the Allies without a proportionate political debt when the fighting was over. Lawrence would therefore be proud to think that he made his little go such a long way—even the total of ten million pounds and the score or so of British casualties that the Arab Revolt cost Great Britain was a flea-bite compared with, for instance, the monthly cost of the Mesopotamian Expeditionary Force in lives and cash—and that politically he made so much ado out of what had begun as little or nothing.

From the point of view of tactics, his conduct is far less clear. A casual reading of his books might lead one to suppose that he fought his battles with bluff and crimson banners for main argument; or even that the hypnotic effect that his presence seems to have had on the Arabs extended to the enemy, who were fascinated into stupidity—that the moon herself came under the influence and consented to open one of the more difficult gates to Akaba for him. But actually his tactics were, I believe, thought out with the same care and artifice, not to say humour, as his general strategic principles. And his reasons for slurring over the ways and means of fighting are connected with the political relations between the Syrian Government and the French in 1919 when he first wrote his book. Both sides were preparing for armed struggle in Syria and it looks as if Lawrence set himself to contribute nothing in the form of a manual of warfare that could be used in this struggle. His late re-draftings of the book at a time when the danger had become less acute only modified the literary style without adding (or taking away) much of the content. He had to select the materials to be used with great severity. His two active years provided enough for ten books of the size to which he limited himself—his memory was uncomfortably clear and full—so that wherever possible he sacrificed the details of the fighting.

He mentions, for instance, no more than three or four armoured-car actions in which he took part; but it seems that he fought at least fifty, enough to evolve a whole system and scheme of battle for them. (Readers of *Revolt in the Desert* will have found no more than two or three occasions mentioned on which Lawrence was wounded, against the four or five mentioned in the *Seven Pillars*; but the total number was nine times, including the occasion of Minifer when he had five bullet grazes, cuts from flying boiler-plate and a broken toe.) Nor is adequate mention made in either book of the numerous engagements in which he tempered his body-guard into a real fighting weapon. We can only gather, from casual allusions, that he did not leave the tactics of the desert as he found them.

He based his strategy on an exhaustive study of the geography of his area, of the Turkish Army; of the nature of the

Bedouin tribes and their distribution. So he based his desert tactics on a study of the raiding parties of the Arabs. As we have seen, one of his first actions on being posted as military adviser to Feisal was to accompany a raid on the Turkish force attacking Rabegh. And he continued this self-education, in the school of Auda and Zaal and Nasir, until after the occupation of Akaba. Only by graduating in this Bedouin school could he win the experience and prestige that would allow him to modify its traditions.

Exactly what these modifications were is nowhere explained, though they seem to have achieved a greater unity of purpose among the members of the raiding party, at the more critical moments before and after the attack, without impairing the self-reliance and self-sufficiency of any individual. His English companions knew the difference between an Arab raid when he was present and one when he was not present; but they were not professional soldiers, nor students of war, so could not put their finger on the precise points of difference. And he himself, except in the battle fought north of Tafileh, withholds any account of himself in command. This battle proves what we knew already, that he relied on automatic rifles and not on ordinary rifles. The rapid-fire exercise, with an ordinary rifle, of fifteen to thirty aimed shots a minute, saved the British Expeditionary Force at the first battle of Ypres in face of enormously superior machine-gun fire; but it was only perfected by years of intense musketry training. The Bedouin Arabs would never have had the patience to master it and in any case it would have been of little use to them in camel-fighting.

Bayonets he scornfully rejected with the memorandum (to General Headquarters!) that they were 'unintelligent masses of steel, generally fatal to the fools behind them.' He might have added that the Turk, a good man with the bayonet, would have welcomed this choice of weapons. Machine-guns, except when armoured, were less suited for his battles than automatics because their longer bursts of fire did not make up for their greater weight and cumbersomeness. There is one recorded case of a British machine-gun sergeant, in France, picking up his weapon and using it like a rifle, but he was a giant. When it came to a choice between Lewis and Hotchkiss automatic rifles, he preferred the Hotchkiss, because it was not so easily jammed by mud and sand; but the files of the Egyptian Expeditionary Force Headquarter Office were full of his demands for quantities of either or both. The battle of Tafileh is a neat example, though not, one gathers, his first, of what is technically known as 'attack by infiltration,' with automatic rifles to the fore. Lawrence seems, before this, to have reduced his gun-crews to two men and a gun. His body-guard of forty-eight men had in one fight with a Turkish cavalry regiment (place and date unfortunately are not available) twenty-one automatics. He himself carried an 'air-Lewis' (borrowed from the Air Force) in a bucket on his camel-saddle. He once said that if he could get control of an arms-factory to make him Hotchkiss guns he would supersede the use of the rifle in war. A pleasant gift to civilization!

Lawrence's attitude to war, by the way, seems to be that he has no stronger objection to war, as war, than to the human race as the human race; but he does not like wars in which the individual is swallowed up in the mass. He commented to me once on the anti-war poetry of Siegfried Sassoon, who had the misfortune to serve, on the Western Front, in divisions that were accustomed to lose the equivalent of their full strength every four or five months, that had Sassoon been serving with him in Arabia he would have written in a completely different vein. That is very likely true. On the other hand, Lawrence's revolt in the desert was a form of fighting so unlike 'civilized' war, and so romantically appealing, that it is perhaps fortunate that Siegfried Sassoon, Wilfred Owen, Edmund Blunden, and the other poets who got badly involved in the war were all infantrymen in France.

Lawrence's use of heavy machine-guns (Vickers'), in the armoured cars, developed from the first experimental raids after Akaba until he could use them in combined operations of camelry, armoured cars and aeroplanes. He was also able to improve on the regulation uses of high explosive as laid down in the Manual of Field-Engineering. He discovered how to fire electric mines along the telegraph wires and how to introduce petards into the fire-boxes of railway locomotives by 'salting' their wood-fuel piles with infernal contraptions that would escape the notice of the firemen. But so strongly was he moved by a sense of what we may call the 'literary style' of the epical romance in which he found himself a leading character—a 'many-wiled Odysseus' let us say—that he always saw his own scientific ingenuities as things alien and incongruous in the Arab setting. We are therefore left with only shadowy clues as to their importance and effectiveness in the campaign.

XXXI

In August 1922 Lawrence, having finally renounced the use of that name, enlisted in the Royal Air Force. He did all the usual duties of a man in the lowest grade of the Force and steadfastly refused promotion. For six months he raised no suspicion at all about his identity. He got on well with the men, though he was very raw and clumsy at the new life. Unfortunately an officer recognized him and sold the information for thirty pounds to a daily paper, with the result that there was an unwelcome publicity-stunt made of it and the suspicion then arose among the men that Lawrence was an Air Force spy! The Secretary of State for Air feared that questions might be asked in the House of Commons as to what he was doing there under an assumed name, so he judged it necessary to dismiss him in February 1923. This was most disappointing to Lawrence, who had got through the first hardship and bitterness of his recruit's training, with a stainless character, only to be thrown out.

He had been stationed at Uxbridge, where his knowledge of photography seems to have put him into a section of photographic specialists. He disguised his previous history with half-truths, accounting, for instance, for his too accurate rifle-shooting at the range by saying that he had done some big-game shooting (perhaps he meant by 'big-game' some of the staff- officers on the train derailed at Minifer). He accurately informed the recruiting officer that he had previously *served in no regiment*, and so framed his explanations that apparently they noted down that he was interned by the Turks during the greater part of the War. At Uxbridge he nearly outdid himself in self-effacing efficiency. He was chosen as one of the squad to rehearse arms-drill for the Cenotaph ceremony at Armistice. He was unwilling to take part in it for fear of being recognized; fortunately his height saved him. He was rejected for not being five-foot-eight.

I am sure, by the way, that Lawrence would not, if he could, 'by taking thought add a cubit' (even an inch or two) 'to his stature.' Height is rarely useful to a man except in crowds and in games (both of which Lawrence avoids) and makes him conspicuous. I remember his saying once of an official: 'Six-foot-three; and yet has brains': being six-foot-two myself I uncomfortably wondered at what height upward Lawrence regards normal intelligence as usually ending.

At Uxbridge, on the first Commanding Officer's Hut-inspection, the Wing-Commander was asking all the recruits personal questions. He noticed a few unusual books in Lawrence's locker (where they were quite in order) and said: 'Do you read that sort of thing? What were you in civil life?'

'Nothing special, sir.'

'What were you doing last?'

'Working in an architect's office, sir.' (This was true enough. Sir Herbert Baker had lent a room of his office in Barton Street for Lawrence to write *Seven Pillars* in.)

'Why did you join the Air Force?'

'I think I must have had a mental break-down, sir.'

'What! What! Sergeant-Major, take this man's name; gross impertinence!'

The next day Lawrence was 'up' and was able to explain that the Wing-Commander had misunderstood him.

At school in Uxbridge—the Royal Air Force makes much of education—the master, a civilian, asked the recruits to write a confidential first essay, for his eye alone, giving details of previous education. As he was obviously a decent and sincere man, Lawrence wrote truthfully that he had got scholarships and exhibitions from the age of thirteen onwards, which had helped to pay school and university bills until he had taken honours in history and been elected to a research-fellowship in political theory. That later events arising out of the War had constrained him to enlist and that he found himself over-educated for his present part in life. The master respected the confidence and instead of lessons gave Lawrence books to read in school hours and a quiet place to sit in.

A month after being dismissed from the Air Force he re-enlisted, with War-Office permission, in the Royal Tank Corps. He had got a qualified assurance that if he served without incident for a while in the Army, his return to the Air Force might be considered. He remained in it for more than two years, stationed near Dorchester. He found life rough but made many friends among the soldiers and was fortunate to be near Mr. and Mrs. Thomas Hardy, to whom I had the satisfaction of introducing him.

It happened more than once that journalists and celebrity hunters would break in on Mr. Hardy's quiet and meeting there a little figure in clumsy khaki with a quiet, almost filial regard for the old poet, would not give him a second glance.

Whereas, as Mrs. Hardy has told me, 'they would have given their ears, almost, for a conversation with him had they known who he was.'

Lawrence was never without a Brough-Superior racing motor-bicycle. Each year he used to wheedle a next year's model from the makers—and ride it to death—to report on it. He nicknamed his machines 'Boanerges' (sons of thunder) and they carried him well. He had five of them in four years and rode 100,000 miles on them, making only two insurance claims (for superficial damage to the machine after skids) and hurting nobody. The greatest pleasure of his recent life has been speed on the road. The bicycle would do a hundred miles an hour, but he is not, he says, a racing man. The first time that he really let Boanerges the Third go, in the early dawn on a long stretch of road near Winchester, he was curious to see the speed-dial make two complete revolutions. It did, and broke with a scream, so he flattered himself that he covered an unknown number of miles beyond the hundred an hour. But this was not his daily practice.

He wrote to me in a letter:

'It's usually my satisfaction to purr along gently about 60 m.p.h. drinking in the air and the general view. I lose detail even at such moderate speeds but gain comprehension. When I open out a little more, as for instance across Salisbury Plain at 80 or so, I feel the earth moulding herself under me. It is *me* piling up this hill, hollowing this valley, stretching out this level place. Almost the earth comes alive, heaving and tossing on each side like a sea. That's a thing that the slow coach will never feel. It is the reward of speed. I could write you pages on the lustfulness of moving swiftly.'

He had at least one serious conflict with authority in the Royal Tank Corps, when he was brought up on the charge of insubordination towards a corporal. (Probably more. But none of them seem to have had unfortunate sequels, for when he left the Tank Corps his character-sheet was free of major entries.)

Of this occasion a comrade, Private Palmer, writes:

'The corporal was a Scotsman of the old school, an ex-officer, overbearing, with a wonderful idea of his own importance. T.E. used to rag him unmercifully. The corporal had a habit of laying the dust in the hut with a bowl of water sprinkled on the floor. This performance annoyed T.E. and everybody else, so one day T.E. got up early and swamped the hut with I forget now how many bowls of water. We all paddled. Later a man in the hut received a few days "Confined to Barracks" unfairly, through the Corporal. T.E. simply slung the corporal's suit-case into the sanitary bin.'

Private Palmer has very kindly given me further amusing if slight details of Lawrence's life in the Tank Corps:

'He did the normal work of a private soldier even to receiving "three days confined to barracks" for leaving overalls on his bed. After "passing off the square" he did fatigues. That is how I met him. We began talking about Thomas Hardy. I was employed in the quarter-master's stores and T.E. joined me there. He did his work well; he had to mark recruits' kits with their numbers, fit them with clothing, boots, etc. In the afternoons sometimes, we used to solve cross-word puzzles together. Generally, however, T.E. would work on sections of the *Seven Pillars*. He did correcting, etc., in the Quartermaster's office, of an evening, and sometimes early morning.

'One day I "pulled his leg" and he beat me with a slipper—after a struggle, mind you. The Quarter-master walked in and wanted to know whether the store was a gymnasium. "No, sir," said T.E., "I'm sorry; I was only correcting Private Palmer with this slipper!" The Quartermaster laughed and said "Carry on!"

'When rumours started in the camp as to who he was, it was amusing to see the troops studying photo-graphs of him in the *Daily* . . . and comparing them with the original. "It's not him!" "I bet you a dollar it is him"; these were the sort of remarks that passed between the troops. T.E. appeared to be indifferent as to what they thought and said about him. This stage of excitement soon passed and he was treated as one of ourselves again. The tradespeople were more polite to him, however.

'His recreations were gramophone music—he loved the Bach concerto for two violins in D minor—and Broughriding. Most Sundays he used to take me, pillion, to breakfast at Corfe: order breakfast first and look at the castle while it was being prepared: he never tired of the castle. Sometimes he took me to cathedrals—Salisbury, Winchester, Wells. Of course we passed everything we met on the road: T.E. couldn't resist a race.

'His passing from the Tank Corps made a nine-days' wonder: I was bombarded with questions. As the people who knew him are scattered now, his name has passed into the legend stage. Strangely enough, he is remembered, not for anything he did during the War, but for his performances on that wonderful motor-cycle.'

That 'T.E. couldn't resist a race' seems to me a misinterpretation of motive. He is not of a competitive nature, but dislikes other people's dust. And he never took the machine out on a dry road without letting it out, all out, at least once for every hundred miles that he rode. Just to keep the two of them from getting sluggish.

In August 1925, through the intercession of a highly-placed friend with the Prime Minister, he was re-transferred to the R.A.F., his ambition for the last two years, and in December 1926 was sent overseas to the Indian frontier, where he now is. He wrote to me some months ago:

'If old P—asks you again why I am in the R.A.F., tell him that it is simply because I *like* the R.A.F. The being cared for, the rails of conduct, the impossibility of doing irregular things, are easements. The companionship of "shop," the enforced routine of simple labour, the occasional leisures are actively pleasant. While my health lasts I'll keep in it. I did not like the Army much, but the R.A.F. is as different from the Army as the air is from the earth. In the Army the person is at a discount: the combined movement, the body of men, is the ideal. In the R.A.F. there are no combined movements: its drill is a joke except when some selected squad is specially trained for a tattoo or a ceremony. The airman is brought up to despise the army. "Soldier" is our chief insult and word of derision.'

I hope that these quotations will not be considered tactless; but will take the risk. He wrote to me a year or two ago in the same strain:

'You were in the regular infantry, so the chances are that you have rather a cock-eyed view of the life we lead in the R.A.F. Our ideal is the skilled mechanic at his bench or machine. Our job is the conquest of the air, our element. That's a more than large enough effort to comprehend all our intelligence. We grudge every routine duty, such as are invented for soldiers to keep them out of mischief, and perform our parades deliberately ill, lest we lose our edges and become degraded into parts of a machine. In the Army the men belong to the machine. In the R.A.F. the machines, upon earth, belong to the men; as in the air they belong to the officers. So the men have the more of them. Drill in the Air Force is punitive, in the eyes of men and officers alike. Whenever the public see a detachment of airmen on a "B-S" (ceremonial) parade, they should realize that these, their very expensive servants, are being temporarily misemployed—as though Cabinet ministers should hump coal in office-hours.'

'T. E.' ON 'BOANERGES,' THE MOTOR-BICYCLE

Sergeant Pugh, of his Flight at Cranwell, in Lincolnshire, has written me a letter about Shaw in the R.A.F., which I print as it stands:

'ARRIVAL AT CRANWELL

'As far as my mind takes me back, it was in the first week of Sept. 1925 that he came to the camp, and although many had heard of his "carryings-on", few had seen him. He was met with all kinds of looks (suspicious): was he finding out who's who and what's what of the R.A.F.? Is that why he was discharged previously? (amazement): we had heard he was a man with a terrible scowl of harshness, etc., etc. (wrath): he is some ex-service guy pulling our legs; and yet! you know his carriage, slight, mild, unassuming, why did he set the camp alive in excitement just to see him?

FIRST FATIGUE. (I was taking names.)

'Perhaps a dozen men were to have a "go" at cleaning the camp fire-buckets. Taking names (you know why) he happened to be the first on the roll and, asked his name, promptly sprang to attention, giving his particulars. The second and third names were taken before the S.M. snapped at those two for not doing likewise and commented on the fact that S. had shown them his military training, by saying "take an example of Shaw, you are letting yourselves down" and possibly stronger words were used. (His start at once told.) Having occasion to call and view the work in progress (and between you and me to get a good "close-up" of this man nobody could weigh up), there he was with bathbrick, polishing and rubbing as though his life depended on the result (eagerness personified) and laughing his heart out in some crude joke of his work-mate; an aircraftman of, to say the best, poor intellect who stood by while our friend grinned and worked.

CREDIT FROM THE TANK CORPS

'It soon flashed through the camp that he was in credit to the tune of £50 from the Tank Corps and at "stand easy" when ordering tea and cakes from the canteen, he asked for about four or five extra teas and *wads* (cakes). Asking a few of the (secretly scrutinising) airmen to "muck in," at least three "lots" were left in sheer wonder and almost embarrassment; smiles and expressions, "Deep B." etc., being used.

CHURCH

'Our camp church he liked—that was all. Always a true soldier preparing for and marching to same, when his turn for it came along. But it was a d—d shame that men of the calibre he went with, should be compelled to listen to the "something rot" that they were attending; for Sermons were not Shaw's strong point. Generosity itself for a just cause. Apparent stupidity (which was amusing to all who "eyed him") for any cause concerning his presence in the above-mentioned place of worship. Politics clashed with divinity—Shaw's view.

JOINS UP IN R.A.F. SECOND TIME

'An amusing item was told of his second admission to the R.A.F. All recruits must pass an educational test before admission. S. had to do a paper of a visit to some place or other and accomplished this with such speed, tact and general show of a born author, that the Officer i/C. asked him why he came to join up and yet could turn out his "stuff" with so much apparent ease. His reply was "Chiefly a mental rest," which took the wind completely out of the officer's sails, and yet the mask of mildness on his face floated him clear of trouble. A lot of heart-to-heart talk took place about various authors to whom he might apply for a job. Finally he was shown a list of R.A.F. trades and I swear he would tackle the lot in turn and decided to be a full blown Air Craft Hand, which means he does all kinds of fatigues and is treated as though he were a mere nothing in uniform.

"B" FLIGHT, CRANWELL

'Being posted to "B" Flight and the way he behaved during his stay was worth a guinea a box. Every conceivable kind of job was put before S. as the office "boy" of our flight. (I could give you a real good list of his duties which he was to do.) He had every job well mastered in a week and "taped" for any clerk who might follow.

Our Flight Lieutenant took to S. and at once realized the asset he must mean to the flight. What "got him" was that S. had more power for getting things than he had himself. (I'm speaking dead honestly now.) He did not on any occasion ever let anyone think that what was given at all was given through thoughts of what he might do or say. His sheer force of personality got him, as you may say, undreamed of odds and ends necessary for us in our work, which seemed unattainable to any Sergeant to say the most, and never an aircraft hand. To know him was to be drawn by his magnetic personality and the heavens fell through, that alone is what made the airmen scratch their heads and THINK.

A GRAMOPHONE WAS BOUGHT

'There is a good story on its own. A beautiful machine with Records. At first we held aloof wondering what class of music appealed to S.—Mozart, Beethoven, Tannhauser? (excuse my ignorance of the classical variety). It left us guessing, but we soon woke up to the fact that he pulled our legs by ordering some of the most awful sounding records possible to get, yet his face was a blank. Should we laugh? moan? or what? That broke all the ice barrier of wondering which had built up between the airmen.

HE STARTS

'No clock was ever made to beat S. for awaking when he wanted, be it any hour. How was it done? Sailors they say do manage it, but at regular intervals. With S. any time was his time. *But* always before reveille. Baths are his god. He bribed the "civvie" stoker to attend to the fires for his bathing "Saloon" before the others; and to see him enjoy a real Turkish variety, gradually cooling to D. cold, was to know when a man is happy. Duty compelled me to have a week of his routine before 6 a.m. So this is authentic. *Bath* is S.'s second name.

'To show there is no ill feeling he starts one of the most appalling records on the market and to hear the various good humoured grumblings of the flight will send S. in fits of laughter. "Onward Christian Soldiers" was his weak or *strong* point. National Anthem he reserved for medical inspection in the huts on Mondays. *Rude but true.* A rather sleepy (at the night time) sailor, whom S. loved to tease was presented by him, S., to a most glorious hand-knitted pair of pink woollen bed socks. He had them specially made in our *Town.*

BROUGHS

'S. had a Brough-Superior 1926 model. You might call that machine his house. To see him ride was enough. To see that baby on a machine like that at speed made the population gasp. Brough junior says that he is the opposite number to his "bus"—"Two Superiors." An insight concerning both is in the following:

'Out riding one summer evening, he came across a smash-up between a car (driven by an oldish man) and a pedestrian. When the unconscious pedestrian had been safely disposed of,—stowed in the back of the car for carriage to hospital—S. was asked to swing the car for the old boy. Nervousness and excitement caused the driver to leave the ignition fully advanced and on S. swinging the starting handle flew back and broke S.'s right arm. Without so much as a sign to show what had taken place S. asked if he would mind retarding the offending lever, and swung the car with his left hand. After the car was at a safe distance S. got an A.A. Scout to "kick over" his Brough, and with his right arm dangling and changing gear with his foot S. got his bus home and parked without a word to a soul of the pain he was suffering. Through some unknown reason the M.O. was away and it was next morning before his arm could be "done." That is a man—S., I mean.

'S. had intended doing a "pull off" from an aeroplane with me and descending by parachute. Unfortunately his arm spoiled it for the pair of us. (Personally I was relying on his personality to get permission for the "drop"), so you see how everyone "fell" for him through his ways. Have served a little while in the R.A.F. but never before have I seen a man refuse to go in Hospital with a broken arm. Yet S. did and "got away with it." Having after 10 days got into the style of writing with his left hand, the good work went on. His skill and supervision in his position astounded one and all. He will want to cancel this but let me tell you as his friend that his broken arm was the 33rd broken bone he has had at various times, including 11 ribs. This last sentence must be known whether he approves or not. In his book *Seven Pillars of Wisdom* he mentions a fact about his capture by a Turkish officer and his treatment under his captor's hands. A bayonet had been forced after two attempts between his ribs,—those scars are on his body still and are very noticeable at once when he is stripped.

"OFFICE BOY"

'As previously stated S. carried out every duty, job or any mortal thing that came his way with amazing speed and accuracy that often we wondered at his reserve power which pointed him out as differently as though he was miles above our standard at anything we tackled. His letters were the joke of the flight, because at every post something or other turned up. Am convinced that had he been given more spare time, the load of letters would not have been littered all over the trays, tables and pigeon-holes—in fact they were everywhere. Mind you his kit was kit, but correspondence he could not keep in check. To see him sign a cheque on his book-account (*Seven Pillars*) for a large amount, with his left hand after his accident made me wonder what proof the bank held of the genuineness of the signature. They used to get through without a line or word of doubt.

FIRES

'S.'s job during cold weather would be to light the fires in the offices. Coal was usually difficult to obtain, but nothing would prevent the fires from being lighted. One day he pulled down a dead tree actually in the Air Officer Commanding's private plantation, walking past flights and offices till he reached the "B" Flight, perspiring like a bull and all smiles. Anyone would think he walked about invisible. He invented a "Shaw mixture" of old oil from aero engines, sawdust and coaldust and mixed it like mortar. So with his trees and mixture fires were kept roaring all day long.

NIGHTS OUT

Asked his idea of a good night out, he told me that to take a man on his Brough to a decent town and give him a good feed and general good time was O.K. to a limit. That limit was that his companion on those rides must be mildly a ruffian, for preference, and his pleasure was derived in studying the man's peculiarities unseen to the man himself.* "There are too many honest men in this world and a few more rogues would make the world a very interesting place." Never sly, he would weigh up a cute scoundrel and gently smile at the result of his observation.

PROMOTION

'At the beginning of each quarter a return is to be submitted stating the particulars of men recommended

---

* Shaw has told me himself that he took out nearly all 'B' Flight at one time or another: all very decent fellows, he said, whom he admired very much.—Sergeant Pugh has made a joke read too seriously, I think.—R. G.

for promotion. Talking it over with the Flight Commander, he asked for S. to see if he had any views
on the matter. S. emphatically refused to hear of any
advance, a thing which made the Flight Commander
nearly curl up, laughing.

NIGHT RIDING

'It sometimes took place that S. felt like a blind into
the night, summer or winter, and would cover as
many miles as safety permitted, arriving in camp dog-
tired and dirty yet cheery and stroll to the canteen
for a couple of packets of "Smith's Crisps"—chipped
potatoes. That would invariably mean his supper. Yet
he would be loaded up with good things for his room-
mates. Fruit he loved, and would go a long way for a
good apple. Other fruits he liked, but the best was the
apple.

OFFER OF AIR OFFICER COMMANDING

'The Air Commodore at Cranwell offered S. his house
for the purpose of spending Christmas, but no! He
was an Aircraft hand and as I've said before he kept
his place as such, never allowing anything to break
him from his position in the R.A.F.

'It seemed his sole purpose was to be an airman of
the lowest grade and rank and to be left alone with
his Brough at "B" Flight, Cranwell. He was hero-wor-
shipped by all the flight for his never failing cheery
disposition, ability to get all he could for their benefit,

never complaining, and his generosity to all concerned till at times it appeared that he was doing too much for everyone and all were out to do their best for him. Quarrels ceased and the flight had to pull together for the sheer joy of remaining in his company and being with him for his companionship, help, habits, fun and teaching one and all to play straight. He fathered us and left us a sorrowful crowd awaiting letters or his return.

FLYING AND SCRUBBING

'When opportunity permitted he made a point of flying with all the officers in the flight so that each knew him well and in my opinion were proud of the fact, the way they used to smile when he climbed in with them. Flying is a very old hobby of his but although he has crashed 7 times, still goes on. He even used to leave the office at times, shove overalls on, and away out into the hangar, scrubbing and washing machines down although there was never any need to do so. Just to feel that he could do any job that came along. The number of times he has corrected mistakes and styles of mine are innumerable but I'm afraid I've slipped back during his absence. His languages got us beat, although he would not shoot out anything out of place unless asked, in that respect.

SCROUNGING

'The hut table could be improved upon, so forthwith S. and a party went away with it to exchange it for a lovely one in the mess-deck. He made his only mistake by taking one that was marked by birds, and was "rumbled," but as usual got away with it. The Quartermaster was a good sort. S. said so.

'S. has been known to lift all manner of articles for our use, sometimes going so far as to speak to the victim and walk away with anything he fancied would be of use to us. Never for himself.

COAL

'A good incident took place when the strike was on; all coal issues were stopped and "B" Flight had only a lot of coal dust and slack.

'S.'s sheer cheek got to work, and calmly filling a huge bucket with dust he inquired the name of a Big officer who had stopped the issue. Walking point blank to his office, he found that the officer had not stopped his own coal ration, so he exchanged his load for some wonderful pieces of coal as big as himself. No one has found out who changed the dust yet. His comments were a broad grin and silence.

CIVIL POLICE

'He was held up on three separate occasions by the same "copper" on point duty in a traffic muddle in *Town* (Sleaford) and reported the matter to the Superintendent. He pointed out that police were the servants of the public, paid by the public, and he did not think that the "copper" on point duty knew his job, that he was decidedly inefficient and a "*Swede*" (Airman's term for villager). The Super. and S. had a grand argument, but S.'s eloquence floored the Super. and left him wondering what the R.A.F. had enlisted. That "copper" is now permanently excused traffic-control.*

AIR DISPLAY

'He took all the flight and wives to Hendon by charabanc although I personally know that his ambition was to charter an Imperial Airways machine and "do" it by air, but he was let down for a "Kite" at the last minute.

'Both going and coming he did not sit down for more than an hour, continually watching traffic and direction, and never turned a hair while the remainder slept or curled up, tired.

JOBS

'On the summer holidays coming round he told us he had got the offer of a job as a Steward aboard a liner going to U.S.A., but finally turned it down owing to work on his book. (Wish this had come off.)

A VISIT

'He used to Brough down to "Smoke" (London)

---

* The point of this story may be lost on most of my readers who are unaware of the cavalier treatment that men in uniform usually get at the hands of jacks-in-office. The Cranwell fellows were astonished that Shaw was not arrested for making a protest against the inefficiency of a police-constable.—R. G.

most Saturdays to look after his book being printed, sleeping at the Union Jack Club. One night it was full, but they shoved him in somewhere. He came back and gave us his views. He said what with sleeping in a dormitory with a drunken sailor one side and a "blind" marine on the other there was nothing to do but swear.'

Here ends Sergeant Pugh's account.

So far as I know Lawrence has only once filled in a confession album; for a comrade in the Royal Air Force. His statements are slight but amusing, and may be taken entirely seriously:

Favourite colour:	Scarlet.
Favourite dish:	Bread and water.
Favourite musician:	Mozart.
Favourite author:	Wm. Morris
Favourite character in history:	Nil.
Favourite place:	London.
Greatest pleasure:	Sleep.
Greatest pain:	Noise.
Greatest fear:	Animal spirits.
Greatest wish:	To be forgotten of my friends.

His future plans are simply to stay out his full time in the Royal Air Force, and afterwards to settle down quietly in some room in London, 'the only possible place to live in permanently,' with a country cottage somewhere for his occasional retreat, and a pair of mechanically driven wheels to tie the

two bedrooms together. But whether he will succeed in set-
tling down quietly is another question. Mr. Winston Churchill's short summary of Lawrence is a very penetrating one: 'A
rare beast; will not breed in captivity.' It has suggested the text
from the Vulgate, which I have made the motto to the book.

APPENDICES

APPENDIX A

OPERATIONS BY BRITISH MOBILE COLUMN AGAINST HEJAZ RAILWAY

SPECIAL INSTRUCTIONS

(1) Two companies, Imperial Camel Corps (Commander, Major R. V. Buxton; strength 16 officers, 300 other ranks, 400 camels, with 6 Lewis guns) have been placed temporarily at the disposal of Hejaz Operations, for the purpose of carrying out the following operations on the Hejaz Railway:

(a) To seize Mudawra,* with the primary object of destroying the enemy's valuable water supply at that place.

(b) To destroy the main railway bridge and tunnel at Kissela, 5 miles south of Amman,

---

* The spelling of this report is not consistent with the spelling I have used: but it does not matter. There is no accurate English spelling of Arabic names.

or

should circumstances arise rendering (b) impracticable—

(c) The demolition of the railway bridge immediately north of Jurf Ed Derwish, and the destruction of the enemy's supply dumps and wells at Jurf Station.

(2) The following instructions and attached march programme are based on the assumption that objectives (a) and (b) will be carried out.

Should it prove necessary, as the second phase of the operations, to substitute (c) for (b), which will be decided solely at the discretion of the O.C., Imperial Camel Corps, these instructions will be amended, and a revised plan prepared by the officer responsible for its execution.

(3) MARCHES.

The column will march, subject to such modifications as may be imposed by circumstances at present unforeseen, in accordance with the march programme and time table attached marked 'A.'

(4) OPERATIONS.

(a) The operations, both at Mudawra and at Kissela (or Jurf Ed Derwish), will be carried out as night attacks, under cover of darkness. In each case, the precise plan of attack will be decided, after personal reconnaissance of the positions to be assaulted by the O.C., I.C.C. In this connection, stress is laid upon the value to be obtained by the element of surprise, the Turks in the Hejaz area being, hitherto, unaccustomed to attack by night, and therefore, probably ill-prepared to resist an operation of this nature.

(b) To provide artillery support during the operation against Mudawra, the Hejaz ten-pounder section will be placed by the O.C. Troops, Northern Hejaz, temporarily at the disposal of the O.C., I.C.C. On the completion of this operation, the section will not proceed east of the Railway, but will return independently to Guweira or elsewhere, under the orders of the O.C. Troops, Northern Hejaz.

(c) For the operation against Kissela, the O.C. Troops, Northern Hejaz, should arrange for the co-operation of a detachment of armoured cars, to be held in readiness at a suitable point east of the Railway to cover the retirement of the column to Bair in the event of pursuit by hostile cavalry from Amman.

(5) SUPPLIES.

The column will march from Akaba, carrying three days' supplies and water for men, and forage for animals. In addition, each man will carry one day's emergency iron ration, to be consumed only by direct order of the O.C. Column.

Dumps for the replenishment of supplies and forage will be established, in advance, under arrangements to be made by the O.C. Troops, Northern Hejaz, as under:

(a) At Rum, 5 days' rations for men and forage for animals.

(b) At El Jefer, 4 days' rations for men and forage for animals.

(c) At Bair, 14 days' rations for men and forage for animals.

(6) WATER.

Plentiful drinking water for men and animals will be found in the following localities: Rum, Mudawra, El Jefer, Bair, Wadi Dakhl (vide attached march tables).

(7) MEDICAL.

A casualty hamla, with capacity for dealing with 24 cases (12 sitting and 12 lying) will be organized at Akaba, to accompany the column, by Major Marshall, M.C., R.A.M.C., under instructions to be issued by the O.C. Troops, Northern Hejaz.

A general scheme for the evacuation of casualties during the operations will be prepared by Major Marshall and forwarded through O.C. Troops, Northern Hejaz, to this office for information as early as possible.

(8) AMMUNITION.

260 rounds S.A.A. per man, and 2,000 rounds per Lewis gun will be carried.

(9) EXPLOSIVES.

(a) Under arrangements to be made by the O.C. Troops, Northern Hejaz, an explosive hamla, carrying 2,500 lb. of gun-cotton, will accompany the column from Akaba to Mudawra. Empty camels and drivers should return from Mudawra to Akaba on the conclusion of that phase of the operations.

(b) For the operation at Kissela, arrangements should be made for an explosive hamla carrying 6,000 lb. of gun-cotton to meet the column on the arrival of the latter at Bair, whence it will accompany the column to Kissela.

(10) GUIDES.

(a) For the first phase of the operations (from Akaba to El Jefer, inclusive), the following arrangements should be made by the O.C. Troops, Northern Hejaz, through Sherif Feisal.

(a) Guides (Amran Howeitat) to meet the column at Akaba and to conduct it thence to Rum.

(b) A suitable Sherif selected by Sherif Feisal, together with the requisite party of guides (Abu Tayi), to join the column at Rum, and to conduct it thence to Mudawra, and subsequently from Mudawra to El Jefer.

Provision of food for Arab guides, and of forage for their camels, whilst employed with the column, should be included in the arrangements to be made in accordance with para. 5 above (Supplies).

(b) The provision of guides required for the march of the column north from El Jefer to Kissela, will be arranged on his arrival, by Lieut.-Col. Lawrence.

(11) COMMUNICATIONS.

The O.C. Troops, Northern Hejaz, should arrange for the closest possible touch to be kept with the column whilst operating east of the Railway, as far north as El Jefer (inclusive), by aeroplanes of the Hejaz Flight.

If possible, similar arrangements will be made direct with G.H.Q. for the maintenance of communication by aeroplane from the Palestine Brigade during the second phase of the operations, north of Bair.

(12) ATTACHED OFFICERS.

The following officers should be detailed by the O.C. Troops, Northern Hejaz, to accompany the column from Akaba:

Political Officer for liaison
with Arabs:

Major Marshall,
M.C., R.A.M.C.
(In addition to
duties as M.O.)

Demolition Officer:	(*Either*) Capt. Scott-Higgins, (*or*) Bimbashi Peake, E.A.
Staff Officer (for 1st phase of operations as far as El Jefer only):	Major Stirling, D.S.O., M.C.

(13) The O.C. Troops, Northern Hejaz, should report by telegram to this office on the completion of the arrangements for which he is responsible, vide paras. 4, 5, 7, 9, 10, 11, and 12 above, confirming in detail all measures taken by mail at first opportunity.

(14) Acknowledge by wire.

If available, it is suggested that the services of Sherif Hazaar, or of Sherif Fahad, might be obtained.

(signed) A. C. DAWNAY.

CAIRO.

SAVOY HOTEL, 16th July, 1918.

Lt.-Col.,
General Staff,
Hejaz Operations.

Copies:
No. 1: Hejaz Operations.
No. 2: Hejaz Operations.
No. 3: O.C. Troops, Northern Hejaz.
No. 4: O.C. Imperial Camel Corps.
No. 5: General Headquarters.

PROVISIONAL MARCH PROGRAMME
AND TIME TABLE

Zero day.	*Column marches from Akaba.*
Z + 1 ⎫ Z + 2 ⎭	Akaba—Rum (11 hours).
Z + 3	Rest day, Rum.
Z + 4 ⎫ Z + 5 ⎭	Rum—position of readiness West of Mudawra.
Night Z5/Z6	Attack on Mudawra.
Z + 6 ⎫ Z + 7 ⎬ Z + 8 ⎭	Mudawra—El Jefer (20 hours).
Z + 9	Rest day, El Jefer.
Z + 10 ⎫ Z + 11 ⎭	El Jefer—Bair (13 hours).
Z + 12	Rest day, Bair.
Z + 13 ⎫ Z + 14 ⎬ Z + 15 ⎭	Bair—position of readiness East of Kissela (30 hours).
Night Z15/Z16	Attack on Kissela bridge and tunnel.
Z + 16 ⎫ Z + 17 ⎬ Z + 18 ⎭	Kissela—Bair (30 hours).

Z + 19 ⎫
Z + 20 ⎭   Rest days, Bair.

Z + 21 ⎫
Z + 22 ⎬   Bair—Wadi Dakhl (24 hours).
Z + 23 ⎭

Z + 24 ⎫
Z + 25 ⎭   Wadi Dakhl—Bir es Aaba (20 hours).

NOTE—All marches are estimated at an average rate of 3½ miles per hour.

SECRET G.S.31

MAJOR R. V.BUXTON,
I.C.C. Ismailia.

In amplification of the special instructions, G.S.31, handed to you on the 16th inst., should unforeseen circumstances arise rendering both (b) and (c) objectives impracticable within the limit of time fixed for these operations, you are authorized, after the attainment of your first objective, to adopt, in consultation with Lieut.-Colonel Joyce and Lieut.-Colonel Lawrence, as an alternative, any modified plan of offensive action against the Hejaz Railway, *North* of Maan, which, in your opinion, the situation justifies, and of which local circumstances allow.

(Sgd.) A. C. DAWNAY.

CAIRO.
22nd July, 1918.

Lieut.-Colonel,
General Staff,
Hejaz Operations.

Copy to: O.C. Troops, Northern Hejaz. For information.

APPENDIX B

LAWRENCE'S LETTER TO THE LONDON *TIMES*

JULY 22ND. 1920

SIR,—

In this week's debate in the Commons on the Middle East a veteran of the House expressed surprise that the Arabs of Mesopotamia were in arms against us despite our well-meant mandate. His surprise has been echoed here and there in the Press, and it seems to me based on such a misconception of the new Asia and the history of the last five years, that I would like to trespass at length on your space and give my interpretation of the situation.

The Arabs rebelled against the Turks during the war not because the Turk Government was notably bad, but because they wanted independence. They did not risk their lives in battle to change masters, to become British subjects or French citizens, but to win a show of their own.

Whether they are fit for independence or not remains to be

tried. Merit is no qualification for freedom. Bulgars, Afghans, and Tahitans have it. Freedom is enjoyed when you are so well armed, or so turbulent, or inhabit a country so thorny that the expense of your neighbour's occupying you is greater than the profit. Feisal's Government in Syria has been completely independent for two years, and has maintained public security and public services in its area.

Mesopotamia has had less opportunity to prove its armament. It never fought the Turks, and only fought perfunctorily against us. Accordingly, we had to set up a war-time administration there. We had no choice; but that was two years ago, and we have not yet changed to peace conditions. Indeed there are yet no signs of change. 'Large reinforcements,' according to the official statement, are now being sent there, and our garrison will run into six figures next month. The expense curve will go up to 50 million pounds for this financial year, and yet greater efforts will be called for from us as the Mesopotamian desire for independence grows.

It is not astonishing that their patience has broken after two years. The Government we have set up is English in fashion, and is conducted in the English language. So it has 450 British executive officers running it, and not a single responsible Mesopotamian. In Turkish days 70 per cent. of the executive civil service was local. Our 80,000 troops there are occupied in police duties, not in guarding the frontiers. They are holding down the people. In Turkish days the two army corps in Mesopotamia were 60 per cent. Arab in officers, 95 per cent. in other ranks. This deprivation of the privilege of sharing the defence and administration of their country is galling to the educated Mesopotamians. It is true we have increased prosperity—but who cares for that when liberty is in the other scale? They waited and welcomed the news of our mandate, because they thought it meant Dominion self-government for themselves. They are now losing hope in our good intentions.

A remedy? I can see a cure only in immediate change of policy. The whole logic of the present thing looks wrong. Why should Englishmen (or Indians) have to be killed to make the Arab Government in Mesopotamia, which is the considered intention of His Majesty's Government? I agree with the intention, but I would make the Arabs do the work. They can. My little experience in helping to set up Feisal showed me that the art of government wants more character than brains.

I would make Arabic the Government language. This would impose a reduction of the British staff, and a return to employment of the qualified Arabs. I would raise two divisions of local volunteer troops, all Arabs, from the senior divisional general to the junior private. (Trained officers and trained N.C.O.'s exist in thousands.) I would entrust these new units with the maintenance of order, and I would cause to leave the country every single British soldier, every single Indian soldier. These changes would take 12 months and we should then hold of Mesopotamia exactly as much (or as little) as we hold of South Africa or Canada. I believe the Arabs in these conditions would be as loyal as anyone in the Empire, and they would not cost us a cent.

I shall be told that the idea of brown Dominions in the British Empire is grotesque. Yet the Montagu scheme and the Milner scheme are approaches to it, and the only alternative seems to be conquest, which the ordinary Englishman does not want, and cannot afford.

Of course, there is oil in Mesopotamia, but we are no nearer that while the Middle East remains at war, and I think if it is so necessary for us, it could be made the subject of a bargain. The Arabs seem willing to shed their blood for freedom; how much more their oil!

T. E. LAWRENCE.

ALL SOULS COLLEGE, *July 22.*

INDEX

Aba el Lissan (place), 193, 194, 200–202, 206, 210, 226, 228, 229, 233, 255, 293, 296, 326, 327, 329, 330, 336, 354, 356, 359, 368, 428

Abd el Aziz (Sheikh), 376

Abd el Kader (the Algerian), 262–270, 273, 274, 276, 290, 291, 374, 386–389, 394, 396

Abd el Kerim (of the Juheina), 111, 112, 122, 137

Abdul Hamid (Sultan), 56–59, 81

Abdulla (Machine-gun officer), 306–307, 300, 367

Abdulla el Zaagi (Captain of bodyguard), 300–302, 313, 345, 350, 367, 368, 376, 380

Abdulla, Emir, 58, 73, 83, 85–88, 110, 126, 131, 145–149, 158, 219, 245, 255, 263, 297, 306, 307, 330, 412, 415–418, 429

Abdulla the Robber, 299–301, 359, 367, 368

Abu Sawana (place), 277–279, 283

Abu Tayi (Howeitat clan), 142, 325. *See also* Auda.

Aden (place), 53

Adhub (Sheikh), 271, 273, 281, 287, 356

Afuleh (place), 366, 369

Ageyl (class of), 116, 128, 129, 134, 136, 140, 141, 145, 159, 162, 164, 166, 171, 172, 175, 199, 200, 224, 226, 254, 255, 264, 298, 300, 306, 307, 310, 345

Ahmed (servant), 22, 23

Aintab (place), 10

Akaba (place), 31, 139, 140, 142, 143, 157–159, 176, 180, 181, 188, 192–196, 199, 201, 206, 207–211, 215–223, 226–230, 234, 249, 251, 255–265, 268, 291, 293, 294, 296, 298, 300, 314, 319, 331–334, 336, 341, 344, 345, 346, 350–356, 391, 402, 415, 417, 420, 428, 430, 431, 433, 461–463, 465,

Aleppo, 18, 21, 22, 25, 28, 82, 93, 124, 135, 180, 194, 223, 255, 259, 281, 318, 329, 360, 425

Alexandretta, 28, 53, 65, 66

Alexandria, 57

Ali (Emir), 67, 71, 72, 87, 88, 91, 111, 125, 126, 219, 297, 330

Ali ibn el Hussein (Sherif), 70, 91, 107, 117, 260– 298, 364,

Ali Riza Pasha (Governor of Damascus), 186, 268, 385, 389, 398, 399, 415

Allenby, Lady, 246

Allenby, Field-Marshal Viscount, xiii, 16, 215–222, 251, 255–260, 266, 271, 273, 283, 284, 293, 296, 304, 312, 317–320, 325–334, 341, 348, 354, 356, 360, 364, 367–370, 372, 374, 381, 384, 385, 395, 397, 399, 400, 426, 427

Amman (place), 187, 194, 226, 305, 319, 321–323, 326, 329, 330, 334, 341, 352, 356–360, 369–371, 384, 415–417, 422, 459, 461

Ammari (place), 272

Anatolia, 56, 78

Annad (Auda's son), 192, 304

Apuleius, Marcus, 339n

Arab Bureau, The, 84, 109, 218, 318

Arab Freedom Societies, 27, 61, 62, 67, 79, 292

Arfaja (place), 168, 174

Aristophanes, 156, 298n

Armenians, 60, 61, 80, 222, 350

Atara (place), 321, 322

Ateiba (tribe), 91, 103, 128, 141, 147, 300, 314, 315

Athens, 77

Auda abu Tayi (Sheikh), 4, 142, 151–155, 167–221, 230–233, 235, 262, 265, 266, 270, 293, 298, 303–305, 323, 325, 329, 346, 356, 373–378, 382, 383, 387, 389, 395, 415, 431

Australians, 65, 322, 369, 382, 385, 388, 391–396, 398

Austrians with Turks, 245, 374, 378

Ayesha, the Lady, 246

Aziz el Masri, 104, 111

Azrak (place), 275

Baalbek (place), 185, 187

Bagdad, 20, 28, 81, 102, 141, 405, 408, 410, 411, 413

Baha (camel), 379, 380

Bair (place), 192–194, 199, 266, 267, 270, 291, 293, 321, 341, 349, 352, 355, 461–463, 465, 466

Baisan (place), 369

Baker, Sir Herbert, 435

Barrow, General, 380–385, 388

Basra, 185, 419

Batra (place), 251

Beersheba, 158, 257, 258, 266, 312, 318, 341, 427, 428

Bell, Miss Gertrude, 26, 27, 168, 274

Bender (Emir Nuri's nephew), 349

Beni Atiyeh (tribe), 142, 254

Beni Sakhr (tribe), 280

Beyrout, 28, 181, 223, 399, 404, 425

Biasha (peasants), 263

Billi, The (tribe), 103, 111, 128, 130, 135, 138, 142, 143

Birejik (place), 11

Blenheim Palace, 45

Blunden, Edmund, 433

Blunts, The, 26, 168

Boanerges, see Brough Superior

Bolsheviki, 183

Borneo, 13

Boyle, Captain, 107, 120, 123, 130, 131, 136

Brough Superior (motor-bicycle), 437, 442, 447–455

Buchan, Colonel J., xiii, 78

Bulgaria, 66, 318, 375

Burckhardt (traveller), 27

Buxton, Colonel, xiii, 322, 330, 331, 341–347, 349–352, 459, 466

Cairo, 28, 75, 76, 81, 82, 89, 93, 106, 108, 139–141, 184, 211, 214–216, 218, 336, 339n, 346, 407, 421, 425, 464, 466

Carchemish, 12–20, 27, 29, 33, 74, 80, 162, 189n, 251
Carson, Lord, 321
Cecil, Lord Robert, 418
Chauvel, General, 382, 288, 392, 395, 400
Churchill, Right Hon. Winston, 42, 408–414, 424, 456
Clausewitz, 146, 308
Clemenceau, 403, 405, 407
Coleridge, 339n
Constantinople, 17, 20, 22, 28, 58, 64–67, 93, 133, 149, 185, 360, 425
Contzen, Herr, 20–24
Cranwell, 422, 423, 433–454
Crusaders, The, 9–12, 51, 316
Cox, Sir Percy, 408
Curzon, Viscount, 409, 417, 418

Dahoum (photographer at Carchemish), 26
Damascus, vii, ix, 28, 55, 56, 66–69, 93, 96, 97, 102, 124, 133, 139, 143, 149, 159, 162, 175, 179–189, 194, 196, 223, 224, 244–251, 255, 258–262, 268, 289, 292, 294, 301, 303, 318, 319, 329–333, 348, 350, 354, 355, 359, 360, 369, 372–374, 382–392, 398–405, 408, 410, 411, 413, 417, 425, 426
Dardanelles, The, 65–66, 121, 227, 259, 366
Davenport, Colonel, 107, 245, 260
Dawnay, Colonel Alan, xiii, 320, 324, 330, 331, 353, 421, 464, 466
Dead Sea, The, 193, 271, 291, 296, 303, 304, 312, 316–319, 336
Deraa (place), 187, 194, 199, 226, 258, 259, 270, 282, 290, 313, 328–330,

352, 353–372, 375, 379–383, 399, 400, 427
Desolate, The (desert), 167, 173
Dinamit (Emir), 4
Distinguished Flying Cross, 335
Distinguished Service Order, 294, 312
Dizad (place), 166
Dorchester, 422, 436
Druse (Mountains and inhabitants), 180, 181, 185, 194, 258, 276, 349, 356, 370, 372, 387, 394, 413
Doughty, C. M., 26, 298

Egyptian gunners, 72, 86, 98, 115, 121, 128, 147
El Arish (place), 228
El Jedha (camel), 236
Enver Pasha, 60, 68, 69, 79, 141, 144, 366
Erzeroum (place), 78
Euphrates (river), 6, 10, 11, 14, 19, 20, 27, 30, 53, 79, 244, 344
Ezraa (place), 373–374

Fahad (Sheikh), 271, 273, 276–282, 287, 288, 325, 329, 356, 364, 464
Faiz, The (clan), 292, 416
Fakhri, Pasha, 149
Falkenhayn, General, 227
Faroun (island), 31
Farraj and Daud, 164, 166, 178, 179, 210, 263, 264, 272, 283, 298, 322, 335
Feisal, Emir, 63, 147–160, 163, 169, 176–181, 184, 185, 216–221, 224, 227, 231–236, 239, 240, 246–272, 289, 297, 300, 303–308, 314–320, 329–333, 346, 348, 353–355, 366, 369–374, 382, 385–390, 400–419, 431, 462, 468, 499

Foch, Marshal, 146, 310, 419
Fontana, Mrs., xiii, 18
Fowle, Mr., 18–20
French Colonel, The, 108, 124, 138, 139, 263

Gadara (place), 235, 262, 273, 276
Galilee, 235, 281, 374, 385
Garland, Captain 110, 111, 123, 144, 149
Gasim, of Maan, 171–173
Gasim abu Dumeik, 233–234
Gaza, 158, 180, 181, 216, 257, 258, 266, 270, 427–428
Geneva Convention, The, 420
George V, H. M. King, 87–88, 407–408
German Detachments, 363, 366, 374, 378, 379, 385, 390, 427
Ghazala (camel), 220, 226, 236, 246, 345
Ghazale (place), 373–374
Goslett, Captain R., xiii, 333
Grey, Sir Edward, 28
Gurkhas, 357, 368
Guweira (place), 193, 207, 211, 219, 221, 227, 230–232, 236, 237, 345, 349, 356, 358, 461

Haifa (town), 10, 258, 329, 369
Hama (town), 187, 223
Hamoudi (headman), 25, 26
Hamra (place), 106
Handley-Page (aeroplane), 369, 370, 407, 421
Harb, The (tribe), 86–91, 110, 114–116, 125–130
Hardinge, H.M.S., 130–136
Hardy, Mr. and Mrs. Thomas, xiii, 436, 437, 439
Harith (clan), 91, 117, 232, 260, 276

Hassan Shah, Jemadar, 262, 278, 289
Hauran, The (district), 224, 237, 258, 290, 356, 363, 364, 369–371, 375
Hedley, Colonel, 74–75
Herbert, Colonel Aubrey, 80
Hermon, Mount, 279
Hesa (place), 329, 355
Hoffman, Herr, 24
Hogarth, Dr. D. G., xiii, 10, 14, 15, 18, 20, 27, 30, 74, 84, 318
Homs (town), 223
Hornby, Captain, 149, 165, 166, 325, 329, 356, 359
Howeimil (Sheikh), 241, 246, 247
Howeitat (tribe), *see also* 'Abu Tayi' and 'Jazi', viii, 4, 142, 143, 157, 158, 162, 171, 174, 176, 178, 181, 192–194, 196, 200, 201, 204–207, 211, 219–221, 223, 230, 231, 233, 241, 262, 266, 269, 292, 304, 305, 315, 323, 325, 349, 350, 356, 374, 462, 463
Huber (traveller), 89
Hussein (Sherif), 58, 59, 64, 65, 67, 70, 71, 81, 82, 85–87, 91, 96, 107, 117, 124, 183, 220, 260–264, 267, 268, 272–286, 289, 291, 298, 330, 353–355, 364, 386, 402, 403

Ibn Saud, Emir of Nejd, 64, 142, 169, 299, 412, 416
Indians, Barrow's, 369, 380, 381, 386
Irak, *see* Mesopotamia
Ismailia (place), 82, 215, 466

Jaafar, Pasha, 141, 219, 226, 227, 303, 320, 323, 334, 353, 359
Jaffa (port), 293, 326

Jane, Mr. Cecil, xiii, 8

Janissaries, The, 76

James, St., 235

Jauf (place), 173, 416

Jazi (clan), 193, 292

Jebel Rudhwa (mountain), 107

Jefer (place), 193, 194, 199–201, 265, 293, 303

Jemal, Pasha, 66–69, 153

Jerablus (place), 20

Jericho, 296, 317, 319, 330, 334, 356

Jersusalem, 223, 258, 259, 293, 294, 326, 328, 361, 395, 419

Jiddah, 55, 71, 82, 85, 87, 96, 107, 108, 120, 125, 219, 223, 263, 299, 330, 417, 422

Jordan, The (river), 304, 317, 322, 360, 415

Joyce, Colonel, 107, 294, 332, 333, 353, 357, 359, 362, 363, 372, 466

Juheina (tribe), 103, 106, 111, 112, 121, 122, 125, 126, 128, 131, 134, 137, 138, 148

Junor, Lieut., 361, 362, 368, 369

Jurf (place), 303, 335, 460

Kaaba, The, 71

Kadesh Barnea, 30

Kemal, Pasha, 348

Kennington, Eric, 313, 423

Kerak (place), 296, 304, 311, 312, 317, 334

Kethera (place), 207

Khartoum, 107

Kirkbride, Lieut., 396, 398

Kissir or Kissela (place), 341, 351, 459–465

Kiswe (place), 385

Kitchener, Earl, 28, 31, 75, 79

Kuneitra (place), 369

Kut, 66, 78–81

Kuweit, 53

Lawrence, Mr. (father), 5, 9

Lawrence, Mrs. (mother), xiii, 5, 8, 267, 338n

Lebanon, 21, 185, 399, 404

Lenin, V., 43

'Lewis,' Sergeant, 230–248, 298

Lloyd George, Right Hon. D., 403–405, 410

Lloyd, Lord, 84, 264, 265

Lucian, 17

Maan (place), 31, 139, 142, 143, 144, 153, 171, 174, 193, 194, 199, 201, 202, 206, 208, 219, 220, 226–231, 251, 253, 256, 296, 297, 314, 319, 320, 323, 325, 326, 329, 330, 334, 341, 344, 345, 352, 355, 356, 360, 417, 466

Mahmas (camel-boy), 309, 313

Malory, Sir Thomas, 155, 156, 298n

Marshall, Major, 462, 463

Masturah (place), 89

Maulud, Pasha, 98–100, 114, 128, 131, 133, 160, 162, 227, 256, 314, 315, 320, 323

Maxwell, General, 75

McMahon, Sir A. H. (High Commissioner of Egypt), xiii, 403

Mecca, 54, 55, 57, 58n, 59, 62, 64, 67, 71, 73, 82, 85–87, 89–91, 99–101, 108, 110, 111, 115, 117, 119, 124, 126, 135, 140, 142, 146, 184, 208, 215, 218–220, 249, 262, 290, 291, 299, 330, 345, 353, 354, 403, 408

Medina, 28, 55, 56, 58, 68–72, 81, 86, 87,

89, 91, 93, 97, 99, 101, 108, 110, 111, 124, 126, 131, 139, 143–150, 158–162, 218, 219, 249, 255, 258, 283, 297, 299, 301, 303, 325, 330, 341, 360, 386, 425–427

Mesopotamia (Irak), 6, 10, 12, 44, 51, 53, 54, 57, 61, 65, 66, 75, 77–81, 98, 100, 104, 142, 153, 180, 183, 402–405, 408–415, 429, 467–469

Mezerib (place), 361, 362, 366, 375, 380, 381

Minifer (place), 195, 197, 284, 430, 435

Moahib (tribe), 142

Mohammed (peasant), 171

Mohammed el Dheilan (Sheikh), 162, 174, 175, 188, 219, 265, 325, 356, 387

Mohammed Said (Algerian), 268, 386, 389, 394

Moor, A, 145

Morris, W., 155, 455

Motalga (clan), 192, 304, 306–308

Mozart, 446, 455

Mudowwara (place), 229, 230, 232, 234, 238–241, 243, 249, 251, 253, 265, 296, 297, 320, 324, 325, 330, 341, 347, 349

Nablus (place), 360, 369

Nakhl Mubarak (place), 112, 113, 125

Napoleon, 42, 146

Nasir (Sherif), 135, 159, 162, 164, 169, 173, 176–181, 185, 188, 196, 199, 201, 203, 204, 206, 207, 208, 210, 211, 218–220, 260, 268, 303, 329, 344, 364, 366, 373, 374, 380–383, 386–390, 431

Nazareth, 360, 363

Nebk (place), 180, 182, 187, 188, 198, 252

Nefudh (district), 168

Nejd (province), 142, 412

Nesib (the Syrian), 158, 162, 169, 175, 176, 178–181, 184, 194, 372

Newcombe, Colonel, 30, 31, 135, 140, 144, 149, 165, 166, 194, 333

New Zealanders, 369–371

Niebuhr (traveller), 27

Nisib (place), 366, 368

Nuri Said (Arab regular officer), 303, 323, 346, 348, 349, 356, 360, 361, 363, 366, 367, 370–372, 374–376, 378–380, 382, 386, 388, 389, 390, 394

Nuri (the Emir of the Ruwalla), 142, 143, 173, 176, 180, 181, 183, 184, 194, 199, 346, 348, 349, 356, 360, 361, 363, 366, 367, 370–372, 374–376, 378–380, 382, 386, 388, 389, 390, 394, 405, 416

Oxford, 4–6, 8, 10, 12, 15, 16, 18, 26, 30, 35, 41, 74, 109, 133, 146, 162, 324, 336, 340, 407, 415, 423

Oxford Book of English Verse, 156, 157, 298n

Oxford Street, London, 295

Owen, Wilfred, 433

Palgrave, William Gifford, 26

Palmer, Pte., xiii, 438, 439

Peace Conference, The, 402, 405–407

Peake, Captain, 464

Petra (place), 30, 228, 276

Petrie, Sir Flinders, 15

Pichon, M., 405

Pisani, Capitaine, 251–254, 356

Poole, R. L., 8, 12

Proverbs, Book of, 424

Pugh, Sergeant, 443, 450n, 455

Quartermaster-General, 328

Rabegh (port), 71–73, 81, 86–89, 92, 96, 99, 101, 104, 106–109, 111, 115, 124–126, 128, 138, 150, 223, 305, 431

Rahail (of the bodyguard), 288, 291–293, 349

Rasim Bey (Gunner officer), 121, 122, 128, 160, 162, 308, 310, 355

Rayak (place), 187

Read, Mr. Herbert, 226, 227

Reading, 421

Remthe (place), 282, 379, 380

Revolt in the Desert, xi, xii, 49, 85, 148, 423, 424, 426, 428, 430

Rheims, 36

Richards, Mr. V. W., xiii, 7, 336

Riddell, Lord, xiii, 406

Rolls, Pte., 357

Ross, Major, 150

Royal Air Force (Lawrence's service in), xi, xiii, 3, 10, 17, 18, 33, 35, 36, 40, 44, 46, 297, 401, 409, 422, 432, 434–436, 441, 455

Royal Tank Corps (Lawrence's service in), xiii, 3, 17, 33, 422, 436, 438, 440, 444

Rumm (place), 232, 234, 235, 236, 238, 249, 251, 264, 276, 293, 341, 343, 346

Ruwalla (tribe), 80, 142, 73, 180, 185, 346, 349, 356, 359, 369–371, 374, 375, 379, 382, 385, 389, 416. *See also* Nuri, Emir

Saladin, 405

Salem (negro), 240, 242, 243, 248, 249

Salem (Sheikh), 254

Salmond, Air-Marshal Sir G., 42, 335

Salonica, 66

Salt (place), 324

Samuel, Sir H., 153

Sassoon, Siegfried, xii, 432, 433

Scott-Higgins, Captain, 464

Semites, The, 51, 61, 133

Semna (hill), 323

Senussi, The, 77, 141, 334

Serahin (tribe), 260, 272–276, 278–284, 286, 356

Seven Pillars of Wisdom, xi, xii, 28, 157, 182, 186, 226, 392, 406, 420, 422–425, 428, 430, 435, 439, 449

Shaalan (tribe), 180

Shakir (Sherif), 147, 148

Shammar (tribe), 142, 166, 174, 350

Sharraf (Sherif), 160, 164, 166, 300

Shaw, G. B., 45

Shedia (place), 264, 265

Sheikh Saad (place), 372, 372, 375

Shelley, 35

Sherarat (tribe), 143, 267

Shobek (place), 356, 359

Shukri Pasha, 385–392

Sinai, 30, 75, 89, 135, 139, 212, 328, 341

Sirhan, 142, 173, 174, 176, 178, 195, 198, 272, 416

Sleaford, 454

Smith's Crisps, 451

Smyrna, 28, 425

Somali camels, 350

Stamfordham, Lord, xiii, 407

Stirling, Major, 464

Stokes (Sergeant), 239–249, 298

Storrs, Sir R., 84, 85

Sudan, 54, 101, 107

Suez (town and canal), 51, 56, 58, 76, 77, 86, 108, 138–141, 158, 211, 212, 214, 215, 218, 331, 341

Swift, Jonathan, 39

Sykes-Picot Treaty, ix, 124, 183, 346, 404, 405

Tafas (place), 290, 375, 378, 379, 382, 427

Tafileh (group of villages), 294, 303–305, 311, 312, 316–319, 341, 355, 356, 359, 396, 431, 432

Taif (place), 85, 87, 111, 114

Tallal (Sheikh), 258, 259, 290, 298, 356, 362, 363, 366, 369, 371, 373–376

Taranto (place), 295

Taurus Mountains, 10

Tebuk (place), 144

Tell Arar (place), 359, 361

Tell el Shehab (place), 273, 276, 278, 279, 364, 366

Themed (place), 212, 334

Thomas, Mr. Lowell, 4, 13, 58n, 96, 186, 187, 332, 419, 436

Thompson, Mr. Campbell, 14, 27

Tigris (river), 51, 53, 78

Tremadoc (place), 4

Trenchard, Sir Hugh, 409–410

Tripoli (port), 399

Trotsky, 43

Turki (boy), 270, 271, 286, 287

Umtaiye (place), 357, 359, 366–369

Urfa (place), 10

Uxbridge, 18, 434–436

Vickery, Major, 131, 133, 137

Victoria Cross, The, 294

Von Moltke, 146

Wadi Safra, 96

Wahabi, The (sect), 416, 417

Wahid (of Carchemish), 21, 22, 25

War Correspondents, 395

Wejh (port), 111, 125–131, 132, 134–145, 149–151, 153, 158–160, 180, 185, 188–190, 194, 200, 206, 209, 214, 218, 219, 223, 254, 262, 300, 399

Wemyss, Admiral Sir Rosslyn, 107, 215

Wilde, Jimmy, 74

Wilson, Colonel C. E., 125, 126, 219

Wilson, Sir Henry, 409

Wilson, Woodrow, 403

Wodheiha (camel), 315–317

Wood, Captain, 262, 264, 278, 281–284

Woolley, Mr. C. Leonard, xiii, 18–22, 24–26, 30, 31

World's End, The, 192, 337

Yarmuk, (river), 187, 259, 260, 263, 265, 279, 290, 291, 293, 312, 351, 360, 361, 386, 394, 415

Yasin (patriot), 186

Yemen, 54, 131

Yenbo (port), 72, 106, 107, 110–112, 115, 120–123, 125–127, 129–131, 134, 149, 150, 214, 218, 223, 297

Young, Major, 331, 334, 361, 363

Ypres, 431

Yusuf (Sheikh), 264

Zaal (Sheikh), 168, 189, 190, 192, 194–198, 202, 219, 234–238, 240, 241, 246, 247, 248, 262, 265, 270, 329, 374, 387, 431

Zeid, Emir, 58, 72, 73, 88, 110, 111, 115, 116, 117, 120, 125, 128, 219, 304–308, 310, 314, 317, 318, 319, 354, 359, 368, 413, 415

Zeki (the Syrian), 159–184

Zerakiye (place), 384

Ziza (place), 187

THE
ROBERT GRAVES
PROJECT

In an unprecedented publishing initiative, Seven Stories pays homage to Robert Graves, one of the English language's greatest practitioners as poet, memoirist, classicist, novelist, and children's book writer. Working in close partnership with Graves's estate, the press is bringing back fourteen major, previously out-of-print titles that express the full range of Graves's restless creativity, most with new introductions by noted authors:

ANN AT HIGHWOOD HALL
POEMS FOR CHILDREN
illustrated by Edward Ardizzone

COUNT BELISARIUS

THE GOLDEN FLEECE
with a new introduction by Dan-el Padilla Peralta

HEBREW MYTHS

HOMER'S DAUGHTER

THE ISLES OF UNWISDOM

LAWRENCE AND THE ARABS
with a new introduction by Dale Maharidge

MYTHS OF ANCIENT GREECE RETOLD FOR THE YOUNG

PROCEED SERGEANT LAMB

SERGEANT LAMB OF THE NINTH

THE READER OVER YOUR SHOULDER
with a new introduction by Patricia T. O'Conner

THE SIEGE AND FALL OF TROY
with a new introduction by Dan-el Padilla Peralta

THEY HANGED MY SAINTLY BILLY

WIFE TO MR. MILTON